YEADON'S REGISTER

of

L N E R

LOCOMOTIVES

Volume Six

THOMPSON B1 CLASS

ACKNOWLEDGEMENTS

Thankfully eighteen months of good health since I wrote this section for Volume 5 has enabled me to present to you a class of no less than 410 engines. I must first pay tribute to my wife for bearing so patiently and with such understanding, the long years of research, and considerable travelling with me, before this Register could be compiled. That involved her in having to take holidays at such places as Aberdeen, Dunfermline, Galashiels, Colchester and Wymondham. Hopefully she found sufficient non–railway interest to have pleasant recollections of all of them.

Some of you who bought Volume 5 have chided me for not including in it a full (and separate) list of the B17 named engines. I overlooked that their numbers and corresponding names are not as familiar to you as they are to me – after I knew them well throughout their lives. You will have no quibble in that respect anent the B1s which were named, and I will take heed of your wishes when I deal with D49 class. Once more I pay tribute to the railwaymen (then a prouder occupational title than it is today) who helped me so cheerfully to compile my Register. They too, like the photographers whose work has been of inestimable value in checking visible evidence of detail changes, are diminishing for, surprisingly as I find it, more than 25 years have passed since a B1 did any real work.

I am sure that Irwell Press will make certain that the reputation they have established for superb production continues in Volume 6, and I am sincerely grateful to them for the effort they put in to their part. That is all the more appreciated when some of them are members of the Thompson Admiration Society, which you will gather I am not.

The Yeadon Collection is available for inspection and anyone who wishes to inspect it should contact:-
The Archivist
Brynmor Jones Library
University of Hull
Hull
HU6 7RX
Tel: 01482-465265
A catalogue of the Yeadon collection is available.

First published in the United Kingdom by Irwell Press
Reprinted by BOOKLAW/RAILBUS 2001 in association with CHALLENGER
382 Carlton Hill, Nottingham NG4 1JA
www.booklawpublications.co.uk
Printed and bound by The Amadeus Press, Cleckheaton.

INTRODUCTION

The B1 class is generally accepted as being Edward Thompson's most useful addition to the LNER locomotive stock. An appraisal of his work by a British Railway Chief Mechanical Engineer, who knew him well, summed it up by saying 'When he wasn't different from Gresley, then he built a good engine'. So it is not surprising that his B1 class acquired a favourable reception when it is appreciated that it was comprised of K2 class cylinders, V2 coupled wheels and a boiler for which Gresley had signed the drawings in April 1939. The chimney – small though it is – can make, or mar, the aesthetic appearance of a locomotive design, and Thompson took no risks; for B1 he used the same as Gresley had put on to his 02 class in 1923. Likewise the tender was substantially the same 4,200 gallons design introduced in September 1924 for the K3 class. Granted, the boiler was to work at 225 instead of Gresley's intended 220lb pressure, the cylinder steam supply passages were smoothed out, and the tender copings differed in detail after 18 years of working experience with it, but a man on a galloping horse would never have noticed any of these alterations. The Chief Draughtsman at Doncaster expected that the lowest vacant 4–6–0 designation, 'B10' would be allocated to it, but seeking official confirmation, was told by Thompson to make it just class B, in his range of proposed standard designs. The first engine entered traffic on 12th December 1942 and carried CLASS B on front buffer beam. Then, on 29th April 1943, Thompson instructed that class B1 should be used and that was applied to the second engine from going into traffic on 12th June 1943, and to all those which were built subsequently.

When Thompson succeeded Gresley in April 1941 he is quoted as saying 'there is so much to do, and so little time in which to do it'. He must have been well aware that his retirement date was no further away than June 1946 and when he took office it was by no means certain that, standing alone and isolated, we should even win the war. As with so many of us, such doubts were not allowed to enter thinking or calculations, but in implementing his programme, he was certainly hampered by the diversion of metal and skilled labour to other necessary activities. When his retirement date duly arrived, only 24 B1 class had been completed, numbered 1000 to 1009 (originally 8301 to 8310) and 1040 to 1053. Thompson had, however, craftily ensured that there would ultimately be at least 310 of that type because by January 1946 he had been able to place orders with outside locomotive builders for 300 similar to the ten which Darlington had built between December 1942 and June 1944. Should a successor wish to cancel even part of those orders, the cost to the LNER would make such an action unthinkable. If such large orders had been placed on LNER workshops, then reduction could have been effected after he had retired without any qualms. Thompson did place an order, on 19th May 1944, for Darlington to built thirty, to be numbered 1010 to 1039 but he reduced that to 26 on 30th November 1945, when he issued another order for the balance of four engines only, specifying that the tenders for them would be obtained from the 6–wheeled type to be released from four A2/1 engines which were to be changed

to 8-wheeled tender instead. The four B1s which had to make do with second hand tenders turned out to be Nos.1010, 1011, 1038 and 1039.

In the final two months of the LNER's existence, Thompson's successor Peppercorn ordered another ten to be built at Darlington and ten more at Gorton works. In September 1948 British Railways ordered an additional forty from the North British Locomotive Co. and finally, on 24th February 1949, ten more from Darlington, both these orders under the signature of Peppercorn as Chief Mechanical Engineer of Eastern and North Eastern Regions. The last 'in–house' engine, No.61409 went into traffic on 15th June 1950 but it was 22nd April 1952 when the last of the 410 was completed by North British.

Even before Darlington finished construction, the class was going to be one short, because on 7th March 1950 No.61057 was so badly damaged in a collision at Marks Tey that engine and tender remains were cut up at Stratford in the following month – though the boiler was to be re–used by five other engines, and was in running service until June 1967.

In the ten years following the completion of the class (with NBL No.61399) changed circumstances of quite unpredictable proportions took place with the swing to dieselisation, so that B1 scrappings had already begun with the withdrawal of No.61085 in November 1961 and all 409 had been taken out of stock by September 1967. Their life span was short, ranging from a mere decade (February 1952 to October 1962) for 61395 to what was still a meagre twenty three and three quarter years, put in by 61002 from 21st September 1943 to 24th June 1967.

61306 spent all except its last three months working from sheds in Hull and was then transferred to Low Moor, the former Lancashire & Yorkshire shed which served the Bradford area. Whilst all the others had been scrapped, or sold for cutting up, 61306 was sold for private preservation in working order on 1st February 1968. With laudable intentions but quite inappropriately, it has subsequently had MAYFLOWER nameplates added. When 61264 was taken out of traffic on 21st November 1965 it remained at Colwick (Nottingham) shed, where it was used as Stationary Boiler No.29 until July 1967 and was then sold in March 1968 to Woodham Bros. of Barry for cutting up. It lingered in their scrapyard, suffering increasing decrepitude, until what remained was re–sold for restoration by some incredible optimists. It left Barry on a low loader in July 1976 for attention by the Main Line Steam Trust at Loughborough but has yet (1993) to be born again. Recently I have been able to help them by identifying the boiler (which had lost its plate) and providing its history.

The first B1 that I registered was the prototype (then showing CLASS B No.8301) on 6th March 1943, arriving in Manchester (London Road) station on the 3.43pm ex–Sheffield (Victoria). I then logged all of them, including 1057 on 4th May 1947 in Liverpool Street station but 61383 persistently eluded me until 19th September 1954, when I caught up with it using the coal stage at Ardsley shed. I see that I was hauled by 127 of them, the first occasion being on 22nd March 1945 when 8309 of Norwich shed took me on the 11.04am from Cambridge to Liverpool Street in London. My final haulage was by 61406 of Doncaster shed on 6th April 1966 when I was in the 8.52am from Hull to Doncaster. Between those dates B1s had taken me into the three London stations of Marylebone, King's Cross and Liverpool Street, as far north as Keith and Fort William, Hull, Cleethorpes, and Norwich in the east but not beyond Manchester in the west, except into Carlisle which is one degree further west, so far as England is concerned. The most surprising place that I saw one was at Castle Bromwich on 7th May 1951 when 61374 was on the 4.45pm from Birmingham to Cleethorpes. For excellent performance I have awarded the accolade to 1213 of Retford shed which I saw arriving in King's Cross station on Monday 1st September 1947 bringing in 12 well–filled coaches on the 3.15pm from Leeds and only 4 minutes late, after a V2 had failed. Where it was put on to that train I did not ascertain, but Retford B1s did not usually appear south of Grantham and 1213 was then less than two months old. My sighting of the youngest engine, however, is held by 61381, which I saw complete in the paint shop at the Queen's Park works of North British on 3rd September 1951, when it was 'no old at all' to quote our daughter's description of another event she had just witnessed.

Despite being designed to work the secondary range of passenger trains and always in the shadow of the Pacifics and V2 classes, in British Railways days B1s were certainly not strangers on named trains carrying headboards. On the former Great Central main line they could be seen regularly on *The Master Cutler* and on *The South Yorkshireman,* and on what was originally the Great Eastern, they frequently hauled the *East Anglian,* as well as *The Hook Continental* and *The Day Continental.* In the North Eastern Region they could be seen on *The Scarborough Flyer,* and in the Scottish Region on *The Queen of Scots;* in all these cases they carried the headboard as of right. The Hull portion of the *Yorkshire Pullman* occasionally had them to and from Doncaster, although not with the headboard, as that stayed with the Leeds portion. In emergency, a B1 even hauled, or assisted, an ailing Pacific on *The Flying Scotsman,* but in such cases I have seen no evidence of the headboard being transferred.

NUMBERING

To eliminate any confusion for younger readers, the re–numbering of the B1 class is explained. The order for the first batch of ten engines was placed on 13th August 1942, and numbers 8301 to 8310 were allocated to them, which were all carried when the engines were new. On 1st June 1943 the Chief Mechanical Engineer's office at Doncaster issued a 'General Plan of Re–Numbering Scheme agreed with the Chief General Manager' in which the 1000 to 1999 range was to include B (including new B1) K and V4 classes. The fully detailed scheme, running to 106 pages 10″ × 7″, was printed in December 1943 but due to wartime shortage of labour, could not be implemented until January 1946. In it, 8301 to 8310 were to become 1000 to 1009 and numbers to 1299 were left blank for the expected augmentation of B1 class. That subsequently proved insufficient and alterations had to be made later to accommodate the number actually built. 8302, 8303, 8304, 8307, 8308 and 8309 changed to 1001, 1002, 1003, 1006, 1007 and 1008 on Sunday 27th January 1946 but 8301, 8305, 8306 and 8309 could not be changed until engines in stock carrying the numbers 1000, 1004, 1005 and 1009 could take the new numbers allocated to them. 8301 and 8306 could be changed in February and the other two in March 1946. Although another thirty were ordered to be built by Darlington on 19th May 1944 and were allotted 1010 to 1039, at that date only 1019, 1020, 1021 and 1038 were not occupied by engines in stock. However no difficulty arose because it was November 1946 before Darlington could turn out the first of those thirty B1s and by then the numbers for them had all been cleared. For the 300 which Thompson ordered from outside contractors, numbers 1040 to 1339 were allocated, so clearly the original scheme would have to be altered with respect to 1300 – 1339, which classes B5, B15 B6 and B8 were originally intended to occupy.

The actual application was not so straightforward as when it was planned, because the last one of which the LNER took delivery was 1273. Whilst awaiting any altered instructions from the new owners, N.B. Loco Co. made delivery up to 1287 still with LNER on the tenders. Ten-

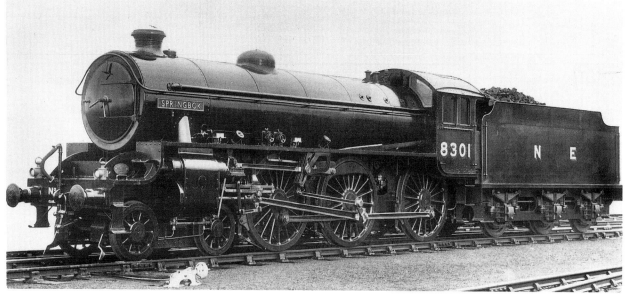

This is the press handout photograph issued on the appearance of the prototype. When new, No.8301's bogie had a 2¾″ deep stay bar across the front to which the usual pair of 14″ wide dust shields were attached. Wartime conditions limited its painting to black without any lining.

Darlington's official photograph of 8309 taken in May 1944 shows the grey paint which they used for such occasions and gives some validity to our choice of colour for the dust wrapper to Volume 6. When released to traffic 8309 was black.

der lettering then became BRITISH RAILWAYS for the rest of the order, but numbers 1288 to 1303 had an E prefix, indicating they were Eastern and North Eastern Region stock, E1303 being delivered on 26th March 1948. By then, the use of a prefix had been discarded in favour of a number and 6 was the figure for the ER and NER, so the remainder of the order came out as 61304 to 61339, and later ones as 61340 to 61409. By the time the prefix was introduced some of the 1946 built engines were due for their first general repair and so 1045, 1046, 1051, 1056, 1064, 1066, 1068, 1069, 1068, 1069, 1072, 1073, 1094 and 1100 acquired the prefix. E1068 was the first on 23rd January and E1064 the last on 13th March 1948. From Gorton works on 15th March No.61063 appeared, and that style then became standard.

NAMING

Whoever decided that the first ten, and the second batch of thirty, should have names of the genus antelope, did not make either an inspired or an attractive choice. The correct pronunciation of some of them was difficult to determine, and one was left to speculate if 1016 being INYALA and 1030 carrying NYALA was an unwitting duplication or if one was the male, and the other the female of the same species. Initially, 1036 was to have been KORRIGUM (for which plates were cast but never fitted) and whether Director Ralph Assheton, son of Baron Clitheroe, was happy to be sandwiched between PRONGHORN and JAIROU has never come to light. Only one more antelope name, the very British ROE-DEER was used, on No.1040, the first of the engines built by outside contractors.

In December 1947, with nationalisation looming, it was thought fitting that all the Directors who were members of the final LNER Board should have an engine named for them. Some were already so honoured on A4 Pacifics but plates for the others were prepared and fitted during December 1947, all on to B1s which had recently been put into traffic. Some made special visits to works simply to have the plates fitted, but others were given rather more

personal treatment. For example, 1189 went new to Stockton shed on 8th August 1947 and after plates were fitted to it in December 1947, the Director for whom it was named (who lived locally) went to Stockton station with his wife and two sons for an official photograph to be taken in front of 'his' engine. For William Henton Carver, who lived in the East Riding of Yorkshire, engine 1215, new on 19th July 1947 and allocated to Hull, was selected. Whilst it was officially photographed, this took place at Darlington Paint Shop, somewhat impersonally. Generally the choice was of engines running in the area for which the nominee was a member of the local Board. Other N.E. Area selected engines were 1237, 1238, 1240 and 1241, followed by 1242–1246 for Scottish Area and 1247–1251 for Southern Area. It will be noted that the continuous run is broken by 1239, which was not used, and it is believed that it was intended to be Rupert E Beckett, who was the only member of the final LNER Board not to have his name on an engine – why has not been divulged. Three of those named actually honoured Directors who were recently deceased, 1221 becoming SIR ALEXANDER ERSKINE–HILL, 1242 ALEXANDER REITH GRAY and 1251 OLIVER BURY. Apart from 1189 already mentioned, only the four Southern Area engines, 1247 to 1250, were given the personal treatment, 1248, 1249 and 1250 with only the nominee present, but for 1247 Lord and Lady Burghley duly posed.

After nationalisation only one more B1 was named, 61379 MAYFLOWER for a ceremony in King's Cross on Friday 13th July 1951 at the request of the Pilgrim Fathers Association. A small plate on the cab side explained that the naming was done as 'a symbol of the ties binding the two towns of Boston, and of the lasting friendship between the U.S.A. and the British Commonwealth'. 61379 then took out the 4.00pm train to Cleethorpes and made the normal call at Boston (Lincs) where the 1951 American Pilgrimage to Boston participants left the train. 61379 was cut up by Doncaster works in August 1962 but after 61306 was restored privately following withdrawal, its owner saw fit to have it named MAYFLOWER, although the U.S. interest had lapsed when 61379 went.

LIST OF NAMES APPLIED TO B1 CLASS ENGINES FROM NEW

The first ten, built at Darlington from December 1942, were given names of mainly African antelopes to commemorate a recent wartime visit to England by South Africa's current Prime Minister – Field Marshal J.C.Smuts. When Darlington built another thirty, from November 1946 to December 1947, they too were allocated names of antelopes, although one, No.1036 had plates cast but never carried them. The multiplicity of languages spoken in Africa accounts for the duplication of names and the various alternatives.

8301/1000	SPRINGBOK	A beautiful South African antelope, whose name was used to typify that country.
8302/1001	ELAND	The South African antelope with a protruberance on its larynx.
8303/1002	IMPALA	A red South African antelope, the size of a fallow deer; only male has horns.
8304/1003	GAZELLE	A small North African antelope, with beautiful dark eyes.
8305/1004	ORYX	A large East African antelope with long horns and a tufted tail.
8306/1005	BONGO	The largest West African bushbuck, of deep chestnut colour.
8307/1006	BLACKBUCK	The Indian antelope, the sole species of its genus.
8308/1007	KLIPSPRINGER	The Boer name for a small mountain antelope of great activity.
8309/1008	KUDU	A large South & East African antelope with long corkscrew horns.
8310/1009	HARTEBEESTE	Red South African antelope with long face & angulated lyrate horns.
1010	WILDEBEESTE	Has neck, body and tail like a horse, but horns similar to a buffalo; widely spread in Africa.
1011	WATERBUCK	A South & East African antelope with long ringed horns.
1012	PUKU	The shortest horned waterbuck – found in the Sudan and in Uganda.
1013	TOPI	East African antelope with lyre shaped ridged horns.
1014	ORIBI	Central & East African antelope whose horns stand up straight.
1015	DUIKER	A small South African antelope of which there are 12 different varieties.
1016	INYALA	The mountain Nyala found in the highlands of North Africa and Ethiopia.
1017	BUSHBUCK	Solitary animal with corkscrew twisted horns found in Central & East Africa.
1018	GNU	The distinctive name given to the black Wildebeeste.
1019	NILGHAI	Indian antelope with shorter, straighter horns than a Bushbuck.
1020	GEMSBOK	The Afrikaaner name for the South African Oryx.
1021	REITBOK	An alternative name for the Reedbuck *(see 1031)*. Should have been spelt RIETBOK.
1022	SASSABY	A South African antelope similar to the East African Topi.
1023	HIROLA	Quite rare species found in Kenya to southern Somalia.
1024	ADDAX	Endangered small groups found on the southern edge of the Sahara desert.
1025	PALLAH	The name for the Impala in the Bantu language.
1026	OUREBI	An alternative name for the Oribi *(see 1014)*.
1027	MADOQUA	One of the East African dik-diks which live in permanent pairs; silver-grey in colour.
1028	UMSEKE	The Zulu tribal name for the Reitbok *(see 1021)*; should have been UMZIKI.
1029	CHAMOIS	An agile dweller of the mountains of southern Europe; also known as the mountain goat.
1030	NYALA	Spiral horned antelope found in small regions of southern Africa.
1031	REEDBUCK	Inhabits grassy swamps across West to East Africa; greyish-brown colour.
1032	STEMBOK	The same animal as the Steinbok *(see 1039)* and the Steenbok.
1033	DIBATAG	Only the male is horned, which are crescent shaped; found in Somalia.
1034	CHIRU	Range limited to the remote higher steppes of Tibet.
1035	PRONGHORN	Last survivor of the antelopes confined to North America.
1036	KORRIGUM	An alternative name for what is usually known as the Topi *(see 1013)*.
1037	JAIROU	The Indian version of Chiru. Proved welcome fresh meat for our troops on jungle training in 1943-45.
1038	BLACKTAIL	Black tailed deer, also the mule deer, of the United States of America.
1039	STEINBOK	The German language name for the Steenbok; found in the Kalahari desert.

Only one more animal name was applied – to No.1040, the first of the order placed with the North British Locomotive Company. It came out new named ROEDEER, a small elegant deer inhabiting the forests of northern Scotland.

I am indebted to Messrs J.C.Dearman, L.R.Peters, L.Perrin and M.Nicholson for very positive help in what proved convoluted – but still fascinating – research.

The forty named after antelopes and the eighteen 'Directors' retained their names until withdrawal; 61243, at Ayr on 28th March 1964, is less than five weeks away from that fate. The length of some of the Director's names made for smaller lettering than had been customary up to then.

NAMES OF L N E R DIRECTORS PUT ON EXISTING B1'S FROM 4TH TO 23RD DEC. 1947

Engine No.	Name	Appointed	Resigned	Died
1036	RALPH ASSHETON	1945	—	21.9.55
1189	SIR WILLIAM GRAY	1933	—	28.1.78
1215	WILLIAM HENTON CARVER	1927	—	28.1.61
1221	SIR ALEXANDER ERSKINE-HILL	1940	—	6.6.47
1237	GEOFFREY H KITSON	1937	—	7.11.74
1238	LESLIE RUNCIMAN	1937 & 1946	1938	1.9.89
1239	*(for RUPERT E BECKETT – not used)*	1923	—	25.4.55
1240	HARRY HINCHLIFFE	1944	—	16.4.80
1241	VISCOUNT RIDLEY	1938	—	25.2.64
1242	ALEXANDER REITH GRAY	1923	—	30.4.46
1243	SIR HAROLD MITCHELL	1939	—	8.4.83
1244	STRANG STEEL	1938	—	14.8.61
1245	MURRAY OF ELIBANK	1923	—	2.6.73
1246	LORD BALFOUR OF BURLEIGH	1937	—	4.6.67
1247	LORD BURGHLEY	1934 & 1945	1943	21.10.81
1248	GEOFFREY GIBBS	1938	—	6.7.75
1249	FITZHERBERT WRIGHT	1943	—	10.4.75
1250	A. HAROLD BIBBY	1924	—	7.3.86
1251	OLIVER BURY	1923	—	21.3.46

One more engine named – by British Railways – 61379 MAYFLOWER was named in July 1951, being the name of the ship in which the Pilgrim Fathers sailed from Plymouth on 6th September 1620.

During the last month of the LNER's existence, eighteen B1s were fitted with plates bearing the names of LNER Directors. The engines selected worked in the Area with which the Director was connected – on the Southern Area examples chosen were Nos.1036 and 1247 to 1251, those in North Eastern Area 1189, 1215, 1237, 1238, 1240 and 1241 and in Scottish Area 1221 and 1242 to 1246. Note the steam turbine driven generator.

LIVERIES

The first ten had unlined black paint and only N E lettering on the tender, but their numbers, 8301 to 8310, and their tender letters were in the customary 12 inch gold blocked transfers. All except 8304 were still in black when they were renumbered 1000 to 1009 in January – March 1946, still with only N E on the tenders. In September 1945 No.8304 was specially repainted green with full black and white lining and with cab roof painted white because it had been selected as Royal Train engine. Even so, it still carried only N E on its tender, and in January 1946 its number changed to 1003. In June Stratford repainted it and restored 'LNER' but in the repainting a change was made to Gill Sans yellow painted numbers and letters, which did not have shading, whilst the cab roof was no longer white, the Royal Train duty having been taken over by B2 class 2871. Apart from 1003 Stratford continued unlined black painting for the other nine, but did restore LNER to their tenders and still used shaded transfers. In April 1946 deliveries began from the order placed with NBL, numbered from 1040 upwards to 1093 on 4th November 1946. All were black but with single red lining and normal gold shaded transfers; by the time that they appeared LNER was standard again. They were however peculiar in having only 10 inch figures on the cab as against 12 inch letters on tender. Beginning with No.1094 delivered on 6th November 1946, lined green passenger livery, and 12 inch cab numbers was the standard painting, although numbers and letters were in Gill Sans style, painted yellow and without back shading. At least to No.1104, on the front buffer beam 4½ inch gold block shaded characters continued to be used, but by No.1111 those had been changed to 6 inch unshaded Gill Sans style. Help with 1105 to 1110 would be appreciated – as to where exactly that change took place, because I lack photographic evidence of them when new. The rest of the order to 1139 then followed the style set by 1094 and was also used by Darlington for 1010 to 1039, except that all that thirty had 6 inch Gill Sans on the front buffer beams. The fifty (1140 to 1189) which Vulcan built were painted the same as 1010 – 1039.

Next came the 150 ordered from NBL numbered from 1190 upwards, which all first acquired green lined painting, although their numbering underwent two changes. Some of those from their first order were also changed from the original black to green when they received their first general repair; those were 1061 and 1067 from Cowlairs, 1062 from Darlington and 1082 from Gorton, all of which retained LNER on the tender. Stratford continued to use unlined black – Doncaster was not concerned with B1 repairs just then although that works called in No.1000 specially at the end of August 1947, to be painted green simply to be photographed officially for record purposes.

After nationalisation on 1st January 1948, at all except Stratford works, green continued to supersede black with 10 inch painted and unshaded BRITISH RAILWAYS on tenders and with an E prefix to the number. From Stratford came unlined black with only 6 inch high lettering for BRITISH RAILWAYS. Then on 19th April 1948 three essays at ownership style were paraded in Liverpool Street station for inspection (by which officials has not been discovered) and two unlined black engines took part. They were from the original batch renumbered to 61001 and 61009 and with the variation limited to the tender sides. 61009 on its left hand side had the 10 inch BRITISH

RAILWAYS as on green painted engines but with a small emblem of a seated lion with one paw on a wheel between the two words. On the opposite side only the emblem appeared but doubled in size. 61001 had the same emblem but in an intermediate size sitting on a small panel enclosing BRITISH RAILWAYS. Instead of the majesty of a lion, it looked more like a kitten playing with a ball of wool, and those emblems were painted over by Stratford on the following day.

On 6th April 1948 the British Railways Chairman Sir Cyril Hurcomb announced that, as an exercise in public relations, about 50 locomotives and 200 coaches were to be specially painted in distinctive colours to work the principal express passenger trains that summer. The trains with which B1 class would be concerned were the 12.30pm from Liverpool Street to Norwich and the 6.25pm return working from Norwich, also the York to Newcastle section of the through Leeds – Glasgow and Liverpool (Exchange) – Newcastle and corresponding return trains. For B1 class the 'distinctive' colour was black because they were rated as mixed traffic rather than express passenger types, but they were to share the same red, cream and grey lining. Darlington specially painted 61012, 61014, 61071 and 61084 for the North Eastern Region trains whilst Stratford dealt with 61040, 61042, 61044, 61048, 61054 and 61057 for Eastern Region trains. That style proved acceptable and along with it, smokebox doors had a cast number plate fitted in place of the painted number on the front buffer beam, so it was adopted as the standard for B1 class. However, NBL were allowed to complete their order to No.61339, delivered on 8th September 1948, in the green painting – so it was May 1951 before the green disappeared, 61320 (it is thought) being the last to wear it.

BRITISH RAILWAYS continued to be displayed on B1 tenders until April 1949 by Doncaster works but Gorton and Darlington applied it until July, 61349 from the former, and 61350 from the latter being the last to get it. In June a lion straddling a wheel emblem was introduced but supplies of the transfers were slow in being delivered so Doncaster sent out 61105, 61165, 61174, 61200, 61201, 61207 and 61212 with plain tender sides, as Darlington did on their new engines 61351 to 61354. The transfer was handed to face forward on both sides, and the larger size, 28 inch high, was used for B1 class. All, including, the ill–fated 61057 wore it.

In 1956 British Railways were accorded a grant of arms by the College of Heralds, and then decided to use the crest from it instead of the emblem. The initial stock of transfers purchased for it showing a lion holding a wheel were handed for the lion to face forward on both sides, so that on the right hand side of tenders the lion faced to the right. That conflicted with the tenets of heraldry, to which a grant of arms was bound to conform and, as objection was raised, correction had to be made. The first transfers began to replace the emblem from April 1957, but it was almost the end of 1958 before the heraldically acceptable variety were seen on the right hand side of B1 tenders. All had at least one repaint in 1959 or later so it is believed that all (except 61057 of course) were duly brought into line. 61402 ex–Cowlairs at the end of March 1959 was unusual, unique maybe, in having the smaller size of crest as applied to tank engines, put on its tender.

It was not only on the emblem/crest that a mistake was made. When the Gill Sans letters and figures were drawn out by Doncaster, the draughtsman added a curled tail to figures 6 and 9 which was definitely wrong. When painted numbers were introduced to save the cost of the expensive

There was less than three weeks difference between 1100 from N.B.Loco. and 1013 from Darlington being put into traffic, but the latter had yellow painted and unshaded characters 12″ high on cab and tender, and 6″ on front buffer beam. 1013 here is leaving Carlisle for Newcastle, but has B1 on the right hand side, and no indication of where it was shedded, although both it and 1100 were at Gateshead.

61400 duly got correct figure 6 both on cab and on smokebox plate but when this official photograph was taken at Darlington Stooperdale, the works number plate on the front end of the frame showed 2101. A reliable observer noted that had been corrected to 2102 when he saw it in the works yard on 26th March 1950, four days prior to it being released to traffic.

gold block shaded transfers, the incorrect 6 and 9 figures not only appeared on cab sides, but also on cast number plates when British Railways began to fit them on smokebox doors. There could be, then, cases of the right hand not knowing what the left hand was doing, as exemplified by the ten new engines from Gorton, Nos.61340 – 61349. The Paint Shop put correct Gill Sans 6 and 9 on their cab sides, but Pattern Shop either had not been advised of the correction, or chose to ignore it, because the plates for all ten were cast, and fitted, with the wrong 6 and 9 on them. 61349 indeed seems to have carried such a plate through to its withdrawal, for it was seen so fitted after its last general repair in June 1963. Modellers need to be wary of the many variations that mistake caused. The curled 6 has also been repeated on the preserved engine, which in its working life was never numbered 1306 or had LNER on its tender, nor was it named

TENDERS

With Thompson having such a fetish for standardisation, we could have expected that only one picture would be required to portray the tender used by B1 class. Certainly all tenders that went into traffic by the date of his retirement were alike, but they only totalled 24, those attached to engines 8301 – 8310 and 1040 – 1053. The basic design was Gresley's because they were Group Standard 4,200 gallons type as introduced for the K3 class in 1924. Even so, Thompson did manage to start a new numbering system for them, as will be detailed later. When the works at Doncaster and Darlington felt that they could breathe again, after 30th June 1946 when Thompson retired, they adhered in general to the standard tender design for B1 class, but managed to introduce some of the fascinating variations which so delight enthusiasts. The order on which North British had started with engine 1040 was continued to 1139: Vulcan followed by supplying 1140 to 1189, then 1190 to 61339 came from NBL and all those 300 had identical tenders. Meanwhile Darlington works had been given Order 1121, dated 19th May 1944, to build thirty to be numbered 1010 to 1039 but on 30th November 1945 Thompson reduced that order to 26 engines and tenders, and issued Order 1182 for four engines only, specifying that the tenders were to come from A2/1 Pacifics which were being given 8-wheeled instead of 6-wheeled type. Darlington did not start delivery against Order 1121 until November 1946 by which date the Group Standard tenders from A2/1 class Nos.3696 and 509 (ex–3696) had become available, so they attached them to engines 1010 and 1011. The 26 new tenders which they built went out with engines 1012 to 1037, leaving provision for 1038 and 1039 when they were completed in December 1947. The tenders from A2/1 Nos.508 and 510 intended for those B1s were not and did not become available until June 1949, so Darlington had to seek tenders suitable for 1038 and 1039. For 1038 they used the C7 class tender from engine 732, which had stood spare since that engine's withdrawal in December 1946, whilst 1039 got a rebuilt tender from C9 class No.2171, scrapped in May 1942. The similar tender from the other C9, No.727, was also rebuilt and it replaced the C7 tender on 1038, which dated from 1920, the change being made at Darlington shed on 9th June 1949. So when the 6–wheeled Group Standard tenders from 60508 and 60510 became available they were additional to requirements, because the rebuilt tenders from C9 class continued to be used by 1038 and 1039 through to 1964. Indeed the tender from 60510 was never

coupled with a B1, K3 class 61873 having it from October 1949 through to its May 1962 withdrawal. The tender from 60508 stood spare from June 1949 until May 1951, when it was put with B1 No.61105 which retained it until they were sold for cutting up in July 1966. That released 61105's original tender for conversion to coal weighing type, and the tender off K3 No.61873 (recognisable by its low front plate and shorter coping) went to 61165 to allow its own tender to be converted to coal weighing too. When completed, the two coal weighing tenders were put with 61210 and 61086, freeing two more B1 tenders for coal weighing. The coupling of these four special tenders were many and varied, two of them going briefly to Peppercorn K1 2–6–0s. Anyone interested in their subsequent usage can find it fully detailed on page 137 of Part 2B of the RCTS *Locomotives of the LNER* but the one attached to 61140 in Scotland from September 1952 to its December 1966 withdrawal is fully illustrated in this volume.

There were some noticeable differences of detail amongst the B1 tenders. Those attached to Nos.1000 to 1037, all built by Darlington, had separate coping plate welded to the top edge of the tank side plate, and the dividing line was easy to see. Tenders built with 1040 to 61349 and 61360 to 61399 had coping integral with the tank side, and all–welded tank. The tenders which Darlington put with 61350 – 61359 had a chequered history. They had rivetted tanks and the four put with 61352, 61353, 61354 and 61357 had very prominent snaphead rivets. They had been partially constructed at Doncaster in 1942 for an O2 class order which was cancelled. Doncaster later sent the parts for the aborted tender order through to Darlington and on the six for which the latter did the tank rivetting, they countersunk the rivets to provide a smooth surface. The intention of sending these sets of tender components to Darlington was to use them with engines being rebuilt to B2 class, in place of the small Great Eastern type tenders with which they had run as B17 class – see *Register 5*.

Apart from the two ex–C9 tenders attached to 1038 and 1039, all B1 tenders had a high front plate but that at the rear of the coal space was much lower. From December 1955 the rear plate was moved two feet further forward and increased in height to match that of the front plate. The pair of ex–C9 tenders also differed in not having any angle iron below the tank sides. The plates across the ends of the tender on which the rear and the intermediate buffers were mounted were square ended on all except the tenders Darlington built for Nos.61400 to 61409; on those the front plate ends were cut diagonally inwards.

Tenders had their own numbers to ease the identification and costing of repairs made to them. When Darlington built the tenders for 8301 to 8310 they continued the series of numbers used for Group Standard 4,200 gallons type, those ten taking 7287 to 7296. For reasons which he thought best, and for which no explanation has ever been put forward, Thompson began a fresh series with 4000 as the starting number. Actually 4000 and 4001 were put on the tenders taken from A2/1 engines which were then coupled with B1s 1010 and 1011, although they had carried 7283 and 7285. Tender numbers 4002 and 4003 were allocated to the other two tenders to come from A2/1 class, which were already plated 7284 and 7286. When they did become available (three years after Thompson had retired) they were able to keep their original tender numbers.

So the tenders built for B1 class took numbers from 4004 upwards, attached in sequence to engines 1012 to

1037. Engine 1038 first had tender 8679 (the ex–C7 type) and then 8684, the number retained by the ex–C9 type. Similarly engine 1039 had 8685. With those complications ironed out 1040 to 61409 got tenders 4030 to 4399. More than half, indeed 236, kept their original tender coupling through to withdrawal, and many more only had a single change. Where coal weighing tenders were concerned many changes were made, except with 61140 in Scotland. On the other hand, Nos.61307, 61347, 61395 and 61401 all ran with five different tenders and, curiously, those four spent almost the whole of their lives in Scotland.

Tucked away in a remote siding somewhere you may still be able to see a B1 tender because there was life after death for two of them, Nos.4040 and 4305 being saved from scrapping to form the base of mobile snow ploughs. It is possible that they were given Departmental numbers 330982 and 330983 and if anybody should now come across either, do please tell me. The preserved engine, now running as LNER 1306, retained its original tender so should still be plated 4296, and the one rescued from Barry scrapyard, 61264, also kept the same tender, 4254, throughout its working life.

The Group Standard tender allocated for engine 1039 had not been released when the engine was ready so an alternative arrangement had to be made. It got one of the two tenders which had been rebuilt after serving as part of the 4–4–4–4 wheel arrangement of booster–fitted Atlantics 727 and 2171. The rebuilds approximated to Group Standard type but could be identified by their very different coping, as seen on this one at Leeds Neville Hill shed, on 9th June 1948.

The tenders put with 61352, 61353, 61354 and 61357 when new were unusual in having snaphead rivets, which showed up quite prominently. This exception arose because the material for them had been prepared at Doncaster in 1942 for an O2 class order; this had then been cancelled as it was found possible to use existing tenders for the 2–8–0s. Normal rivetting was countersunk, but that needed extra work, which had to be saved in the wartime conditions of 1942.

When only two months old, 8301 had the stay bar replaced by a plate 16″ deep, with the dust shields cut short at the top and that revised arrangement was also applied to 8302 when new, in June 1943. No.8301 is leaving Manchester (London Road) station for Sheffield (Victoria) in March 1943, and it can just be discerned that its buffer beam carries only CLASS B and not B1.

1046 out of Doncaster works on 12th October 1946. It had been called in specially to be the first B1 to be fitted with Stone's steam turbine generator and electric lighting. Note no heater connection at front end, which was fitted later.

THE B1 CLASS

8301

SPRINGBOK

Darlington.

To traffic 12/12/42.

REPAIRS:
Str. 8/8–7/9/45.**L.**
Str. 15/2–13/4/46.**G.**
Str. 24/5–15/6/46.**L.**
Str. 28/10–9/11/46.**L.**
Don. 26/8–6/9/47.*Paint.*
Str. 19/4–29/5/48.**G.**
Str. 20/9–22/10/49.**C/L.**
Str. 3/4–27/5/50.**G.**
Str. 19–29/6/51.**C/L.**
Str. 27/8–13/9/51.**C/L.**
Str. 28/1–2/2/52.**C/L.**
Str. 19/5–3/7/52.**G.**
Str. 22–31/7/53.**N/C.**
Str. 27/9–30/10/54.**G.**
Str. 16/11/55–10/1/56.**C/L.**
Str. 22/10–24/11/56.**C/L.**
Str. 25/6–6/9/57.**G.**
Str. 13/10–11/12/59.**G.**
A.T.C. fitted.
Don. 13–14/9/60.*Not Rep.
Sent to works in error.*
Don. 20/12/60–6/1/61.**N/C.**
Don. 26/2/62.*Not repaired.*

BOILERS:
9425.
9439 *(ex1622)* 29/5/48.
5065 *(ex1054)* 27/5/50.
5065 renumbered 28561
29/6/51.
28503 *(ex1271)* 3/7/52.
28502 *(ex1119)* 30/10/54.
28870 *(ex1614)* 6/9/57.
28592 *(ex1228)* 11/12/59.

SHEDS:
Darlington.
Gorton 1/3/43.
Cambridge 11/12/44.
Norwich 29/9/45.
Stratford 21/7/46.
Parkeston 19/10/46.
Stratford 1/2/48.
Colchester 6/1/57.
March 1/11/59.
Doncaster 20/12/59.
Colwick 12/6/60.

RENUMBERED:
1000 22/2/46.
61000 29/5/48.

CONDEMNED:
5/3/62.
Cut up Doncaster.

8302

ELAND

Darlington 1912.

To traffic 12/6/43.

REPAIRS:
Str. 24/1–12/2/44.**N/C.**
Dar. 22/3–7/6/45.**G.**
Str. 15–24/11/45.**L.**
Str. 23/9–9/11/46.**G.**
Str. 9–14/5/47.**L.**
Str. 29/11/48–22/1/49.**G.**
Str. 10–18/1/50.**N/C.**
Str. 18/12/50–3/2/51.**G.**
Str. 13–14/3/51.**C/L.**
Str. 1–12/1/52.**C/L.**
Str. 24–26/6/52.**N/C.**
Don. 3/2–5/3/53.**G.**
Str. 23/8–8/10/54.**G.**
Don. 6–30/1/56.**C/H.**
Don. 20/11–29/12/56.**G.**
Str. 8/9–17/10/58.**G.**
Don. 15/6–23/7/60.**G.**

BOILERS:
9426.
9431 *(new)* 7/6/45.
9426 *(ex-spare)* 9/11/46.
9693 *(ex1104)* 22/1/49.
28529 *(ex1205)* 3/2/51.
28857 *(new)* 5/3/53.
28427 *(ex61364)* 8/10/54.
28276 *(ex1083)* 29/12/56.
28548 *(ex1149)* 17/10/58.
28192 *(ex1658)* 23/7/60.

SHEDS:
Darlington.
Stratford 30/6/43.
Norwich 10/7/43.
Ipswich 25/6/44.
Parkeston 11/1/45.
Ipswich 28/2/45.
Stratford 24/7/46.
Parkeston 7/12/46.
Stratford 1/2/48.
Ipswich 26/3/50.
Stratford 30/4/50.
Neasden 22/6/52.
Peterborough 20/1/57.
Ipswich 3/3/57.
Norwich 27/9/59.
Doncaster 29/11/59.

RENUMBERED:
1001 27/1/46.
61001 10/4/48.

CONDEMNED:
22/9/63.
*Into Doncaster Works for
cut-up 31/10/63.*

8303

IMPALA

Darlington 1916.

To traffic 21/9/43.

REPAIRS:
Dar. 28/10–12/11/43.**L.**
Dar. 9–11/2/44.**N/C.**
Dar. 12/6–12/7/45.**G.**
Cow. 29/7–29/8/46.**L.**
Cow. 28/11/46–10/1/47.**G.**
Cow. 27/8–12/9/47.**L.**
Cow. 5/3–10/4/48.**G.**
Cow. 17/6–1/7/48.**L.**
Cow. 13–30/10/48.**L.**
Cow. 10–13/1/49.**C/L.**
Cow. 3–25/6/49.**H/I.**
Cow. 14/9–19/10/49.**C/L.**
Cow. 9–18/11/49.**C/L.**
Cow. 2–25/2/50.**C/H.**
Cow. 8–26/5/50.**C/H.**
Cow. 23/8–16/9/50.**N/C.**
Cow. 29/6–9/8/51.**L/I.**
Dar. 28/8–28/9/53.**C/L.**
Dar. 4–13/3/54.**C/L.**
Dar. 18/6–14/7/54.**G.**
Dar. 19–20/7/54.**N/C.**
Dar. 21/6–8/8/56.**G.**
Dar. 4/9–3/10/58.**G.**
Dar. 4–17/6/59.**N/C.**
Dar. 10/4–6/5/61.**G.**
Dar. 17–26/5/61.**N/C.**
Dar. 19/11–24/12/64.**G.**

BOILERS:
3391.
3449 *(ex1007)* 25/2/50.
3449 renumbered 28601
9/8/51.
28801 *(ex1125)* 14/7/54.
28227 *(ex1030)* 8/8/56.
28293 *(ex1216)* 3/10/58.
28235 *(ex1061)* 6/5/61.
28588 *(ex1288)* 24/12/64.

SHEDS:
Darlington.
Haymarket 21/11/43.
Perth 4/3/44.
St Margarets 5/2/50.
Dalry Rd 11/3/51.
Darlington 2/9/51.
York 11/11/51.
Hull Dairycoates 6/6/65.

RENUMBERED:
1002 27/1/46.
61002 10/4/48.

CONDEMNED:
24/6/67.
Sold 8/67 for scrap to

*Garnham, Harris & Elton,
Chesterfield.*

8304

GAZELLE

Darlington 1920.

To traffic 22/11/43.

REPAIRS:
Str. 20–21/3/44.**L.** *Front
end heater connection*
Str. 4/6–1/9/45.**G.**
Str. 12–18/9/45. *Paint.(1)*
Str. 14–19/12/45. *Paint.(1)*
Str. 27/5–11/6/46.**N/C.**
Paint.(1)
Str. 9/12/46–18/2/47.**G.**
Str. 13/10–18/12/48.**G.**
Str. 24–28/1/50.**N/C.**
Str. 26/1–3/3/51.**C/L.**
Str. 16/7–18/8/51.**G.**
Str. 7–24/4/53.**N/C.**
Str. 24/11–24/12/53.**G.**
Str. 25/4–14/5/55.**N/C.**
Str. 15/10–1/12/56.**G.**
Str. 11–22/2/57.**N/C.**
Str. 1/12/58–30/1/59.**G.**
Str. 4–25/3/59.**N/C.** *A.T.C.
fitted.*
Don. 4–9/7/60.**N/C.**
Don. 6/10–7/11/61.**G.**

**(1) For Royal Train
working.**

BOILERS:
3415.
3625 *(ex1057)* 18/2/47.
9735 *(new)* 18/12/48.
28560 *(ex1052)* 18/8/51.
28569 *(ex61362)* 24/12/53.
28510 *(ex1671)* 1/12/56.
28808 *(ex1192)* 30/1/59.
28201 *(ex61361)* 7/11/61.

SHEDS:
Darlington.
Norwich 9/1/44.
Ipswich 25/6/44.
Cambridge 13/7/44.
Norwich 28/9/45.
Cambridge 24/7/46.
Stratford 31/1/47.
Parkeston 8/2/47.
Stratford 2/3/58.
Parkeston 13/4/58.
March 1/11/59.
Doncaster 15/11/59.
Immingham 30/12/62.
Colwick 26/9/65.

WORKS CODES:– Cow – Cowlairs. Dar – Darlington. Dee – Dundee. Don – Doncaster. Ghd – Gateshead. Gor – Gorton. Inv – Inverurie. Str – Stratford. SRX – St Rollox.
REPAIR CODES:– **C/H** – Casual Heavy. **C/L** – Casual Light. **G** – General. **H** – Heavy. **H/I** – Heavy Intermediate. **L** – Light. **L/I** – Light Intermediate. **N/C** – Non–Classified.

RENUMBERED:
1003 27/1/46.
6100318/12/48.

CONDEMNED:
26/12/65.
*Sold 2/66 for scrap to
Garnham, Harris & Elton,
Chesterfield./.*

8305

ORYX

Darlington 1922.

To traffic 22/12/43.

REPAIRS:
Str. 4–5/4/44.**L.**
Str. 19/9–20/10/45.**G.**
Str. 10–13/3/47.**L.**
Str. 23/4–18/6/47.**G.** *Front
heater connection fitted.*
Str. 17/8–2/10/48.**H.**
Str. 13/2–29/4/50.**G.**
Str. 9/10–22/11/52.**G.**
Dar. 11/3–20/4/55.**G.**
Str. 6–9/5/57.**N/C.**
Str. 6/8–21/9/57.**G.**
Str. 24/8–16/10/59.**G.**
A.T.C.fitted.
Str. 28/10–6/11/59.**N/C.**

BOILERS:
3419.
5099 *(new)* 18/6/47.
5062 *(ex1050)* 29/4/50.
28578 *(ex1008)* 22/11/52.
28202 *(ex1078)* 20/4/55.
28256 *(ex1058)* 21/9/57.
28173 *(ex1639)* 16/10/59.

SHEDS:
Darlington.
Stratford 14/1/44.
Norwich 2/11/45.
Cambridge 24/7/46.
Parkeston 24/1/47.
Stratford 31/5/47.
Parkeston 7/9/47.
Stratford 2/3/58.
Parkeston 13/4/58.
Stratford 14/12/58.
Parkeston 8/2/59.
March 13/12/59.
Sheffield 10/1/60.
Mexborough 9/9/62.
Canklow 9/12/62.

RENUMBERED:
1004 24/3/46.
61004 2/10/48.

CONDEMNED:
28/12/63.
*Into Darlington for cut-up
21/3/64.*

8306

BONGO

Darlington 1925.

To traffic 19/2/44.

REPAIRS:
Str. 5–22/9/45.**G.**
Str. 13/5–6/6/46.**L.**
Str. 11/3–1/5/47.**G** *Front
heater connection fitted.*
Str. 14/2–17/3/49.**C/H.**
Str. 19/12/49–11/2/50.**G.**
Str. 26/5–4/7/52.**G.**
Str. 3–19/11/54.**N/C.**
Str. 28/2–7/4/55.**G.**
Str. 17–28/7/56.**N/C.**
Str. 25/2–2/3/57.**N/C.**
Str. 19/11–28/12/57.**G.**
Str. 5–16/5/58.**N/C.**
Str. 22/5–11/6/59.**C/L**
A.T.C fitted.
Don. 22/1–24/2/60.**G.**

BOILERS:
3421.
3415 *(ex8304)* 1/5/47.
5074 *(ex1052)* 11/2/50.
28588 *(ex1119)* 4/7/52.
28524 *(ex1233)* 7/4/55.
28502 *(ex1000)* 28/12/57.
28319 *(ex1130)* 24/2/60.

SHEDS:
Darlington.
Stratford 24/3/44.
Cambridge 3/2/46.
Stratford 24/7/46.
Parkeston 19/10/46.
Stratford 7/12/46.
Parkeston 25/1/47.
New England 7/10/56.
Peterborough 3/2/57.
Stratford 16/6/57.
Parkeston 8/2/59.
March 1/11/59.
Cambridge 11/6/61.
Stratford 17/6/62.
March 29/7/62.

RENUMBERED:
1005 24/2/46.
61005 17/3/49.

CONDEMNED:
16/9/62.
*In for cut up Doncaster
21/11/62.*

8307

BLACKBUCK

Darlington 1927.

To traffic 17/3/44.

REPAIRS:
Str. 21/11–21/12/45.**G.**
Str. 13/5–1/8/47.**G.**
Str. 21/12/48–14/1/49.**C/L.**
Str. 28/12/49–18/2/50.**G**

Str. 24/7–5/8/50.**C/L.**
Str. 1–19/1/52.**C/L.**
Str. 1/10–15/11/52.**G.**
Str. 23/5–1/7/55.**G.**
Don. 8–23/11/56.**C/L.**
Str. 10/12/57–15/2/58.**G.**
Don. 23/2–26/3/60.**G.**
Don. 18–27/1/61**N/C.**

BOILERS:
3446.
3421 *(ex8306)* 1/8/47.
3446 *(ex1009)* 18/2/50.
3446 renumbered 28574
19/1/52.
28256 *(ex1672)* 15/11/52.
28554 *(ex1050)* 1/7/55.
28573 *(ex1252)* 15/2/58.
28352 *(ex3982)* 26/3/60.

SHEDS:
Darlington.
Gorton 3/8/44.
Ipswich 11/12/44.
Parkeston 5/1/45.
Ipswich 28/2/45.
Stratford 14/8/46.
Parkeston 25/1/47.
New England 7/10/56.
Peterborough 6/1/57.
Stratford 16/6/57.
Parkeston 8/2/59.
March 8/11/59.
Lincoln 7/2/60.

RENUMBERED:
1006 27/1/46.
61006 14/1/49.

CONDEMNED:
22/9/63.
*Sold 1/64 for scrap to
R.A.King, Norwich.*

8308

KLIPSPRINGER

Darlington 1928.

To traffic 14/4/44.

REPAIRS:
Dar. 21/9–20/10/45.**G.**
Dar. 25/3–6/4/46.**N/C.** *For
self cleaning smokebox.*
Cow. 23/4–8/5/47.**H.**
Cow. 8/12/48–29/1/49.**G.**
Cow. 13/3–5/4/51.**H/I.**
Cow. 11/2–14/3/53.**G.**
Hay. 5–22/10/54.**C/L.**
Hay. 7–18/6/55.**C/L.**
Cow. 27/7–27/8/55.**H/I.**
Hay. 17–30/5/57.**C/L.**
Cow. 28/8–13/9/57.**N/C.**
Cow. 15/10–23/11/57.**G.**
Hay. 19–22/10/58.**C/L.**
StRx. 30/3–25/4/59.**N/C.**
Cow. 18/6–10/7/59.**H/I.**
Cow. 8/1–3/2/62.**C/L.**
Cow. 14–16/2/62.**C/L.**
Cow. 13–28/12/63.**N/C.**

BOILERS:
3449.
9856 *(ex1219)* 29/1/49.
9856 renumbered 28625
5/4/51.
28702 *(ex1262)* 14/3/53.
28543 *(ex1191)* 23/11/57.
28614 *(ex1132)* 3/2/62.

SHEDS:
Darlington.
Haymarket 15/5/44.
Dundee 28/6/48.
Haymarket 25/7/48.
Dalry Rd. 30/6/60.
St Margarets 1/10/61.
Eastfield 29/12/62.
Ayr 21/1/63.

RENUMBERED:
1007 27/1/46.
61007 29/1/49.

CONDEMNED:
6/2/64.
*Sold 6/64 for scrap to
Geo.H.Campbell, Airdrie.*

8309

KUDU

Darlington 1931.

To traffic 13/5/44.

REPAIRS:
Dar. 2–18/10/44.**L.**
Str. 25/2–18/4/46.**G.**
Str. 3–21/12/46.**L.**
Str. 6/4–11/5/48.**G.** *Front
end heater connection
fitted.*
Str. 7–8/4/49.**C/L.**
Str. 17/4–10/6/50.**G.**
Str. 26/6–1/7/50.**N/C.**
Str. 31/7–4/8/50.**N/C.**
Str. 21/1–2/2/52.**C/L.**
Str. 21/7–30/8/52.**G.**
Str. 29/9–10/10/53.**N/C.**
Str. 12/8–2/10/54.**G.**
Str. 10–24/6/55.**N/C.**
Dar. 12/2–14/3/57.**G.**
Dar. 6–9/5/57.**N/C.**
Dar. 17/9–23/10/58.**G.**
Dar. 16/8–23/9/60.**G.**
Dar. 20/10–20/11/61.**C/L.**

BOILERS:
3464.
3606 *(ex1043)* 11/5/48.
3415 *(ex1005)* 10/6/50.
3415 renumbered 28578
2/2/52.
28518 *(ex1272)* 30/8/52.
28869 *(new)* 2/10/54.
28431 *(ex1157)* 14/3/57.
28461 *(ex61367)* 23/10/58.
28131 *(ex1236 & spare)*
23/9/60.

SHEDS:
Darlington.
Gateshead 3/6/44.

Neville Hill 18/8/44.
Parkeston 3/1/45.
Stratford 3/3/45.
Norwich 29/9/45.
Stratford 17/8/46.
Parkeston 25/1/47.
Stratford 16/5/48.
Kings Cross 23/10/55.
Leicester 10/6/56.
Agecroft 26/9/59.
Woodford 21/7/62.
Eastfield 16/3/63.
Carstairs 13/6/66.

RENUMBERED:
1008 27/1/46.
61008 11/5/48.

CONDEMNED:
9/12/66.
Sold 2/67 for scrap to
J.McWilliam, Shettleston.

8310

HARTEBEESTE

Darlington 1934.

To traffic 19/6/44.

REPAIRS:
Str. 26/11/45–12/1/46.**G.**
Str. 19/8–25/10/47.**G.**
Str. 16–18/4/48.**N/C.**
Str. 3/10–5/11/49.**G.**
Str. 21/8–6/10/51.**G.**
Don. 19/8–4/9/52.**C/L.**
Don. 5/10–2/11/53.**G.**
Don. 18/4–16/5/55.**G.**
Dar. 6/12/56–15/1/57.**G.**
Don. 28/8–18/9/58.**C/L.**
Str. 2/3–17/4/59.**G.**
Don. 15–24/9/59.**N/C.**
Don. 9–19/8/60.**N/C.**

BOILERS:
3456.
3446 *(ex8307)* 25/10/47.
3753 *(ex2817)* 5/11/49.
28523 *(ex1301)* 6/10/51.
28172 *(ex1266)* 2/11/53.
28525 *(ex1015)* 15/1/57.
28295 *(ex61361)* 17/4/59.

SHEDS:
Darlington.
Neville Hill 6/7/44.
Parkeston 3/1/45.
Stratford 3/3/45.
Neasden 22/6/52.
Leicester 25/7/54.
Neasden 5/12/54.
Sheffield 10/6/56.
Doncaster 29/9/57.
Lincoln 10/11/57.

RENUMBERED:
1009 2/3/46.
61009 18/4/48.

CONDEMNED:
16/9/62.

Sold 5/64 for scrap to Cox
& Danks, Wadsley Bridge.

1010

WILDEBEESTE

Darlington 1990.

To traffic 2/11/46.

REPAIRS:
Don. 28/4–10/5/47.**N/C.**
Stone's elec.light fitted.
Gor. 17/4–8/5/48.**G.**
Dar. 12/6–7/7/50.**G.**
Ghd. 11–14/7/50.**N/C.**
Dar. 30/7–1/8/51.**C/L.**
Dar. 26/2–21/3/52.**G.**
Dar. 6–27/11/52.**N/C.**
Dar. 11/2–6/3/54.**G.**
Dar. 20/9–15/10/55.**G.**
Dar. 17–18/10/55.**N/C.**
Dar. 20/12/56–16/1/57.**C/L.**
Dar. 14/6–31/7/57.**G.**
Dar. 7–13/8/57.**N/C.**
Dar. 8/9–3/10/59.**G.**
Complete A.T.C.fitted.
Dar. 5/7–29/8/62.**G.**
Dar. 20/9–2/10/62.**N/C.**

BOILERS:
3716.
5075 *(ex1065)* 8/5/48.
3684 *(ex1084)* 7/7/50.
28404 *(ex1131)* 21/3/52.
28235 *(ex1108)* 6/3/54.
28260 *(ex1053)* 15/10/55.
28369 *(ex1295)* 31/7/57.
28874 *(ex1176)* 3/10/59.
28302 *(ex1080)* 29/8/62.

SHEDS:
Hull Botanic Gdns.
Hull Dairycoates 14/6/59.

RENUMBERED:
61010 8/5/48.

CONDEMNED:
7/11/65.
Sold 12/65 for scrap to
A.Draper, Hull. Cut-up
28/2/66.

1011

WATERBUCK

Darlington 1991.

To traffic 30/11/46.

REPAIRS:
Dar. 11/3–23/4/48.**G.**
Ghd. 18/1–1/2/49.**L/I.**
Dar. 9/6–6/7/49.**G.**
Ghd. 8–15/8/50.**C/L.**
Dar. 31/1–24/2/51.**G.**
Ghd. 16–30/5/52.**C/L.**
Dar. 12/8–6/9/52.**G.**
Dar. 8–10/9/52.**N/C.**
Dar. 18/3–10/4/54.**G.**

Dar. 20/7–9/8/55.**C/L.**
Dar. 24/2–23/3/56.**G.**
Dar. 13/3–10/4/58.**G.**
Dar. 4–14/4/60.**C/L.**
Dar. 13/9–15/10/60.**G.**

BOILERS:
3717.
9728 *(ex1142)* 6/7/49.
28133 *(ex1166)* 24/2/51.
28266 *(ex1154)* 6/9/52.
28602 *(ex1061)* 10/4/54.
28102 *(ex1253)* 23/3/56.
28191 *(ex1124)* 10/4/58.
28508 *(ex1641)* 15/10/60.

SHEDS:
Gateshead.
Ardsley 23/9/56.
Wakefield 22/2/59.
Mirfield 22/3/59.
Gorton 15/7/60 *(on loan).*
Gorton 17/7/60.
Woodford 5/8/61.
Gorton 13/1/62.

RENUMBERED:
61011 23/4/48.

CONDEMNED:
2/11/62.
27/11/62 in for cut up
Darlington.

1012

PUKU

Darlington 1992.

To traffic 30/11/46.

REPAIRS:
Dar. 7/5–4/6/48.**G.**
Dar. 8/11–3/12/49.**G.**
Dar. 8–22/12/49.**N/C.**
Dar. 21–27/3/50.**C/L.**
Dar. 6–13/6/50.**C/L.**
Dar. 15/3–13/4/51.**G.**
Ghd. 8–13/11/51.**C/L.**
Dar. 16/9–11/10/52.**G.**
Dar. 13–14/10/52.**N/C.**
Dar. 20/4–15/5/54.**G.**
Dar. 17–21/5/54.**N/C.**
Dar. 31/5–9/6/54.**N/C.**
Ghd. 12/4–31/5/55.**C/L.**
Ghd. 2–24/5/56.**C/L.**
Dar. 12/10–15/11/56.**G.**
Dar. 8/1–15/2/57.**C/L.**
Dar. 4/11–5/12/58.**G.**
A.T.C. Mech.Fitted.
Dar. 9–23/6/59.**N/C.**
A.T.C. Elec.Fitted.
Dar. 6–14/4/61.**C/L.**
Dar. 28/4–25/5/61.**G.**
Dar. 4/11–21/12/63.**G.**
Dar. 24–28/2/64.**C/L.**

BOILERS:
3723.
5078 *(ex1069)* 3/12/49.
28205 *(ex1199)* 13/4/51.
28107 *(ex1016)* 11/10/52.
28322 *(ex3796)* 15/5/54.

28224 *(ex61338)* 15/11/56.
28216 *(ex1138)* 5/12/58.
28134 *(ex61309)* 25/5/61.
28801 *(ex1069)* 21/12/63.

SHEDS:
Gateshead.
Hull Dairycoates 17/7/60.
York 18/12/66.

RENUMBERED:
61012 4/6/48.

CONDEMNED:
12/6/67.
Sold 8/67 for scrap to
Hughes, Bolckow, N.Blyth.

1013

TOPI

Darlington 1993.

To traffic 14/12/46.

REPAIRS:
Gor. 17/4–15/5/48.**G.**
Dar. 26/8–22/9/49.**G.**
Dar. 19/2–17/3/51.**G.**
Dar. 17/6–12/7/52.**G.**
Dar. 4–27/3/54.**G.**
Dar. 10/11–9/12/55.**G.**
Dar. 19–22/12/55.**N/C.**
Dar. 14–24/7/56.**C/L.**
Dar. 3–7/12/56.**C/L.**
Dar. 19/3–3/4/57.**C/L.**
Dar. 1/7–15/8/58.**G.**
Dar. 1–5/9/58.**N/C.**
Dar. 30/4–13/5/59.**N/C.**
A.T.C. Mech.fitted.
Dar. 5–9/6/59.**N/C. A.T.C.**
Elec.fitted.
Dar. 20/3–27/4/62.**G.**
Dar. 3–9/5/62.**N/C.**
Dar. 6–27/1/64.**N/C.**

BOILERS:
3725.
9678 *(ex1079)* 15/5/48.
9852 *(ex1215)* 22/9/49.
28201 *(ex1018)* 17/3/51.
28658 *(ex61353)* 12/7/52.
28421 *(ex1071)* 27/3/54.
28700 *(ex61387)* 9/12/55.
28261 *(ex1030)* 15/8/58.
28126 *(ex1161)* 27/4/62.

SHEDS:
Gateshead.
Ardsley 23/9/56.
Wakefield 31/10/65.

RENUMBERED:
61013 15/5/48.

CONDEMNED:
6/12/66.
Sold 2/67 for scrap to
A.Draper, Hull.

1014

ORIBI

Darlington 1994.

To traffic 23/12/46.

REPAIRS:
Dar. 29/5–18/6/48.**G.**
Gor. 17–25/12/48.**L.**
Dar. 2–30/9/49.**G.**
Dar. 11–18/10/49.**N/C.**
Dar. 28/3–28/4/51.**G.**
Dar. 7–11/1/52.**C/L.**
Dar. 26/9–18/10/52.**G.**
Dar. 20–23/10/52.**N/C.**
Dar. 23/3–1/4/54.**C/L.**
Dar. 1–28/7/54.**G.**
Dar. 10/4–8/5/56.**G.**
Dar. 9/10–11/11/58.**G.**
A.T.C. Mech.fitted.
Dar. 24/2–9/3/59.**N/C.**
A.T.C. Elec.fitted.
Dar. 25/7–19/8/61.**G.**

BOILERS:
3729.
5058 *(ex1071)* 18/6/48.
3703 *(ex1035)* 30/9/49.
3703 renumbered 28210
28/4/51.
28450 *(ex1038)* 18/10/52.
28454 *(ex1035)* 28/7/54.
28545 *(ex61380)* 8/5/56.
28227 *(ex1002)* 11/11/58.
28155 *(ex1269)* 19/8/61.

SHEDS:
Gateshead.
Tweedmouth 17/1/54.
Gateshead 14/6/59.
Tyne Dock 10/9/61.
Low Moor 7/6/64.
North Blyth 21/8/66.

RENUMBERED:
61014 18/6/48.

CONDEMNED:
31/12/66.
Sold 3/67 for scrap to
Hughes,Bolckow, North
Blyth.

1015

DUIKER

Darlington 1995.

To traffic 4/1/47.

REPAIRS:
Gor. 21/8–18/9/48.**G.**
Dar. 8/2–5/3/49.**L.**
Ghd. 27/3–26/4/50.**C/L.**
Don. 30/10–24/11/50.**G.**
Dar. 16/12/52–14/1/53.**G.**
Dar. 19–26/7/54.**C/L.**

Dar. 11/12/54–12/1/55.**G.**
Dar. 30/10–27/11/56.**G.**
Dar. 27/4–28/5/59.**G.**
A.T.C. Mech.fitted.
Dar. 5–18/6/59.**N/C.**
A.T.C. Elec.fitted.

BOILERS:
3727.
9696 *(ex1108)* 18/9/48.
28113 *(ex1137)* 24/11/50.
28114 *(ex1074)* 14/1/53.
28525 *(ex1032)* 12/1/55.
28137 *(ex1130)* 27/11/56.
28128 *(ex61353)* 28/5/59.

SHEDS:
York.
Southern Region 17/5/53.
York 21/6/53.
Neville Hill 15/11/53.
York 21/2/54.
Darlington 25/9/55.
Wakefield 8/6/58.

RENUMBERED:
61015 18/9/48.

CONDEMNED:
19/11/62.
In 1/63 for cut up
Darlington.

1016

INYALA

Darlington 1996.

To traffic 16/1/47.

REPAIRS:
Gor. 23/10–20/11/48.**G.**
Don. 13/9–10/10/50.**G.**
Ghd. 4–28/9/51.**C/L.**
Ghd. 1–4/10/51.**N/C.**
Dar. 1–27/9/52.**G.**
Dar. 30/6–24/7/54.**G.**
Dar. 21–27/10/55.**C/L.**
Dar. 14–22/12/55.**C/L.**
Dar. 27/3–25/4/56.**C/L.**
Dar. 3/10–1/11/56.**G.**
Dar. 2/9–2/10/58.**G.**
A.T.C. Mech.fitted.
Dar. 16–24/10/58.**N/C.**
Dar. 1/12/58.Weigh.
Dar. 25/6–6/7/59.**N/C.**
A.T.C. Elec.fitted.
Dar. 15/10–18/11/60.**G.**
Dar. 20/4–21/5/64.**C/L.**

BOILERS:
3730.
5090 *(ex1087)* 20/11/48.
28107 *(ex1126)* 10/10/50.
28453 *(ex1085)* 27/9/52.
28107 *(ex1012)* 24/7/54.
28458 *(ex61304)* 1/11/56.
28244 *(ex61334)* 2/10/58.
28439 *(ex1241)* 18/11/60.

SHEDS:
York.
Neville Hill 5/5/57.
Gateshead 15/1/61.
Copley Hill 13/8/61.
Mirfield 8/9/63.
Low Moor 12/4/64.

RENUMBERED:
61016 16/11/48.

CONDEMNED:
31/10/65.
Sold 12/65 for scrap to
Hughes,Bolckow, North
Blyth.

1017

BUSHBUCK

Darlington 1997.

To traffic 28/1/47.

REPAIRS:
Gor. 23/10–27/11/48.**G.**
Dar. 6/2–1/3/50.**C/L.** After
derailment.
Ghd. 6–8/3/50.**N/C.**
Dar. 28/5–22/6/51.**G.**
Dar. 2–10/5/52.**C/L.**
Dar. 5–30/5/53.**G.**
Dar. 19–26/10/53.**N/C.**
Dar. 5/11–2/12/53.**C/L.**
Dar. 13–22/1/54.**N/C.** Prep.
for dyno. car trials.
Dar. 2/11–3/12/54.**C/L.**
Dar. 28/5–1/7/55.**G.**
Dar. 30/11–16/12/55.**C/L.**
Dar. 13–23/11/56.**C/L.**
Dar. 17/12/56–18/1/57.**C/L.**
Dar. 26–29/6/57.**N/C.**
Dar. 13/1–6/2/58.**G.**
Dar. 24/4–11/5/59.**N/C.**
A.T.C. Mech.fitted.
Dar. 12–16/6/59.**N/C.**
A.T.C. Elec.fitted.
Dar. 30/8–23/9/61.**G.**
Dar. 28/9–19/10/61.**N/C.**
Dar. 21/10–3/11/61.**N/C.**

BOILERS:
3732.
9743 *(ex1157)* 27/11/48.
28216 *(ex1023)* 22/6/51.
28550 *(ex1141)* 30/5/53.
28408 *(ex61305)* 1/7/55.
28518 *(ex1090)* 6/2/58.
28513 *(ex1255)* 23/9/61.

SHEDS:
York.
Neville Hill 30/5/48.
Stockton 6/2/49.
Neville Hill 23/8/53.
York 20/11/55.
Copley Hill 8/6/58.
Wakefield 22/2/59.

Ardsley 25/11/62.
York 31/10/65.

RENUMBERED:
61017 27/11/48.

CONDEMNED:
15/11/66.
Sold 1/67 for scrap to A.
Draper, Hull.

1018

GNU

Darlington 1998.

To traffic 4/2/47.

REPAIRS:
Gor. 25/12/48–22/1/49.**G.**
Dar. 14/2–13/3/51.**G.**
Ghd. 19–29/3/51.**N/C.**
Dar. 3–4/4/51.**N/C.**
Dar. 11/12/52–17/1/53.**G.**
Dar. 22–27/1/53.**N/C.**
Dar. 4–28/1/55.**H/I.**
Dar. 31/1–1/2/55.**N/C.**
Dar. 19/1–14/2/57.**N/C.**
Dar. 17/12/58–23/1/59.**G.**
A.T.C. Mech.fitted.
Dar. 15–24/6/59.**N/C.**
A.T.C. Elec.fitted.
Dar. 18/6–3/8/62.**G.**
Dar. 13–23/8/62.**N/C.**
Dar. 12–26/9/62.**N/C.** After
derailment.

BOILERS:
3733.
3687 *(ex1062)* 22/1/49.
28132 *(ex1011)* 13/3/51.
28455 *(ex1122)* 17/1/53.
28172 *(ex1009)* 14/2/57.
28429 *(ex61367)* 23/1/59.
28427 *(ex61376)* 3/8/62.

SHEDS:
York.
Neville Hill 30/5/48.
Stockton 6/2/49.
Haverton Hill 8/6/58.
Thornaby 14/6/59.
Darlington 20/9/59.
Wakefield 12/6/60.
York 11/9/60.

RENUMBERED:
61018 22/1/49.

CONDEMNED:
7/11/65.
Sold 12/65 for scrap to
A.Draper, Hull.

WORKS CODES:– Cow – Cowlairs. Dar – Darlington. Dee – Dundee. Don – Doncaster. Ghd – Gateshead. Gor – Gorton. Inv – Inverurie. Str – Stratford. SRX – St Rollox.

REPAIR CODES:– **C/H** – Casual Heavy. **C/L** – Casual Light. **G** – General. **H** – Heavy. **H/I** – Heavy Intermediate. **L** – Light. **L/I** – Light Intermediate. **N/C** – Non–Classified.

1019

NILGHAI

Darlington 1999.

To traffic 24/2/47.

REPAIRS:
Dar. 2/6–2/7/48.**G.**
Ghd. 12–25/1/50.**C/L.**
Dar. 9/8–1/9/50.**G.**
Dar. 6–12/9/50.**N/C.**
Ghd. 23/1–1/2/52.**N/C.**
Dar. 15/4–10/5/52.**G.**
Dar. 15–20/5/52.**N/C.**
Dar. 10–15/10/52.**C/L.**
Dar. 10–19/2/53.**C/L.**
Dar. 18–26/8/53.**C/L.**
Ghd. 15–18/3/54.**N/C.**
Ghd. 28/5–15/6/54.**C/L.**
Dar. 7/9–8/10/54.**G.**
Ghd. 7–24/11/55.**C/L.**
Ghd. 9–25/1/56.**C/L.**
Dar. 9–17/2/56.**C/L.**
Ghd. 30/10–7/12/56.**G.**
Dar. 7/1–6/2/57.**C/L.** *After collision.*
Ghd. 10–25/3/58.**N/C.**
Dar. 9/3–9/4/59.**G.** *A.T.C. Mech fitted.*
Dar. 15–28/4/59.**N/C.**
Dar. 29–30/6/59.**N/C.**
A.T.C. Elec.fitted.
Dar. 12/2–17/3/62.**G.**
Dar. 19/8–2/9/63.**C/L.**

BOILERS:
3734.
3708 *(ex1084)* 2/7/48.
5075 *(ex1010)* 1/9/50.
28280 *(ex1187)* 10/5/52.
28182 *(ex1267)* 8/10/54.
28175 *(ex1152)* 7/12/56.
28238 *(ex61337)* 9/4/59.
28346 *(ex1303)* 17/3/62.

SHEDS:
Heaton.
Haymarket 29/8/48.
Darlington 31/10/48.
Tweedmouth 2/1/49.
Gateshead 17/1/54.
Blaydon 10/2/57.
Gateshead 1/11/59.
Blaydon 11/9/60.
Alnmouth 4/11/62.
Heaton 24/2/63.
Gateshead 16/6/63.
York 3/10/65.

RENUMBERED:
61019 2/7/48.

CONDEMNED:
12/3/67.
Sold 7/67 for scrap to A.Draper,Hull.

1020

GEMSBOK

Darlington 2000.

To traffic 28/2/47.

REPAIRS:
Dar. 30–30/9/47.**N/C.** *Elec. generator fitted.*
Dar. 24/6–9/7/48.**L.**
Dar. 1/2–12/3/49.**G.**
Ghd. 25/5–9/6/50.**C/L.**
Dar. 18/4–17/5/51.**G.**
Dar. 26/1–27/2/53.**G.**
Dar. 2/9–6/10/54.**G.**
Dar. 11/6–10/7/56.**G.**
Dar. 22/3–8/4/57.**C/L.**
Dar. 17/10–17/11/58.**C/L.**
Dar. 24/2–31/3/59.**G.**
A.T.C. Mech.fitted.
Dar. 8–15/4/59.**N/C.**
Dar. 28/2–7/3/60.**N/C.**
Dar. 11–13/10/60.**N/C.**
A.W.S. Elec.fitted.
Dar. 1/8–23/11/61.**C/H.**

BOILERS:
3763.
9771 *(ex1185)* 12/3/49.
28211 *(ex1112)* 17/5/51.
28276 *(ex1145)* 27/2/53.
28601 *(ex1002)* 6/10/54.
28170 *(ex1022)* 10/7/56.
28641 *(ex1259)* 31/3/59.

SHEDS:
Heaton.
Darlington 7/11/48.
York 17/7/49.
Neville Hill 15/11/53.
York 21/2/54.
Darlington 25/9/55.
Low Moor 8/6/58.
Wakefield 8/11/59.
York 11/9/60.

RENUMBERED:
61020 9/7/48.

CONDEMNED:
26/11/62.
In 1/63 for cut up Darlington.

1021

REITBOK

Darlington 2001.

To traffic 12/3/47.

REPAIRS:
Gor. 10/11–31/12/48.**G.**
Ghd. 16–26/5/49.**C/L.**
Dar. 5/3–4/4/51.**G.**
Dar. 2–18/10/52.**N/C.**
Dar. 27/3–25/4/53.**G.**
Dar. 7–7/5/53.*Weigh.*
Dar. 18/4–13/5/55.**G.**
Dar. 3–29/6/57.**G.**
Dar. 1–2/7/57.**N/C.**

Dar. 21/9–30/10/59.**G.**
Complete A.T.C. fitted.
Dar. 1/10–1/11/62.**G.**

BOILERS:
3766.
28202 *(ex1065)* 4/4/51.
28125 *(ex1129)* 25/4/53.
28154 *(ex1177)* 13/5/55.
28516 *(ex1041)* 29/6/57.
28603 *(ex1100)* 30/10/59.
28874 *(ex1010)* 1/11/62.

SHEDS:
Heaton.
Darlington 7/11/48.
Gateshead 6/7/52.
Darlington 14/9/52.
York 26/6/55.
Darlington 25/9/55.
Haverton Hill 8/6/58.
Thornaby 14/6/59.
Darlington 20/9/59.
Wakefield 12/6/60.
York 11/9/60.

RENUMBERED:
61021 31/12/48.

CONDEMNED:
6/6/67.
Sold 8/67 for scrap to Hughes,Bolckow, N.Blyth.

1022

SASSABY

Darlington 2002.

To traffic 22/3/47.

REPAIRS:
Dar. 3/1–3/2/49.**G.**
Dar. 15–24/6/49.**C/L.**
Dar. 4–16/9/50.**C/L.**
Dar. 23/5–22/4/51.**G.**
Dar. 7–7/11/52.*Weigh.*
Dar. 5–30/5/53.**G.**
Dar. 5/8–15/9/54.**G.**
Ghd. 11–12/8/55.**C/L.**
Ghd. 6–18/10/55.**C/L.**
Dar. 30/4–29/5/56.**G.**
Ghd. 28/11–4/12/56.**C/L.**
Dar. 10/12/56–4/1/57.**C/L.**
Dar. 17/11–16/12/58.**G.**
A.T.C. Mech.fitted.
Dar. 22–30/6/59.**N/C.**
A.T.C. Elec.fitted.
Dar. 21/9–14/10/61.**G.**
Dar. 24/9–1/10/62.**C/L.**

BOILERS:
3768.
3705 *(ex1080)* 3/2/49.
28213 *(ex1020)* 22/4/51.
28304 *(ex1110)* 30/5/53.
28170 *(ex1265)* 15/9/54.
28454 *(ex1014)* 29/5/56.
28700 *(ex1013)* 16/12/58.
28408 *(ex1123)* 14/10/61.

SHEDS:
Heaton.

Darlington 7/11/48.
York 6/7/52.
Darlington 14/9/52.
Heaton 19/7/53.
Gateshead 26/7/53.
Tyne Dock 10/9/61.
Alnmouth 4/11/62.
Heaton 24/2/63.
Gateshead 16/6/63.
Wakefield 31/1/65.

RENUMBERED:
61022 3/2/49.

CONDEMNED:
25/11/66.
Sold 2/67 for scrap to Arnott Young, Parkgate.

1023

HIROLA

Darlington 2003.

To traffic 1/4/47.

REPAIRS:
Dar. 15/6–2/7/48.**L.**
Dar. 11/3–9/4/49.**G.**
Dar. 17–26/5/49.**N/C.**
Dar. 5/4–2/5/50.**C/L.**
Dar. 7/5–2/6/51.**G.**
Dar. 20/4–20/5/53.**G.**
Dar. 25–28/5/53.**N/C.**
Dar. 4–30/4/55.**G.**
Dar. 2–3/5/55.**N/C.**
Dar. 19/6–3/8/57.**G.**
Dar. 16/12/60–28/1/61.**G.**
Complete A.W.S. fitted.
Dar. 29/12/61–11/1/62.**N/C.**

BOILERS:
3770.
3763 *(ex1020)* 9/4/49.
28212 *(ex1100)* 2/6/51.
28110 *(ex1060)* 20/5/53.
28126 *(ex1174)* 30/4/55.
28863 *(ex1127)* 3/8/57.
28434 *(ex1084)* 28/1/61.

SHEDS:
Heaton.
Darlington 7/11/48.
Gateshead 6/7/52.
Darlington 14/9/52.
York 26/6/55.
Darlington 25/9/55.
Low Moor 8/6/58.
Ardsley 8/11/59.
Copley Hill 17/6/62.
Low Moor 8/9/63.
Mirfield 5/1/64.
Low Moor 12/4/64.

RENUMBERED:
61023 2/7/48.

CONDEMNED:
31/10/65.
Sold 12/65 for scrap to Hughes,Bolckow, N.Blyth.

1024

ADDAX

Darlington 2004.

To traffic 12/4/47.

REPAIRS:
Dar. 29/9–28/10/49.**G.**
Dar. 14/9–6/10/51.**G.**
Dar. 8–10/10/51.**N/C.**
Dar. 14–14/10/53.*Weigh.*
Dar. 30/10–21/11/53.**G.**
Dar. 1–28/2/56.**G.**
Dar. 28/3–17/4/58.**C/L.**
Dar. 23/5–23/6/58.**G.**
Dar. 30/6–13/8/58.**N/C.**
Dar. 11–24/3/59.**N/C.**
A.T.C. Mech. fitted.
Dar. 25–27/5/59.**N/C.**
A.T.C. Elec fitted.
Dar. 31/10–25/11/61.**G.**

BOILERS:
3772.
5077 *(ex1068)* 28/10/49.
28222 *(ex1068)* 6/10/51.
28815 *(ex1179)* 21/11/53.
28463 *(ex61320)* 28/2/56.
28440 *(ex1255)* 23/6/58.
28700 *(ex1022)* 25/11/61.

SHEDS:
Tweedmouth.
Gateshead 1/7/51.
Darlington 2/9/51.
York 6/7/52.
Darlington 14/9/52.
Haverton Hill 8/6/58.
Thornaby 14/6/59.
Darlington 20/9/59.
Wakefield 12/6/60.
Ardsley 25/11/62.
Wakefield 31/3/63.

RENUMBERED:
61024 17/12/48.

CONDEMNED:
15/5/66.
*Sold 7/66 for scrap to Birds,
Long Marston.*

1025

PALLAH

Darlington 2005.

To traffic 22/4/47.

REPAIRS:
Gor. 20/11–25/12/48.**G.**
Cow. 20/10–30/11/50.**H/I.**
Dar. 25/2–26/3/53.**G.**
Dar. 31/3–2/4/53.**N/C.**
Dar. 25/5–13/6/53.**C/L.**
Ghd. 3/1–4/2/55.**C/H.**
Dar. 5–30/7/55.**G.**
Dar. 2–3/8/55.**N/C.**
Dar. 14/8–7/9/57.**G.**
Dar. 9–11/9/57.**N/C.**
Dar. 22/11–28/1/60.**G.**

A.W.S. Mech fitted.
Dar. 11–18/2/60.**N/C.**
Dar. 18–21/10/60.**N/C.**
A.W.S. Elec.fitted.
Dar. 26/4–12/5/61.**C/L.**

BOILERS:
3773.
28211 *(ex1020)* 26/3/53.
28401 *(ex1173)* 30/7/55.
28126 *(ex1023)* 7/9/57.
28162 *(ex1051)* 28/1/60.

SHEDS:
Tweedmouth.
Haymarket 29/8/48.
Tweedmouth 31/10/48.
Blaydon 12/6/60.
Alnmouth 4/11/62.

RENUMBERED:
61025 24/12/48.

CONDEMNED:
2/12/62.
*In 3/63 for cut up
Darlington.*

1026

OUREBI

Darlington 2006.

To traffic 28/4/47.

REPAIRS:
Don. 2/12/48–3/1/49.**G.**
Don. 15–17/11/49.**C/L.**
Don. 21/11–15/12/50.**G.**
Don. 10/12/52–7/1/53.**G.**
Don. 8–17/6/53.**C/L.**
Dar. 20/12/54–21/1/55.**G.**
Dar. 31/1–22/2/57.**G.**
Str. 14/5–27/6/59.**G.**
complete A.T.C. fitted.
Don. 19–30/9/59.**N/C.**
Don. 7/3–12/4/62.**G.**

BOILERS:
3737.
9750 *(ex1164)* 3/1/49.
28120 *(ex1139)* 15/12/50.
28115 *(ex1090)* 7/1/53.
28280 *(ex1019)* 21/1/55.
28115 *(ex1096)* 22/2/57.
28871 *(ex1232)* 27/6/59.
28505 *(ex1042)* 12/4/62.

SHEDS:
Doncaster.
Lincoln 10/11/57.
Immingham 29/11/59.
Lincoln 6/3/60.
Immingham 22/9/63.
Colwick 26/9/65.
Immingham 19/12/65.

RENUMBERED:
61026 3/1/49.

CONDEMNED:
10/2/66.
*Sold 3/66 for scrap to
A.Draper, Hull.*

1027

MADOQUA

Darlington 2007.

To traffic 11/5/47.

REPAIRS:
Dar. 3–8/6/47.**L.**
Don. 20/4–19/5/49.**G.**
Don. 9/4–4/5/51.**G.**
Don. 23/3–17/4/53.**G.**
Don. 25/1–22/2/55.**G.**
Don. 21/2–23/3/57.**G.**
Str. 28/5–3/7/59.**G.**
complete A.T.C. fitted.

BOILERS:
3747.
9842 *(ex1205)* 19/5/49.
28140 *(ex1170)* 4/5/51.
28144 *(ex1196)* 17/4/53.
28306 *(ex1619)* 22/2/55.
28127 *(ex1142)* 23/3/57.
28420 *(ex1096)* 3/7/59.

SHEDS:
New England.
Hitchin 17/5/53.
Sheffield 12/7/59.

RENUMBERED:
61027 19/5/49.

CONDEMNED:
16/9/62.
*Sold 3/63 for scrap to
J.Cashmore, Great Bridge.*

1028

UMSEKE

Darlington 2008.

To traffic 30/5/47.

REPAIRS:
Don. 25/11–10/12/47.**C/L.**
Don. 17/3–13/4/49.**G.**
Don. 10–24/6/49.**C/L.**
Don. 4–30/8/50.**G.**
Don. 24/1–21/2/52.**G.**
Don. 11/6–29/7/53.**G.**
Dar. 20/1–19/2/55.**G.**
Don. 17/6–4/7/55.**C/L.**
Don. 17/1–8/2/56.**C/H.**
Don. 15–23/5/56.**C/L.**
Don. 12–20/7/56.**C/L.**
Don. 5–27/2/57.**G.**
Dar. 9/2–3/3/59.**G.**
Dar. 14–24/4/59.**C/L.**
Dar. 14/8–24/9/59.**C/H.**
Dar. 29/5–23/6/61.**G.**

BOILERS:
3741.
5061 *(ex1097)* 13/4/49.
9831 *(ex1163)* 30/8/50.
28176 *(ex1031)* 21/2/52.
28865 *(new)* 29/7/53.
28460 *(ex1086)* 19/2/55.
28348 *(ex1122)* 27/2/57.

28602 *(ex61383)* 3/3/59.
28949 *(ex1666)* 23/6/61.

SHEDS:
Neasden.
Leicester 4/7/54.
Neasden 21/11/54.
Leicester 12/2/59.
Woodford 2/7/59.

RENUMBERED:
61028 13/4/49.

CONDEMNED:
8/10/62.
*In 22/3/63 for cut up
Darlington.*

1029

CHAMOIS

Darlington 2009.

To traffic 7/6/47.

REPAIRS:
Gor. 15/8–17/9/49.**G.**
Don. 7/10–1/11/51.**G.**
Don. 13–16/11/51.**N/C.**
Dar. 19/6–11/7/53.**G.**
StM. 25/10–4/11/54.**C/L.**
Cow. 5/7–20/8/55.**H/I.**
Cow. 29/8–3/9/55.**N/C.**
Cow. 17/8–15/9/56.**C/L.**
Cow. 11/9–12/10/57.**G.**
Cow. 24–26/10/57.**N/C.**
Cow. 30/4–14/5/59.**N/C.**
Cow. 20–28/5/59.**N/C.**
Cow. 25/11–25/12/59.**L/I.**
Cow. 7/9–28/10/61.**H/I.**
Cow. 3–8/11/61.**N/C.**
Cow. 5/7–24/8/63.**G.**
Cow. 11–19/12/63.**N/C.**
Inv. 20/10–6/11/64.**N/C.**
Cow. 22/6–5/8/66.**C/L.**

BOILERS:
3744.
9846 *(ex1209)* 17/9/49.
28155 *(ex1083)* 1/11/51.
28212 *(ex1023)* 11/7/53.
28620 *(ex1147)* 12/10/57.
28800 *(ex spare 1.5 years)*
24/8/63.

SHEDS:
Kings Cross.
Hitchin 11/3/48.
Gorton 23/1/49.
Copley Hill 2/10/49.
Ardsley 4/6/50.
Copley Hill 24/9/50.
Ardsley 18/2/51.
Sheffield 13/12/51.
St Margarets 13/9/53.
Thornton Jct 3/4/66.
Dunfermline 6/11/66.
Dundee 4/12/66.

RENUMBERED:
61029 12/9/49.

CONDEMNED:
31/12/66.
*Sold 2/67 for scrap to
J.McWilliam, Shettleston.*

1030

NYALA

Darlington 2010.

To traffic 26/6/47.

REPAIRS:
Dar. 15/11–10/12/49.**G.**
Dar. 10/12/51–10/1/52.**G.**
Dar. 4–24/12/53.**G.**
Dar. 25/4–28/5/56.**G.**
Dar. 26/4–23/5/58.**G.**
Dar. 7–9/7/58.**N/C.**
Dar. 18/10–23/12/60.**G.**
Complete A.W.S. fitted.
Dar. 14/6–5/7/62.**C/L.**
Dar. 22/6–4/9/64.**G.**

BOILERS:
 3740.
 4015 *(New)* 10/12/49.
28244 *(ex1108)* 10/1/52.
28227 *(ex1218)* 24/12/53.
28261 *(ex1138)* 28/5/56.
28264 *(ex1121)* 23/5/58.
28449 *(ex1298)* 23/12/60.
28309 *(ex1289)* 4/9/64.

SHEDS:
Stockton.
Thornaby 14/6/59.
Darlington 20/9/59.
Neville Hill 11/6/61.
Ardsley 25/11/62.
Wakefield 31/10/65.
York 22/1/67.
Low Moor 25/6/67.

RENUMBERED:
61030 10/12/49.

CONDEMNED:
30/9/67.
*Sold 11/67 for scrap to
Garnham,Harris & Elton,
Chesterfield.*

1031

REEDBUCK

Darlington 2011.

To traffic 10/7/47.

REPAIRS:
Dar. 22/7–9/8/47.**N/C.**
Don. 22/11–22/12/49.**G.**
Gor. 7–31/1/52.**G.**
Gor. 9/10–13/11/54.**G.**
Dar. 12/4–10/5/57.**G.**
Dar. 27/4–7/5/59.**N/C.**
A.T.C.Mech. fitted.
Dar. 25–27/5/59.**N/C.**
A.T.C.Elec. fitted.
Dar. 9/11–10/12/59.**G.**

Dar. 23/11–28/12/62.**G.**

BOILERS:
 3750.
 9888 *(ex1251)* 22/12/49.
28516 *(ex1051)* 31/1/52.
28404 *(ex1010)* 13/11/54.
28528 *(ex1128)* 10/5/57.
28281 *(ex1240)* 10/12/59.
28279 *(ex1206)* 28/12/62.

SHEDS:
Copley Hill.
Ardsley 4/6/50.
Bradford 13/5/51.
Low Moor 12/1/58.
Darlington 14/9/58.
Thornaby 30/11/58.
York 11/9/60.
Copley Hill 7/6/64.
Ardsley 6/9/64.

RENUMBERED:
61031 22/12/49.

CONDEMNED:
9/11/64.
*Sold 1/65 for scrap to
A.Draper, Hull.*

1032

STEMBOK

Darlington 2012.

To traffic 7/8/47.

REPAIRS:
Dar. 15/12/49–13/1/50.**G.**
Dar. 21/4–10/5/52.**G.**
Dar. 12–13/5/52.**N/C.**
Dar. 14/5–12/6/54.**G.**
Dar. 14–16/6/54.**N/C.**
Dar. 8/8–6/9/56.**G.**
Dar. 23/5–20/6/58.**G.**
Dar. 27/6–9/7/58.**N/C.**
Dar. 2–10/4/59.**N/C.**
A.T.C.Mech. fitted.
Dar. 2–4/6/59.**N/C.**
A.T.C.Elec. fitted.
Dar. 23/1–24/2/61.**G.**
Dar. 3–10/3/61.**N/C.**
Dar. 3/2–21/3/64.**G.**

BOILERS:
 3739.
 3723 *(ex1012)* 13/1/50.
28525 *(ex1049)* 10/5/52.
28414 *(ex1049)* 12/6/54.
28426 *(ex61353)* 6/9/56.
28106 *(ex61309)* 20/6/58.
28187 *(ex1289)* 24/2/61.
28228 *(ex1199)* 21/3/64.

SHEDS:
Stockton.
Thornaby 14/6/59.
Darlington 20/9/59.
Hull Dairycoates 15/12/63.

RENUMBERED:
61032 13/1/50.

CONDEMNED:
27/11/66.
*Sold 2/67 for scrap to
A.Draper, Hull.*

1033

DIBATAG

Darlington 2013.

To traffic 29/8/47.

REPAIRS:
Don. 12/12/49–17/1/50.**G.**
Don. 24/3–23/4/52.**L/I.**
Gor. 28/10/53–9/1/54.**G.**
Gor. 12–19/1/54.**N/C.**
Gor. 20–21/1/54.**N/C.**
Gor. 29/1–6/2/54.**N/C.**
Str. 13/11/55–11/2/56.**G.**
Dar. 8/4–6/5/58.**G.**
Don. 20/5–17/6/60.**G.**

BOILERS:
 3712.
 9866 *(ex1229)* 17/1/50.
 9866 renumbered 28187
23/4/52.
28374 *(ex3803)* 9/1/54.
28816 *(ex1051)* 11/2/56.
28574 *(ex1173)* 6/5/58.
28982 *(new)* 17/6/60.

SHEDS:
Bradford.
Copley Hill 21/9/47.
Ardsley 4/6/50.
Copley Hill 15/10/50.
Ardsley 6/1/52.
Stratford 22/9/52.
Colwick 19/10/52.
Cambridge 24/10/54.
Sheffield 28/10/56.
Lincoln 4/11/62.
Canklow 2/12/62.

RENUMBERED:
61033 17/1/50.

CONDEMNED:
25/3/63.
*In 25/3/63 for cut up
Doncaster.*

1034

CHIRU

Darlington 2014.

To traffic 3/10/47.

REPAIRS:
Dar. 12/7–22/8/49.**G.**
Dar. 1–27/6/51.**G.**
Dar. 12/8–1/9/53.**G.**
Dar. 12/12/55–11/1/56.**G.**
Dar. 18/11–14/12/57.**G.**
Dar. 16–17/12/57.**N/C.**
Dar. 11–27/5/59.**N/C.**
A.T.C. fitted.
Dar. 10/7–6/10/59.**C/H.**
After collision.

Dar. 7/11/60–25/1/61.**G.**

BOILERS:
 3599.
 9836 *(ex1199)* 22/8/49.
28220 *(ex1017)* 27/6/51.
28216 *(ex1017)* 1/9/53.
28168 *(ex1150)* 11/1/56.
28315 *(ex1126)* 14/12/57.
28398 *(ex1271)* 25/1/61.

SHEDS:
York.
Neville Hill 29/11/47.
Stockton 6/2/49.
Thornaby 14/6/59.
Ardsley 25/11/62.
Wakefield 5/1/64.

RENUMBERED:
61034 22/8/49.

CONDEMNED:
21/12/64.
*Sold 2/65 for scrap to
A.Draper, Hull.*

1035

PRONGHORN

Darlington 2015.

To traffic 31/10/47.

REPAIRS:
Dar. 28/4–25/5/49.**G.**
Dar. 31/5–9/6/49.**N/C.**
Dar. 30/4–31/5/51.**G.**
Dar. 30/12/52–29/1/53.**G.**
Dar. 9–11/4/53.**N/C.**
Dar. 1/6–2/7/54.**G.**
Dar. 8–12/7/54.**N/C.**
Dar. 2–26/11/55.**G.**
Dar. 28–29/11/55.**N/C.**
Dar. 1–8/3/56.**N/C.**
Dar. 17/1–14/2/57.**C/L.**
Dar. 3/9–2/10/57.**G.**
Dar. 14/10–6/11/57.**N/C.**
Dar. 30/6–15/8/59.**G.**
Complete A.T.C. fitted.
Dar. 15/1–16/2/62.**G.**

BOILERS:
 3703.
 9877 *(ex1240)* 25/5/49.
28641 *(ex61307)* 31/5/51.
28454 *(ex61381)* 29/1/53.
28428 *(ex1275)* 2/7/54.
28110 *(ex1023)* 26/11/55.
28444 *(ex1268)* 2/10/57.
28113 *(ex1065)* 15/8/59.
28333 *(ex1129)* 16/2/62.

SHEDS:
York.
Neville Hill 5/4/48.
Blaydon 15/1/61.
Heaton 10/2/63.
Gateshead 16/6/63.
York 3/10/65.

RENUMBERED:
61035 25/5/49.

CONDEMNED:
12/12/66.
*Sold 2/67 for scrap to
A.Draper, Hull.*

1036

RALPH ASSHETON
*(was to have been
KORRIGUM)*

Darlington 2016.

To traffic 20/11/47.

REPAIRS:
Gor. 28/2–1/3/49.**N/C.**
Don. 29/3–3/5/50.**G.**
Don. 2–25/1/52.**G.**
Don. 7/12/53–1/1/54.**G.**
Don. 29/11–23/12/55.**G.**
Don. 12–16/11/56.**N/C.**
Don. 19/3–19/4/58.**G.**
Don. 27/8–5/9/59.**N/C.**
Don. 14/3–21/4/60.**G.**

BOILERS:
3755.
9680 *(ex1083)* 3/5/50.
28171 *(ex1206)* 25/1/52.
28100 *(ex1142)* 1/1/54.
28757 *(ex1113)* 23/12/55.
28169 *(ex61394)* 19/4/58.
28241 *(ex61394)* 21/4/60.

SHEDS:
Gorton.
Doncaster 3/7/49.
Stratford 25/8/49.
Cambridge 20/11/49.
Doncaster 2/12/49.

RENUMBERED:
61036 3/5/50.

CONDEMNED:
16/9/62.
*In 1/11/62 for cut up
Doncaster.*

1037

JAIROU

Darlington 2017.

To traffic 28/11/47.

REPAIRS:
Dar. 6/1–15/2/50.**G.**
Dar. 18/2–8/3/52.**G.**
Dar. 10–13/3/52.**N/C.**
Dar. 24/2–20/3/54.**G.**
Dar. 22–27/3/54.**N/C.**
Dar. 8/5–7/6/56.**G.**
Dar. 12/4–9/5/58.**G.**
Dar. 7–9/7/58.**N/C.**
Dar. 4–14/5/59.**N/C.**
A.T.C.Mech. fitted.

Dar. 4–5/6/59.**N/C.**
A.T.C.Elec. fitted.
Dar. 26/1–25/2/61.**G.**

BOILERS:
3604.
3740 *(ex1030)* 15/2/50.
28407 *(ex61325)* 8/3/52.
28400 *(ex1214)* 20/3/54.
28513 *(ex61334)* 7/6/56.
28232 *(ex1209)* 9/5/58.
28127 *(ex spare)* 25/2/61.

SHEDS:
Darlington.
Stockton 22/8/48.
Haverton Hill 8/6/58.
Thornaby 14/6/59.
Darlington 11/9/60.

RENUMBERED:
61037 15/2/50.

CONDEMNED:
18/5/64.
*Sold 8/64 for scrap to
Hughes,Bolckow, Blyth.*

1038

BLACKTAIL

Darlington 2018.

To traffic 5/12/47.

REPAIRS:
Cow. 24/10–25/11/50.**G.**
Dar. 26/6–19/7/52.**G.**
Dar. 25/9–13/10/53.**N/C.**
Dar. 31/8–29/9/54.**G.**
Dar. 29/8–28/9/56.**G.**
Dar. 1–2/10/56.**N/C.**
Dar. 4/7–19/8/58.**G.**
Dar. 3–3/12/58.*Weigh.*
Dar. 16–27/2/59.**N/C.**
A.T.C. Mech. fitted.
Dar. 4–15/6/59.**N/C.**
A.T.C.Elec. fitted.
Dar. 17–25/9/59.**N/C.** *B16
type waterscoop fitted.*
Dar. 13/9–28/10/60.**H/I.**
Dar. 28/4–29/9/64.*Not
repaired.*

BOILERS:
3709.
9896 *(ex1257)* 25/11/50.
28443 *(ex1291)* 19/7/52.
28181 *(ex61379)* 29/9/54.
28189 *(ex1272)* 28/9/56.
28416 *(ex61377)* 19/8/58.

SHEDS:
Darlington.
York 17/7/49.
Neville Hill 5/5/57.
Gateshead 15/1/61.
Sunderland 30/4/61.

Blaydon 17/6/62.
Heaton 9/9/62.
Blaydon 4/11/62.
Heaton 24/2/63.
Gateshead 16/6/63.

RENUMBERED:
61038 25/11/50.

CONDEMNED:
1/5/64.
*Sold 9/64 for scrap to
Arnott,Young & Co,
Fighting Cocks.*

1039

STEINBOK

Darlington 2019.

To traffic 12/12/47.

REPAIRS:
Dar. 21/6–2/7/49.**C/L.**
Dar. 23/11–21/12/49.**G.**
Dar. 28/12/49–9/1/50.**N/C.**
Dar. 30/1–29/2/52.**G.**
Ghd. 9–18/6/52.**N/C.**
Dar. 8/3–3/4/54.**G.**
Dar. 6–20/4/56.**C/L.**
Dar. 1–31/8/56.**G.**
Dar. 10–12/9/56.**N/C.**
Dar. 13/10–14/11/58.**G.**
Dar. 20/11–3/12/58.**N/C.**
Dar. 8–17/10/59.**N/C.**
Complete A.T.C. fitted.
Dar. 2/2–9/3/62.**G.**
Dar. 15–22/3/62.**N/C.**

BOILERS:
3600.
9926 *(ex1289)* 21/12/49.
28402 *(ex61312)* 29/2/52.
28209 *(ex61319)* 3/4/54.
28535 *(ex1299)* 31/8/56.
28342 *(ex61304)* 14/11/58.
28172 *(ex61382)* 9/3/62.

SHEDS:
Darlington.
York 6/7/52.
Darlington 14/9/52.
Low Moor 8/6/58.
Ardsley 8/11/59.
York 11/9/60.
Woodford 6/8/62.
Gorton 10/11/62.
Canklow 1/12/63.
Doncaster 28/3/65.

RENUMBERED:
61039 21/12/49.

CONDEMNED:
27/6/65.
*Sold 8/65 for scrap to
T.W.Ward, Beighton.*

1040

ROEDEER

North British Loco. 25796.

To traffic 16/4/46.

REPAIRS:
Dar. 6–7/5/46.*Weigh.*
Str. 3–13/9/47.**H.**
Str. 26/4–12/6/48.**G.**
Str. 30/12/48–18/1/49.**L.**
Str. 12/5–24/6/50.**G.**
Str. 20–31/8/51.**C/L.**
Dar. 14/12/51–19/1/52.**G.**
Dar. 21/2–6/3/52.**N/C.**
Dar. 21/10–16/11/53.**C/L.**
Dar. 26/2–5/3/54.**C/L.**
Dar. 4–29/5/54.**G.**
Dar. 31/5–1/6/54.**N/C.**
Dar. 8/6–10/7/56.**G.**
Dar. 19/9–24/10/58.**G.**
A.T.C. Mech. fitted.
Dar. 26/10–5/11/60.**N/C.**
A.T.C. Elec. fitted.
Dar. 26/4–31/5/62.**G.**
Dar. 6–29/6/62.**N/C.**

BOILERS:
5062.
5067 *(ex1047)* 13/9/47.
3704 *(ex2832)* 12/6/48.
3606 *(ex1008)* 24/6/50.
3606 renumbered 28565
31/8/51.
28240 *(ex1189)* 19/1/52.
28447 *(ex1115)* 29/5/54.
28406 *(ex1238)* 10/7/56.
28458 *(ex1016)* 24/10/58.
28440 *(ex1024)* 31/5/62.

SHEDS:
Stratford.
Norwich 21/7/46.
Darlington 2/9/51.
York 6/7/52.
Darlington 14/9/52.
Low Moor 8/6/58.
Wakefield 15/3/59.
Mirfield 22/3/59.
Low Moor 20/8/61.
Wakefield 10/9/61.

RENUMBERED:
61040 12/6/48.

CONDEMNED:
10/7/66.
*Sold 8/66 for scrap to
R.A.King, Norwich.*

1041

North British Loco. 25797.

To traffic 26/4/46.

continued on page 23

WORKS CODES:– Cow – Cowlairs. Dar – Darlington. Dee – Dundee. Don – Doncaster. Ghd – Gateshead. Gor – Gorton. Inv – Inverurie. Str – Stratford. SRX – St Rollox.
REPAIR CODES:– C/H – Casual Heavy. C/L – Casual Light. G – General. H – Heavy. H/I – Heavy Intermediate. L – Light. L/I – Light Intermediate. N/C – Non–Classified.

The initial engine of the class was sent from Parkeston shed to Doncaster works on 26th August 1947 specifically for painting in the standard green livery, to then be officially photographed to represent the class for record purposes.

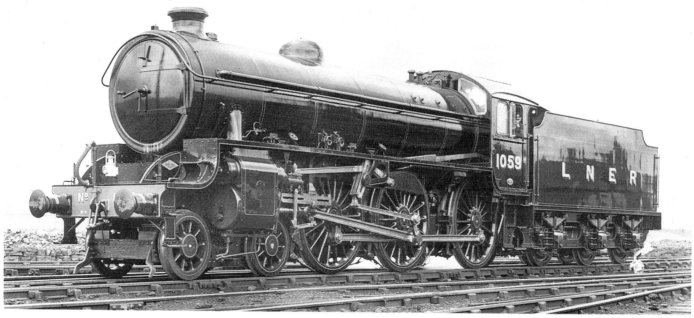

1059 shedded at Ipswich was regarded as their best engine, and its exterior also received special care and cleaning. That enables the single red lining applied by N.B.Loco.Co. to show clearly, and the panel of it on the cylinder casing is seen to advantage here. Note preparation has been made for electric lighting to be applied but neither generator nor lamps have been fitted.

1072 is representative of the first batch built by North British, on which the firm used the normal shaded numbers on the cab side but only 10″ high instead of 12″ as for the tender letters. Group Standard buffers with circular heads were normal equipment throughout the class. 1072 is at Haymarket on 6th April 1947.

Some of the earliest delivered engines from NBL had their first heavy repair at Stratford whilst still in LNER ownership. Their red lining disappeared and cab numbers went from 10″ to 12″ and they, and LNER were changed to yellow painted and unshaded Gill Sans.

Green passenger livery was applied on 1094 and subsequent engines, as here on 1100 at Newcastle in August 1947. This view illustrates what was then being put on the front buffer beam. 4½″ shaded transfers were still being used for the number, and on the left hand side just B1 appeared, because Thompson ordered CLASS to be dropped as un—necessary in a 30th July 1944 instruction. Its loss enabled the shed allocation to be stencilled on the right hand side.

1061 was one of the very few to be changed from black to green livery and LNER on the tender, being ex–Cowlairs works only four days before nationalisation. It is at Perth (Gilmerton) shed (hence the LMS background though its home shed was the former North British establishment where, along with 1002, it had taken over the daily Perth – Edinburgh (Waverley) workings from D49 4–4–0s.

1044 went to Stratford again on 7th March 1948 for a light repair, and when ex works on 2nd April, its B.R. number had been put on, but no alteration was made to LNER on the tender. The added figure 6 was also the modification to true Gill Sans which Doncaster had made on their drawing dated 21st February 1945.

After being in service for 16 months, 1072 in black, went to Cowlairs for its first general repair. They changed it to green lined livery, added the prefix to its number and changed the ownership on its tender, before sending it back to traffic on 6th March 1948.

1066 at Woodford on 15th May 1948. When it entered traffic it was similar to 1072, but by this time had changed from black to green painting, with new ownership shown on tender, and Regional prefix added to the number. The engine returned to traffic so altered by Gorton on 21st February 1948. That works also changed the buffer heads to the oval Great Central design, but no others are known to have been so altered.

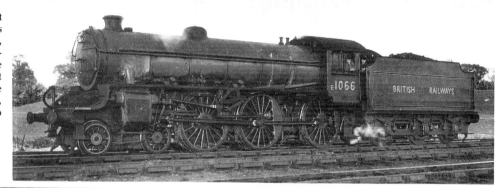

In April 1948 two of the first batch of the class were the subject of essays for demonstrating the new ownership. 61009 was changed to its BR number (put on in the Doncaster modified style instead of true Gill Sans for 6 and 9) and on the left hand side of the tender had a small emblem between BRITISH and RAILWAYS. The right hand side was without lettering but with an appreciably larger emblem. The lettering and its spacing proved acceptable, and was adopted and in use until July 1949, but without any emblem between the two words. That emblem too clearly resembled a kitten playing with a ball of wool, and Stratford no doubt relished obliterating the samples next day.

The other engine displayed for inspection in Liverpool Street station on 19th April 1948 was 61001, also with a false 6 added to its LNER number. The smaller version of the emblem was seated on a panel showing BRITISH RAILWAYS in small capital letters, and on both sides the emblem was handed to face forward. That too was discarded but it probably did have a faint influence on the emblem which was adopted in June 1949, having a more virile lion straddling a wheel across which was a square (not round) ended panel bearing BRITISH RAILWAYS. This was in standard use until April 1957, applied as a transfer.

Stratford turned out 61057 on 13th April 1948 from a general repair, then on 21st May called it back for the special painting as shown here in Liverpool Street station because it was amongst those selected for parading the chosen standard livery on the G.E. main line. Note it had also been fitted with cast number plate on its smokebox door, superseding painted number on front buffer beam. On that, and on the cab, Stratford had used the modified figure 6.

Although the highest numbered in the class, at 61400 – 61409, Darlington had put the batch into traffic from March to June 1950, almost two years prior to 61399's appearance. They were unusual in not being fitted with any electric lighting equipment, but they did have standard black lined livery with correct 6 and 9 numbering throughout. 61400 has just been coaled at Kittybrewster shed, in August 1950.

61344 at St Margarets shed in 1963 shows some interesting details. The box below the cab housed the batteries which were connected with the installation of the Automatic Warning System. The additional information above and below the number on the cab was a Cowlairs works custom. 5MT was its British Railways power class and RA5 below the number indicated its Route Availability.

Almost the whole of 61402's work was done from Dundee shed, and Cowlairs was responsible for all its maintenance. It was unusual, if not actually unique, in its tender having the smaller size of crest applied; that size was used for tank engines.

1041 continued

REPAIRS:
Str. 3/10–22/11/47.**G.**
Str. 5–22/4/48.**N/C.**
Str. 19/7–21/8/48.**L.**
Str. 10/10–12/11/49.**G.**
Str. 22–28/11/49.**N/C.**
Don. 16/8–12/9/50.**C/L.**
Str. 23/4–26/5/51.**G.**
Str. 9/3–2/5/53.**G.** *Modified bogie springs.*
Dar. 23/6–21/7/55.**G.**
Dar. 26/4–23/5/57.**G.**
Dar. 30–31/5/57.**N/C.**
Dar. 18/2–19/3/59.**G.**
Don. 25/3–22/4/61.**G.**

BOILERS:
5065.
3456 *(ex8310)* 22/11/47.
9901 *(ex1264)* 12/11/49.
28553 *(ex1287)* 26/5/51.
28552 *(ex1059)* 2/5/53.
28516 *(ex1031)* 21/7/55.
28206 *(ex1185)* 23/5/57.
28864 *(ex1062)* 19/3/59.
28360 *(ex1657)* 22/4/61.

SHEDS:
Stratford.
Norwich 19/7/46.
Southern Region 18/5/53.
Norwich 27/5/53.
Sheffield 7/6/53.
Staveley 3/6/62.
Lincoln 27/1/63.
New England 24/11/63.

RENUMBERED:
61041 22/4/48.

CONDEMNED:
19/4/64.
Sold 6/64 for scrap to Central Wagon Co, Ince.

1042

North British Loco. 25799.

To traffic 4/5/46.

REPAIRS:
Str. 17–28/6/47.**H.**
Str. 3/5–2/7/48.**G.**
Str. 8–13/1/50.**N/C.**
Str. 28/2–6/5/50.**G.**
Str. 6–23/9/50.**C/L.**
Str. 1/1–9/2/52.**G.**
Str. 13–15/1/53.**N/C.**
Gor. 7/7–29/8/53.**G.**
Str. 10/5–11/6/55.**G.**
Str. 4/3–26/4/57.**G.**
Str. 21/10–23/11/57.**C/L.**
Str. 26/1–13/3/59.**G.**
B.T.H. speed indic. part A.T.C. modified bogie springs.
Don. 14–26/3/60.**N/C.**

Don. 1–21/4/60.**C/L.**
Don. 16–26/1/61.**N/C.**
Don. 18/10–2/12/61.**G.**

BOILERS:
5064.
5104 *(new)* 28/6/47.
5067 *(ex1040)* 2/7/48.
5099 *(ex1004)* 6/5/50.
28575 *(ex1054)* 9/2/52.
28349 *(ex1184)* 29/8/53.
28588 *(ex1005)* 11/6/55.
28841 *(ex61329)* 26/4/57.
28505 *(ex1066)* 13/3/59.
28452 *(ex1089)* 2/12/61.

SHEDS:
Cambridge.
Norwich 22/7/46.
Yarmouth 6/1/57.
Norwich 24/2/57.
March 29/11/59.
Lincoln 21/2/60.
Immingham 22/9/63.
Colwick 26/9/65.
Doncaster 28/11/65.

RENUMBERED:
61042 2/7/48.

CONDEMNED:
17/4/66.
Sold 5/66 for scrap to Geo.Cohen, Kettering.

1043

North British Loco. 25800.

To traffic 14/5/46.

REPAIRS:
Str. 21/3–22/4/48.**G.** *Front heat. fitted.*
Str. 25/9–29/10/49.**G.**
Str. 22/1–3/2/50.**C/L.**
Str. 6/7–24/11/50.**C/H.**
Str. 12/7–25/8/51.**C/L.**
Str. 11/1–26/2/52.**G.**
Str. 13/10–21/11/53.**G.**
Str. 20/9–29/10/55.**G.**
Str. 16/9–19/10/57.**G.**
Str. 21/10–31/12/59.**G.**
Don. 4/7/62.*Not repaired.*

BOILERS:
3606.
5066 *(ex1052)* 22/4/48.
3419 *(ex1045)* 29/10/49.
3419 renumbered 28505 24/11/50.
28577 *(ex61360)* 26/2/52.
28514 *(ex1632)* 21/11/53.
28541 *(ex1617)* 29/10/55.
28530 *(ex1616)* 19/10/57.
28256 *(ex1004)* 31/12/59.

SHEDS:
Norwich.
March 4/2/62.

RENUMBERED:
61043 17/4/48.

CONDEMNED:
9/7/62.
Cut up Doncaster.

1044

North British Loco. 25801.

To traffic 20/5/46.

REPAIRS:
Str. 27/10–13/12/47.**G.** *Front heater fitted.*
Str. 7/3–2/4/48.**C/L.**
Str. 11/7–15/9/48.**C/L.** *Special painting.*
Str. 4/2–9/4/49.**C/L.** *After collision.*
Str. 14/5–30/6/50.**G.**
Str. 24/2–17/3/51.**C/L.**
Str. 6/5–13/6/51.**C/L.**
Str. 5/8–13/9/52.**G.**
Gor. 9/8–14/11/53.**C/H.**
Gor. 17–19/11/53.**N/C.**
Gor. 21–22/11/53.**N/C.**
Gor. 24–27/11/53.**N/C.**
Gor. 10–15/5/54.**N/C.**
Don. 14/10–11/11/54.**G.**
Dar. 1–12/3/55.**N/C.**
Dar. 10/6–30/7/56.**H/I.**
Dar. 25/6–8/8/58.**G.**
Dar. 15–25/8/58.**N/C.**
Don. 9/12/60–14/1/61.**G.**

BOILERS:
3619.
5069 *(ex1048)* 13/12/47.
5104 *(ex1053)* 30/6/50.
5104 renumbered 28543 17/3/51.
28591 *(ex1005)* 13/9/52.
28258 *(ex1641)* 11/11/54.
28220 *(ex1061)* 8/8/58.
28591 *(ex3935)* 14/1/61.

SHEDS:
Norwich.
Sheffield 7/6/53.
Canklow 7/4/63.

RENUMBERED:
61044 2/4/48.

CONDEMNED:
17/3/64.
Sold 5/64 for scrap to Central Wagon Co, Ince.

1045

North British Loco. 25802

To traffic 24/5/46.

REPAIRS:
Cow. 2–6/6/46.**N/C.**

Str. 17/6–5/7/47.**H.**
Str. 8/1–11/2/48.**H.** *Front heat. fitted.*
Str. 22/8–25/9/48.**L.**
Str. 8/5–18/6/49.**G.**
Str. 22/7–19/8/49.**C/L.**
Str. 5–19/5/50.**C/L.**
Str. 28/11/50–20/1/51.**G.**
Str. 15–22/3/51.**C/L.**
Str. 27/9–6/10/51.**N/C.**
Str. 1/7–22/8/52.**G.**
Str. 13/1–13/2/54.**G.**
Str. 17/10/55–25/11/56.**G.**
Str. 3/2–3/4/58.**G.** *Mod. bogie springs.*
Str. 19/5–5/6/58.**C/L.**
Str. 23/9–16/10/59.**C/L.**
Don. 2/6–9/7/60.**G.**

BOILERS:
5066.
3419 *(ex8305)* 5/7/47.
3619 *(ex1055)* 18/6/49.
28521 *(ex1254)* 20/1/51.
28589 *(ex61372)* 22/8/52.
28166 *(ex1206)* 13/2/54.
28517 *(ex1135)* 25/1/56.
28445 *(ex1228)* 3/4/58.
28218 *(ex61399)* 9/7/60.

SHEDS:
Norwich.
March 4/2/62.
Stratford 29/7/62.

RENUMBERED:
E1045 11/2/48.
61045 25/9/48.

CONDEMNED:
16/9/62.
In 26/11/62 for cut up Doncaster.

1046

North British Loco. 25798.

To traffic 29/5/46*.

REPAIRS:
Don. 24/9–12/10/46.**L.** *Stone's Elec. fitted.*
Str. 18/1–23/2/48.**G.** *Front Heat fitted.*
Str. 5/10–12/11/49.**G.**
Str. 5/10–11/11/50.**C/L.**
Str. 17/7–24/8/51.**G.**
Str. 3/8/52–27/3/53.**G.** *Mod. bogie springs.*
Str. 24/8–29/9/54.**N/C.**
Str. 21/3–30/4/55.**G.**
Str. 7/5–21/6/57.**G.**
Str. 6/8–12/9/58.**C/L.**
Str. 25/5–30/7/59.**G.** *Part A.T.C. fitted.*
Str. 16/3–9/4/60.**N/C.** *A.T.C. completed.*
Don. 11–16/8/60.**N/C.**
Don. 17/4/62.*Not repaired.*

WORKS CODES:– Cow – Cowlairs. Dar – Darlington. Dee – Dundee. Don – Doncaster. Ghd – Gateshead. Gor – Gorton. Inv – Inverurie. Str – Stratford. SRX – St Rollox.

REPAIR CODES:– **C/H** – Casual Heavy. **C/L** – Casual Light. **G** – General. **H** – Heavy. **H/I** – Heavy Intermediate. **L** – Light. **L/I** – Light Intermediate. **N/C** – Non–Classified.

BOILERS:
3610.
5073 *(ex1055)* 23/2/48.
9969 *(ex61332)* 12/11/49.
9969 renumbered 28509
11/11/50.
28564 *(ex61332)* 24/8/51.
28264 *(ex61329)* 27/3/53.
28558 *(ex1639)* 30/4/55.
28262 *(ex1232)* 21/6/57.
28526 *(ex1205)* 30/7/59.

SHEDS:
Norwich.
Cambridge 12/6/60.
March 20/11/60.
Cambridge 11/6/61.

RENUMBERED:
E1046 23/2/48.
61046 12/11/49.

CONDEMNED:
24/4/62.
Cut up Doncaster.
* *No maker's plate was ever*
fitted.

1047

North British Loco. 25803.

To traffic 3/6/46.

REPAIRS:
Str. 4–21/8/47.**H.**
Str. 25/1–28/2/48.**H.** *Front*
heat. fitted.
Str. 17/9–10/11/48.**G.**
Str. 13–18/12/49.**N/C.**
Str. 25/6–19/8/50.**G.**
Str. 30/3–7/4/51.**N/C.**
Str. 29/8–28/9/51.**C/L.**
Str. 11/10–1/12/51.**C/L.**
Str. 11–24/5/52.**C/L.**
Str. 15/12/52–7/2/53.**G.**
Don. 25/10–19/11/54.**G.**
Don. 12/1–9/2/55.**C/L.**
Don. 3–24/4/56.**C/L.**
Don. 25/7–22/8/57.**G.**
Don. 20/1–20/2/60.**G.**
Don. 6–11/1/61.**N/C.**

BOILERS:
5067.
5050 *(ex1052)* 21/8/47.
3680 *(ex1058)* 10/11/48.
5050 *(ex1119)* 19/8/50.
5050 renumbered 28548
7/4/51.
28563 *(ex1617)* 7/2/53.
28561 *(ex1205)* 19/11/54.
28529 *(ex1073)* 22/8/57.
28556 *(ex1602)* 20/2/60.

SHEDS:
Norwich.
Lincoln 27/5/51.
Norwich 24/6/51.
New England 25/10/53.
Peterborough 27/11/55.
Sheffield 14/12/58.

RENUMBERED:
61047 6/11/48.

CONDEMNED:
16/9/62.
Sold 3/63 for scrap to
J.Cashmore, Great Bridge.

1048

North British Loco. 25804.

To traffic 6/6/46.

REPAIRS:
Str. 12/8–1/9/47.**H.**
Str. 30/3–29/4/48.**G.** *Front*
heat. fitted.
Str. 22/5–11/6/48.**N/C.**
Specially painted.
Str. 29/7–13/8/49.**C/L.**
Str. 27/11/49–7/1/50.**G.**
Str. 14–28/6/50.**C/L.**
Str. 5–24/10/50.**C/L.**
Don. 18/6–20/7/51.**G.**
Don. 25–30/7/51.**N/C.**
Str. 28/1–20/3/53.**G.** *Mod.*
bogie springs.
Str. 14/2–1/4/55.**G.**
Str. 24/4–14/6/57.**G.**
Str. 21/7–13/8/58.**C/L.**
Str. 27/7–5/9/59.**G.**
Complete A.T.C. fitted.
Str. 13/4–14/5/60.**C/L.**

BOILERS:
5069.
5064 *(ex1042)* 1/9/47.
5066 *(ex1043)* 7/1/50.
28147 *(ex1196)* 20/7/51.
28555 *(ex1282)* 20/3/53.
28292 *(ex1160)* 1/4/55.
28186 *(ex1233)* 14/6/57.
28541 *(ex1615)* 5/9/59.

SHEDS:
Norwich.
Cambridge 12/6/60.
March 20/11/60.
Cambridge 11/6/61.
Stratford 17/6/62.

RENUMBERED:
61048 24/4/48.

CONDEMNED:
16/9/62.
In 3/12/62 for cut up
Doncaster.

1049

North British Loco. 25805.

To traffic 11/6/46.

REPAIRS:
Str. 26/3–21/5/47.**L.**
Str. 25/2–20/3/48.**G.**
Str. 14/2–19/3/49.**C/L.**
Str. 29/11–5/12/49.**N/C.**
Str. 20/6–5/8/50.**G.**
Str. 12–16/12/50.**C/L.**

Str. 16–24/2/51.**C/L.**
Dar. 24/3–18/4/52.**G.**
Dar. 31/3–1/5/54.**G.**
Dar. 30/7–29/8/56.**G.**
Dar. 3/2–11/3/58.**C/L.**
Derailment damage.
Dar. 11/3–15/4/59.**G.**
A.T.C.Mech. fitted.
Dar. 23/4–15/5/59.**N/C.**
Dar. 28–29/7/59.**N/C.**
A.T.C.Elec. fitted.
Dar. 12/10–14/11/62.**G.**
Dar. 24–31/5/63.**N/C.**

BOILERS:
5068.
3610 *(ex1046)* 20/3/48.
5067 *(ex1042)* 5/8/50.
5067 renumbered 28525
16/12/50.
28414 *(ex1063)* 18/4/52.
28353 *(ex3571)* 1/5/54.
28447 *(ex1040)* 29/8/56.
28214 *(ex61322)* 15/4/59.
28429 *(ex1018)* 14/11/62.

SHEDS:
Norwich.
Darlington 2/9/51.
Low Moor 8/6/58.
Mirfield 8/11/59.
York 11/9/60.

RENUMBERED:
61049 20/3/48.

CONDEMNED:
7/11/65.
Sold 12/65 for scrap to
A.Draper, Hull.

1050

North British Loco. 25806.

To traffic 17/6/46.

REPAIRS:
Str. 2/11–31/12/47.**G.**
Str. 1/48 at shed. *Front*
heat. fitted.
Str. 25/6–19/8/48.**L.** *Still*
LNER on tender.
Str. 27/1–25/4/50.**G.**
Don. 16/9–11/10/51.**G.**
Str. 3/3–25/4/53.**G.**
Str. 20/4–28/5/54.**C/L.**
Str. 13/4–14/5/55.**G.**
Dar. 18/7–9/8/56.**C/L.**
Dar. 14/6–11/7/57.**G.**
Dar. 15–17/7/57.**N/C.**
Don. 20/8–22/9/59.**G.**
Don. 30/1–11/2/61.**N/C.**
Don. 4/6–31/7/62.**G.**

BOILERS:
5070.
5062 *(ex1040)* 31/12/47.
3836 *(ex1051)* 25/4/50.
28152 *(ex1207)* 11/10/51.
28554 *(ex1052)* 25/4/53.
28555 *(ex1088)* 14/5/55.
28568 *(ex1088)* 11/7/57.
28978 *(new)* 22/9/59.

28869 *(ex1250)* 31/7/62.

SHEDS:
Norwich.
Ardsley 13/5/51.
Norwich 28/10/51.
Southern Region 18/5/53.
Norwich 23/5/53.
Sheffield 10/6/56.
Canklow 16/6/63.
Retford 28/3/65.
Doncaster 13/6/65.
Langwith 11/7/65.

RENUMBERED:
61050 18/8/48.

CONDEMNED:
10/2/66.
Made S.B. Departmental
No.30.
Sold for scrap, engine only,
to G.Haslewood,
Attercliffe, 10/68.
Tender to snowplough.

1051

North British Loco. 25807.

To traffic 20/6/46.

REPAIRS:
Str. 9/8–11/9/46.**L.**
Str. 25/9–12/10/46.**L.**
Str. 9/12/47–4/2/48.**G.**
Str. 10/1–11/3/50.**G.**
Str. 4–14/6/50.**C/L.**
Str. 10/10–4/11/50.**C/L.**
Str. 21/2–22/3/51.**C/L.**
Don. 19/12/51–17/1/52.**G.**
Str. 1/10–7/11/53.**G.**
Str. 11/6/55–20/1/56.**G.**
Dar. 31/8–7/9/56.**N/C.**
Dar. 7–15/8/57.**N/C.**
Dar. 11/3–10/4/58.**G.**
Dar. 2/11–4/12/59.**G.**
Don. 19/1–1/2/61.**N/C.**
Don. 21/12/61–26/1/62.**G.**

BOILERS:
5071.
3836 *(new)* 4/2/48.
3456 *(ex1041)* 11/3/50.
3456 renumbered 28516
4/11/50.
28168 *(ex1208)* 17/1/52.
28816 *(ex1114)* 7/11/53.
28564 *(ex61362)* 20/1/56.
28162 *(ex1137)* 10/4/58.
28180 *(ex61391)* 4/12/59.
28569 *(ex61323)* 26/1/62.

SHEDS:
Norwich.
Ardsley 13/5/51.
Norwich 16/12/51.
Sheffield 10/6/56.
Canklow 16/6/63.
Doncaster 28/3/65.
Langwith 11/7/65.

RENUMBERED:
E1051 31/1/48.
61051 11/3/50.

CONDEMNED:
10/2/66.
*Made S.B.Departmental
No.31.
Sold for scrap to Arnott
Young, Parkgate, 5/66.*

1052

North British Loco. 25808.

To traffic 24/6/46.

REPAIRS:
Str. 18/7–2/8/47.**H.**
Str. 29/2–27/3/48.**G.** *Front
Heat. fitted.*
Str. 9–21/5/49.**L/I.**
Str. 4/9–28/10/49.**G.**
Str. 21–22/2/50.**Weigh.**
Str. 29/4–22/6/51.**G.**
Str. 26/1–13/3/53.**G.**
Str. 13/9–23/10/54.**G.**
Str. 22/5–21/7/56.**G.**
Str. 10–20/12/56.**N/C.**
Str. 11/6–14/8/58.**G.**
Str. 22/9–22/10/58.**C/L.**
Don. 4–29/10/60.**G.**

BOILERS:
  5050.
  5066 *(ex1045)* 2/8/47.
  5074 *(ex1056)* 27/3/48.
  9923 *(ex1286)* 28/10/49.
  28554 *(ex1141)* 22/6/51.
  28527 *(ex1252)* 13/3/53.
  28452 *(ex61376)* 23/10/54.
  28595 *(ex1104)* 21/7/56.
  28517 *(ex1045)* 14/8/58.
  28253 *(ex61325)* 29/10/60.

SHEDS:
Ipswich.
Norwich 17/8/46.
Ipswich 24/9/50.
March 1/11/59.

RENUMBERED:
61052 25/3/48.

CONDEMNED:
16/9/62.
*Sold 6/63 for scrap to
Central Wagon Co, Ince.*

1053

North British Loco. 25809.

To traffic 27/6/46.

REPAIRS:
Str. 15/1–8/3/47.**L.**
Str. 31/5–30/7/48.**G.**
Str. 4–22/4/49.**C/L.**
Don. 8/7–16/9/49.**C/L.**
Str. 24/4–10/6/50.**G.**
Str. 26/9–14/11/50.**C/L.**

Str. 29/3–27/4/51.**H.**
Str. 18–20/7/51.**N/C.**
Dar. 10/4–8/5/52.**G.**
Dar. 29/4–22/5/54.**G.**
Dar. 24–26/5/54.**N/C.**
Dar. 8/3–5/4/56.**G.**
Dar. 13–29/5/57.**C/L.**
Dar. 16/5–18/6/58.**G.**
Dar. 5/12/60–19/1/61.**G.**
A.W.S. fitted.

BOILERS:
  3675.
  5104 *(ex1042)* 30/7/48.
  3421 *(ex1006)* 10/6/50.
  *3421 renumbered 28507
  14/11/50.*
  28551 *(ex1045)* 27/4/51.
  28260 *(ex1150)* 8/5/52.
  28551 *(ex spare 2 years)*
  22/5/54.
  28155 *(ex1084)* 5/4/56.
  28816 *(ex1033)* 18/6/58.
  28308 *(ex61321)* 19/1/61.

SHEDS:
Ipswich.
York 2/9/51.

RENUMBERED:
61053 30/7/48.

CONDEMNED:
25/2/63.
*In 13/3/63 for cut up
Darlington.*

1054

North British Loco. 25810.

To traffic 2/7/46.

REPAIRS:
Str. 12/10–16/12/47.**G.**
Front heat. fitted.
Str. 5–21/4/48.**N/C.**
Str. 5–19/6/48.**N/C.** *Spec.
painting only.*
Str. 29/1–17/3/49.**L.**
Str. 28/6–5/8/49.**C/H.**
Str. 15/1–15/4/50.**G.**
Str. 4/9–13/10/51.**G.**
Str. 4–28/3/52.**C/L.**
Str. 29/4–20/6/53.**G.**
Str. 6/12/54–22/1/55.**G.**
Str. 11/6–11/8/56.**G.**
Str. 3/3–30/5/58.**G.** *Mod.
bogie springs.*
Str. 7–16/10/59.**C/L.** *After
collision.*
Str. 13/11/59–24/2/60.**G.**

BOILERS:
  5072.
  5065 *(ex1041)* 16/12/47.
  9684 *(ex1089)* 15/4/50.
  28567 *(ex61333)* 13/10/51.
  28152 *(ex1050)* 20/6/53.
  28501 *(ex1059)* 22/1/55.
  28147 *(ex1301)* 11/8/56.
  28524 *(ex1005)* 30/5/58.
  28870 *(ex1000)* 24/2/60.

SHEDS:
Ipswich.
Norwich 26/7/59.
Lowestoft 3/4/60.
Norwich 11/9/60.
March 4/2/62.

RENUMBERED:
61054 17/4/48.

CONDEMNED:
16/9/62.
*Sold 6/63 for scrap to
Central Wagon Co, Ince.*

1055

North British Loco. 25811.

To traffic 4/7/46.

REPAIRS:
Str. 31/3–23/4/47.**L.**
Str. 7/12/47–16/1/48.**G.**
Front heat. fitted.
Str. 1/4–4/6/49.**G.**
Str. 9–23/7/49.**C/L.**
Str. 24/11–2/12/49.**N/C.**
Str. 26/3–12/5/50.**C/L.**
Str. 19/2–7/4/51.**G.**
Str. 19–22/8/52.**N/C.**
Str. 24/11/52–10/1/53.**G.**
Mod. bogie springs.
Str. 26/5–24/7/53.**C/L.**
Str. 22/11/54–1/1/55.**G.**
Str. 5–29/9/55.**C/L.**
Str. 11/12/55–25/1/57.**G.**
Str. 15/9–24/10/58.**G.**
Str. 4–5/11/58.**N/C.**
Don. 4–15/7/60.**N/C.**
Don. 6/7–3/8/61.**G.**

BOILERS:
  5073.
  3619 *(ex1044)* 16/1/48.
  9863 *(ex1226)* 4/6/49.
  28538 *(ex1149)* 7/4/51.
  28594 *(ex1005)* 10/1/53.
  28145 *(ex1164)* 1/1/55.
  28569 *(ex1003)* 25/1/57.
  28835 *(ex1287)* 24/10/58.
  28579 *(ex61312)* 3/8/61.

SHEDS:
Ipswich.
Doncaster 8/11/59.
Retford 16/9/62.
Doncaster 13/6/65.

RENUMBERED:
61055 3/6/49.

CONDEMNED:
27/2/66.
*Sold 4/66 for scrap to
T.W.Ward, Beighton.*

1056

North British Loco. 25812.

To traffic 4/7/46.

REPAIRS:
Str. 27/9–23/10/46.**L.** *After
collision.*
Str. 2/1–18/2/48.**G.** *Front
heater fitted.*
Str. 8/5–6/8/49.**G.**
Str. 6–13/12/49.**N/C.**
Str. 4/2–16/3/51.**G.**
Str. 6/4–8/5/52.**N/C.**
Str. 9/9–4/10/52.**C/H.**
Str. 9/5–9/6/53.**C/L.** *After
collision.*
Gor. 6/2–20/3/54.**G.**
Gor. 21/8–4/9/54.**C/L.**
Dar. 26/11–7/12/55.**C/L.**
Dar. 21/11–18/12/56.**G.**
Str. 6/10–5/12/58.**G.** *Mod.
bogie springs.*
Don. 16/6–22/7/61.**G.**

BOILERS:
  5074.
  3841 *(new)* 18/2/48.
  3762 *(ex1607)* 6/8/49.
  28537 *(ex1201)* 16/3/51.
  28850 *(new)* 20/3/54.
  28575 *(ex1092)* 18/12/56.
  28347 *(ex1211)* 22/7/61.

SHEDS:
Ipswich.
Ardsley 13/5/51.
Ipswich 16/12/51.
Colwick 29/6/52.
Ipswich 6/10/57.
March 22/11/59.
Sheffield 24/1/60.
Immingham 4/11/62.

RENUMBERED:
E1056 18/2/48.
61056 6/8/49.

CONDEMNED:
19/4/64.
*Sold 6/64 for scrap to
Central Wagon Co, Ince.*

1057

North British Loco. 25813.

To traffic 8/7/46.

REPAIRS:
Str. 25/10–26/12/46.**H.**
Str. 5/3–13/4/48.**G.** *Front
Heat. fitted.*
Str. 21/5–10/6/48.**N/C.**
Painting only.
Don. 1/7–19/8/49.**G.**

BOILERS:
  3625.
  3404 *(ex2822)* 26/12/46.
  5124 *(new)* 13/4/48.
  9751 *(ex1165)* 19/8/49.

SHED:
Ipswich.

RENUMBERED:
61057 10/4/48.

CONDEMNED:
17/4/50.
Engine and tender cut up at Stratford after damage in collision at Marks Tey 7/3/50. Boiler re-used.

1058

North British Loco. 25814.

To traffic 10/7/46.

REPAIRS:
Str. 24/4–11/5/47.**L.**
Str. 23/8–25/9/48.**G.** *Front heater fitted.*
Str. 19/2–12/5/50.**G.**
Str. 25/11/51–4/1/52.**G.**
Str. 6–17/5/52.**N/C.**
Str. 13–31/1/53.**N/C.**
Str. 1/7–29/8/53.**G.**
Str. 6–22/12/54.**C/L.**
Str. 27/6–20/8/55.**G.**
Str. 13/5–28/6/57.**G.**
Str. 14/1–20/2/59.**G.** *Mod. bogie springs. Part A.T.C. fitted.*
Don. 29–31/8/60.**N/C.**
Don. 22/2–3/4/62.**G.**

BOILERS:
3680.
3832 *(new)* 25/9/48.
28507 *(ex1053)* 4/1/52.
28337 *(ex1186)* 29/8/53.
28256 *(ex1006)* 20/8/55.
28292 *(ex1048)* 28/6/57.
28538 *(ex61336)* 20/2/59.
28146 *(ex1158)* 3/4/62.

SHEDS:
Ipswich.
March 22/11/59.
Lincoln 27/3/60.
Retford 5/1/64.
Doncaster 13/6/65.
Immingham 3/10/65.

RENUMBERED:
61058 25/9/48.

CONDEMNED:
10/2/66.
Sold 3/66 for scrap to A.Draper, Hull.

1059

North British Loco. 25815.

To traffic 27/7/46.

REPAIRS:
Str. 21–31/5/47.**L.**
Str. 11/4–9/6/48.**G.**
Str. 3–24/12/48.**L.**
Str. 3/1–4/3/50.**G.**
Str. 15/4–23/5/51.**G.**

Str. 21/1–6/3/53.**G.**
Str. 23/11–12/12/53.**C/L.**
Str. 25/10–27/11/54.**G.**
Str. 9/12/55–13/1/56.**C/H.**
Str. 24/1–2/3/57.**G.**
Str. 23/5–4/7/58.**C/L.**
Str. 1/1–13/2/59.**G.** *Part A.T.C. fitted. B.T.H.speed indicator.*
Don. 9/5–3/7/62.**G.**

BOILERS:
3683.
3404 *(ex1057)* 9/6/48.
5064 *(ex1048)* 4/3/50.
28552 *(ex1226)* 23/5/51.
28501 *(ex1109)* 6/3/53.
28131 *(ex1090)* 27/11/54.
28557 *(ex1300)* 2/3/57.
28510 *(ex1003)* 13/2/59.
28808 *(ex1003)* 3/7/62.

SHEDS:
Ipswich.
March 29/11/59.
Kings Lynn 31/1/60.
March 3/7/60.

RENUMBERED:
61059 5/6/48.

CONDEMNED:
25/11/63.
Made S.B.Departmental No.17. Withdrawn 4/66. Sold 5/66 for scrap to Birds, Long Marston.

1060

North British Loco. 25816.

To traffic 1/8/46.

REPAIRS:
Dar. 11/3–23/4/48.**G.**
Dar. 27/4–4/5/48.**N/C.**
Don. 19/10–14/11/50.**G.**
Don. 21–28/12/50.**C/L.**
Dar. 11–16/6/51.**C/L.**
Dar. 12/12/52–15/1/53.**G.**
Dar. 3–5/3/53.**Weigh.**
Dar. 31/12/53–12/1/54.**N/C.**
Dar. 17/9–14/10/54.**G.**
Dar. 12–25/1/56.**C/L.**
Dar. 17/10–14/11/56.**G.**
Str. 1/6–30/7/59.**G.** *A.T.C. fitted.*
Don. 13–25/5/60.**C/L.**

BOILERS:
3684.
3711 *(new)* 23/4/48.
28110 *(ex1087)* 14/11/50.
28208 *(ex1100)* 15/1/53.
28108 *(ex1170)* 14/10/54.
28658 *(ex1303)* 14/11/56.
28593 *(ex1252)* 30/7/59.

SHEDS:
Neville Hill.
Hull Dairycoates 16/5/48.
Grantham 24/2/57.
New England 6/10/57.
Lincoln 20/11/60.

RENUMBERED:
61060 23/4/48.

CONDEMNED:
16/9/62.
Sold 1/63 for scrap to Cox & Danks, Wadsley Bridge.

1061

North British Loco. 25817.

To traffic 3/8/46.

REPAIRS:
Cow. 5–27/12/47.**G.**
Cow. 23/3–7/5/49.**H/I.**
Cow. 23–26/12/49.**N/C.**
Cow. 28/5–7/7/51.**G.**
Dar. 5–14/8/52.**C/L.**
Dar. 23/12/52.**Weigh.**
Dar. 28/9–17/10/53.**G.**
Dar. 19–20/10/53.**N/C.**
Ghd. 17/2–23/3/55.**C/L.**
Dar. 10/10–4/11/55.**G.**
Dar. 17/9–1/12/56.**C/L.**
Dar. 10/4–7/5/58.**G.**
Dar. 13–19/5/58.**N/C.**
Dar. 21/5–5/6/59.**N/C.** *A.T.C. Elec. fitted.*
Dar. 31/1–3/3/61.**G.**

BOILERS:
3681.
3681 *renumbered* 28602 7/7/51.
28364 *(ex1078)* 17/10/53.
28220 *(ex1100)* 4/11/55.
28235 *(ex1063)* 7/5/58.
28430 *(ex1071)* 3/3/61.

SHEDS:
Perth.
St Margarets 5/2/50.
Darlington 2/9/51.
Low Moor 8/6/58.
Darlington 14/9/58.
West Hartlepool 5/10/58.
Ardsley 25/11/62.

RENUMBERED:
61061 7/5/49.

CONDEMNED:
13/9/65.
Sold 10/65 for scrap to Garnham, Harris & Elton, Chesterfield.

1062

North British Loco. 25818.

To traffic 7/8/46.

REPAIRS:
Dar. 26/9–14/11/47.**G.**
Gor. 11/12/48–8/1/49.**G.**
Dar. 20/6–14/7/50.**G.**
Dar. 1–4/8/50.**N/C.**
Dar. 29/9–25/10/51.**G.**
Dar. 29–31/10/51.**N/C.**
Dar. 3–31/12/52.**G.**
Dar. 9–11/4/53.**N/C.**
Dar. 30/3–30/4/54.**C/L.**
Dar. 26/11–23/12/54.**G.**
Dar. 13/1–2/2/55.**N/C.**
Dar. 1/4–10/5/55.**C/H.**
Dar. 25/10–21/11/56.**G.**
Dar. 1/12/58–6/1/59.**G.** *A.T.C.Mech. fitted.*
Dar. 14/5–19/6/59.**C/H.** *A.T.C.Elec. fitted.*
Dar. 31/7–31/8/61.**G.**
Dar. 6–14/9/61.**N/C.**

BOILERS:
3687.
9739 *(ex1153)* 8/1/49.
9928 *(ex1291)* 14/7/50.
28225 *(ex1069)* 25/10/51.
28456 *(ex1290)* 31/12/52.
28105 *(ex1268)* 23/12/54.
28864 *(ex1271)* 21/11/56.
28224 *(ex1012)* 6/1/59.
28216 *(ex1012)* 31/8/61.

SHEDS:
Neville Hill.
Thornaby 1/11/59.
York 11/9/60.

RENUMBERED:
61062 8/1/49.

CONDEMNED:
3/8/64.
In 8/9/64 for cut up Darlington.

1063

North British Loco. 25819.

To traffic 10/8/46.

REPAIRS:
Gor. 9/2–15/3/48.**G.**
Gor. 11/10–12/11/49.**G.**
Dar. 27/1–1/3/52.**G.**
Dar. 3–4/3/52.**N/C.**
Gor. 6/3–3/4/54.**G.**
Dar. 7/2–5/3/56.**G.**
Dar. 17/2–15/3/58.**G.**
Dar. 19/10–18/11/59.**G.**
Dar. 12/12/60–9/1/61.**C/L.**
Dar. 20/3–28/4/61.**C/L.**
Derailment damage.

WORKS CODES:– Cow – Cowlairs. Dar – Darlington. Dee – Dundee. Don – Doncaster. Ghd – Gateshead. Gor – Gorton. Inv – Inverurie. Str – Stratford. SRX – St Rollox.

REPAIR CODES:– **C/H** – Casual Heavy. **C/L** – Casual Light. **G** – General. **H** – Heavy. **H/I** – Heavy Intermediate. **L** – Light. **L/I** – Light Intermediate. **N/C** – Non–Classified.

BOILERS:
5059.
5125 *(new)* 15/3/48.
9865 *(ex1228)* 12/11/49.
28249 *(ex1078)* 1/3/52.
28187 *(ex1033)* 3/4/54.
28235 *(ex1010)* 5/3/56.
28834 *(ex1210)* 15/3/58.
28369 *(ex1010)* 18/11/59.

SHEDS:
Sheffield.
Woodford 27/4/47.
Annesley 19/6/49.
Colwick 21/10/56.
Leicester 11/11/56.
Neasden 6/3/60.
Leicester 30/9/60.
Woodford 17/3/62.

RENUMBERED:
61063 27/3/48.

CONDEMNED:
26/3/62.
In 13/4/62 for cut up
Darlington.

1064

North British Loco. 25820.

To traffic 14/8/46.

REPAIRS:
Inv. 4/9/46.**N/C.**
Inv. 10/9/46.**N/C.**
Inv. 17/10/46.**N/C.**
Inv. 5–8/2/47.**L.** *Tablet*
app. fitted.
Cow. 19/1–13/3/48.**G.**
Cow. 7/2–18/3/50.**H/I.**
Cow. 17/10–10/11/51.**H/I.**
Cow. 12/2–5/3/53.**L/I.**
Cow. 28/4–31/5/54.**H/I.**
After collision with 62012.
Cow. 28/6–6/8/55.**G.**
Cow. 8/6–12/7/57.**L/I.**
Cow. 11/2–11/3/59.**L/I.**
Cow. 22/8–7/10/60.**G.**

BOILERS:
5063.
5063 renumbered 28606
10/11/51.
28878 *(new)* 6/8/55.
28622 *(ex1133)* 7/10/60.

SHEDS:
Kittybrewster.
Keith 14/4/47.
Eastfield 28/8/49.
Carlisle Canal 18/5/55.
Eastfield 15/7/62.
Carlisle Canal 12/8/62.

RENUMBERED:
E1064 13/3/48.
61064 23/10/48.

CONDEMNED:
15/10/62.
Cut up Cowlairs 7/63.

1065

North British Loco. 25821.

To traffic 15/8/46.

REPAIRS:
Gor. 28/2–27/3/48.**G.**
Dar. 1–25/6/49.**G.**
Dar. 27–29/6/49.**N/C.**
Dar. 29/8–2/9/50.**C/L.**
Dar. 7/2–8/3/51.**G.**
Dar. 15–27/10/51.**C/L.**
Dar. 30/1–14/2/52.**C/L.**
Dar. 19/8–6/9/52.**G.**
Dar. 15–18/9/52.**N/C.**
Dar. 27/11–24/12/53.**G.**
Dar. 22/6–16/7/55.**G.**
Dar. 25–29/7/55.**N/C.**
Dar. 5–12/8/55.**N/C.**
Dar. 29/8–21/9/55.**N/C.**
Dar. 6–30/3/57.**G.**
Dar. 1/5/57.**N/C.**
Dar. 13–17/9/57.**N/C.**
Dar. 11/2–12/3/59.**G.**
A.T.C. Mech.fitted.
Dar. 18/3–1/4/59.**N/C.**
Dar. 31/7–13/8/59.**C/L.**
A.T.C. Elec.fitted.
Dar. 10/10–4/11/61.**G.**

BOILERS:
5075.
5123 *(new)* 27/3/48.
9759 *(ex1173)* 25/6/49.
28200 *(ex1129)* 8/3/51.
28277 *(ex1123)* 6/9/52.
28213 *(ex1022)* 24/12/53.
28125 *(ex1021)* 16/7/55.
28113 *(ex1259)* 30/3/57.
28858 *(ex1237)* 12/3/59.
28601 *(ex1192)* 4/11/61.

SHEDS:
Neville Hill.
Heaton 19/11/50.
Neville Hill 1/1/51.
Gateshead 15/9/57.
Hull Dairycoates 14/9/58.

RENUMBERED:
61065 25/3/48.

CONDEMNED:
1/9/64.
Sold 11/64 for scrap to
A.Draper, Hull.

1066

North British Loco. 25822.

To traffic 19/8/46.

REPAIRS:
Gor. 1/1–21/2/48.**G.**
Gor. 27/3–29/4/50.**G.**
Gor. 3–6/5/50.**N/C.**
Dar. 12/4–10/5/52.**G.**
Dar. 12–13/5/52.**N/C.**
Dar. 22/12/52–4/2/53.**C/L.**
After collision.
Gor. 31/7–11/9/54.**G.**
Gor. 11–30/9/54.**N/C.**

Don. 3–12/3/55.**N/C.**
Dar. 24/10–20/11/56.**G.**
Str. 17/11/58–9/1/59.**G.**
Mod. bogie springs.
Str. 20/4–15/5/59.**N/C.**
Complete A.T.C. fitted.
Don. 9/3–8/4/61.**G.**

BOILERS:
5076.
9710 *(ex1078)* 29/4/50.
28436 *(ex1204)* 10/5/52.
28405 *(ex1131)* 11/9/54.
28505 *(ex1074)* 20/11/56.
28104 *(ex1164)* 9/1/59.
28220 *(ex1044)* 8/4/61.

SHEDS:
Sheffield.
Woodford 27/4/47.
Annesley 19/6/49.
Colwick 7/10/56.
Cambridge 6/10/57.
Stratford 14/9/58.
Cambridge 21/9/58.
March 20/11/60.

RENUMBERED:
E1066 21/2/48.
61066 29/4/50.

CONDEMNED:
16/9/62.
Sold 6/63 for scrap to
Central Wagon Co,Ince.

1067

North British Loco. 25823.

To traffic 22/8/46.

REPAIRS:
Inv. 15–18/1/47. *Tablet*
apparatus fitted.
Cow. 27/10–5/12/47.**G.**
Cow. 16–23/4/49.**C/L.**
Cow. 8–30/3/50.**L/I.**
Cow. 21/12/50–19/1/51.**G.**
Cow. 9–30/6/51.**C/L.**
Cow. 25/11–12/12/51.**H/I.**
Cow. 3/11/53.**N/C.**
Cow. 28/12/53–6/2/54.**G.**
Cow. 13/3–14/4/56.**H/I.**
Water Pick-up gear
removed.
Cow. 18–26/10/56.**C/L.**
Cow. 18–22/6/57.**N/C.**
Cow. 28/2–22/3/58.**H/I.**
Cow.
17/12/58–14/1/59.**C/L.**
Cow. 28/3–10/4/59.**N/C.**
A.W.S. fitted.
Cow. 19/1–19/3/60.**G.**

BOILERS:
3691.
3391 *(ex1002)* 19/1/51.
3391 renumbered 28600
12/12/51.
28661 *(ex61356)* 6/2/54.
28635 *(ex61354)* 19/3/60.

SHEDS:
Kittybrewster.
St Margarets 25/9/49.
Eastfield 4/3/51.
Parkhead 18/3/51.

RENUMBERED:
61067 13/11/48.

CONDEMNED:
29/12/62.
Into Cowlairs for cut-up
1/63.

1068

North British Loco. 25824

To traffic 23/8/46.

REPAIRS:
Dar. 27/11/47–23/1/48.**G.**
Dar. 16/9–14/10/49.**G.**
Dar. 29/5–23/6/51.**G.**
Dar. 13/4/53–9/5/53.**G.**
Dar. 11–12/5/53.**N/C.**
Dar. 20/11–4/12/53.**C/L.**
Dar. 27/1–18/2/55.**G.**
Dar. 28/2–1/3/55.**N/C.**
Dar. 27/3–10/4/56.**N/C.**
Dar. 8/10–8/11/56.**G.**
Dar. 20/6–1/8/58.**G.**
Dar. 5–17/3/59.**N/C.**
A.T.C. Mech.fitted.
Dar. 18/2/60.**Weigh.**
Dar. 12/10–7/11/61.**G.**
A.T.C. Elec.fitted.

BOILERS:
5077.
9678 *(ex1013)* 14/10/49.
28217 *(ex61320)* 23/6/51.
28210 *(ex1014)* 9/5/53.
28456 *(ex1062)* 18/2/55.
28417 *(ex1291)* 8/11/56.
28400 *(ex1215)* 1/8/58.
28348 *(ex1186)* 7/11/61.

SHEDS:
Neville Hill.
Hull Dairycoates 16/5/48.
Hull Botanic Gardens
14/2/54.
Scarborough 14/6/59.
Darlington 27/3/60.
Thornaby 3/4/60.
York 11/9/60.
Ardsley 25/11/62.

RENUMBERED:
E1068 23/1/48.
61068 14/10/49.

CONDEMNED:
17/6/63.
Into Darlington for cut-up
2/7/63.

1069

North British Loco. 25825.

To traffic 26/8/46.

REPAIRS:
Dar. 2/1–26/2/48.**G.**
Gor. 1–29/5/48.**L.** *After collision.*
Dar. 26/4–14/5/49.**C/L.**
Dar. 16–25/5/49.**N/C.**
Dar. 7/10–5/11/49.**G.**
Dar. 7–10/11/49.**N/C.**
Dar. 22/11–8/12/49.**C/L.**
Dar. 18/6–10/7/51.**G.**
Dar. 30/8–2/9/51.**C/L.**
Dar. 4/10/51.**N/C.**
Dar. 8–27/9/52.**G.**
Dar. 29–30/9/52.**N/C.**
Dar. 10–18/6/53.**N/C.**
Dar. 1–8/7/53.**C/L.**
Dar. 25/9–7/10/53.**C/L.**
Dar. 18/2–13/3/54.**G.**
Dar. 15–17/3/54.**N/C.**
Dar. 25/3/54.*Weigh.*
Dar. 27/3–2/4/54.**N/C.**
Dar. 5–10/4/54.**N/C.**
Dar. 21/7–28/9/55.**C/L.**
Dar. 28/6–10/8/56.**G.**
Dar. 21/3–18/4/58.**G.**
Dar. 8/12/58.*Weigh.*
Dar. 16/2–18/3/60.**G.**
Complete A.W.S. fitted.
Dar. 2/11–6/12/62.**G.**
Dar. 12–20/12/62.**N/C.**
Dar. 19/8/63.*Not repaired.*

BOILERS:
5078.
3772 *(ex1024)* 5/11/49.
28218 *(ex1022)* 10/7/51.
28448 *(ex61337)* 27/9/52.
28233 *(ex1255)* 13/3/54.
28453 *(ex1215)* 10/8/56..
28551 *(ex1183)* 18/4/58.
28125 *(ex1085)* 18/3/60.
28801 *(ex61388)* 6/12/62.

SHEDS:
Neville Hill.
York 25/1/59.

RENUMBERED:
E1069 26/2/48.
61069 29/5/48.

CONDEMNED:
26/8/63.
Cut up Darlington.

1070

North British Loco. 25826.

To traffic 28/8/46.

REPAIRS:
Don. 17/2–23/3/48**G.**
Don. 17/12/49–20/1/50.**G.**
Don. 20–22/9/50.**C/L.**
Don. 17/3–18/4/52.**G.**
Str. 12/4–4/6/54.**G.**
Don. 11/10–10/11/56.**G.**

Don. 20/11–24/12/58.**G.**
Don. 23–31/8/60.**N/C.**
Don. 3–31/8/61.**G.**

BOILERS:
5088.
3750 *(ex1031)* 20/1/50.
28186 *(ex1654)* 18/4/52.
28868 *(new)* 4/6/54.
28436 *(ex1630)* 10/11/56.
28567 *(ex1142)* 24/12/58.

SHEDS:
Eastfield.
Gorton 16/9/46.
New England 4/5/47.
Colwick 3/1/65.

RENUMBERED:
61070 23/3/48.

CONDEMNED:
22/8/65.
Sold 9/65 for scrap to Hughes, Bolckow, N. Blyth.

1071

North British Loco. 25827.

To traffic 29/8/46.

REPAIRS:
Dar. 23/3–30/4/48.**G.**
Special painting.
Dar. 7/10–5/11/49.**G.**
Dar. 7–10/11/49.**N/C.**
Dar. 24/4–25/5/50.**C/L.**
Ghd. 11/9–12/10/50.**C/L.**
Dar. 21/3–12/4/52.**G.**
Dar. 15–16/4/52.**N/C.**
Dar. 11/1–4/2/54.**G.**
Dar. 8–11/2/54.**N/C.**
Dar. 7–19/3/55.**C/L.**
Dar. 24/1–22/2/56.**G.**
Dar. 20/2–19/3/58.**G.**
Dar. 1/12/60–14/1/61.**G.**
A.W.S. fitted.
Dar. 1–6/6/61.**N/C.**

BOILERS:
5058.
3702 *(new)* 30/4/48.
4008 *(new)* 5/11/49.
28421 *(ex1223)* 12/4/52.
28277 *(ex1065)* 4/2/54.
28237 *(ex1283)* 22/2/56.
28430 *(ex1288)* 19/3/58.
28433 *(ex61386)* 14/1/61.

SHEDS:
Eastfield.
Hull Botanic Gardens 30/8/46.
York 16/5/48.

RENUMBERED:
61071 30/4/48.

CONDEMNED:
11/2/63.
Into Darlington for cut-up 11/3/63.

1072

North British Loco. 25828.

To traffic 7/9/46.

REPAIRS:
Cow. 22–23/3/47.**C/L.**
Cow. 20/1–6/3/48.**G.**
Cow. 30/12/49–21/1/50.**L/I.**
Cow. 13/2–21/3/52.**G.**
Cow. 5–8/8/53.**N/C.**
Cow. 24/3–24/4/54.**H/I.**
Thj. 4–15/1/55.**C/L.**
Thj. 16/5–21/6/55.**C/L.**
Cow. 18/7–28/8/56.**G.**
Cow. 23/5–14/6/58.**H/I.**
Cow. 17–18/7/58.**N/C.**
Cow. 22–30/6/59.**N/C.**
Cow. 4/10–4/11/60.**G.**
Cow. 24/12/62–19/1/63.**H/I.**
Cow. 15/4–7/5/66.**C/L.**

BOILERS:
3693.
28614 *(ex1118)* 21/3/52.
28706 *(ex61398)* 28/8/56.
28873 *(ex1134)* 4/11/60.

SHEDS:
Eastfield.
Haymarket 21/9/46.
Thornton Junction 28/3/48.
Dunfermline 25/8/58.
Dundee 6/11/66.
Aberdeen 4/12/66.
Dundee 6/1/67.

RENUMBERED:
E1072 6/3/48.
61072 12/6/48.

CONDEMNED:
1/5/67.
Sold 14/7/67 for scrap to Motherwell Machinery & Scrap Co. Wishaw.

1073

North British Loco. 25829.

To traffic 6/9/46.

REPAIRS:
Don. 19/1–26/2/48.**G.**
Don. 14/2–3/3/49.**C/L.**
Don. 29/11/49–4/1/50.**G.**
Don. 19/11–14/12/51.**G.**
Don. 22–30/10/52.**N/C.**
Don. 16/7–13/8/53.**G.**
Don. 5–21/10/53.**N/C.**
Don. 21/3–15/4/55.**G.**
Don. 13/3–11/4/57.**G.**
Don. 15/1–13/2/59.**G.**
Don. 9/4–3/5/60.**C/L.**
Don. 3/3–1/4/61.**G.**

BOILERS:
3695.
9931 *(ex1294)* 4/1/50.
28160 *(ex1048)* 14/12/51.
28315 *(ex1652)* 13/8/53.
28529 *(ex1095)* 15/4/55.

28156 *(ex1205)* 11/4/57.
28803 *(ex1609)* 13/2/59.
28153 *(ex1251)* 1/4/61.

SHEDS:
Eastfield.
Gorton 16/9/46.
New England 4/5/47.

RENUMBERED:
E1073 26/2/48.
61073 3/3/49.

CONDEMNED:
22/9/63.
Sold 2/64 for scrap to R.A. King & Sons, Norwich.

1074

North British Loco. 25830.

To traffic 7/9/46.

REPAIRS:
Dar. 3/4–1/5/47.**L.**
Gor. 28/2–20/3/48.**G.**
Ghd. 13/1–15/2/50.**C/L.**
Don. 1–24/11/50.**G.**
Dar. 24/9–24/10/52.**G.**
Dar. 22/12/53–5/1/54.**C/L.**
Dar. 22/7–13/8/54.**G.**
Dar. 6/9–5/10/56.**G.**
Don. 7/4–12/5/59.**G.**
Don. 6/6–14/7/61.**G.**

BOILERS:
9676.
5126 *(new)* 20/3/48.
28114 *(ex2954)* 24/11/50.
28123 *(ex1115)* 24/10/52.
28505 *(ex1193)* 13/8/54.
28414 *(ex1032)* 5/10/56.
28109 *(ex1200)* 12/5/59.
28860 *(ex1120)* 14/7/61.

SHEDS:
Hull Botanic Gardens.
Hull Dairycoates 16/5/48.
Grantham 24/2/57.
New England 6/10/57.

RENUMBERED:
61074 20/3/48.

CONDEMNED:
4/9/63.
Sold 1/64 for scrap to R.A. King & Sons, Norwich.

1075

North British Loco. 25831.

To traffic 16/9/46.

REPAIRS:
Don. 5/4–12/5/48.**G.**
Don. 18–20/1/49.**C/L.**
Don. 8/5–8/6/50.**G.**
Don. 23/11–21/12/51.**G.**

Don. 25/8–2/10/53.**G.**
Don. 11/5–11/6/55.**G.**
Don. 15/2–16/3/57.**G.**
Don. 6/2–19/3/59.**G.**
Don. 26/8–30/9/61.**G.**

BOILERS:
 3623.
 9886 *(ex1249)* 8/6/50.
 28162 *(ex1029)* 21/12/51.
 28352 *(ex1204)* 2/10/53.
 28875 *(new)* 11/6/55.
 28150 *(ex1136)* 16/3/57.
 28156 *(ex1073)* 19/3/59.
 28405 *(ex1175)* 30/9/61.

SHEDS:
Gorton.
New England 9/5/47.
Kings Cross 13/6/54.
New England 9/10/60.
Kings Cross 3/6/62.
Mexborough 16/6/63.

RENUMBERED:
61075 12/5/48.

CONDEMNED:
22/9/63.
*Sold 12/63 for scrap to
G.Haslewood, Attercliffe,
Sheffield.*

1076

North British Loco. 25832.

To traffic 17/9/46.

REPAIRS:
Cow. 26/1–26/3/48.**G.**
Cow. 13/9–8/10/49.**L/I.**
Cow. 3/9–30/10/51.**G.**
Cow. 26/10–5/12/53.**H/I.**
*Heater connection fitted to
front.*
Cow. 12/5–11/6/54.**C/L.**
Cow. 11/10–12/11/55.**G.**
Cow. 29/3–26/4/58.**L/I.**
Cow. 28/1–13/2/59.**N/C.**
A.T.C. fitted.
Cow. 8/6–6/8/60.**G.** *Mod.
bogie springs.*
Inv. 4/6–19/7/63.**L/I.**

BOILERS:
9677.
 9677 renumbered 28607
30/10/51.
28667 *(ex61402)* 12/11/55.
28646 *(ex61359)* 6/8/60.

SHEDS:
Haymarket.
St Margarets 23/9/62.

RENUMBERED:
61076 26/3/48.

CONDEMNED:
10/9/65.
*Sold 11/65 for scrap to
Shipbreaking Industries,
Faslane.*

1077

North British Loco. 25833.

To traffic 18/9/46.

REPAIRS:
Don. 22/3–7/5/48.**G.**
Don. 4/6–10/7/50.**G.**
Don. 19/2–18/3/52.**G.**
Don. 3/9–8/10/53.**G.**
Don. 21/2–18/3/55.**G.**
Don. 17/7–17/8/56.**G.**
Don. 10/2–8/3/58.**G.**
Dar. 25/9–23/10/59.**G.**
Dar. 28/10–2/11/59.**N/C.**
Dar. 20/7–10/12/60.**C/L.**
*Collision damage. Tender
rebuilt.*

BOILERS:
 5060.
 3716 *(ex1086)* 10/7/50.
 28181 *(ex1113)* 18/3/52.
 28199 *(ex1144)* 8/10/53.
 28296 *(ex1612)* 18/3/55.
 28324 *(ex1149)* 17/8/56.
 28305 *(ex1166)* 8/3/58.
 28170 *(ex1020)* 23/10/59.

SHEDS:
Gorton.
Neasden 18/5/47.
Leicester 13/11/61.
Gorton 21/3/62.

RENUMBERED:
61077 7/5/48.

CONDEMNED:
14/5/62.
*21/6/62 in for cut up
Darlington.*

1078

North British Loco. 25834.

To traffic 23/9/46.

REPAIRS:
Gor. 12/4–22/5/48.**G.**
Gor. 11/3–1/4/50.**G.**
Gor. 10/11–8/12/51.**G.**
Gor. 11–19/12/51.**N/C.**
Dar. 13/5–13/6/53.**G.**
Dar. 17–22/6/53.**N/C.**
Dar. 10/1–5/2/55.**G.**
Dar. 20/2–1/3/56.**C/L.**
Dar. 21/9–18/10/56.**G.**
Dar. 19/12/57–20/1/58.**C/H.**
Dar. 31/10–3/12/58.**G.**
Dar. 12/8–16/9/60.**G.**
Dar. 24/8–20/9/62.**C/L.**

BOILERS:
 3699.
 9710 *(ex1122)* 22/5/48.
 9965 *(ex61328)* 1/4/50.
 28364 *(ex1184)* 8/12/51.
 28202 *(ex1021)* 13/6/53.
 28270 *(ex1123)* 5/2/55.
 28117 *(ex1188)* 18/10/56.
 28406 *(ex1040)* 3/12/58.

28560 *(ex61335)* 16/9/60.

SHEDS:
Gorton.
Woodford 2/3/47.
Colwick 19/6/49.
Leicester 27/1/52.
Woodford 11/5/52.
Leicester 6/7/52.
Woodford 14/9/52.

RENUMBERED:
61078 22/5/48.

CONDEMNED:
8/10/62.
*22/3/63 in for cut up
Darlington.*

1079

North British Loco. 25835.

To traffic 24/9/46.

REPAIRS:
Gor. 14/3–19/4/48.**G.**
Gor. 20/10–19/11/49.**G.**
Gor. 22–29/11/49.**N/C.**
Gor. 1/4–9/6/51.**G.**
Gor. 10–14/6/51.**N/C.**
Gor. 16–17/6/51.**N/C.**
Don. 16/1–11/2/53.**G.**
Don. 8/7/53.*Weigh.*
Don. 15/10/53.*Weigh.*
Dar. 18/7–12/8/54.**G.**
Dar. 14–16/8/54.**N/C.**
Don. 25/12/55–2/2/56.**G.**
Don. 10–15/2/56.**N/C.**
Dar. 22/10–23/11/57.**G.**
Dar. 15–23/12/57.**N/C.**
Dar. 6/6–3/7/58.**C/L.**
Don. 4–11/6/59.**N/C.**
Don. 23/12/59–30/1/60.**G.**
Don. 7–11/11/60.**N/C.**
Don. 13/6/62.*Not repaired.*

BOILERS:
 9678.
 5059 *(ex1063)* 19/4/48.
 5125 *(ex1063)* 19/11/49.
 28320 *(ex1190)* 9/6/51.
 28134 *(ex1167)* 11/2/53.
 28814 *(ex1198)* 12/8/54.
 28149 *(ex1144)* 2/2/56.
 28317 *(ex61387)* 23/11/57.
 28304 *(ex1183)* 30/1/60.

SHEDS:
Gorton.
Immingham 17/5/47.

RENUMBERED:
61079 17/4/48.

CONDEMNED:
18/6/62.
Cut up Doncaster.

1080

North British Loco.25836

To traffic 26/9/46.

REPAIRS:
Dar. 10–14/4/47.*Tender
change.*
Dar. 12/7–27/8/48.**G.**
Dar. 29/11–28/12/49.**C/L.**
Don. 10/1–1/2/51.**G.**
Dar. 23/1–21/2/53.**G.**
Dar. 24/3–20/4/55.**G.**
Dar. 25–26/4/55.**N/C.**
Dar. 2–6/5/55.**N/C.**
Dar. 11–17/5/55.**N/C.**
Dar. 25/6–10/8/57.**G.**
Dar. 15–28/11/57.**C/L.**
Dar. 22–26/9/58.**C/L.**
Dar. 24/10–6/11/58.**N/C.**
Dar. 5/5–15/6/59.**N/C.**
Complete A.T.C. fitted.
Dar. 18/9–2/10/59.**C/L.**
Dar. 4/1–8/2/60.**G.**
Dar. 25/4–4/5/61.**C/L.**
Dar. 24/4–24/5/62.**G.**
Dar. 30/5–5/6/62.**N/C.**
Dar. 30/11/62–22/1/63.**C/L.**

BOILERS:
 3705.
 3729 *(ex1014)* 27/8/48.
 28126 *(ex1194)* 1/2/51.
 28291 *(ex1106)* 21/2/53.
 28267 *(ex1163)* 20/4/55.
 28586 *(ex1085)* 10/8/57.
 28302 *(ex1086)* 8/2/60.
 28353 *(ex61383)* 24/5/62.

SHEDS:
Hull Botanic Gardens.
Hull Dairycoates 16/5/48.
Hull Botanic Gardens
15/12/57.
Hull Dairycoates 14/6/59.

RENUMBERED:
61080 27/8/48.

CONDEMNED:
30/3/64.
*Sold for scrap 5/64 to
G.W.Butler, Otley.*

1081

North British Loco. 25837.

To traffic 3/10/46.

REPAIRS:
Cow. 16/2–27/3/48.**G.**
Cow. 1–26/8/49.**L/I.**
Cow. 21/9–20/11/51.**G.**
Cow. 30/12/53–8/1/54.**C/L.**
Hay. 25/1–5/2/54.**C/L.**
Cow. 15/4–8/5/54.**L/I.**
Cow. 13/9–15/10/55.**G.**
Cow. 17/7–4/8/56.**C/L.**
Hay. 18–21/3/57.**C/L.**
Cow. 20–28/8/57.**N/C.**

continued on page 34

Carriage warming connection and hose were not fitted as original equipment, but it was added to quite a number, 61043 gaining it at an April 1948 general repair.

In July 1950 Doncaster fitted 61164 with this chime whistle on the side of the smokebox, although the normal whistle in front of the cab was retained. The engine worked from Neasden shed but the experiment ended in December when the chime was removed, and it was the only B1 so fitted.

The pitfalls for precision modellers are illustrated by this photograph of 61017 at York North shed on 16th February 1958. In 1954 seven B1s, 61035, 61258, 61284, 61311, 61360, 61362 and 61394 had extra balancing plates fitted on to the face of those cast in the wheel centres. A glass shows quite clearly that 61017 had also acquired them and the explanation is that it had exchanged coupled wheels with 61258 whilst both were having general repairs in Darlington, during January 1958. Note also that whilst 61017 has the correct figure 6 on the cab, its smokebox number plate still has the wrong one with curled tail, and the door also carries an SC, indicating self–cleaning box.

At its March 1957 general repair at Cowlairs, 61243 was given an appreciably increased radius to the angle at each end of its running plate. This particular detail was introduced in 1956 on engines maintained by that works to help cure frequent cracking at those points. 61243, at Eastfield shed in June 1957, has also been fitted with a B.T.H. speed indicator operated from the coupling pin of the rear wheel. The other workshops which repaired B1s did not apply that extra radius.

On 8303 to 8310 the bogie front was a concave stretcher plate 14″ deep at the sides and 10″ deep at the centre, but when Darlington built 1010 t0 1039 the stretcher plate was superseded by a casting 10½″ deep with a level top edge. 1018 at York on 31st July 1947 shows the Metropolitan Vickers axle mounted generator for electric lighting, and also the shortest LNER name and plate.

On 61340 to 61349 built by Gorton, and also on 61400 – 61409 which Darlington built, as well as on the latter's 61350 – 61359, the bogie front end stay was 14½″ deep at the sides but only 9″ at the centre, and it had two slots in it.

61350 to 61409 had a different design of smokebox door, with curvature of only 6ft. 5-½ns. radius instead of 11ft. as used previously, and the hinge straps were 15ins. instead of 24ins. apart. The number plate and top lamp iron on this batch were higher.

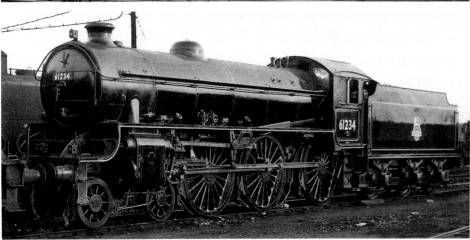

On engines with the earlier design of smokebox door, it was found possible to fit the cast number plate between the top hinge strap and the twin handles for fastening the door; that enabled the top lamp iron position to be retained.

The two smokebox door types were quite interchangeable – witness 61237 at Sunderland on 9th July 1961, wearing the later type instead of that first fitted to it. Note that although named after one of the LNER Directors, this gave it no preference in the matter of painting or cleaning. The Automatic Train Control apparatus was operative from July 1959 and a protection plate was fitted to prevent damage from the swinging front coupling.

Beginning with No.1190 a step was added near the bottom of the smokebox door to provide easier access to the top lamp iron. At Doncaster shed on Sunday 8th June 1947, and only just one month old, its washout plugs do not appear to be in the best condition. Despite the electric generator being fitted, conduit and lamps for electric lighting have yet to be installed at the front end.

Even where the full electric lighting equipment had been fitted, it was still necessary for normal oil lamps to be carried, to indicate the class of train being worked, and irons suitable for them were fitted. Above the buffer beam they were combined, but separate ones were fitted for the upper indication.

1081 continued
Cow. 6/9–9/10/57.**H/I.**
Cow. 23/5–13/6/59.**G.**
Mod.bogie springs
Cow. 19/8–23/9/60.**C/L.**
Cow. 31/5–5/7/62.**L/I.**
Cow. 10/7–1/8/62.**C/L.**

BOILERS:
9679.
28616 *(ex1134)* 20/11/51.
28659 *(ex61354)* 15/10/55.
28665 *(ex61402 141 tubes)*
13/6/59.

SHEDS:
Haymarket.
Dalry Road 9/9/63.
St Margarets 18/11/63.
Dundee 15/6/64.

RENUMBERED:
61081 27/3/48.

CONDEMNED:
29/6/64.
Sold for scrap 8/64 to
Motherwell Machinery &
Scrap Co. Wishaw.

1082

North British Loco. 25839.

To traffic 4/10/46.

REPAIRS:
Gor. 18/10–6/12/47.**G.**
Gor. 7–18/12/47.**N/C.**
Gor. 6/8–3/9/49.**G.**
Gor. 25/3–22/4/50.**C/L.**
Gor. 13/10–10/11/51.**G.**
Gor. 5–12/1/52.**C/L.**
Don. 15–17/1/52.**N/C.**
Don. 11–29/8/52.**N/C.**
Don. 6/10–3/11/52.**C/H.**
Don. 21/9–20/10/53.**G.**
Don. 22/12/54–5/1/55.**C/L.**
Don. 10/2–12/3/55.**G.**
Don. 4/9–13/10/56.**G.**
Don. 15/9–17/10/58.**G.**
Don. 13–27/1/59.**N/C.**
Don. 31/5–7/7/60.**G.**
Don. 5–30/10/61.**C/H.**

BOILERS:
3706.
9702 *(ex1114)* 3/9/49.
28357 *(ex1181)* 10/11/51.
28331 *(ex61409)* 20/10/53.
28144 *(ex1027)* 12/3/55.
28506 *(ex1643)* 13/10/56.
28231 *(ex61389)* 17/10/58.
28865 *(ex1168)* 7/7/60.
28807 *(ex1188)* 30/10/61.

SHEDS:
Gorton.
Immingham 17/5/47.

RENUMBERED:
61082 3/9/49.

CONDEMNED:
29/12/62.
Sold for scrap 2/63 to
J.Cashmore, Great Bridge.

1083

North British Loco. 25838.

To traffic 7/10/46.

REPAIRS:
Don. 5/6–23/7/48.**G.**
Don. 3/3–21/4/50.**G.**
Don. 29/9–26/10/51.**G.**
Don. 23/4–20/5/53.**G.**
Don. 24/11–22/12/54.**G.**
Don. 30/5–7/7/56.**G.**
Str. 2/6–1/8/58.**G.**
Don. 12/12/60–12/1/61.**G.**

BOILERS:
9680.
3712 *(ex1033)* 21/4/50.
28154 *(ex1165)* 26/10/51.
28752 *(ex1126)* 20/5/53.
28276 *(ex1020)* 22/12/54.
28100 *(ex1036)* 7/7/56.
28515 *(ex61360)* 1/8/58.
28952 *(ex61366)* 12/1/61.

SHEDS:
Gorton.
Neasden 16/6/47.
Peterborough 20/1/57.
Sheffield 14/12/58.
Mexborough 24/5/59.
Millhouses 30/7/61.
Canklow 31/12/61.

RENUMBERED:
61083 23/7/48.

CONDEMNED:
22/9/63.
Sold for scrap 12/63 to
Marples & Gillott,
Sheffield.

1084

North British Loco. 25841.

To traffic 9/10/46.

REPAIRS:
Dar. 14/4–14/5/48.**G.**
Dar. 18–28/5/48.**N/C.**
Special painting.
Dar. 1–27/5/50.**G.**
Dar. 27/3–25/4/52.**G.**
Dar. 3–27/2/54.**G.**
Dar. 1–2/3/54.**N/C.**
Dar. 20/1–20/2/56.**G.**
Dar. 29/2–6/3/56.**N/C.**

Dar. 22–29/8/57.**N/C.**
Dar. 17/4–14/5/58.**G.**
Dar. 24/6–6/7/59.**N/C.**
Complete A.T.C. fitted.
Dar. 14/9–22/10/60.**G.**

BOILERS:
3708.
3684 *(ex1060)* 14/5/48.
9775 *(ex1189)* 27/5/50.
28419 *(ex1010)* 25/4/52.
28155 *(ex1029)* 27/2/54.
28319 *(ex1110)* 20/2/56.
28434 *(ex1238)* 14/5/58.
28524 *(ex1054)* 22/10/60.

SHEDS:
Hull Botanic Gardens.
York 16/5/48.

RENUMBERED:
61084 14/5/48.

CONDEMNED:
29/6/64.
7/9/64 in for cut up
Darlington.

1085

North British Loco. 25842.

To traffic 11/10/46.

REPAIRS:
Don. 20/6–4/8/48.**G.**
Don. 20/6–21/7/50.**G.**
Dar. 20/8–12/9/52.**G.**
Don. 3–30/11/54.**G.**
Don. 24/1–8/2/56.**C/L.**
Dar. 8/5–5/6/57.**G.**
Dar. 8/12/58–15/1/59.**C/L.**
Dar. 9/9–15/10/59.**G.**
Dar. 8/11–22/12/60.**C/L.**
Dar. 31/8–5/10/61.**C/L.**

BOILERS:
9681.
9443 *(new)* 4/8/48.
9933 *(ex1296)* 21/7/50.
28272 *(ex1185)* 12/9/52.
28586 *(ex1201)* 30/11/54.
28125 *(ex1065)* 5/6/57.
28280 *(ex1256)* 15/10/59.

SHEDS:
Gorton.
Woodford 2/3/47.
Neasden 9/3/47.
Gorton 4/2/49.
Ardsley 17/7/49.
Copley Hill 7/8/49.
Ardsley 4/6/50.
New England 20/9/53.
Lincoln 26/6/55.
Leicester 1/6/58.
Woodford 7/11/59.
Leicester 6/10/60.

RENUMBERED:
61085 4/8/48.

CONDEMNED:
27/11/61.
7/12/61 in for cut up
Darlington.

1086

North British Loco. 25840.

To traffic 14/10/46.

REPAIRS:
Gor. 1–29/5/48.**G.**
Gor. 4/9/48.**C/L.**
Don. 23/5–16/6/50.**G.**
Don. 17/12/51–11/1/52.**G.**
Don. 25/2–15/3/52.**C/L.**
Don. 26/11–13/12/52.**C/L.**
Dar. 30/4–29/5/53.**G.**
Dar. 6/12/54–7/1/55.**G.**
Dar. 23/5–19/6/56.**G.**
Dar. 13/3–2/4/57.**C/L.**
Dar. 9–14/5/57.**N/C.**
Dar. 30/9–1/10/57.**N/C.**
Dar. 4–28/2/58.**G.**
Dar. 7/12/59–9/1/60.**G.**
Dar. 3–12/10/60.**N/C.**
A.W.S.Elec. fitted.

BOILERS:
9682.
3716 *(ex1010)* 29/5/48.
3623 *(ex1075)* 16/6/50.
28167 *(ex1075)* 11/1/52.
28460 *(ex1025)* 29/5/53.
28128 *(ex1168)* 7/1/55.
28424 *(ex1151)* 19/6/56.
28302 *(ex1258)* 28/2/58.
28834 *(ex1083)* 9/1/60.

SHEDS:
Gorton.
Leicester 1/6/47.
Doncaster 6/2/49.
Neville Hill 27/1/52.
York 25/1/59.

RENUMBERED:
61086 29/5/48.

CONDEMNED:
3/12/62.
18/12/62 in for cut up
Darlington.

1087

North British Loco. 25843.

To traffic 16/10/46.

REPAIRS:
Gor. 20/9–6/11/48.**G.**
Don. 5–17/3/50.**C/L.**
Don. 12/8–19/9/50.**G.**

WORKS CODES:– Cow – Cowlairs. Dar – Darlington. Dee – Dundee. Don – Doncaster. Ghd – Gateshead. Gor – Gorton. Inv – Inverurie. Str – Stratford. SRX – St Rollox.

REPAIR CODES:– **C/H** – Casual Heavy. **C/L** – Casual Light. **G** – General. **H** – Heavy. **H/I** – Heavy Intermediate. **L** – Light. **L/I** – Light Intermediate. **N/C** – Non–Classified.

Don. 12/5–4/6/52.**G.**
Dar. 5–30/4/54.**G.**
Don. 1/5–1/6/56.**G.**
Don. 14/7–15/8/58.**G.**
Don. 18/8–30/9/60.**G.**
Don. 12/6–15/7/61.**C/H.**
Don. 8/1–16/2/63.**G.**

BOILERS:
  5090.
  9436 (ex6624) 6/11/48.
28100 (ex1127) 19/9/50.
28194 (ex1128) 4/6/52.
28817 (ex1198) 30/4/54.
28215 (ex61390) 1/6/56.
28589 (ex1113) 15/8/58.
28149 (ex1121) 30/9/60.
28250 (ex spare) 15/7/61.
28306 (ex1210) 16/2/63.

SHEDS:
Sheffield.
Woodford 27/4/47.
Leicester 14/11/48.
Doncaster 6/2/49.

RENUMBERED:
61087 6/11/48.

CONDEMNED:
5/12/65.
Sold for scrap 1/66 to
Garnham, Harris & Elton,
Chesterfield.

1088

North British Loco. 25844.

To traffic 18/10/46.

REPAIRS:
Gor. 19/7–4/9/48.**G.**
Gor. 21/7–19/8/50.**G.**
Dar. 9/12/51–10/1/52.**C/L.**
Dar. 6–28/2/53.**G.**
Dar. 2–3/3/53.**N/C.**
Dar. 6/12/54–4/1/55.**G.**
Dar. 11–24/2/55.**C/L.**
Dar. 5–11/12/56.**N/C.**
Dar. 14/5–7/6/57.**G.**
Dar. 18–24/6/57.**N/C.**
Don. 2/3–9/4/59.**G.**
Don. 19/6–8/7/59.**C/L.**
Don. 9–18/2/60.**C/L.**
Don. 21–30/9/60.**N/C.**
Don. 15/7–12/8/61.**G.**

BOILERS:
  9683.
  9682 (ex1086) 4/9/48.
  9950 (ex61313) 19/8/50.
  9950 renumbered 28401
10/1/52.
28293 (ex1182) 28/2/53.
28568 (ex61314) 4/1/55.
28900 (ex1256) 7/6/57.
28183 (ex1643) 9/4/59.
28814 (ex1093) 12/8/61.

SHEDS:
Sheffield.
Woodford 27/4/47.
Leicester 13/3/49.

Woodford 3/4/49.
Colwick 19/6/49.
Leicester 12/3/50.
Colwick 18/11/56.

RENUMBERED:
61088 4/9/48.

CONDEMNED:
22/9/63.
Sold for scrap 1/64 to
J.Cashmore, Great Bridge.

1089.

North British Loco. 25845.

To traffic 22/10/46.

REPAIRS:
Don. 3/2–20/3/48.**G.**
Gor. 7–11/6/49.**C/L.**
Str. 16/1–1/4/50.**G.**
Str. 3/7–11/8/51.**C/L.**
Str. 17/3–19/4/52.**G.**
Str. 12/1–6/2/54.**G.**
Str. 3/3–12/5/55.**C/L.**
Str. 23/3–14/5/56.**G.**
Str. 12–16/11/56.**N/C.**
Str. 19–23/5/58.**N/C.**
Str. 15/12/58–6/2/59.**G.**
Mod. bogie springs.
B.T.H. speed indicator.
Str. 16–19/2/59.**N/C.**
Str. 11–12/3/59.**N/C.**
Str. 27/4–15/5/59.**N/C.**
Complete A.T.C. fitted.
Don. 11/10–10/11/61.**G.**
Don. 30/4–17/5/62.**C/L.**
Don. 17/12/62–9/1/63.**N/C.**

BOILERS:
  9684.
  5073 (ex1046) 1/4/50.
  5073 renumbered 28562
11/8/51.
28584 (ex61311) 19/4/52.
28570 (ex1227) 6/2/54.
28572 (ex61361) 14/5/56.
28452 (ex1300) 6/2/59.
28872 (ex1122) 10/11/61.

SHEDS:
Sheffield.
Hitchin 20/11/46.
Gorton 26/12/48.
Stratford 28/8/49.
Immingham 27/5/51.
Stratford 24/6/51.
Colchester 6/1/57.
Stratford 29/9/57.
Lincoln 27/11/60.
Immingham 22/9/63.
Colwick 11/7/65.
To LM.Reg Book Stock
2/1/66.

RENUMBERED:
61089 20/3/48.

CONDEMNED:
2/4/66.
Sold for scrap 5/66 to
J.Cashmore, Great Bridge.

1090

North British Loco.25846.

To traffic 24/10/46.

REPAIRS:
Don. 7/11–24/12/48.**G.**
Don. 1/11–4/12/50.**G.**
Don. 28/11–24/12/52.**G.**
Str. 20/9–29/10/54.**G.**
Dar. 4–29/11/57.**G.**
Don. 21/3–22/4/60.**G.**
Don. 2–22/8/60.**C/L.**

BOILERS:
  5091.
  9713 (ex1125) 24/12/48.
28115 (ex1015) 4/12/50.
28131 (ex1203) 24/12/52.
28518 (ex1008) 29/10/54.
28116 (ex61310) 29/11/57.
28221 (ex1210) 22/4/60.

SHEDS:
Sheffield.
Hitchin 20/11/46.
Mexborough 14/6/59.
Sheffield 15/5/60.
Mexborough 9/9/62.

RENUMBERED:
61090 24/12/48.

CONDEMNED:
22/9/63.
In 22/9/63 for cut up
Darlington.

1091

North British Loco. 25847.

To traffic 28/10/46.

REPAIRS:
Don. 30/7–18/8/47.**L.**
Don. 5/12/48–14/1/49.**G.**
Don. 7/11–6/12/50.**G.**
Don. 25/8–25/9/52.**G.**
Don. 17–26/3/53.**N/C.**
Str. 25/1–6/2/54.**C/L.**
Don. 26/8–1/10/54.**G.**
Don. 25/7–29/8/56.**G.**
Str. 13/10–21/11/58.**G.**
Don. 18–31/8/60.**N/C.**
Don. 22/8/62.Not repaired.

BOILERS:
  9685.
  5091 (ex1090) 14/1/49.
28117 (ex1143) 6/12/50.
28512 (ex1144) 25/9/52.
28833 (ex61405) 1/10/54.
28584 (ex1212) 29/8/56.
28410 (ex1104) 21/11/58.

SHEDS:
Sheffield.
Hitchin 20/11/46.
New England 7/8/60.

RENUMBERED:
61091 14/1/49.

CONDEMNED:
10/9/62.
Cut up Doncaster.

1092

North British Loco. 25848.

To traffic 30/10/46.

REPAIRS:
Don. 12/9–27/10/48.**G.**
Gor. 28/11/49–28/1/50.**G.**
Gor. 31/1–2/2/50.**N/C.**
Gor. 5–10/2/50.**N/C.**
Dar. 28/9–3/11/51.**G.**
Gor. 12/9–17/10/53.**G.**
Dar. 8/9–5/10/55.**G.**
Dar. 12–20/4/56.**C/L.**
Dar. 14–16/5/57.**N/C.**
Dar. 1–26/10/57.**G.**
Don. 3/7–5/8/59.**G.**
Don. 12–30/1/60.**C/L.**
Don. 12/10–4/11/60.**G.**
Don. 27/2–4/4/62.**G.**

BOILERS:
  5089.
  9700 (ex1112) 27/10/48.
  9860 (ex1223) 28/1/50.
28232 (ex1024) 3/11/51.
28575 (ex1042) 17/10/53.
28211 (ex1025) 5/10/55.
28294 (ex1206) 26/10/57.
28958 (new) 5/8/59.
28171 (ex3932) 4/4/62.

SHEDS:
Sheffield.
Hitchin 20/11/46.
Colwick 22/11/48.
Leicester 12/3/50.
Colwick 19/12/54.
To LM.Reg Book Stock
2/1/66.

RENUMBERED:
61092 27/10/48.

CONDEMNED:
19/2/66.
Sold for scrap 5/66 to Birds,
Long Marston.

1093

North British Loco. 25849.

To traffic 4/11/46.

REPAIRS:
Don. 26/1–1/3/49.**G.**
Don. 20/7–18/8/49.**C/L.**
Don. 16/1–6/2/51.**G.**
Don. 17/12/52–16/1/53.**G.**
Don. 4/10–3/11/54.**G.**
Don. 25/1–1/2/55.**C/L.**
Don. 6/11–8/12/56.**G.**
Don. 29/5–8/7/58.**G.**
Don. 29/12/60–26/1/61.**G.**

BOILERS:
  9686.

9755 *(ex1169)* 1/3/49.
28127 *(ex1175)* 6/2/51.
28300 *(ex1628)* 16/1/53.
28344 *(ex1171)* 8/12/56.
28814 *(ex1211)* 8/7/58.
28413 *(ex61409)* 26/1/61.

SHEDS:
Doncaster.
Hitchin 20/11/46.
Mexborough 14/6/59.
Millhouses 30/7/61.
Canklow 31/12/61.
Doncaster 28/3/65.
Langwith 11/7/65.

RENUMBERED:
61093 1/3/49.

CONDEMNED:
25/7/65.
*Sold for scrap 9/65 to
Geo.Cohen, Sheffield.*

1094

North British Loco. 25850.

To traffic 6/11/46.

REPAIRS:
Gor. 4–16/5/47.**L.**
Don. 11/9–3/10/47.**L.**
Don. 25/2–12/3/48.**L.**
Don. 1/3–1/4/49.**G.**
Don. 1–29/12/50.**G.**
Don. 30/9–24/10/52.**G.**
Don. 13–24/11/52.**N/C.**
Don. 31/8–6/10/54.**G.**
Don. 22/8–29/9/56.**G.**
Don. 18/8–30/9/58.**G.**
Don. 27/3–29/4/61.**G.**
Dar. 13–21/11/64.**C/L.**

BOILERS:
5092.
9749 *(ex1163)* 1/4/49.
28122 *(ex1091)* 29/12/50.
28506 *(ex1098)* 24/10/52.
28523 *(ex1009)* 6/10/54.
28157 *(ex1143)* 29/9/56.
28215 *(ex1087)* 30/9/58.
28104 *(ex1066)* 29/4/61.

SHEDS:
Doncaster.
Hitchin 20/11/46.
Hull Botanic Gardens
5/2/48.
Hitchin 13/2/48.
Sheffield 16/8/59.
Canklow 16/6/63.
Colwick 13/6/65.

RENUMBERED:
E1094 12/3/48.
61094 1/4/49.

CONDEMNED:
20/6/65.
*Sold for scrap 8/65 to
T.W.Ward, Sheffield.*

1095

North British Loco. 25851.

To traffic 11/11/46.

REPAIRS:
Don. 27/2–30/3/49.**G.**
Don. 2/4–2/5/50.**C/L.** *After
collision.*
Don. 14/3–11/4/51.**G.**
Don. 25/2–23/3/53.**G.**
Don. 15–17/10/53.*Tender
change.*
Don. 28/2–25/3/55.**G.**
Don. 28/5–5/7/57.**G.**
Str. 6/4–21/5/59.**G.**
Complete A.T.C. fitted.
Don. 10/5–9/6/61.**G.**
Don. 4/2/63–5/3/63.**C/H.**

BOILERS:
9687.
9827 *(ex1190)* 30/3/49.
28136 *(ex1096)* 11/4/51.
28529 *(ex1001)* 23/3/53.
28272 *(ex1085)* 25/3/55.
28236 *(ex1116)* 5/7/57.
28841 *(ex1042)* 21/5/59.
28349 *(ex1300)* 9/6/61.
28241 *(ex1036)* 5/3/63.

SHEDS:
Doncaster.
Hitchin 20/11/46.
New England 17/5/53.
Peterborough 3/3/57.
March 31/1/60.
Norwich 3/12/61.
March 4/2/62.
Lincoln 20/1/63.

RENUMBERED:
61095 30/3/49.

CONDEMNED:
28/12/63.
*31/1/64 into Doncaster for
cut up.*

1096

North British Loco. 25852.

To traffic 12/11/46.

REPAIRS:
Gor. 28/11/48–15/1/49.**G.**
Don. 7/2–9/3/51.**G.**
Gor. 28/3–25/4/53.**G.**
Gor. 28/4–29/5/53.**N/C.**
Dar. 17/2–16/3/55.**G.**
Dar. 21–29/3/55.**N/C.**
Dar. 2–3/4/55.**N/C.**
Dar. 12/12/56–9/1/57.**G.**
Dar. 13/2–8/3/57.**C/L.** *After
collision.*
Str. 11/11–21/12/57.**C/L.**
Str. 20/1–6/3/59.**G.**
*Mod.bogie springs. Part
A.T.C. fitted.*
Str. 13–16/3/59.**N/C.**
Don. 13–21/7/60.**N/C.**
Don. 20/1–22/2/61.**G.**

BOILERS:
9688.
9731 *(ex1145)* 15/1/49.
28130 *(ex1097)* 9/3/51.
28394 *(ex3670)* 25/4/53.
28115 *(ex1026)* 16/3/55.
28420 *(ex1230)* 9/1/57.
28557 *(ex1059)* 6/3/59.
28276 *(ex1270)* 22/2/61.

SHEDS:
Hitchin.
March 17/6/48.
Gorton 31/10/48.
Ardsley 17/7/49.
Copley Hill 7/8/49.
Ardsley 4/6/50.
Sheffield 23/12/51.
Cambridge 29/9/57.
Stratford 14/9/58.
Cambridge 21/9/58.
Peterborough 14/12/58.
March 31/1/60.

RENUMBERED:
61096 15/1/49.

CONDEMNED:
16/9/62.
*Sold for scrap 6/63 to
Central Wagon Co. Ince.*

1097

North British Loco. 25853.

To traffic 15/11/46.

REPAIRS:
Don. 29/5–11/6/47.**L.**
Don. 25/2–9/3/48.**L.**
Don. 13/2–24/3/49.**G.**
Don. 31/1–19/2/51.**G.**
Don. 8/1–14/2/53.**G.**
Don. 16/12/54–14/1/55.**G.**
Don. 21/1–10/2/55.**C/L.**
Don. 30/4–16/5/56.**C/L.**
Don. 1–29/8/57.**G.**
Don. 17/9–4/10/58.**C/L.**
Str. 8/6–6/8/59.**G.** *A.T.C.
fitted.*
Don. 28/8–1/9/59.**N/C.**
Don. 12/11–11/12/62.**G.**

BOILERS:
5061.
9717 *(ex1129)* 24/3/49.
28129 *(ex1093)* 19/2/51.
28137 *(ex1200)* 14/2/53.
28254 *(ex1655)* 14/1/55.
28193 *(ex1665)* 29/8/57.
28402 *(ex61405)* 6/8/59.
28899 *(ex3768)* 11/12/62.

SHEDS:
Hitchin.
New England 7/8/60.
Colwick 22/9/63.
New England 24/11/63.

RENUMBERED:
61097 24/3/49.

CONDEMNED:
3/1/65.
*Sold for scrap 2/65 to
R.A.King, Norwich.*

1098

North British Loco. 25854.

To traffic 19/11/46.

REPAIRS:
Don. 2/7–20/8/48.**G.**
Str. 17/9–4/11/50.**G.**
Str. 23/10–16/11/51.**C/L.**
Don. 14/5–9/6/52.**G.**
Don. 18/8–23/9/53.**G.**
Don. 23–30/11/53.**N/C.**
Don. 4–15/1/54.**C/L.**
Gor. 20–27/3/54.**C/L.**
Don. 1/6–7/7/55.**G.**
Don. 9–24/1/56.**N/C.**
Don. 19/9–19/10/57.**G.**
Don. 9–26/8/58.**C/L.**
Don. 13/4–14/5/59.**G.**
Don. 15–26/8/60.**N/C.**
A.W.S. fitted.
Don. 17/8–28/9/61.**G.**

BOILERS:
9689.
9716 *(ex1128)* 20/8/48.
28506 *(ex1047)* 4/11/50.
28195 *(ex1248)* 9/6/52.
28174 *(ex1163)* 23/9/53.
28750 *(ex61409)* 7/7/55.
28866 *(ex1158)* 19/10/57.
28955 *(new)* 14/5/59.
28536 *(ex61372)* 28/9/61.

SHEDS:
Hitchin.
March 17/6/48.
Gorton 31/10/48.
Stratford 31/7/49.
Immingham 21/10/51.

RENUMBERED:
61098 20/8/48.

CONDEMNED:
11/7/65.
*Sold for scrap 8/65 to
A.Draper, Hull.*

1099

North British Loco. 25855.

To traffic 21/11/46.

REPAIRS:
Don. 6/3–7/4/49.**G.**
Don. 10/4–7/5/51.**G.**
Don. 14/2–12/3/53.**G.**
Don. 12–19/5/53.**C/L.**
Cow. 18/6–1/7/54.**N/C.**
Cow. 9/11–4/12/54.**H/I.**
Cow. 23/12/55–14/1/56.**C/L.**
Cow. 12/8–5/10/57.**G.**
Cow. 24/12/57–16/1/58.**N/C.**
Cow. 31/3–15/4/59.**N/C.**
Cow. 10/8–5/9/59.**L/I.**

Cow. 16/2–15/4/61.**G.**
Cow. 22/2–3/3/62.**N/C.**
Cow. 30/4–8/6/63.**L/I.**
Cow. 18/4–1/5/64.**N/C.**
Cow. 3–19/2/66.**N/C.**
Cow. 17–26/3/66.**N/C.**

BOILERS:
9690.
9687 *(ex1095)* 7/4/49.
28141 *(ex1095)* 7/5/51.
28207 *(ex1112)* 12/3/53.
28639 *(ex61347)* 5/10/57.
28609 *(ex1117)* 15/4/61.

SHEDS:
Hitchin.
Kings Cross 11/1/53.
St Margarets 13/9/53.
Bathgate 9/1/66.
Thornton Junction 24/4/66.

RENUMBERED:
61099 7/4/49.

CONDEMNED:
2/9/66.
*Sold for scrap 10/66 to
Shipbreaking Industries,
Faslane.*

1100

North British Loco. 25856.

To traffic 26/11/46.

REPAIRS:
Dar. 23/12/47–6/2/48.**G.**
Gor. 23–30/10/48.**L.**
Dar. 12/5–3/6/49.**G.**
Dar. 13–17/6/49.**N/C.**
Dar. 16–25/8/49.*Painting
only.*
Ghd. 27/4–19/5/50.**C/L.**
Ghd. 25/8–5/9/50.**C/L.**
Dar. 11/4–4/5/51.**G.**
Dar. 9–10/5/51.**N/C.**
Ghd. 16/4–15/5/52.**C/L.**
After collision.
Dar. 30/9–25/10/52.**G.**
Dar. 1–13/7/53.**C/L.**
Dar. 11/3–3/4/54.**G.**
Dar. 5–7/4/54.**N/C.**
Dar. 8–30/9/55.**G.**
Dar. 10/5–7/6/56.**C/L.**
Dar. 19/8–14/9/57.**G.**
Dar. 21/5–8/6/59.**N/C.**
A.T.C.Elec. fitted.
Dar. 2–29/9/59.**G.**
Dar. 5–12/10/59.**N/C.**

BOILERS:
5093.
9744 *(ex1158)* 3/6/49.
28208 *(ex1173)* 4/5/51.
28218 *(ex1069)* 25/10/52.
28220 *(ex1034)* 3/4/54.
28550 *(ex1017)* 30/9/55.
28603 *(ex1131)* 14/9/57.
28249 *(ex1186)* 29/9/59.

SHEDS:
Gateshead.

Blaydon 10/2/57.
Gateshead 1/11/59.
Copley Hill 13/8/61.

RENUMBERED:
E1100 6/2/48.
61100 5/8/48.

CONDEMNED:
19/11/62.
*21/2/63 into Darlington for
cut up.*

1101

North British Loco. 25857.

To traffic 28/11/46.

REPAIRS:
Cow. 25/5–26/6/48.**G.**
Cow. 26/5–16/6/50.**L/I.**
Cow. 3/3–15/4/52.**G.**
Cow. 1/2–6/3/54.**H/I.**
Cow. 25–31/8/54.**N/C.**
Cow. 8–19/3/55.**N/C.**
Cow. 9–24/9/55.**N/C.**
Cow. 10/11–17/12/55.**G.**
Cow. 11/7–10/8/57.**C/L.**
Cow. 14/5–7/6/58.**H/I.**
Cow. 15/5–3/6/59.**N/C.**
Cow. 20–30/12/60.**C/L.**
Cow. 21/6–19/8/61.**G.**
Cow. 19/9–23/11/63.**L/I.**
Cow. 2–10/2/66.**N/C.**
Cow. 7–12/3/66.**N/C.**

BOILERS:
3700.
28611 *(ex1133)* 15/4/52.
28626 *(ex1134)* 17/12/55.
28633 *(ex1245)* 19/8/61.

SHEDS:
Dundee.
Dunfermline 25/4/55.

RENUMBERED:
61101 26/6/48.

CONDEMNED:
31/12/66.
*Sold for scrap 27/2/67 to
J.McWilliam, Shettleston.*

1102

North British Loco. 25862.

To traffic 2/12/46.

REPAIRS:
Cow. 16/6–17/7/48.**G.**
Cow. 31/10–16/12/50.**H/I.**
Cow. 20/10–8/11/52.**G.**
Cow. 5/2–13/3/54.**C/L.**
Cow. 19/1–19/2/55.**L/I.**
Cow. 27/2–14/4/56.**L/I.**
Cow. 24/5–2/6/56.**N/C.**
Cow. 16/8–13/9/58.**G.**
Cow. 12–16/10/59.**N/C.**
Cow. 8/2–18/3/61.**L/I.**
Cow. 13/12/62–26/1/63.**G.**
Cow. 5–27/6/64.**C/L.**

BOILERS:
9691.
28617 *(ex1147)* 8/11/52.
28619 *(ex1102)* 13/9/58.
28844 *(ex61308)* 26/1/63.

SHED:
Dundee.

RENUMBERED:
61102 17/7/48.

CONDEMNED:
22/4/67.
*Sold for scrap 7/7/67 to P &
W McLellan, Langloan.*

1103

North British Loco. 25863.

To traffic 4/12/46.

REPAIRS:
Cow. 27/7–27/8/48.**G.**
Cow. 17/4–6/5/50.**L/I.**
Cow. 19/3–3/5/52.**G.**
Cow. 16/11–12/12/53.**L/I.**
Thj. 29/6–3/7/54.**C/L**.*
Cow. 29/11–25/12/54.**N/C.**
Cow. 25/4–6/5/55.**N/C.**
Cow. 3–29/10/55.**G.**
Thj. 15–27/8/56.**C/L**.*
Cow. 30/7–30/8/57.**L/I.**
Cow. 23/8–20/9/58.**H/I.**
Cow. 3–27/8/59.**C/L.**
Cow. 8/11–3/12/60.**G.**
Inv. 28/5–12/7/63.**L/I.**
* Thornton Junction shed.

BOILERS:
9692.
28604 *(ex1072)* 3/5/52.
28666 *(ex61401)* 29/10/55.
28667 *(ex1076)* 3/12/60.

SHED:
Thornton Junction.

RENUMBERED:
61103 27/8/48.

CONDEMNED:
14/7/66.
*Sold for scrap 9/66 to
G.H.Campbell, Airdrie.*

1104

North British Loco. 25864.

To traffic 6/12/46.

REPAIRS:
Str. 11/2–20/3/48.**H.**
Str. 2/11–21/12/48.**G.**
Str. 8/8–9/9/50.**G.**
Str. 3/6–26/7/52.**G.**
Str. 30/3–18/5/54.**G.**
Str. 11/4–29/5/56.**G.**
Str. 24/7–5/9/58.**G.**
Mod.bogie springs.
Don. 4/11–6/12/60.**G.**

BOILERS:
9693.
3625 *(ex1003)* 21/12/48.
28500 *(ex1144)* 9/9/50.
28556 *(ex61335)* 26/7/52.
28595 *(ex61384)* 18/5/54.
28410 *(ex1632)* 29/5/56.
28166 *(ex1632)* 5/9/58.
28517 *(ex1052)* 6/12/60.

SHEDS:
Stratford.
Parkeston 7/9/47.
Stratford 1/2/48.
Cambridge 8/2/59.
Sheffield 3/5/59.
Mexborough 29/11/59.
Sheffield 10/1/60.
Mexborough 9/9/62.
Canklow 9/12/62.

RENUMBERED:
61104 18/12/48.

CONDEMNED:
18/4/64.
*Sold for scrap 6/64 to
W.F.Smith, Ecclesfield.*

1105

North British Loco. 25858.

To traffic 9/12/46.

REPAIRS:
Don. 15/5–5/7/49.**G.**
Don. 29/3–1/5/51.**G.**
Don. 23/4–18/5/53.**G.**
Don. 26–28/5/53.**N/C.**
Don. 5–27/8/53.**C/L.**
Don. 1–25/2/55.**G.**
Don. 16/10–2/11/56.**C/L.**
Don. 25/9–24/10/57.**G.**
Dar. 16/12/58–15/1/59.**C/L.**
Dar. 10/11–11/12/59.**G.**
Dar. 18–30/12/59.**N/C.**
Don. 3–19/10/60.**C/L.**
Don. 24/10–29/11/62.**G.**

BOILERS:
9694.
9753 *(ex1167)* 5/7/49.
28139 *(ex1182)* 1/5/51.
28140 *(ex1027)* 18/5/53.
28508 *(ex1282)* 25/2/55.
28756 *(ex1633)* 24/10/57.
28189 *(ex1038)* 11/12/59.
28121 *(ex61394)* 29/11/62.

SHEDS:
Hitchin.
Kings Cross 11/1/53.
Hitchin 13/6/54.
Sheffield 13/7/58.
Canklow 16/6/63.
New England 10/11/63.

RENUMBERED:
61105 5/7/49.

CONDEMNED:
26/12/64.
*Made S.B Departmental
No.27 8/3/65. Sold for scrap
7/66 to R.A.King, Norwich.*

1106

North British Loco. 25859.

To traffic 11/12/46.

REPAIRS:
Don. 1–27/5/48.**G.**
Gor. 4/4–7/5/49.**G.**
Gor. 21/2–1/4/50.**C/L.**
Gor. 10/1–24/2/51.**G.**
Gor. 3–5/3/51.**N/C.**
Gor. 13–14/3/51.**N/C.**
Dar. 22/12/52–24/1/53.**G.**
Gor. 16/10–20/11/54.**G.**
Dar. 3/7–15/8/57.**G.**
Dar. 22–28/10/57.**N/C.**
Dar. 10/6–8/8/59.**G.**
Dar. 28/11–24/12/60.**G.**

BOILERS:
9695.
9774 *(ex1188)* 7/5/49.
28291 *(ex1187)* 24/2/51.
28269 *(ex1153)* 24/1/53.
28205 *(ex1162)* 20/11/54.
28279 *(ex1188)* 15/8/57.
28270 *(ex1201)* 8/8/59.
28211 *(ex1214)* 24/12/60.

SHEDS:
Hitchin.
Gorton 23/1/49.
Leicester 15/5/49.
Colwick 12/10/52.
Leicester 15/2/53.
Colwick 28/2/54.
Leicester 8/12/57.
Woodford 4/11/59.

RENUMBERED:
61106 27/5/48.

CONDEMNED:
2/11/62.
27/11/62 into Darlington for cut up.

1107

North British Loco. 25861.

To traffic 13/12/46.

REPAIRS:
Don. 20–30/1/48.**L.**
Don. 11/9–28/10/48.**G.**
Gor. 10–23/12/48.**L.**
Don. 2–26/10/50.**G.**
Don. 12/11–18/12/50.**C/L.**
Don. 22/9–17/10/52.**G.**
Don. 26/1/53.*Weigh.*
Don. 6/12/54–5/1/55.**G.**
Don. 30–31/1/55.*Weigh.*
Dar. 1–28/3/57.**G.**
Don. 20/5–13/6/59.**G.**
Don. 11/8–1/9/60.**C/L.**
Don. 20/10–7/12/61.**G.**

BOILERS:
3701.
9708 *(ex1120)* 28/10/48.
28108 *(ex1138)* 26/10/50.
28121 *(ex1193)* 17/10/52.

28752 *(ex1083)* 5/1/55.
28282 *(ex1196)* 28/3/57.
28531 *(ex1649)* 13/6/59.
28327 *(ex1249)* 7/12/61.

SHEDS:
Hitchin.
Leicester 14/11/48.
Doncaster 27/2/49.
Retford 13/3/49.
Doncaster 7/5/50.
Immingham 30/9/51.
Doncaster 11/11/51.
Lincoln 29/4/62.
Retford 5/1/64.
Doncaster 13/6/65.

RENUMBERED:
61107 28/10/48.

CONDEMNED:
15/8/65.
Sold for scrap 9/65 to Hughes,Bolckow, N.Blyth.

1108

North British Loco. 25860.

To traffic 16/12/46.

REPAIRS:
Gor. 19/7–28/8/48.**G.**
Gor. 26/9–19/11/49.**G.**
Gor. 24–25/11/49.**N/C.**
Dar. 19/11–12/12/51.**G.**
Cow. 30/6–8/8/53.**G.**
Cow. 13/9–22/10/55.**L/I.**
Cow. 8–12/11/55.**N/C.**
Cow. 9/11–14/12/57.**L/I.**
Cow. 23/8–13/9/58.**C/H.**
StRx. 30/3–23/4/59.**C/L.**
Cow. 15–23/9/59.**N/C.**
Cow. 22/11–30/12/60.**H/I.**

BOILERS:
9696.
3725 *(ex1013)* 28/8/48.
9699 *(ex1204)* 19/11/49.
28235 *(ex1092)* 12/12/51.
28167 *(ex1086)* 8/8/53.
28649 *(ex61324)* 13/9/58
(141 tubes).

SHEDS:
Sheffield.
Woodford 8/5/47.
Leicester 13/3/49.
St Margarets 13/9/53.

RENUMBERED:
61108 28/8/48.

CONDEMNED:
29/12/62.
1/63 into Cowlairs for cut up.

1109

North British Loco. 25865.

To traffic 18/12/46.

REPAIRS:
Don. 19/8–1/10/48.**G.**
Str. 4–12/5/50.**C/L.**
Str. 18/6–12/8/50.**G.** *Speed indicator fitted. Front heater connection fitted.*
Str. 26/8–8/9/50.**N/C.**
Str. 5/7–18/8/51.**C/L.**
Str. 17/3–3/5/52.**C/H.**
Str. 24–29/10/52.**N/C.**
Str. 1/12/52–17/1/53.**G.**
Str. 23/11/54–8/1/55.**G.**
Str. 13/11–29/12/56.**G.**
Str. 3–18/12/58.**C/L.**
Str. 4/5–12/6/59.**G.**
Complete A.T.C. fitted.
Str. 4/5–28/6/60.**C/L.**
Don. 10/5–16/6/62.**G.**

BOILERS:
9697.
9714 *(ex1126)* 1/10/48.
3704 *(ex1048)* 12/8/50.
3704 renumbered 28501
8/9/50.
28510 *(ex1236)* 17/1/53.
28520 *(ex61336)* 8/1/55.
28163 *(ex61371)* 29/12/56.
28848 *(ex1119)* 12/6/59.
28141 *(ex1174)* 16/6/62.

SHEDS:
Sheffield.
Neasden 15/5/47.
Gorton 13/3/49.
LM Region. 3/7/49.
Gorton 17/7/49.
Stratford 28/8/49.
Southern Region 18/5/53.
Stratford 23/5/53.
Sheffield 27/11/60.
Canklow 16/6/63.
New England 10/11/63.

RENUMBERED:
61109 1/10/48.

CONDEMNED:
12/7/64.
Sold for scrap 8/64 to R.A.King, Norwich.

1110

North British Loco. 25866.

To traffic 20/12/46.

REPAIRS:
Gor. 13/7–7/10/47.**L.**
Gor. 10/11–31/12/48.**G.**
Gor. 9/2–14/4/51.**G.**
Dar. 16/3–11/4/53.**G.**
Dar. 13–14/4/53.**N/C.**
Dar. 20/9–14/10/55.**G.**
Dar. 15/5–22/6/57.**C/L.**
Dar. 4/6–1/7/58.**G.**
Dar. 6/10–2/11/61.**G.**
Dar. 14–24/11/61.**N/C.**

BOILERS:
9698.
9832 *(ex1195)* 31/12/48.
28304 *(ex1155)* 14/4/51.

28319 *(ex1159)* 11/4/53.
28552 *(ex1041)* 14/10/55.
28237 *(ex1071)* 1/7/58.
28133 *(ex1116)* 2/11/61.

SHEDS:
Sheffield.
Leicester 1/6/47.
Colwick 22/1/50.
Woodford 30/9/51.
Colwick 25/11/51.
Norwich 9/12/51.
Ardsley 27/1/52.

RENUMBERED:
61110 31/12/48.

CONDEMNED:
31/10/65.
Sold for scrap 12/65 to Hughes,Bolckow, N.Blyth.

1111

North British Loco. 25867.

To traffic 24/12/46.

REPAIRS:
Gor. 8/12/47–19/1/48.**L.**
Gor. 23/5–22/6/48.**G.**
Gor. 2–8/9/48.**L.**
Gor. 21/10–2/12/49.**G.**
Gor. 5–8/12/49.**N/C.**
Gor. 27/6–1/9/51.**G.**
Gor. 4–14/9/51.**N/C.**
Dar. 21/5–15/6/53.**G.**
Dar. 13–17/7/53.**N/C.** *After collision.*
Gor. 20/4–15/5/54.**N/C.**
Dar. 29/8–21/9/55.**G.**
Str. 19/12/57–14/2/58.**G.**
Don. 8/4–6/5/60.**G.**

BOILERS:
9699.
3699 *(ex1078)* 22/6/48.
3725 *(ex1108)* 2/12/49.
28814 *(new)* 1/9/51.
28333 *(ex1181)* 15/6/53.
28213 *(ex1065)* 21/9/55.
28202 *(ex1004)* 14/2/58.
28397 *(ex1253)* 6/5/60.

SHEDS:
Sheffield.
Leicester 1/6/47.
Colwick 21/11/48.
Woodford 7/9/52.
Colwick 14/9/52.
Leicester 7/12/52.
Colwick 28/1/53.
Woodford 9/1/55.
Colwick 6/2/55.
Kings Cross 7/10/56.
Neasden 2/12/56.
Kings Cross 27/1/57.
Stratford 10/2/57.
Parkeston 8/2/59.
Sheffield 24/5/59.

RENUMBERED:
61111 19/6/48.

CONDEMNED:
16/9/62.
Sold for scrap 3/63 to
J.Cashmore, Great Bridge.

1112

North British Loco. 25868.

To traffic 27/12/46.

REPAIRS:
Don. 14/9–15/10/48.**G.**
Dar. 15/3–28/4/51.**G.**
Don. 11–28/8/52.**N/C.**
Don. 27/1–20/2/53.**G.**
Don. 24/2–2/3/53.**N/C.**
Don. 3–28/1/55.**G.**
Dar. 22/3–18/4/57.**H/I.**
Dar. 28–30/4/57.**N/C.**
Don. 23/3–28/4/60.**G.**

BOILERS:
9700.
9715 *(ex1127)* 15/10/48.
28207 *(ex1012)* 28/4/51.
28282 *(ex1600)* 20/2/53.
28119 *(ex1630)* 28/1/55.
28199 *(ex3961)* 28/4/60.

SHEDS:
Kings Cross.
March 12/6/49.
Lincoln 20/10/49.
Norwich 28/10/51.
Lincoln 27/1/52.
Mexborough 4/10/53.
Sheffield 24/5/59.
Canklow 2/12/62.
Mexborough 9/12/62.

RENUMBERED:
61112 15/10/48.

CONDEMNED:
29/12/62.
Sold for scrap 6/63 to
J.Cashmore, Great Bridge.

1113

North British Loco. 25869.

To traffic 31/12/46.

REPAIRS:
Don. 28/3–21/5/48.**G.**
Don. 27/3–28/4/50.**G.**
Don. 29/1–26/2/52.**G.**
Don. 8/2–15/3/54.**G.**
Don. 18/11–17/12/55.**G.**
Don. 8–29/5/57.**C/L.**
Don. 31/5–4/6/57.**N/C.**
Don. 7/3–5/4/58.**G.**
Don. 23/9–3/10/59.**N/C.**
Don. 14/3–20/4/60.**G.**

BOILERS:
9701.
5088 *(ex1070)* 28/4/50.
28177 *(ex1163)* 26/2/52.
28757 *(ex61393)* 15/3/54.
28589 *(ex1139)* 17/12/55.

28239 *(ex1622)* 5/4/58.
28200 *(ex1285)* 20/4/60.

SHEDS:
Kings Cross.
New England 28/12/52.
Norwich 5/9/54.
New England 5/12/54.
Lincoln 20/11/60.

RENUMBERED:
61113 21/5/48.

CONDEMNED:
22/9/63.
17/9/63 into Darlington for
cut up.

1114

North British Loco. 25870.

To traffic 8/1/47.

REPAIRS:
Don. 3/12/47–15/1/48.**L.**
Gor. 8/6–23/7/49.**G.**
Gor. 17–18/8/49.**N/C.**
Gor. 28–29/3/51.**C/L.**
Gor. 21/9–3/11/51.**G.**
Gor. 6–8/11/51.**N/C.**
Gor. 10–13/11/51.**N/C.**
Gor. 15–16/11/51.**N/C.**
Str. 10/2–7/3/53.**C/L.** *After*
collision.
Str. 8/9–10/10/53.**G.**
Don. 15/6–19/7/55.**G.**
Dar. 9/7–24/8/57.**H/I.**
Don. 6–19/6/59.**C/L.**
Don. 5/11–3/12/59.**G.**
Don. 21–22/8/61.*Weigh.*

BOILERS:
9702.
9768 *(ex1182)* 23/7/49.
28816 *(new)* 3/11/51.
28528 *(ex1149)* 10/10/53.
28876 *(new)* 19/7/55.
28568 *(ex1050)* 3/12/59.

SHEDS:
Kings Cross.
Hitchin 5/2/48.
Kings Cross 19/2/48.
Hitchin 11/3/48.
Gorton 23/1/49.
Stratford 5/10/52.
Doncaster 28/2/54.
Immingham 13/12/59.

RENUMBERED:
61114 23/7/49.

CONDEMNED:
16/9/62.
Sold for scrap 1/63 to
Geo.Cohen, Rotherham.

1115

North British Loco. 25871.

To traffic 10/1/47.

REPAIRS:
Gor. 25/9–30/10/48.**G.**
Dar. 21/6–2/7/49.**C/L.** *After*
collision.
Don. 11/12/50–8/1/51.**G.**
Dar. 5–27/9/52.**G.**
Dar. 29–30/9/52.**N/C.**
Dar. 8/4–13/5/54.**G.**
Dar. 13/10–5/11/55.**G.**
Dar. 7–8/11/55.**N/C.**
Dar. 6–13/12/55.**N/C.**
Dar. 30/10–22/11/57.**G.**
Dar. 5–18/8/59.**N/C.**
Complete A.T.C. fitted.
Dar. 8/7–26/8/60.**G.**
Dar. 24/9–9/11/63.**G.**

BOILERS:
9703.
9718 *(ex1131)* 30/10/48.
28123 *(ex1125)* 8/1/51.
28447 *(ex1220)* 27/9/52.
28419 *(ex1084)* 13/5/54.
28146 *(ex1298)* 5/11/55.
28309 *(ex61390)* 22/11/57.
28850 *(ex1267)* 26/8/60.
28226 *(ex1187)* 9/11/63.

SHEDS:
York.
Copley Hill 8/6/58.
Low Moor 8/9/63.
Mirfield 5/1/64.
Low Moor 12/4/64.
Wakefield 13/11/66.

RENUMBERED:
61115 30/10/48.

CONDEMNED:
8/5/67.
Sold for scrap 21/7/67 to
Arnott Young, Parkgate.

1116

North British Loco. 25872.

To traffic 13/1/47.

REPAIRS:
Cow. 8/6–10/7/48.**G.**
Cow. 17–21/1/49.**C/L.**
Cow. 15/4/49.**N/C.**
Cow. 23/3–8/4/50.**L/I.**
Cow. 14/9/50.**N/C.**
Cow. 2/7/51.**N/C.**
Cow. 9/7/51.**N/C.**
Cow. 22–25/1/52.**N/C.**
Cow. 5/3–9/4/52.**G.**
Str. 6/2–19/3/54.**G.**
Don. 29/8–1/10/55.**G.**
Don. 10–12/10/55.**N/C.**
Don. 28/10–12/11/55.**N/C.**
Don. 18/4–31/5/57.**G.**
Don. 8–28/2/58.**C/L.**
Str. 24/2–24/4/59.**G.**
Str. 10–25/11/59.**C/L.**
Dar. 11/8–9/9/61.**G.**

BOILERS:
9704.
28822 *(new)* 9/4/52.
28540 *(ex61361)* 19/3/54.

28236 *(ex1158)* 1/10/55.
28133 *(ex1162)* 31/5/57.
28154 *(ex 2 years spare)*
9/9/61.

SHEDS:
Eastfield.
Neasden 18/5/52.
Leicester 3/10/59.
Neasden 7/11/59.
Leicester 17/9/60.
Neasden 24/9/60.
Woodford 15/3/62.
Eastfield 10/3/63.
Carstairs 26/6/66.

RENUMBERED:
61116 10/7/48.

CONDEMNED:
17/7/66.
Sold for scrap 10/66 to
Motherwell Machinery &
Scrap Co. Wishaw.

1117

North British Loco. 25873.

To traffic 15/1/47.

REPAIRS:
Cow. 30/4–12/6/48.**G.**
Cow. 9–28/1/50.**L/I.**
Cow. 19/12/51–25/1/52.**G.**
Cow. 11–29/8/53.**H/I.**
Cow. 2/7–7/8/54.**N/C.**
Cow. 30/11–31/12/54.**L/I.**
W.P.U. gear removed
9/4/55.
Cow. 28/11–29/12/56.**G.**
Cow. 18/4–1/5/58.**N/C.**
Cow. 11/12/58–7/1/59.**H/I.**
Mod. bogie springs.
Cow. 16–20/2/59.**N/C.**
A.T.C. fitted.
Cow. 4–14/5/59.**N/C.**
Cow. 25/11–14/1/61.**G.**
Cow. 8/2–13/3/61.**C/L.**
Cow. 11/9–6/10/62.**C/L.**
Cow. 21/1–2/3/63.**C/L.**

BOILERS:
9705.
28631 *(ex1245)* 25/1/52.
28609 *(ex1132)* 29/12/56.
28878 *(ex1064)* 14/1/61.

SHEDS:
Eastfield.
Parkhead 7/11/55.
St Margarets 13/8/62.

RENUMBERED:
61117 12/6/48.

CONDEMNED:
6/2/64.
2/64 into Inverurie for cut
up.

1118

North British Loco. 25874.

To traffic 17/1/47.

REPAIRS:
Cow. 7/3/47.**L.**
Cow. 21/6–13/8/48.**G.**
Cow. 5–27/1/50.**L/I.**
Cow. 11/12/51–16/1/52.**G.**
Cow. 12–29/8/53.**H/I.**
Cow. 31/8–1/10/55.**L/I.**
W.P.U. gear removed.
Cow. 13/12/56–12/1/57.**G.**
Cow. 24/6–11/7/57.**N/C.**
Cow. 9/2–31/5/58.**H/I.**
Cow. 13–29/4/59.**N/C.**
Mod. bogie springs.
A.W.S. fitted.
Cow. 5–12/5/59.**N/C.**
Cow. 6/2–26/3/60.**H/I.**
Cow. 1–16/8/60.**N/C.**
Cow. 27/3–12/4/61.**N/C.**
Cow. 3/2–3/3/62.**N/C.**
Cow. 10–26/1/63.**N/C.**

BOILERS:
9706.
28823 *(new)* 16/1/52.
28608 *(ex1245)* 12/1/57.
28412 *(ex1191)* 3/3/62.

SHED:
Thornton Junction.

RENUMBERED:
61118 13/8/48.

CONDEMNED:
23/7/64.
Cut up Darlington 10/64.
Tender to snowplough.

1119

North British Loco. 25875.

To traffic 20/1/47.

REPAIRS:
Str. 14/10–4/12/48.**G.**
Str. 29/3–1/4/49.**C/L.**
Str. 29/6–26/7/49.**C/L.**
Str. 27/4–27/5/50.**G.**
Str. 4/4–30/5/52.**G.**
Str. 14–25/10/52.**C/L.**
Str. 26/7–11/9/54.**G.**
Str. 23/7–25/8/56.**G.**
Str. 2–7/12/57.**N/C.**
Str. 18–20/6/58.**N/C.**
Str. 22/1–13/3/59.**G.** *Mod. bogie springs. Part A.T.C. fitted.*
Str. 18/12/59–29/1/60.**L/I.**
Don. 16–21/9/60.**N/C.**
Don. 19/7–19/8/61.**G.**
Don. 23/5–20/6/62.**C/L.**

BOILERS:
9707.
5050 *(ex1047)* 4/12/48.
9751 *(ex1057)* 27/5/50.

28502 *(ex1121)* 30/5/52.
28101 *(ex1143)* 11/9/54.
28848 *(ex61312)* 25/8/56.
28161 *(ex61384)* 13/3/59.
28835 *(ex1055)* 19/8/61.

SHEDS:
Stratford.
Parkeston 24/5/59.
Stratford 14/6/59.
March 16/9/62.

RENUMBERED:
61119 4/12/48.

CONDEMNED:
25/11/63.
14/1/64 into Doncaster for cut up.

1120

North British Loco. 25876.

To traffic 22/1/47.

REPAIRS:
Don. 23/8–8/10/48.**G.**
Don. 21/7–22/8/50.**G.**
Don. 13–16/11/50.**N/C.**
M.V.Elec. removed.
Don. 28/4–23/5/52.**G.**
Gor. 5/6–31/7/54.**H/I.**
Don. 7/8–18/9/56.**G.**
Don. 11–13/12/56.**N/C.**
Don. 30/4–18/5/57.**C/L.**
Don. 6/1–11/2/59.**G.**
Don. 30/5–6/7/61.**G.**

BOILERS:
9708.
9722 *(ex1136)* 8/10/48.
9689 *(ex1136)* 22/8/50.
28109 *(ex1124)* 23/5/52.
28833 *(ex1091)* 18/9/56.
28860 *(ex1640)* 11/2/59.
28841 *(ex1095)* 6/7/61.

SHEDS:
Doncaster.
Retford 22/11/59.

RENUMBERED:
61120 8/10/48.

CONDEMNED:
31/1/65.
Sold for scrap 3/65 to Marples & Gillott, Sheffield.

1121

North British Loco. 25877.

To traffic 24/1/47.

REPAIRS:
Don. 25/9–4/11/48.**G.**
Str. 14/8–23/9/50.**G.** *All M.V. lighting removed.*

Str. 28/3–3/5/52.**G.**
Str. 1–3/7/53.**N/C.**
Str. 2/9–3/10/53.**G.**
Str. 8–17/9/54.**N/C.**
Str. 15/2–24/6/55.**C/H.**
Don. 5/12/55–7/1/56.**G.**
Don. 19/4–11/5/56.**C/L.**
Dar. 25/11–20/12/57.**G.**
Don. 18/8–3/9/58.**C/L.**
Don. 22/7–27/8/60.**G.**
Don. 6–18/2/61.**C/L.**
Don. 25/4–19/6/63.**G.**

BOILERS:
9709.
5089 *(ex1092)* 4/11/48.
28502 *(ex1109)* 23/9/50.
28585 *(ex61314)* 3/5/52.
28538 *(ex61333)* 3/10/53.
28264 *(ex1046)* 24/6/55.
28149 *(ex1079)* 20/12/57.
28120 *(ex1302)* 27/8/60.
28803 *(ex1211)* 19/6/63.

SHEDS:
Kings Cross.
March 12/6/49.
Lincoln 20/10/49.
Cambridge 20/11/49.
Doncaster 28/10/56.
Sheffield 25/1/59.
Doncaster 8/2/59.

RENUMBERED:
61121 4/11/48.

CONDEMNED:
17/4/66.
Sold for scrap 5/66 to Geo.Cohen, Kettering.

1122

North British Loco. 25878.

To traffic 28/1/47.

REPAIRS:
Gor. 8/3–14/4/48.**G.**
Gor. 9–19/3/49.**C/L.**
Gor. 20/7–24/8/50.**G.**
Gor. 26/8–1/9/50.**N/C.**
Dar. 29/8–20/9/52.**G.**
Don. 1/12/54–6/1/55.**G.**
Don. 17/1–15/2/57.**G.**
Don. 20/12/58–24/1/59.**G.**
Don. 29/4–2/6/61.**G.**

BOILERS:
9710.
9676 *(ex1074)* 14/4/48.
9683 *(ex1131)* 24/8/50.
28446 *(ex1303)* 20/9/52.
28348 *(ex1602)* 6/1/55.
28861 *(ex61409)* 15/2/57.
28872 *(ex1621)* 24/1/59.
28157 *(ex1162)* 2/6/61.

SHEDS:
Sheffield.
Leicester 4/6/47.
Colwick 8/1/50.
Ardsley 30/9/51.

New England 20/9/53.
Sheffield 26/6/55.
Doncaster 23/10/55.
New England 16/9/62.

RENUMBERED:
61122 14/4/48.

CONDEMNED:
25/11/63.
30/1/64 into Doncaster for cut up.

1123

North British Loco. 25879.

To traffic 30/1/47.

REPAIRS:
Gor. 20/9–13/11/48.**G.**
Gor. 15/10–9/12/50.**G.**
Gor. 13–18/12/50.**N/C.**
Dar. 6–28/6/52.**G.**
Dar. 4–13/12/52.**C/L.**
Gor. 10–17/4/54.**C/L.**
Dar. 27/11–23/12/54.**G.**
Dar. 13/1–1/2/55.**N/C.**
Dar. 10/2–1/3/55.**N/C.**
Dar. 3–11/7/57.**N/C.**
Dar. 14/2–15/3/58.**G.**
Dar. 17/3–21/4/61.**G.**
Complete A.W.S. fitted.
Dar. 14/10–21/11/64.**G.**
Dar. 23–26/11/64.**N/C.**

BOILERS:
9711.
9703 *(ex1115)* 13/11/48.
28277 *(ex1161)* 9/12/50.
28270 *(ex1161)* 28/6/52.
28134 *(ex1079)* 23/12/54.
28408 *(ex1017)* 15/3/58.
28424 *(ex1238)* 21/4/61.
28454 *(ex61388)* 21/11/64.

SHEDS:
Sheffield.
Leicester 4/6/47.
Colwick 1/1/50.
Ardsley 30/9/51.
Copley Hill 17/6/62.
Wakefield 5/1/64.
York 22/1/67.

RENUMBERED:
61123 13/11/48.

CONDEMNED:
11/5/67.
Sold for scrap 21/7/67 to A.Draper, Hull.

1124

North British Loco. 25880.

To traffic 4/2/47.

REPAIRS:
Don. 15–23/6/47.**C/L.** *After collision.*

Don. 6/9–26/10/48.**G.**
Don. 8–23/12/48.**L.**
Don. 13–20/4/50.**C/L.**
Don. 10–30/10/50.**G.**
Don. 7/4–1/5/52.**G.**
Don. 3–13/6/52.**N/C.**
Dar. 26/2–20/3/54.**H/I.**
Dar. 23–29/3/54.**N/C.**
Don. 25/4–5/5/55.**C/L.**
Don. 21/2–27/3/56.**G.**
Dar. 30/12/57–1/2/58.**G.**
Don. 29/2–31/3/60.**G.**

BOILERS:
9712.
 9697 (ex1109) 26/10/48.
28109 (ex1016) 30/10/50.
28191 (ex3924) 1/5/52.
28168 (ex1034) 1/2/58.
28255 (ex1637) 31/3/60.

SHED:
Doncaster.

RENUMBERED:
61124 26/10/48.

CONDEMNED:
16/9/62.
1/11/62 into Doncaster for
cut up.

1125

North British Loco. 25881.

To traffic 6/2/47.

REPAIRS:
Don. 3/10–9/11/48.**G.**
Don. 28–29/3/49.**Weigh.**
Don. 13/11–13/12/50.**G.**
Don. 5–29/8/52.**G.**
Dar. 13/4–13/5/54.**G.**
Don. 27/9–5/10/55.**C/L.**
Don. 8/5–9/6/56.**G.**
Don. 2–9/1/57.**N/C.**
Don. 6/8–5/9/58.**G.**
Don. 15/11–14/12/60.**G.**
Don. 22/7–8/8/63.**N/C.**

BOILERS:
9713.
 9712 (ex1124) 9/11/48.
28119 (ex1090) 13/12/50.
28801 (ex1630) 29/8/52.
28423 (ex1150) 13/5/54.
28522 (ex61394) 9/6/56.
28956 (new) 5/9/58.
28193 (ex spare & 1097)
14/12/60.

SHEDS:
Doncaster.
Retford 8/6/50.
Doncaster 16/7/50.

RENUMBERED:
61125 9/11/48.

CONDEMNED:
28/12/63.
8/1/64 into Doncaster for
cut up.

1126

North British Loco. 25882.

To traffic 7/2/47.

REPAIRS:
Don. 19/7–3/9/48.**G.**
Don. 6–13/10/48.**N/C.**
Don. 2–31/8/50.**G.**
Don. 24/3–20/4/53.**G.**
Don. 30/3–30/4/55.**G.**
Dar. 15/10–8/11/57.**G.**
Dar. 10–28/11/57.**N/C.**
Don. 11–17/6/58.**N/C.**
Don. 22–26/11/58.**C/L.**
Don. 6/8–13/9/60.**G.**

BOILERS:
9714.
 9681 (ex1085) 3/9/48.
 9947 (ex61310) 31/8/50.
28860 (new) 20/4/53.
28315 (ex1073) 30/4/55.
28110 (ex1035) 8/11/57.
28503 (ex61362) 13/9/60.

SHEDS:
Doncaster.
Retford 3/12/50.

RENUMBERED:
61126 3/9/48.

CONDEMNED:
22/9/63.
Sold for scrap 1/64 to
W. Rigley, Bulwell Forest.

1127

North British Loco. 25883.

To traffic 12/2/47.

REPAIRS:
Don. 9–27/5/47.**L.**
Don. 7/8–18/9/48.**G.**
Don. 18/7–16/8/50.**G.**
Don. 16/4–9/5/52.**G.**
Don. 7/1–4/2/54.**G.**
Don. 25/10–19/11/55.**G.**
Dar. 28/5–27/6/57.**G.**
Don. 8/6–11/7/59.**G.**
Don. 17/8–23/9/61.**G.**

BOILERS:
9715.
 9442 (new) 18/9/48.
 9437 (ex3962) 16/8/50.
28192 (ex1140) 9/5/52.
28231 (ex1258) 4/2/54.

28863 (ex1605) 19/11/55.
28394 (ex1176) 27/6/57.
28135 (ex1612 & spare)
11/7/59.
28981 (ex1185) 23/9/61.

SHEDS:
Doncaster.
Retford 16/9/62.
Doncaster 13/6/65.
Frodingham 11/7/65.

RENUMBERED:
61127 18/9/48.

CONDEMNED:
15/8/65.
Sold 11/65 for scrap to
Hughes, Bolckow, N. Blyth.

1128

North British Loco. 25884

To traffic 14/2/47.

REPAIRS:
Don. 7/6–6/8/48.**G.**
Don. 1–10/12/48.**L.**
Don. 14/6–19/7/50.**G.**
Don. 24/4–23/5/52.**G.**
Don. 23/1–18/2/54.**G.**
Don. 1/9/54.**Weigh.**
Don. 21/2/55.**Weigh.**
Don. 14/7–12/8/55.**G.**
Dar. 6/2–6/3/57.**G.**
Don. 27/9–28/10/58.**G.**
Don. 6–17/10/59.**N/C.**
Don. 28/9–22/10/60.**G.**

BOILERS:
9716.
 9441 (ex spare New 9/44)
6/8/48.
 9885 (ex1248) 19/7/50.
28193 (ex1164) 23/5/52.
28192 (ex1127) 18/2/54.
28528 (ex1114) 12/8/55.
28425 (ex61382) 6/3/57.
28252 (ex1634) 28/10/58.
28589 (ex1087) 22/10/60.

SHEDS:
Sheffield.
Leicester 4/5/47.
Doncaster 13/2/49.

RENUMBERED:
61128 6/8/48.

CONDEMNED:
29/12/62.
Sold 6/63 for scrap to
J. Cashmore, Great Bridge.

1129

North British Loco. 25885

To traffic 18/2/47.

REPAIRS:
Don. 10/2–11/3/49.**G.**
Don. 4–25/1/51.**G.**
Dar. 19/2–14/3/53.**G.**
Don. 15/6–3/7/54.**L.**
Dar. 21/11–16/12/55.**G.**
Ghd. 19/3–3/5/57.**C/L.**
Dar. 6/5–6/6/58.**H/I.**
Dar. 28–30/7/58.**N/C.**
Dar. 16–26/2/59.**N/C.**
A.T.C. Mech. fitted.
Dar. 16–19/6/59.**N/C.**
A.T.C. Elec. fitted.
Dar. 23/10–18/11/61.**G.**

BOILERS:
9717.
 9686 (ex1093) 11/3/49.
28125 (ex1094) 25/1/51.
28318 (ex1183) 14/3/53.
28333 (ex1111) 16/12/55.
28535 (ex1198) 18/11/61.

SHEDS:
Kings Cross.
Ardsley 11/11/51.
Copley Hill 29/6/52.
Wakefield 5/1/64.

RENUMBERED:
61129 11/3/49.

CONDEMNED:
13/9/65.
Sold 10/65 for scrap to
Garnham Harris &
Elton, Chesterfield.

1130

North British Loco. 25886

To traffic 24/2/47.

REPAIRS:
Gor. 18/9–16/10/48.**G.**
Str. 18/10–2/12/50.**G.**
Gor. 1–12/1/52.**C/L.**
Don. 19/8–8/10/52.**G.**
Don. 30/9–2/11/53.**G.**
Gor. 9–23/10/54.**C/L.**
Don. 1/4–7/5/55.**G.**
Don. 7–16/5/56.**C/L.**
Dar. 11/10–9/11/56.**G.**
Don. 26/3/57.**Weigh.**
Dar. 26/4–29/5/58.**G.**
Don. 2–14/2/59.**N/C.**
Don. 29/12/59–29/1/60.**G.**

BOILERS:
5094.
 9736 (ex1150) 16/10/48.
28511 (ex1233) 2/12/50.
continued on page 44

WORKS CODES:– Cow – Cowlairs. Dar – Darlington. Dee – Dundee. Don – Doncaster. Ghd – Gateshead. Gor – Gorton. Inv – Inverurie. Str – Stratford. SRX – St Rollox.
REPAIR CODES:– C/H – Casual Heavy. C/L – Casual Light. G – General. H – Heavy. H/I – Heavy Intermediate. L – Light. L/I – Light Intermediate. N/C – Non–Classified.

41

Between September 1951 and April 1952 Doncaster rebuilt four B1 tenders for coal weighing and this is No.4219, which was coupled with engine 61140 from April 1952 to withdrawal in December 1966 except for a month, when 61172 had it.

This view of 1123 at Leicester on 14th July 1947 clearly shows the arrangement and low rear division plate on the tender, which was applicable to all except 1038 and 1039 when they were built. Note the conduit for electric wiring, though no lamps have been fitted, nor does the engine have a generator.

Although allocated to Mexborough shed for many years, Nos.61165 to 61168 worked regularly to Hull on the passenger trains from and to Sheffield Victoria and 61165 has one of them at Hessle on 7th September 1954. At that period it was coupled with the tender taken from K3 class 61873, which could be recognised by its coping being shorter than on the normal B1 tender.

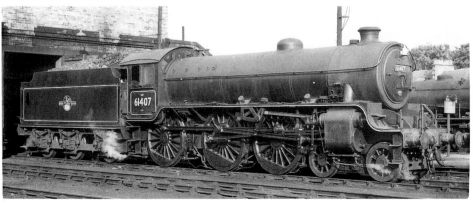

The tenders which Darlington built for engines 61400 to 61409 had a slight detail difference from all the other Group Standard type which ran with B1s. The plate across the front end, on which the intermediate buffers were mounted, had its ends cut away on a slant, as can be seen clearly on 61407 at Dunfermline Upper on 20th June 1959. The plate on all the others was square ended.

After coal weighing tender No.4095 was transferred to engine 61258, based at Lincoln in November 1955, they remained attached in normal service until withdrawn together for scrapping in January 1964. Here on 27th April 1960 the loco is at Grantham, attached to the Engineer's Inspection Saloon.

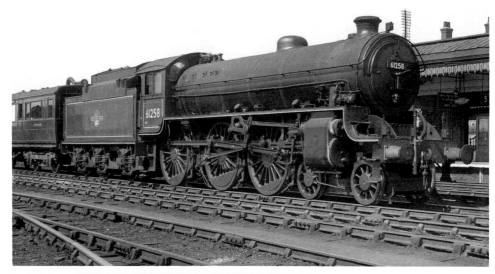

61300 at Cambridge shed on 23rd April 1962 shows the higher rear division plate, and its more forward position, an alteration which began to be made from December 1955. The engine has electric generator, and the rear of the tender is equipped for full electric lighting with four white marker lights and one red one.

In January 1964 No.61039's tender was transferred to 61013, with which it ran until May 1966. On 18th July 1965 in Ardsley shed the absence of angle iron below the tank side can be seen clearly. On 16th May 1966 this tender was put with No.61024, to be sold with that engine for scrapping. A useful life of nineteen years after rebuilding must have well justified the cost of it.

1130 continued

28834 (new) 8/10/52.
28136 (ex1095) 2/11/53.
28137 (ex1097) 7/5/55.
28181 (ex1038) 9/11/56.
28319 (ex1084) 29/5/58.
28422 (ex1247) 29/1/60.

SHEDS:
Gorton.
Leicester 1/6/47.
Gorton 6/2/49.
Stratford 21/8/49.
March 8/10/50.
Stratford 15/10/50.
Immingham 21/10/51.

RENUMBERED:
61130 16/10/48.

CONDEMNED:
16/9/62.
Sold 1/63 for scrap to
T.W.Ward, Broughton
Lane, Sheffield.

1131

North British Loco. 25887

To traffic 25/2/47.

REPAIRS:
Gor. 12/8–25/9/48.G.
Gor. 3/6–22/7/50.G.
Gor. 27–30/7/50.N/C.
Dar. 24/12/51–30/1/52.G.
Dar. 4–7/2/52.N/C.
Dar. 11–15/2/52.N/C.
Gor. 13/3–17/4/54.G.
Dar. 28/6–9/8/57.G.
Dar. 12–13/8/57.N/C.
Dar. 18/1–12/2/60.G.
A.W.S.Mech.fitted.
Dar. 25–29/10/60.N/C.
A.W.S.Elec.fitted.
Dar. 19/11–24/12/64.G.
Dar. 29–31/12/64.N/C.

BOILERS:
9718.
9683 (ex1088) 25/9/48.
5076 (ex1066) 22/7/50.
28405 (ex1082) 30/1/52.
28603 (ex1199) 17/4/54.
28457 (ex1186) 9/8/57.
28756 (ex1105) 12/2/60.
28412 (ex1118) 24/12/64.

SHEDS:
Gorton.
Woodford 4/6/47.
Colwick 19/6/49.
Stratford 14/9/52.
Ardsley 19/10/52.
Bradford 15/9/57.
Low Moor 12/1/58.
Wakefield 1/3/59.
Ardsley 25/11/62.
Wakefield 31/3/63.

RENUMBERED:
61131 25/9/48.

CONDEMNED:
6/12/66.
Sold 16/2/67 for scrap to
A.Draper, Hull.

1132

North British Loco. 25888

To traffic 26/2/47.

REPAIRS:
Inv. 26–28/3/47.L.
Tab.catcher fitted.
Cow. 30/6–11/8/48.H/I.
Cow. 15/9–8/10/49.L/I.
Cow. 10–26/8/50.H/I.
Cow. 20/11–27/12/52.G.
Cow. 12–28/8/54.N/C.
Cow. 2–12/2/55.C/L.
Cow. 17–3/9/4/55.L/I.
Cow. 19/9–29/10/55.C/L.
Cow. 31/10–24/11/56.G.
Cow. 14–24/5/57.N/C.
Cow. 19–28/2/58.N/C.
Cow. 6–31/1/59.H/I.
Cow. 15–22/8/59.N/C.
Cow. 27/1–31/3/60.C/L.
Cow. 24/3–21/4/61.N/C.
Cow. 29/5–8/7/61.G.
Inv. 25/11/63–3/1/64.L/I.

BOILERS:
9719.
28609 (ex1102) 27/12/52.
28614 (ex1072) 24/11/56.
28668 (ex1243) 8/7/61.

SHEDS:
Kittybrewester.
Aberdeen 16/5/49.
Dundee 14/1/51.
Thornton Jct. 11/1/60.

RENUMBERED:
61132 28/8/48.

CONDEMNED:
2/9/66.
Sold 10/66 for scrap to
Shipbreaking Industries,
Faslane.

1133

North British Loco. 25889

To traffic 28/2/47.

REPAIRS:
Inv. 5/4/47.L. Tab.catcher
fitted.
Cow. 8/9–9/10/48.G.
Cow. 9/12/48–21/1/49.C/H.
Inv. 3/2–1/3/49.N/C.
Cow. 13/9–18/10/50.L/I.
Cow. 31/3–11/4/51.C/L.
Cow. 20/4–5/5/51.C/L.
Cow. 29/6–4/8/51.C/L.
Inv. 24/10/51.N/C.
Inv. 12–14/11/51.N/C.
Inv. 26/11–5/12/51.N/C.

Cow. 25/1–1/3/52.C/H.
Perth. 14–26/8/52.C/L.
Cow. 8–31/1/53.L/I.
Cow. 11/1–13/2/54.H/I.
Cow. 26/2/54.N/C.
Cow. 3/4/54.N/C.
Cow. 2–18/12/54.N/C.
Cow. 29/12/54.N/C.
Cow. 19/4–21/5/55.C/L.
Cow. 9/4–19/5/56.G.
Cow. 16–31/10/57.N/C.
Cow. 31/3–26/4/58.H/I.
Cow. 30/8–13/9/58.C/L.
Cow. 25/11–13/12/58.C/L.
Cow. 24/2–13/3/59.N/C.
Cow. 30/11–3/12/59.N/C.
Cow. 16/5–2/7/60.G.
Cow. 3/9–19/10/62.H/I.
Inv. 14/12/64–25/1/65.L/I.
Inv. 23/8–20/9/65.C/L.

BOILERS:
5095.
Renumbered 28611 (–)
11/4/51.
28613 (ex1117) 1/3/52.
28622 (ex1172) 19/5/56.
28606 (ex61395) 2/7/60.

SHEDS:
Kittybrewster.
Aberdeen 16/5/49.
Kittybrewster 19/8/51.
Eastfield 1/2/53.
Southern Region 20/5/53.
Eastfield 21/6/53.
Thorton Jct 27/1/56.

RENUMBERED:
61133 3/4/48.

CONDEMNED:
2/9/66.
Sold 10/66 for scrap to
Shipbreaking Industries,
Faslane.

1134

North British Loco. 25890

To traffic 4/3/47.

REPAIRS:
Inv. 5/4/47.L. Tab.catcher
fitted.
Cow. 24/2–6/4/48.G.
Cow. 20/3–6/4/50.L/I.
Cow. 20/9–16/10/51.G.
Cow. 3–28/11/53.H/I.
Cow. 16/8–18/9/54.N/C.
Cow. 11/2–19/3/55.G.
Cow. 23–26/3/55.N/C.
Cow. 28/11–22/12/56.H/I.
Cow. 9/7–16/8/58.H/I.
Cow. 5–20/10/59.N/C.
A.W.S.fitted.
Cow. 18/11–18/12/59.N/C.
Mod.bogie springs.
Cow. 7/4–21/5/60.G.
Cow. 10/12/62–12/1/63.L/I.
Cow. 14–26/11/63.N/C.
Cow. 4/65.C/L.

BOILERS:
9720.
28626 (ex1221) 16/10/51.
28873 (new) 19/3/55.
28661 (ex1067) 21/5/60.

SHEDS:
Kittybrewster.
Aberdeen 16/5/49.
Kittybrewster 9/10/49.
Eastfield 22/2/53.
Thornton Jct 21/1/56.
Eastfield 18/4/60.
Corkerhill 31/12/62.
Ayr 11/3/63.
Dalry Road 31/7/64.

RENUMBERED:
61134 6/4/48.

CONDEMNED:
5/10/65.
Sold 11/65 for scrap to
Shipbreaking Industries,
Faslane.

1135

North British Loco. 25891

To traffic 10/3/47.

REPAIRS:
Str. 11/11–31/12/48.G.
Front heat.fitted.
Str. 24–28/1/50.N/C.
Str. 22/1–9/3/51.G.
Str. 27/4–12/6/53.G.
Modified bogie springs.
Str. 23/8–1/10/55.G.
Str. 10/9–19/10/56.C/L.
After collision.
Str. 28/5–25/7/58.G.
Don. 10/1–11/2/61.G.
Don. 23–26/4/63.N/C.

BOILERS:
9721.
9707 (ex1119) 31/12/48.
28536 (ex1253) 9/3/51.
28517 (ex1603) 12/6/53.
28539 (ex61329) 1/10/55.
28867 (ex1280) 25/7/58.
28504 (ex1664) 11/2/61.

SHEDS:
Stratford.
Parkeston 31/5/47.
Stratford 2/3/58.
Parkeston 8/2/59.
Doncaster 25/10/59.

RENUMBERED:
61135 31/12/48.

CONDEMNED:
22/9/63.
30/10/93 In for cut up
Doncaster.

1136

North British Loco. 25892

To traffic 18/3/47.

REPAIRS:
Don. 13/8–17/9/48.**G.**
Don. 4–26/7/50.**G.**
Don. 25/3–24/4/52.**G.**
Don. 4–28/11/53.**G.**
Don. 7–10/12/53.**N/C.**
Str. 17/3–1/4/54.**N/C.**
Don. 7/4–14/5/55.**G.**
Don. 16/10–23/11/56.**G.**
Str. 17/11/58–16/1/59.**G.**
Dar. 28/12/60–10/2/61.**G.**
Dar. 15/11–1/12/61.**C/L.**
Dar. 27/7–21/8/62.**C/L.**

BOILERS:
9722.
9689 (ex1098) 17/9/48.
3701 (ex1164) 26/7/50.
28188 (ex61331) 24/4/52.
28150 (ex3950) 28/11/53.
28804 (ex1619) 23/11/56.
28634 (ex61323) 16/1/59.
28178 (ex spare & 1204)
10/2/61.

SHEDS:
Gorton.
Kings Cross 16/6/47.
Neasden 18/5/52.
Leicester 28/9/59.
Neasden 16/11/59.
Woodford 15/3/62.

RENUMBERED:
61136 17/9/48.

CONDEMNED:
22/10/62.
22/11/62 In for cut up at
Darlington.

1137

North British Loco. 25898

To traffic 19/3/47.

REPAIRS:
Don. 19/10–3/12/48.**G.**
Don. 16/11–14/12/49.**C/L.**
Don. 23/8–21/9/50.**G.**
Don. 2/4–1/5/52.**G.**
Don. 22/2–22/3/54.**G.**
Don. 21/12/55–26/1/56.**G.**
Dar. 10/2–7/3/58.**G.**
Don. 16/8–19/9/58.**C/L.**
Don. 18/12/59–23/1/60.**G.**

BOILERS:
9723.
9709 (ex1121) 3/12/48.
28102 (ex1140) 21/9/50.
28190 (ex1070) 1/5/52.
28511 (ex61374) 22/3/54.
28162 (ex1251) 26/1/56.
28399 (ex1153) 7/3/58.
28176 (ex1225) 23/1/60.

SHEDS:
Gorton.
Kings Cross 16/6/47.
Doncaster 21/12/52.
Leicester 14/12/58.
Gorton 18/3/62.

RENUMBERED:
61137 3/12/48.

CONDEMNED:
28/5/62.
17/8/62 In for cut up at
Darlington.

1138

North British Loco. 25894

To traffic 31/3/47.

REPAIRS:
Don. 28/11–31/12/48.**G.**
Don. 15/8–15/9/50.**G.**
Don. 23/4–21/5/52.**G.**
Str. 17/3–24/4/54.**G.**
Dar. 16/2–14/3/56.**G.**
Dar. 7/6–13/7/57.**C/L.**
Dar. 7/7–22/8/58.**G.**
Dar. 26–28/8/58.**N/C.**
Don. 30/12/59–29/1/60.**C/L.**
Don. 10–13/6/60.**N/C.**
Don. 8/2–10/3/61.**G.**

BOILERS:
9724.
9723 (ex1137) 31/12/48.
28101 (ex1120) 15/9/50.
28102 (ex1137) 21/5/52.
28261 (ex1195) 24/4/54.
28216 (ex1034) 14/3/56.
28426 (ex1032) 22/8/58.
28557 (ex1096) 10/3/61.

SHEDS:
Gorton.
Sheffield 6/4/47.
Kings Cross 16/6/47.
New England 28/12/52.
Sheffield 26/6/55.
Millhouses 6/12/59.
Canklow 31/1/60.
Sheffield 23/4/61.
Mexborough 9/9/62.
New England 26/1/64.

RENUMBERED:
61138 31/12/48.

WITHDRAWN:
3/1/65.
Made S.B.Dept'l No.26.
4/1/65.
CONDEMNED:
8/67
Sold 11/67 for scrap to
T.W.Ward, Killamarsh.

1139

North British Loco. 25895

To traffic 1/4/47.

REPAIRS:
Don. 1/1–2/2/49.**G.**
Don. 21/7–2/9/49.**C/L.**
Don. 25/10–23/11/50.**G.**
Don. 14/7–18/8/52.**G.**
Str. 2/3–9/4/54.**G.**
Don. 15/11–16/12/55.**G.**
Don. 6/2–1/3/58.**G.**
Don. 22/4–20/5/60.**G.**

BOILERS:
9725.
9685 (ex1091) 2/2/49.
28112 (ex61309) 23/11/50.
28589 (ex1045) 9/4/54.
28755 (ex61392) 16/12/55.
28540 (ex61393) 1/3/58.
28116 (ex1090) 20/5/60.

SHEDS:
Sheffield.
Kings Cross 16/6/47.
New England 14/12/52.
Kings Cross 8/3/53.
Hitchin 1/2/59.
Sheffield 14/6/59.·

RENUMBERED:
61139 2/2/49.

CONDEMNED:
16/9/62.
Sold 3/63 for scrap to
J.Cashmore, Great Bridge.

1140

Vulcan 5498

To traffic 11/4/47.

REPAIRS:
Don. 23/4–24/4/47**N/C.**
Don. 20/12/48–19/1/49.**G.**
Don. 26–27/4/49.**N/C.**
Don. 17/7–11/8/50.**G.**
Don. 13/3–9/4/52.**G.** Coal
Weighing tender fitted.
Cow. 11–12/9/52.**N/C.**
Cow. 27–28/5/53.**N/C.**
Cow. 14/9–17/10/53.**L/I.**
Cow. 20–28/8/54.**N/C.**
Cow. 21–22/9/54.**N/C.**
Cow. 12/4–7/5/55.**H/I.**
Cow. 2–3/3/56.**N/C.**
Cow. 24/12/56–26/1/57.**G.**
Cow. 23/6–12/7/58.**L/I.**
Cow. 17–28/11/58.**C/L.**
Cow. 2–11/3/59.**N/C.**
Cow. 27/5–4/6/59.**N/C.**
Cow. 22/6–15/7/60.**L/I.**
Cow. 3–4/8/60.**N/C.**
Cow. 10–14/10/60.**N/C.**
Cow. 22/11–17/12/60.**C/L.**
Cow. 31/7–17/8/61.**N/C.**
Cow. 15/8–15/9/62.**G.**
Inv. 9–11/9/65.**N/C.**
Cow. 15–18/11/65.**N/C.**
Cow. 28/6–20/8/66.**C/L.**

BOILERS:
9726.
3737 (ex1026) 19/1/49.
9441 (ex1128) 11/8/50.
28185 (ex1077) 9/4/52.
28629 (ex1262) 26/1/57.
28654 (ex61356) 15/9/62.

SHEDS:
Gorton.
Sheffield 23/4/47.
Neasden 16/6/47.
Eastfield 18/5/52.
Motherwell 10/11/66.

RENUMBERED:
61140 19/1/49.

CONDEMNED:
31/12/66.
Sold 2/67 for scrap to
J.McWilliam, Shettleston.

1141

Vulcan 5499

To traffic 11/4/47.

REPAIRS:
Gor. 20/9–6/11/48.**G.**
Str. 19/3–5/5/51.**G.**
M.V.elect. lighting
removed.
Dar. 8/4–9/5/52.**C/L.**
Dar. 11/3–4/4/53.**G.**
Dar. 7–9/4/53.**N/C.**
Dar. 7/1–5/2/55.**G.**
Dar. 20/11–19/12/56.**G.**
Dar. 7–9/1/57.**N/C.**
Don. 12/11–13/12/58.**G.**
Don. 18–27/2/60.**C/L.**
Don. 16/12/60–18/1/61.**G.**
Don. 10–15/7/61.**N/C.**

BOILERS:
9727.
5094 (ex1130) 6/11/48.
28550 (ex1055) 5/5/51.
28808 (ex1152) 4/4/53.
28641 (ex1215) 5/2/55.
28108 (ex1060) 19/12/56.
28753 (ex1605) 13/12/58.
28354 (ex3925) 18/1/61.

SHEDS:
Gorton.
Sheffield 23/4/47.
Woodford 16/6/47.
Leicester 14/11/48.
Colwick 5/2/50.
Leicester 12/3/50.
Colwick 11/11/56.

RENUMBERED:
61141 6/11/48.

CONDEMNED:
25/7/65.
Sold 9/65 for scrap to
Geo.Cohen, Ickles,

1142

Vulcan 5500

To traffic 15/4/47.

REPAIRS:
Dar. 9/1–15/3/49.**G.**
Gor. 2/12/50–27/1/51.**G.**
Gor. 1–5/2/51.**N/C.**
Gor. 6/9–20/10/51.**C/L.**
Gor. 23–28/10/51.**N/C.**
Gor. 23/11–8/12/51.**C/L.**
Gor. 16–20/12/51.**N/C.**
Don. 3/6–4/7/52.**G.**
Don. 16/9–29/10/53.**G.**
Don. 3–4/2/54.**Weigh.**
Dar. 19/3–23/4/55.**G.**
Don. 4–31/8/55.**N/C.**
Don. 1/11/56–9/1/57.**G.**
Don. 11–12/1/57.**N/C.**
Don. 14/10–22/11/58.**G.**
Don. 6–20/2/59.**N/C.**
Don. 11/11–13/12/60.**G.**

BOILERS:
9728.
9767 *(ex1181)* 15/3/49.
28285 *(ex1123)* 27/1/51.
28100 *(ex1087)* 4/7/52.
28263 *(ex61325)* 29/10/53.
28127 *(ex1166)* 23/4/55.
28567 *(ex1227)* 9/1/57.
28522 *(ex1125)* 22/11/58.
28950 *(ex61331)* 13/12/60.

SHEDS:
Gorton.
Sheffield 27/4/47.
Immingham 16/6/47.
Colwick 6/12/59.

RENUMBERED:
61142 15/3/49.

CONDEMNED:
22/9/63.
*Sold 12/63 for scrap to
J.Cashmore, Great Bridge.*

1143

Vulcan 5501

To traffic 15/4/47.

REPAIRS:
Don. 18/9/47.**N/C.**
Elec.lighting.
Don. 27/11/48–6/1/49.**G.**
Don. 23–24/3/49.**N/C.**
Elec.generator.
Don. 24–25/10/49.**C/L.**
Elec.generator.
Don. 17/10–16/11/50.**G.**
B.T.H speed indic.fitted.
Don. 28/5–1/7/52.**G.**
Don. 29/12/52–2/1/53.**N/C.**
Str. 12/6–24/7/54.**G.**
Don. 27/7–30/8/56.**G.**
Don. 8–26/11/56.**C/L.**
Don. 25/10–6/11/57.**C/L.**
Don. 16/3–18/4/59.**G.**
Don. 4–17/11/59.**C/L.**

Don. 31/7–25/8/61.**G.**
Don. 19/10–8/11/61.**N/C.**

BOILERS:
9729.
9724 *(ex1138)* 6/1/49.
28111 *(ex1107)* 16/11/50.
28101 *(ex1138)* 1/7/52.
28157 *(ex1212)* 24/7/54.
28296 *(ex1077)* 30/8/56.
28861 *(ex1122)* 18/4/59.
28161 *(ex1119)* 25/8/61.

SHEDS:
Gorton.
Sheffield 23/4/47.
New England 16/6/47.
Grantham 6/3/51.
New England 9/9/51.
Lincoln 26/6/55.
Immingham 17/11/57.

RENUMBERED:
61143 6/1/49.

CONDEMNED:
24/2/64.
*13/3/64 In for cut up at
Doncaster.*

1144

Vulcan 5502

To traffic 17/4/47.

REPAIRS:
Don. 6/1–11/2/49.**G.**
Str. 14/10–2/12/50.**G.**
Don. 23/7–20/8/52.**G.**
Don. 17/8–29/9/53.**G.**
Gor. 11–18/9/54.**C/L.**
Don. 12/4–17/5/55.**G.**
Dar. 10/1–7/2/57.**G.**
Don. 24/2–26/3/59.**G.**
Don. 15/3–19/4/61.**G.**

BOILERS:
9730.
9726 *(ex1140)* 11/2/49.
28512 *(ex1098)* 2/12/50.
28199 *(ex61330)* 20/8/52.
28149 *(ex1246)* 29/9/53.
28269 *(ex1106)* 17/5/55.
28182 *(ex1019)* 7/2/57.
28337 *(ex1646)* 26/3/59.

SHEDS:
Gorton.
Sheffield 8/5/47.
New England 16/6/47.
Grantham 4/1/48.
Stratford 18/11/49.
Immingham 21/10/51.

RENUMBERED:
61144 11/2/49.

CONDEMNED:
19/4/64.
*Sold 6/64 for scrap to
Central Wagon Co., Ince.*

1145

Vulcan 5503

To traffic 17/4/47.

REPAIRS:
Gor. 31/10–15/12/48.**G.**
Gor. 10–20/1/50.**C/L.**
Gor. 23–28/1/50.**N/C.**
Gor. 21/9–23/11/50.**G.**
Gor. 25/11–1/12/50.**N/C.**
Dar. 29/12/52–24/1/53.**G.**
Don. 18/1–11/2/55.**G.**
Don. 23/2–3/3/55.**N/C.**
Don. 29/6–18/7/56.**C/L.**
Dar. 15/2–14/3/57.**G.**
Don. 30/11–19/12/57.**C/L.**
Don. 21/4–21/5/59.**G.**
Don. 12/9–13/10/61.**G.**

BOILERS:
9731.
3732 *(ex1017)* 15/12/48.
28276 *(ex1185)* 23/11/50.
28302 *(ex1156)* 24/1/53.
28874 *(new)* 11/2/55.
28405 *(ex1066)* 14/3/57.
28150 *(ex1075)* 21/5/59.
28156 *(ex1075)* 13/10/61.

SHEDS:
Gorton.
Sheffield 15/5/47.
Ardsley 30/9/51.
Bradford 18/11/51.
Doncaster 6/12/53.
Immingham 30/12/62.
Canklow 10/1/65.
Colwick 28/3/65.

RENUMBERED:
61145 15/12/48.

CONDEMNED:
2/1/66.
*Sold 3/66 for scrap to
Geo.Cohen, Kettering.*

1146

Vulcan 5504

To traffic 22/4/47.

REPAIRS:
Inv. 11–14/6/47.**L.**
Tab.catcher fitted.
Cow. 7/10–12/11/48.**G.**
Cow. 5–24/6/50.**L/I.**
Cow. 18/2–28/3/52.**H/I.**
Cow. 3/2–13/3/54.**G.**
Thj. 24–29/12/54.**C/L.**
Thj. 28/4–11/5/55.**C/L.**
Cow. 5/1–4/2/56.**H/I.**
W.P.U.Gear removed.
Thj 24/5–11/6/57.**C/L.**
Cow. 28/10–30/11/57.**H/I.**
Cow.
22/12/58–19/1/59.**C/L.**
Cow. 26/1–21/2/59.**G.**
Mod.bogie springs.
Cow. 3–16/6/59.**N/C.**
A.T.C.fitted.

Cow. 25/10–30/11/61.**L/I.**
Cow. 11–30/11/63.**N/C.**

BOILERS:
9732.
9854 *(ex1217)* 12/11/48.
Renumbered 28624 *(–)*
28/3/52.
28651 *(ex61346)* 13/3/54.
28657 *(ex61341)*
21/2/59.141 tubes.

SHEDS:
Kittybrewster.
Thornton Jct 3/7/49.
Dalry Road 5/9/60.
Thornton Jct 2/11/60.

RENUMBERED:
61146 28/8/48.

CONDEMNED:
12/3/64.
*Sold 6/64 for scrap to
T.W.Ward, Inverkeithing.*

1147

Vulcan 5505

To traffic 22/4/47.

REPAIRS:
Inv. 12–13/6/47.**L.**
Tab.catcher fitted.
Cow. 2–27/11/48.**G.**
Cow. 8–26/8/50.**L/I.**
Cow. 1–26/9/52.**G.**
Thj. 26/10–7/11/53.**C/L.**
Cow. 19/5–19/6/54.**H/I.**
Cow. 19/8–8/10/55.**N/C.**
Thj. 14/10–18/11/55.**C/L.**
Cow. 12/12/55–14/1/56.**H/I.**
Cow. 27/7–31/8/57.**G.**
Cow. 21/10–2/11/57.**C/L.**
Cow. 24/4–15/5/59.**H/I.**
Cow. 29/10–19/11/59.**N/C.**
Cow. 9/11–10/12/60.**C/H.**
Cow. 6–29/4/61.**N/C.**
Cow. 28/8–7/10/61.**L/I.**
Cow. 27/3–6/4/63.**N/C.**
Inv. 23/1–21/2/64.**L/I.**

BOILERS:
9733.
9732 *(ex1146)* 27/11/48.
28620 *(ex1172)* 26/9/52.
28637 *(ex61345)* 31/8/57.
28604 *(ex1172)* 10/12/60.

SHEDS:
Kittybrewster.
Dundee 3/7/49.
Thornton Jct 14/10/51.
Dundee 4/4/65.

RENUMBERED:
61147 27/11/48.

CONDEMNED:
16/12/65.
*Sold 1/66 for scrap to
Shipbreaking Industries,
Faslane.*

1148

Vulcan 5506

To traffic 25/4/47.

REPAIRS:
Inv. 15–18/6/47.**L.**
Tab.catcher fitted.
Cow. 28/1–11/3/49.**G.**
Cow. 17/4–10/5/51.**G.**
Cow. 5/3–4/4/53.**H/I.**
Cow. 4–30/10/54.**H/I.**
Thj. 23–28/5/55.**C/L.**
Cow. 19/12/55–7/1/56.**N/C.**
Cow. 2/5–9/6/56.**G.**
Cow. 15–20/6/56.**N/C.**
Cow. 3–22/6/57.**C/L.**
Cow. 17/12/57–25/1/58.**L/I.**
Cow. 14–21/5/58.**N/C.**
Cow. 4–16/10/58.**N/C.**
Cow. 19/5–6/6/59.**L/I.**
Cow. 16/6/59.**N/C.**
Cow. 26–30/6/59.**N/C.**
Cow. 4–6/8/59.**N/C.**
Cow. 7–21/4/61.**N/C.**
Cow. 8/9–3/11/61.**G.**
Cow. 26/10–15/11/61.**C/L.**
Cow. 25/2–8/3/63.**N/C.**
Cow. 10/4–20/6/64.**H/I.**
Inv. 21–29/12/64.**N/C.**
Inv. 9/4–1/5/65.**C/L.**
Cow. 4–12/3/66.**N/C.**

BOILERS:
9734.
28634 *(ex1262)* 10/5/51.
28628 *(ex1221)* 9/6/56.
28656 *(ex61396)* 3/11/61.

SHEDS:
Kittybrewster.
Eastfield 11/9/49.
Thornton Jct 29/1/50.
Southern Region 20/5/53.
Thornton Jct 21/6/53.

RENUMBERED:
61148 11/3/49.

CONDEMNED:
2/9/66.
Sold 11/66 for scrap to
Shipbreaking Industries,
Faslane.

1149

Vulcan 5507

To traffic 25/4/47.

REPAIRS:
Str. 27/10/47.**N/C.** *Stub axle*
re-welded.
Str. 23/9–26/11/48.**G.**
Str. 19/12/48–3/1/49.**L.**
Str. 25/9–29/10/49.**C/L.**
Str. 14/1–24/2/51.**G.**
Str. 23/6–18/8/53.**G.**

Don. 17/1–17/2/56.**G.**
Str. 24/6–22/8/58.**G.**
Mod.bogie springs.
Str. 13–30/4/59.**N/C.**
Complete A.T.C.fitted.
Str. 31/7–11/8/59.**C/L.**
Don. 29/9–28/10/60.**G.**

BOILERS:
9735.
9431 *(ex1671)* 26/11/48.
28528 *(ex1614)* 24/2/51.
28324 *(ex1191)* 18/8/53.
28548 *(ex1226)* 17/2/56.
28184 *(ex1607)* 22/8/58.
28374 *(ex1160)* 28/10/60.

SHEDS:
Stratford.
Parkeston 31/5/47.
Stratford 1/1/61.
March 16/9/62.

RENUMBERED:
61149 26/11/48.

CONDEMNED:
23/9/62.
Sold 6/63 for scrap to
Central Wagon Co., Ince.

1150

Vulcan 5508

To traffic 29/4/47.

REPAIRS:
Gor. 1/8–18/9/48.**G.**
Gor. 4–12/2/49.**C/L.** *Stub*
axle to repair.
Gor. 2/8–30/9/50.**G.**
Gor. 6–7/10/50.**N/C.**
Dar. 26/2–20/3/52.**G.**
Dar. 29/5–8/7/53.**C/L.**
Gor. 5/12/53–16/1/54.**G.**
Gor. 19/1–6/2/54.**N/C.**
Gor. 17/2–5/3/54.**N/C.**
Dar. 15/10–17/11/55.**G.**
Dar. 21/9–24/10/57.**G.**
Ghd. 27/10–5/11/57.**N/C.**
Don. 8/12/59–2/1/60.**G.**
Don. 4/2–2/3/61.**N/C.**

BOILERS:
9736.
9841 *(ex1204)* 18/9/48.
28260 *(ex1157)* 30/9/50.
28423 *(ex1159)* 20/3/52.
28168 *(ex1051)* 16/1/54.
28151 *(ex1284)* 17/11/55.
28820 *(ex1154)* 24/10/57.
28580 *(ex61390)* 2/1/60.

SHEDS:
Gorton.
Sheffield 1/6/47.

RENUMBERED:
61150 18/9/48.

CONDEMNED:
16/9/62.
Sold 3/63 for scrap to
J.Cashmore, Great Bridge.

1151

Vulcan 5509

To traffic 29/4/47.

REPAIRS:
Gor. 15/8–9/10/48.**G.**
Gor. 6–9/4/49.**L.** *Stub axle*
to weld.
Gor. 12/6–4/8/50.**G.**
Gor. 6–11/8/50.**N/C.**
Gor. 4–16/9/50.**N/C.**
Dar. 15/5–7/6/52.**G.**
Gor. 1/1–20/2/54.**G.**
Gor. 23–26/2/54.**N/C.**
Gor. 27/2–2/3/54.**N/C.**
Gor. 5–19/3/54.**N/C.**
Dar. 4/7–12/8/55.**N/C.**
Dar. 20/2–22/3/56.**G.**
Dar. 1/12/57–3/1/58.**G.**
Dar. 7–17/10/58.**C/L.**
Don. 14/1–11/2/60.**G.**
Don. 16–18/2/60.**N/C.**
Don. 17–21/12/60.**N/C.**

BOILERS:
9737.
3727 *(ex1015)* 9/10/48.
28261 *(new)* 4/8/50.
28434 *(ex1019)* 7/6/52.
28424 *(ex1187)* 20/2/54.
28253 *(ex1228)* 22/3/56.
28559 *(ex1241)* 3/1/58.
28267 *(ex1154)* 11/2/60.

SHEDS:
Gorton.
Sheffield 1/6/47.

RENUMBERED:
61151 9/10/48.

CONDEMNED:
16/9/62.
Sold 3/63 for scrap to
J.Cashmore, Great Bridge.

1152

Vulcan 5510.

To traffic 2/5/47.

REPAIRS:
Gor. 28/11/48–15/1/49.**G.**
Gor. 18/1–10/3/51.**G.**
Gor. 15–16/3/51.**N/C.**
Dar. 12/2–13/3/53.**G.**
Dar. 8/1–4/2/55.**G.**
Dar. 28/9–26/10/56.**G.**
Dar. 25/6–13/8/58.**G.**
Dar. 12–25/2/59.**C/L.**
Dar. 23/6–7/7/59.**C/L.**

Don. 1/1–3/2/60.**C/L.**
Don. 22/10–19/11/60.**G.**

BOILERS:
9738.
9698 *(ex1110)* 15/1/49.
28808 *(new)* 10/3/51.
28113 *(ex1015)* 13/3/53.
28175 *(ex61374)* 4/2/55.
28103 *(ex1276)* 26/10/56.
28364 *(ex1289)* 13/8/58.
28563 *(ex61406)* 19/11/60.

SHEDS:
Gorton.
Sheffield 4/6/47.
Doncaster 29/9/57.
Sheffield 17/11/57.
Millhouses 8/11/59.
Sheffield 23/4/61.
Immingham 3/3/63.

RENUMBERED:
61152 15/1/49.

CONDEMNED:
19/4/64.
Sold 6/64 for scrap to
Central Wagon Co., Ince.

1153

Vulcan 5511

To traffic 2/5/47.

REPAIRS:
Gor. 31/10–10/12/48.**G.**
Gor. 4/9–21/10/50.**G.**
Gor. 24–29/10/50.**N/C.**
Gor. 8/5–9/6/51.**C/L.**
Dar. 21/8–13/9/52.**G.**
Gor. 6/2/54.**C/L.**
Gor. 8/5–12/6/54.**G.**
Dar. 26/1–27/2/56.**G.**
Dar. 13/11–12/12/57.**G.**
Don. 10/12/59–5/1/60.**G.**
Don. 18/5–17/7/62.**G.**

BOILERS:
9739.
3730 *(ex1016)* 10/12/48.
28269 *(ex1122)* 21/10/50.
28800 *(ex1195)* 13/9/52.
28440 *(ex1154)* 12/6/54.
28399 *(ex61388)* 27/2/56.
28151 *(ex1150)* 12/12/57.
28500 *(ex3945)* 5/1/60.
28848 *(ex1109)* 17/7/62.

SHEDS:
Gorton.
Sheffield 4/6/47.
Langwith 23/10/60.
Sheffield 10/9/61.
Canklow 16/6/63.

RENUMBERED:
61153 10/12/48.

WORKS CODES:– Cow – Cowlairs. Dar – Darlington. Dee – Dundee. Don – Doncaster. Ghd – Gateshead. Gor – Gorton. Inv – Inverurie. Str – Stratford. SRX – St Rollox.

REPAIR CODES:– **C/H** – Casual Heavy. **C/L** – Casual Light. **G** – General. **H** – Heavy. **H/I** – Heavy Intermediate. **L** – Light. **L/I** – Light Intermediate. **N/C** – Non–Classified.

CONDEMNED:
17/1/65.
*Sold 3/65 for scrap to
Marples & Gillott,
Sheffield.*

1154

Vulcan 5512

To traffic 6/5/47.

REPAIRS:
Gor. 11/10–27/11/48.**G.**
Gor. 28/8–12/10/50.**G.**
Gor. 14–23/10/50.**N/C.**
Dar. 29/5–26/6/52.**G.**
Gor. 20/3–24/4/54.**G.**
Dar. 2/12/55–3/1/56.**G.**
Dar. 23/8–18/9/57.**G.**
Dar. 25–30/9/57.**N/C.**
Don. 2–26/12/59.**G.**
Don. 9/9–1/10/60.**C/L.**
Don. 27/12/61–4/1/62.**C/L.**
Don. 5–16/3/62.**N/C.**

BOILERS:
9740.
9727 *(ex1141)* 27/11/48.
28266 *(ex1088)* 12/10/50.
28440 *(ex1032)* 26/6/52.
28434 *(ex1151)* 24/4/54.
28820 *(ex1189)* 3/1/56.
28267 *(ex1080)* 18/9/57.
28521 *(ex61365)* 26/12/59.

SHEDS:
Gorton.
Sheffield 4/6/47.

RENUMBERED:
61154 27/11/48.

CONDEMNED:
16/9/62.
*Sold 3/63 for scrap to
J.Cashmore, Great Bridge.*

1155

Vulcan 5513

To traffic 6/5/47.

REPAIRS:
Gor. 7/11–18/12/48.**G.**
Gor. 3–13/1/49.**N/C.**
Gor. 12–27/2/49.**N/C.**
Gor. 15/1–3/3/51.**G.**
Gor. 8–9/3/51.**N/C.**
Gor. 3–29/3/52.**C/L.**
Gor. 9–10/1/53.**N/C.**
Gor. 15/3–18/4/53.**G.**
Gor. 21/4–1/5/53.**N/C.**
Gor. 9–12/5/53.**C/L.**
Gor. 11–12/7/53.**N/C.**
Gor. 1/9–1/10/53.**C/L.**
Dar. 28/4–3/6/55.**G.**
Dar. 23/10–16/11/57.**G.**
Dar. 27–30/11/57.**N/C.**
Dar. 5–13/12/57.**N/C.**
Don. 9/12/59–6/1/60.**G.**
Don. 13–17/8/60.**C/L.**

BOILERS:
9741.
9740 *(ex1154)* 18/12/48.
28294 *(ex1237)* 3/3/51.
28307 *(ex3868)* 18/4/53.
28263 *(ex1142)* 3/6/55.
28259 *(ex1218)* 16/11/57.
28122 *(ex1627)* 6/1/60.

SHEDS:
Gorton.
Copley Hill 13/6/54.
Doncaster 28/11/54.
Sheffield 12/6/60.
Canklow 2/12/62.
Mexborough 9/12/62.

RENUMBERED:
61155 18/12/48.

CONDEMNED:
1/3/64.
*Sold 5/64 for scrap to
Geo.Cohen, Ickles,
Rotherham.*

1156

Vulcan 5514

To traffic 9/5/47.

REPAIRS:
Gor. 19/12/48–29/1/49.**G.**
Gor. 2–3/9/49.**Weigh.**
Gor. 13–14/9/49.**C/L.**
Gor. 25–26/1/50.**N/C.**
Gor. 1–2/4/50.**Weigh.**
Gor. 7–12/12/50.**N/C.**
Gor. 5/2–13/4/51.**G.**
Gor. 16–17/4/51.**N/C.**
Gor. 26–28/1/52.**N/C.**
Dar. 7–29/11/52.**G.**
Gor. 6–27/2/54.**C/L.**
Gor. 2/10–6/11/54.**G.**
Dar. 29/3–6/4/55.**C/L.**
Dar. 23–27/4/56.**C/L.**
Dar. 10/12/56–11/1/57.**G.**
Str. 21/4–5/6/59.**G.**
*Mod.bogie springs.
A.T.C.fitted.*
Don. 30/3–5/5/62.**G.**

BOILERS:
9742.
9688 *(ex1096)* 29/1/49.
28302 *(ex1106)* 13/4/51.
28200 *(ex1065)* 29/11/52.
28266 *(ex1011)* 11/1/57.
28278 *(ex1174)* 11/1/57.
28525 *(ex1009)* 5/6/59.
28865 *(ex1082)* 5/5/62.

SHEDS:
Gorton.
Sheffield 13/6/54.
Peterborough 29/9/57.
March 31/1/60.
Stratford 19/2/61.
March 16/9/62.

RENUMBERED:
61156 29/1/49.

CONDEMNED:
25/11/63.
13/1/64 *In for cut up at
Doncaster.*

1157

Vulcan 5515

To traffic 9/5/47.

REPAIRS:
Gor. 26/9–30/10/48.**G.**
Gor. 13–14/6/49.**C/L.**
Gor. 24/1/50.**N/C.**
Gor. 30/7–6/9/50.**G.**
Gor. 8–13/9/50.**N/C.**
Gor. 21/9–24/11/51.**C/L.**
Gor. 19–20/3/52.**N/C.**
Dar. 28/4–22/5/52.**G.**
Dar. 26–29/5/52.**N/C.**
Gor. 29/5–10/7/54.**L/I.**
Don. 27/10–6/11/54.**C/L.**
Dar. 8/1–1/2/57.**G.**
Don. 1–30/5/59.**G.**
Don. 27/6–26/7/61.**G.**
Don. 1/3–4/4/63.**C/L.**

BOILERS:
9743.
9737 *(ex1151)* 30/10/48.
28251 *(ex1151)* 6/9/50.
28431 *(ex1084)* 22/5/52.
28435 *(ex1170)* 1/2/57.
28108 *(ex1141)* 30/5/59.
28159 *(ex61378)* 26/7/61.

SHEDS:
Gorton.
Stratford 5/10/52.
Doncaster 19/10/52.

RENUMBERED:
61157 30/10/48.

CONDEMNED:
1/8/65.
*Sold 9/65 for scrap to
T.W.Ward, Beighton.*

1158

Vulcan 5516

To traffic 14/5/47.

REPAIRS:
Dar. 11/1–19/2/49.**G.**
Gor. 9/3–28/4/51.**G.**
Gor. 28/11–15/12/51.**C/L.**
Gor. 19–21/12/51.**N/C.**
Dar. 6/3–9/4/53.**G.**
Dar. 15–20/4/53.**N/C.**
Don. 28/3–25/4/55.**G.**
Don. 16/7–16/8/57.**G.**
Don. 20/12/58–13/1/59.**C/L.**
Don. 23/9–20/10/59.**G.**
Don. 15/2–16/3/62.**G.**

BOILERS:
9744.
3870 *(new)* 19/2/49.
28308 *(ex61329)* 28/4/51.

28236 *(ex61368)* 9/4/53.
28866 *(ex61365)* 25/4/55.
28751 *(ex1203)* 16/8/57.
28146 *(ex1195)* 20/10/59.
28866 *(ex1207)* 16/3/62.

SHEDS:
Gorton.
Doncaster 18/10/53.

RENUMBERED:
61158 19/2/49.

CONDEMNED:
17/4/66.
*Sold 5/66 for scrap to
Geo.Cohen, Kettering.*

1159

Vulcan 5517

To traffic 14/5/47.

REPAIRS:
Gor. 29/7–4/9/48.**L.** *After
collision.*
Gor. 8/6–30/7/49.**G.**
Gor. 7–8/2/51.**N/C.**
Gor. 23/4–2/6/51.**G.**
Gor. 5–7/6/51.**N/C.**
Dar. 16/1–7/2/53.**G.**
Gor. 27–28/10/53.**N/C.**
Gor. 23/2–10/4/54.**C/L.**
Dar. 2–29/10/54.**G.**
Dar. 19/2–19/3/56.**G.**
Dar. 7–20/6/56.**N/C.**
Don. 14/3–17/4/57.**G.**
Don. 6/1–7/2/59.**G.**
Don. 21–26/2/59.**N/C.**
Don. 27/4–20/5/61.**G.**

BOILERS:
9745.
9428 *(ex1497)* 30/7/49.
28319 *(ex1160)* 2/6/51.
28278 *(ex1162)* 7/2/53.
28304 *(ex1022)* 29/10/54.
28178 *(ex1218)* 19/3/56.
28875 *(ex1075)* 17/4/57.
28271 *(ex61331)* 7/2/59.
28421 *(ex61363)* 20/5/61.

SHEDS:
Gorton.
Immingham 13/6/54.

RENUMBERED:
61159 4/9/48.

CONDEMNED:
22/9/63.
*Sold 11/63 for scrap to
J.Cashmore, Great Bridge.*

1160

Vulcan 5518

To traffic 16/5/47.

REPAIRS:
Gor. 4/4–7/5/49.**G.**

Gor. 28/3–22/4/50.**C/L.**
Gor. 17/2–14/4/51.**G.**
Gor. 19–21/4/51.**N/C.**
Gor. 1–2/11/52.**N/C.**
Dar. 17/11–18/12/52.**G.**
Gor. 14–29/8/53.**C/L.**
Gor. 29/3–27/5/54.**C/L.**
Str. 6/9–15/10/54.**G.**
Str. 10/3–4/5/56.**G.**
Str. 17/2–2/5/58.**G.**
Mod.bogie springs.
Str. 24/12/58–12/1/59.**N/C.**
Str. 15/6–1/7/59.**N/C.**
A.T.C.fitted.
Don. 14/9–8/10/60.**G.**

BOILERS:
9746.
9765 *(ex1179)* 7/5/49.
28305 *(ex1168)* 14/4/51.
28292 *(ex1169)* 18/12/52.
28857 *(ex1001)* 15/10/54.
28514 *(ex1043)* 4/5/56.
28374 *(ex61317)* 2/5/58.
28548 *(ex1001)* 8/10/60.

SHEDS:
Gorton.
Cambridge 20/6/54.
Colwick 28/10/56.
Ipswich 6/10/57.
Lowestoft 19/7/59.
Lincoln 13/3/60.
Colwick 20/3/60.
Lincoln 27/3/60.
Colwick 1/7/62.

RENUMBERED:
61160 7/5/49.

CONDEMNED:
22/9/63.
*Sold 1/64 for scrap to
J.Cashmore, Great Bridge.*

1161

Vulcan 5519

To traffic 16/5/47.

REPAIRS:
Dar. 2/1–12/2/49.**G.**
Gor. 19/9–28/10/50.**G.**
Gor. 1–8/11/50.**N/C.**
Dar. 5–30/5/52.**G.**
Dar. 5–12/6/52.**N/C.**
Gor. 30/1–13/3/54.**G.**
Gor. 31/7–7/8/54.**C/L.**
Gor. 29/9–1/10/55.**C/L.**
Dar. 12/1–16/2/57.**C/L.**
Dar. 7/3–11/4/58.**G.**
Dar. 4/5–8/6/60.**G.**
Complete A.W.S.fitted.
Dar. 1–3/8/61.**N/C.**
Dar. 4/1–3/2/62.**G.**
Dar. 14–20/2/62.**N/C.**

BOILERS:
9747.
3868 *(new)* 12/2/49.
28270 *(ex1150)* 28/10/50.
28439 *(ex1066)* 30/5/52.
28222 *(ex1024)* 13/3/54.

28204 *(ex1195)* 11/4/58.
28126 *(ex1025)* 8/6/60.
28243 *(ex1291)* 3/2/62.

SHEDS:
Gorton.
Leicester 30/5/59.
Gorton 25/7/59.
Mirfield 17/7/60.
Low Moor 20/8/61.
Wakefield 10/9/61.

RENUMBERED:
61161 12/2/49.

CONDEMNED:
6/12/66.
*Sold 2/67 for scrap to
Arnott,Young, Parkgate.*

1162

Vulcan 5520

To traffic 21/5/47.

REPAIRS:
Dar. 2/1–4/2/49**G.**
Dar. 18–25/2/49.**N/C.**
Gor. 10/8–3/9/49.**C/H.**
Gor. 21/9–18/11/50.**G.**
Gor. 22–24/11/50.**N/C.**
Gor. 30/11–1/12/50.**N/C.**
Gor. 18/8–29/9/51.**C/L.**
Gor. 2–4/10/51.**N/C.**
Gor. 26/11–1/12/51.**C/L.**
Gor. 10–23/2/52.**C/L.**
Gor. 19/4–8/5/52.**C/L.**
Dar. 17/11–6/12/52.**G.**
Gor. 14/8–25/9/54.**G.**
Don. 12/12/56–18/1/57.**G.**
Don. 9/12/58–16/1/59.**G.**
Complete A.T.C.fitted.
Dar. 28/7–5/8/59.**C/L.**
Don. 6/4–11/5/61.**G.**
Don. 21/10–7/11/61.**C/L.**

BOILERS:
9748.
3734 *(ex1019)* 4/2/49.
28278 *(ex1153)* 18/11/50.
28205 *(ex1012)* 6/12/52.
28133 *(ex1169)* 25/9/54.
28427 *(ex1001)* 18/1/57.
28157 *(ex1094)* 16/1/59.
28215 *(ex1094)* 11/5/61.

SHEDS:
Gorton.
Copley Hill 13/6/54.
Doncaster 24/10/54.
Sheffield 8/2/59.
Staveley 3/6/62.
Lincoln 27/1/63.
New England 24/11/63.

RENUMBERED:
61162 4/2/49.

CONDEMNED:
8/12/64.
*Sold 2/65 for scrap to
Hughes,Bolckow, North
Blyth.*

1163

Vulcan 5521

To traffic 23/5/47.

REPAIRS:
Don. 17/10/47.**N/C.**
Elec.lighting.
Gor. 12/4–14/5/48.**L.**
Gor. 15/2–23/3/49.**G.**
Don. 24/7–24/8/50.**G.**
Don. 15/1–10/2/52.**G.**
Don. 14–20/2/52.**N/C.**
Don. 28/7–28/8/53.**G.**
Don. 19–21/9/53.**N/C.** *For
Works Centenary exhib.*
Dar. 10/2–12/3/55.**G.**
Dar. 15–16/3/55.**N/C.**
Dar. 18–23/3/55.**N/C.**
Dar. 19/10–29/11/56.**C/L.**
Dar. 16/11–14/12/57.**G.**
Don. 19/9–17/10/59.**G.**
Don. 20/2–3/3/60.**N/C.**
Don. 5–20/10/60.**N/C.**

BOILERS:
9749.
9831 *(ex1194)* 23/3/49.
9967 *(ex61330)* 24/8/50.
28174 *(ex1036)* 10/2/52.
28267 *(ex1657)* 28/8/53.
28865 *(ex1028)* 12/3/55.
28219 *(ex1266)* 14/12/57.
28562 *(ex1193)* 17/10/59.

SHEDS:
Gorton.
Neasden 23/6/47.
Leicester 4/7/54.
Colwick 19/12/54.

RENUMBERED:
61163 14/5/48.

CONDEMNED:
16/9/62.
*Sold 2/63 for scrap to Albert
Looms, Spondon.*

1164

Vulcan 5522

To traffic 23/5/47.

REPAIRS:
Don. 22/10/47.**N/C.**
Elec.lighting.
Don. 19/10–1/12/48.**G.**
Don. 19–24/5/49.**C/L.**
Don. 11/6–18/7/50.**G.**
*Chime whistle fitted –
removed 12/50.*
Don. 20/12/51–17/1/52.**G.**
Don. 26/5–29/6/53.**G.**
Str. 2/11–18/12/54.**G.**
Don. 6/12/56–12/1/57.**G.**
Don. 2–8/2/57.**N/C.**
Str. 20/5–1/6/57.**C/L.** *After
collision.*
Str. 25/11/58–23/1/59.**G.**
Mod.bogie springs.
Don. 27/8/62. *Not repaired.*

1165

Vulcan 5523

To traffic 28/5/47.

REPAIRS:
Don. 14/10/47.**N/C.**
Elec.lighting.
Don. 14/7–5/8/49.**G.**
Don. 2/9–2/10/51.**G.**
Don. 16/11–12/12/53.**G.**
Don. 31/1–22/2/55.**C/L.**
Don. 20/10–17/11/55.**G.**
Dar. 18/3–17/4/58.**H/I.**
Dar. 28/10/59–1/1/60.**C/H.**
Don. 25/1–24/2/61.**G.**

BOILERS:
9751.
9838 *(ex1201)* 5/8/49.
28151 *(ex1079)* 2/10/51.
28176 *(ex1028)* 12/12/53.
28331 *(ex1082)* 17/11/55.
28857 *(ex1279)* 24/2/61.

SHEDS:
Gorton.
Mexborough 14/6/47.
Canklow 11/3/62.

RENUMBERED:
61165 5/8/49.

CONDEMNED:
1/11/64.
*Sold 1/65 for scrap to
A.Draper, Hull.*

1166

Vulcan 5524

To traffic 30/5/47.

REPAIRS:
Don. 13/10/47.**N/C.**
Elec.lighting.
Don. 6/2–17/3/49.**G.**
Don. 23–24/8/49.**C/L.**

BOILERS:
9750.
3701 *(ex1107)* 1/12/48.
5060 *(ex1077)* 18/7/50.
28169 *(ex1086)* 17/1/52.
28145 *(ex1247)* 29/6/53.
28534 *(ex1286)* 18/12/54.
28104 *(ex61366)* 12/1/57.
28164 *(ex61372)* 23/1/59.

SHEDS:
Gorton.
Neasden 23/6/47.
Stratford 17/2/57.
Sheffield 3/5/59.

RENUMBERED:
61164 1/12/48.

CONDEMNED:
10/9/62.
Cut up at Doncaster Works.

Don. 14–16/8/50.**C/L.**
Don. 31/12/50–24/1/51.**G.**
Don. 23/12/52–23/1/53.**G.**
Don. 16–19/9/53.**N/C.**
Gor. 10/5–12/6/54.**C/L.**
Gor. 15–18/6/54.**N/C.**
Dar. 6/2–4/3/55.**G.**
Don. 2–18/5/56.**C/L.**
Don. 11/1–16/2/57.**G.**
Dar. 11/11–17/12/59.**G.**

BOILERS:
9752.
9757 (ex1171) 17/3/49.
28124 (ex1026) 24/1/51.
28127 (ex1093) 23/1/53.
28305 (ex1182) 4/3/55.
28179 (ex61406) 16/2/57.
28444 (ex1035) 17/12/59.

SHEDS:
Gorton.
Mexborough 16/6/47.
Millhouses 6/8/61.
Sheffield 10/9/61.

RENUMBERED:
61166 17/3/49.

CONDEMNED:
16/9/62.
Sold 5/63 for scrap to Albert Looms, Spondon.

1167

Vulcan 5525

To traffic 30/5/47.

REPAIRS:
Don. 16/10/47.**N/C.**
Elec.lighting.
Don. 21/4–18/5/49.**G.**
Don. 26/2–20/3/51.**G.**
Don. 2–29/1/53.**G.**
Don. 31/12/54–29/1/55.**G.**
Don. 3–10/2/55.**N/C.**
Don. 12–20/3/56.**C/L.**
Don. 29/10–1/12/56.**G.**
Dar. 10/2–6/3/59.**G.**
Don. 31/5–11/7/61.**G.**

BOILERS:
9753.
9690 (ex1099) 18/5/49.
28134 (ex1203) 20/3/51.
28120 (ex1026) 29/1/53.
28121 (ex1107) 29/1/55.
28868 (ex1070) 1/12/56.
28752 (ex61306) 6/3/59.
28403 (ex61327) 11/7/61.

SHEDS:
Gorton.
Mexborough 16/6/47.
Immingham 21/6/53.
Mexborough 4/10/53.
Canklow 1/3/64.

RENUMBERED:
61167 18/5/49.

CONDEMNED:
6/12/64.
Sold 2/65 for scrap to Hughes,Bolckow, N.Blyth.

1168

Vulcan 5526

To traffic 4/6/47.

REPAIRS:
Don. 15/10/47.**N/C.**
Elec.lighting.
Don. 31/3–3/5/49.**G.**
Don. 23/1–23/2/51.**G.**
Don. 3–27/2/53.**G.**
Dar. 12/10–4/11/54.**H.**
Dar. 27/3–23/4/56.**G.**
Dar. 10/1–7/2/58.**G.**
Don. 17–28/11/58.**C/L.**
Don. 17–28/4/59.**N/C.**
Don. 3–31/10/59.**G.**
Don. 29/8–16/9/60.**N/C.**
Don. 17/1–16/2/62.**G.**

BOILERS:
9754.
5092 (ex1094) 3/5/49.
28128 (ex1080) 23/2/51.
28123 (ex1074) 4/11/54.
28277 (ex1071) 23/4/56.
28865 (ex1163) 7/2/58.
28859 (ex1250) 31/10/59.
28114 (ex61375) 16/2/62.

SHEDS:
Gorton.
Mexborough 16/6/47.
Immingham 21/6/53.

RENUMBERED:
61168 3/5/49.

CONDEMNED:
3/10/65.
Sold 11/65 for scrap to T.W.Ward, Killamarsh.

1169

Vulcan 5527

To traffic 6/6/47.

REPAIRS:
Gor. 19/4–22/5/48.**L.**
Prep.for trials.
Don. 7/1–16/2/49.**G.**
Gor. 15/1–17/2/51.**G.**
Gor. 20–27/2/51.**N/C.**
Dar. 11/9–4/10/52.**G.**
Gor. 19/6–7/8/54.**G.**
Dar. 22/3–18/4/56.**G.**
Dar. 13/2–19/3/57.**C/H.**
Dar. 24/2–22/3/58.**G.**
Dar. 26–31/3/58.**N/C.**
Don. 17/2–17/3/60.**G.**

BOILERS:
9755.
9725 (ex1139) 16/2/49.
28292 (ex1195) 17/2/51.

28133 (ex1011) 4/10/52.
28800 (ex1153) 7/8/54.
28187 (ex1063) 18/4/56.
28277 (ex1168) 22/3/58.
28502 (ex1005) 17/3/60.

SHEDS:
Gorton.
Neasden 23/6/47.
Gorton 6/3/49.
Sheffield 19/6/49.
Canklow 2/12/62.
Mexborough 9/12/62.

RENUMBERED:
61169 18/5/48.

CONDEMNED:
28/12/63.
17/2/64 In for cut up at Doncaster.

1170

Vulcan 5528

To traffic 6/6/47.

REPAIRS:
Don. 17/9/47.**N/C.**
Don. 30/8–7/10/49.**G.**
Don. 24/2–5/4/51.**G.**
Don. 20/10/52–13/11/52.**G.**
Dar. 4/8–4/9/54.**G.**
Don. 14/3/55. Weigh.
Dar. 26/11–21/12/56.**G.**
Don. 10/3–11/4/59.**G.**
Don. 14–28/9/60.**C/L.**
Don. 3/7/62. Not repaired.

BOILERS:
9756.
9847 (ex1210) 7/10/49.
28135 (ex1169) 5/4/51.
28108 (ex1107) 13/11/52.
28435 (ex1291) 4/9/54.
28322 (ex1012) 21/12/56.
28833 (ex1120) 11/4/59.

SHEDS:
Gorton.
Doncaster 20/7/47.

RENUMBERED:
61170 7/10/49.

CONDEMNED:
9/7/62.
Cut up at Doncaster Works.

1171

Vulcan 5529

To traffic 11/6/47.

REPAIRS:
Don. 14–19/9/47.**N/C.**
Elec.lighting.
Don. 25/1–3/3/49.**G.**
Str. 31/12/50–10/2/51.**G.**
Don. 31/3–29/4/53.**G.**
Don. 18/11–16/12/54.**G.**

Don. 23/10–23/11/56.**G.**
Don. 27–28/11/56.**N/C.**
Str. 20/10–5/12/58.**G.**
Don. 18/7–18/8/60.**G.**
Don. 12–27/10/61.**C/L.**

BOILERS:
9757.
9830 (ex1193) 3/3/49.
28522 (ex1272) 10/2/51.
28861 (new) 29/4/53.
28344 (ex1642) 16/12/54.
28114 (ex1190) 23/11/56.
28587 (ex1603) 5/12/58.
28594 (ex1182) 18/8/60.

SHEDS:
Gorton.
Grantham 4/7/47.
Stratford 11/12/49.
Lincoln 21/10/51.
Doncaster 19/12/54.
Stratford 16/6/57.
Cambridge 12/4/59.
March 20/11/60.

RENUMBERED:
61171 3/3/49.

CONDEMNED:
16/9/62.
Sold 6/63 for scrap to Central Wagon Co., Ince.

1172

Vulcan 5530

To traffic 9/6/47.

REPAIRS:
Cow. 14/9–21/10/48.**G.**
Cow. 7–29/4/50.**L/I.**
Cow. 23/6–16/8/52.**G.**
Cow. 20/8–11/9/52.**C/L.**
Cow. 30/4–13/6/53.**C/L.**
Cow. 2/2/54.**N/C.**
Cow. 15/2/54.**N/C.**
Cow. 21/6–7/8/54.**H/I.**
Cow. 17–21/8/54.**N/C.**
Cow. 27/5–22/6/55.**C/L.**
Cow. 8/7–13/8/55.**C/L.**
Cow. 12–17/9/55.**N/C.**
Cow. 28/1–3/3/56.**G.**
Cow. 5/7–2/8/57.**C/L.**
Cow. 15/2–8/3/58.**L/I.**
Cow. 8–23/9/59.**N/C.**
Cow. 14/5–25/6/60.**G.**
Cow. 10/1–16/2/63.**L/I.**
Cow. 7–13/7/65.**N/C.**

BOILERS:
9758.
28622 (ex1180) 16/8/52.
28604 (ex1103) 3/3/56.
28663 (ex61342) 25/6/60.

SHEDS:
Gorton.
Eastfield 13/6/47.
Dundee 27/1/56.

RENUMBERED:
61172 21/10/48.

CONDEMNED:
16/12/65.
Sold 1/66 for scrap to Shipbreaking Industries, Faslane.

1173

Vulcan 5531

To traffic 9/6/47.

REPAIRS:
Dar. 16–17/9/47.**N/C.** *Stub axle to weld.*
Dar. 2/4–3/5/49.**G.**
Dar. 19/3–13/4/51.**G.**
Dar. 7–10/11/51.**C/L.**
Dar. 9–11/10/52.**C/L.**
Dar. 24/3–23/4/53.**G.**
Dar. 23/5–18/6/55.**G.**
Dar. 15/9–12/10/56.**C/H.**
Dar. 14/1–8/2/58.**G.**
Dar. 29/6–9/7/59.**N/C.**
Complete A.T.C.fitted.
Dar. 5/5–9/6/60.**G.**
Dar. 10/2–25/3/61.**C/L.**
Dar. 31/10/64–15/1/65.**L/I.**

BOILERS:
9759.
9769 *(ex1183)* 3/5/49.
28206 *(ex1021)* 13/4/51.
28401 *(ex1088)* 23/4/53.
28574 *(ex1179)* 18/6/55.
28263 *(ex1155)* 8/2/58.
28551 *(ex1069)* 9/6/60.

SHEDS:
Gorton.
Darlington 13/6/47.
Stockton 4/11/51.
Thornaby 14/6/59.
Ardsley 25/11/62.
Wakefield 5/1/64.
York 13/11/66.

RENUMBERED:
61173 3/5/49.

CONDEMNED:
23/1/67.
Sold 3/67 for scrap to T.W.Ward, Beighton.

1174

Vulcan 5532

To traffic 18/6/47.

REPAIRS:
Gor. 16/9/47.**N/C.**
Don. 2–10/10/47.**N/C.**
Elec.lighting.
Don. 24/5–4/7/49.**G.**
Don. 15/4–9/5/51.**G.**
Dar. 25/2–21/3/53.**G.**
Dar. 22/3–1/4/53.**C/L.**
Dar. 11/11–9/12/54.**G.**
Dar. 20/9–4/10/55.**C/L.**
Dar. 7/9–11/10/56.**G.**

Don. 28/1–4/3/59.**G.**
Don. 21/3–28/4/62.**G.**

BOILERS:
9760.
9763 *(ex1177)* 4/7/49.
28142 *(ex1191)* 9/5/51.
28126 *(ex1080)* 21/3/53.
28278 *(ex1159)* 9/12/54.
28438 *(ex61337)* 11/10/56.
28141 *(ex61409)* 4/3/59.
28875 *(ex1179)* 28/4/62.

SHEDS:
Gorton.
Doncaster 20/7/47.
Mexborough 5/11/47.
Sheffield 24/2/52.
Kings Cross 19/10/58.
New England 9/10/60.

RENUMBERED:
61174 4/7/49.

CONDEMNED:
28/12/63.
28/2/64 In for cut up at Doncaster.

1175

Vulcan 5533

To traffic 18/6/47.

REPAIRS:
Don. 10/12/48–24/1/49.**G.**
Str. 8/10–25/11/50.**G.**
Dar. 24/12/51–15/i/52.**N/C.**
Dar. 19–31/3/52.**C/L.**
Don. 28/8–26/9/52.**G.**
Don. 7–10/10/52.**N/C.**
Don. 3–25/2/54.**G.**
Dar. 19/12/54–5/1/55.**C/L.**
Don. 12/5–18/6/55.**G.**
Don. 30/1–9/2/56.**N/C.**
Don. 23/7–10/8/56.**C/L.**
Don. 27/3–1/5/57.**G.**
Don. 9–26/2/58.**C/L.**
Don. 18/6–23/7/59.**G.**
Don. 27/7/59.**N/C.**
Don. 16/8–29/9/61.**G.**

BOILERS:
9761.
9729 *(ex1143)* 24/1/49.
28513 *(ex1104)* 25/11/50.
28330 *(ex61405)* 26/9/52.
28153 *(ex1211)* 25/2/54.
28352 *(ex1075)* 18/6/55.
28121 *(ex1167)* 1/5/57.
28405 *(ex1145)* 23/7/59.
28610 *(ex1204)* 29/9/61.

SHEDS:
Gorton.
Grantham 20/7/47.
Stratford 7/12/49.
Immingham 21/10/51.
Colwick 16/10/60.

RENUMBERED:
61175 24/1/49.

CONDEMNED:
28/12/63.
11/2/64 In for cut up at Doncaster.

1176

Vulcan 5534

To traffic 17/6/47.

REPAIRS:
Dar. 22/9/47.**N/C.** *Stub axle to weld.*
Dar. 11/8–9/9/49.**G.**
Dar. 7–14/10/50.**N/C.**
Dar. 7/7–17/8/51.**G.**
Dar. 11/6–4/7/53.**G.**
Dar. 13–22/1/54.**C/L.**
Mod.bogie springs.
Ghd. 10–22/9/54.**N/C.**
Dar. 13/4–13/5/55.**G.**
Dar. 10/4–4/5/57.**G.**
Dar. 6–8/5/57.**N/C.**
Dar. 23–24/3/59.**N/C.**
Dar. 30/7–29/8/59.**G.**
Complete A.T.C.fitted.
Dar. 8–16/9/59.**N/C.**
Dar. 21/5–20/6/62.**G.**

BOILERS:
9762.
3599 *(ex1034)* 9/9/49.
28221 *(ex1034)* 17/8/51.
28206 *(ex1173)* 4/7/53.
28394 *(ex1096)* 13/5/55.
28874 *(ex1145)* 4/5/57.
28175 *(ex1019)* 29/8/59.
28227 *(ex1014)* 20/6/62.

SHEDS:
Darlington.
St Margarets 29/8/48.
Darlington 31/10/48.
York 19/7/53.
Darlington 25/9/55.
West Hartlepool 16/6/63.
Hull Dairycoates 15/12/63.
York 6/9/64.

RENUMBERED:
61176 9/9/49.

CONDEMNED:
7/11/65.
Sold 12/65 for scrap to A.Draper, Hull.

1177

Vulcan 5535

To traffic 25/6/47.

REPAIRS:
Don. 4/5–3/6/49.**G.**
Str. 31/12/50–10/2/51.**G.**
Don. 5–29/5/53.**G.**
Don. 26/10–3/11/54.**C/L.**
Don. 27/2–31/3/55.**G.**
Don. 11–12/4/55.**N/C.**
Dar. 5/2–1/3/57.**G.**
Don. 22/10–27/11/58.**G.**

Don. 19–26/2/60.**N/C.**
Don. 6/12/60–10/1/61.**G.**

BOILERS:
9763.
9754 *(ex1168)* 3/6/49.
28532 *(ex1171)* 10/2/51.
28154 *(ex1083)* 29/5/53.
28808 *(ex1141)* 31/3/55.
28585 *(ex1201)* 1/3/57.
28506 *(ex1082)* 27/11/58.
28370 *(ex61374)* 10/1/61.

SHEDS:
Gorton.
Grantham 20/7/47.
Stratford 29/9/49.
Lincoln 21/10/51.
Cambridge 23/10/55.
Colwick 28/10/56.

RENUMBERED:
61177 3/6/49.

CONDEMNED:
22/9/63.
Sold 12/63 for scrap to J.Cashmore, Great Bridge.

1178

Vulcan 5536

To traffic 23/6/47.

REPAIRS:
Cow. 14/9–21/10/48.**G.**
Cow. 16–18/11/48.**L.**
Cow. 26/2–17/3/51.**L/I.**
Cow. 27–29/3/51.**N/C.**
Cow. 26/4–5/5/51.**C/H.**
Cow. 19/5–12/6/52.**C/L.**
Cow. 7–29/8/53.**G.**
Hay. 27/2–7/3/55.**C/L.**
Cow. 6–31/12/55.**H/I.**
Cow. 4–11/2/56.**C/L.**
Cow. 5–10/11/56.**C/L.**
Cow. 21/11–15/12/56.**L/I.**
Cow. 5–9/2/57.**N/C.**
Cow. 22–30/3/57.**N/C.**
Cow. 14–24/5/57.**N/C.**
Cow. 4–8/2/58.**N/C.**
Cow. 3–26/9/58.**G.**
Mod.bogie springs.
Cow. 29/1–17/2/59.**N/C.**
A.T.C.fitted.
Cow. 16–27/10/59.**N/C.**
Cow. 24/1–18/2/61.**L/I.**
Cow. 28/8–28/9/61.**C/L.**
Cow. 17–27/10/61.**C/L.**
Cow. 19–23/11/63.**C/L.**

BOILERS:
9764.
Renumbered 28621 17/3/51.
28660 *(ex61355)* 29/8/53.
28615 *(ex61308)* 26/9/58.
141 Tubes.

SHEDS:
Haymarket.
Dalry Road 9/9/63.
St Margarets 18/11/63.

RENUMBERED:
61178 21/10/48.

CONDEMNED:
13/2/64.
*Sold 5/64 for scrap to
Geo.H.Campbell, Airdrie.*

1179

Vulcan 5537

To traffic 27/6/47.

REPAIRS:
Gor. 13/2–26/3/49.**G.**
Gor. 6/9–27/10/51.**G.**
Gor. 30–31/10/51.**N/C.**
Gor. 1–2/11/51.**N/C.**
Dar. 25/11–11/12/52.**C/L.**
Dar. 1/7–12/8/53.**G.**
Dar. 24–26/8/53.**N/C.**
Gor. 16–23/1/54.**C/L.**
Dar. 2–30/4/55.**G.**
Dar. 31/10–6/12/55.**C/L.**
Dar. 22/5–21/6/57.**G.**
Don. 19/2–26/3/59.**G.**
Don. 1/3–6/4/62.**G.**

BOILERS:
9765.
9839 *(ex1202)* 26/3/49.
28815 *(new)* 27/10/51.
28574 *(ex1006)* 12/8/53.
28580 *(ex1190)* 30/4/55.
28404 *(ex1031)* 21/6/57.
28875 *(ex1159)* 26/3/59.
28538 *(ex1058)* 6/4/62.

SHEDS:
Gorton.
Sheffield 10/8/47.
Kings Cross 19/10/58.
Doncaster 16/6/63.
Immingham 14/6/64.

RENUMBERED:
61179 26/3/49.

CONDEMNED:
10/1/65.
*Sold 2/65 for scrap to
A.Draper, Hull.*

1180

Vulcan 5538

To traffic 30/6/47.

REPAIRS:
Cow. 2/11–4/12/48.**G.**
Cow. 12/6–1/7/50.**L/I.**
Cow. 22/6–14/7/52.**G.**
Cow. 12/12/53–16/1/54.**L/I.**
Cow. 14/1–22/2/56.**L/I.**
Cow. 1/2–4/3/58.**G.**
Cow. 30/9–9/11/60.**L/I.**
Cow. 19/4–30/5/63.**G.**
Cow. 10/64.**C/L.**
BOILERS:
9766
28643 *(ex61323)* 14/7/52.

28519 *(ex61333)* 4/3/58.
28635 *(ex1067)* 30/5/63.

SHEDS:
Eastfield.
Dundee 20/6/55.
Dunfermline Upper
28/8/66.
Dundee 6/11/66.
Aberdeen 27/11/66.
Dundee 12/3/67.

RENUMBERED:
61180 4/12/48.

CONDEMNED:
1/5/67.
*Sold 7/67 for scrap to
Motherwell Machinery &
Scrap Co., Wishaw*

1181

Vulcan 5539

To traffic 2/7/47.

REPAIRS:
Dar. 6/1–26/2/49.**G.**
Gor. 17–19/1/50.**N/C.**
Gor. 12/6–4/8/51.**G.**
Gor. 7–14/8/51.**N/C.**
Dar. 10/4–9/5/53.**G.**
Dar. 16/11–16/12/54.**G.**
Dar. 27/7–27/8/56.**G.**
Dar. 21/4–22/5/58.**G.**
Don. 5/8–3/9/60.**G.**

BOILERS:
9767.
3768 *(ex1022)* 26/2/49.
28333 *(ex1191)* 4/8/51.
28142 *(ex1174)* 9/5/53.
28208 *(ex1060)* 16/12/54.
28801 *(ex1002)* 27/8/56.
28564 *(ex1051)* 22/5/58.
28190 *(ex3983)* 3/9/60.

SHEDS:
Gorton.
Sheffield 24/8/47.
March 20/1/63.

RENUMBERED:
61181 26/2/49.

CONDEMNED:
25/11/63.
*Made S.B.Dept'l No.18.
Sold 12/65 for scrap to
Garnham Harris & Elton,
Chesterfield.*

1182

Vulcan 5540

To traffic 4/7/47.

REPAIRS:
Gor. 25/4–28/5/49.**G.**
Gor. 21–30/6/49.**N/C.**
Gor. 17–18/2/50.**N/C.**

Gor. 2/6/50. *Weigh.*
Gor. 13/12/50–3/3/51.**G.**
Gor. 7–8/3/51.**N/C.**
Gor. 22–23/2/52.**N/C.**
Dar. 2–28/1/53.**G.**
Gor. 30/3–1/4/53.**N/C.**
Gor. 13/3/54.**C/L.**
Dar. 27/12/54–26/1/55.**G.**
Don. 8–22/3/55.**C/L.**
Dar. 29/6–15/8/56.**G.**
Str. 18/9–24/10/58.**G.**
Mod.bogie springs.
Str. 4–14/11/58.**N/C.**
Don. 13/6–16/7/60.**G.**

BOILERS:
9768.
9695 *(ex1106 & spare)*
28/5/49.
28293 *(ex1202)* 3/3/51.
28305 *(ex1160)* 28/1/53.
28142 *(ex1181)* 26/1/55.
28601 *(ex1020)* 15/8/56.
28594 *(ex1617)* 24/10/58.
28231 *(ex1082)* 16/7/60.

SHEDS:
Gorton.
Norwich 28/10/51.
Gorton 27/1/52.
Immingham 13/6/54.
Stratford 17/2/57.
Cambridge 10/8/58.
March 20/11/60.

RENUMBERED:
61182 28/5/49.

CONDEMNED:
16/9/62.
*Sold 2/63 for scrap to
Central Wagon Co., Ince.*

1183

Vulcan 5541

To traffic 9/7/47.

REPAIRS:
Dar. 6/1–4/3/49.**G.**
Gor. 20/4–26/5/51.**G.**
Dar. 4/12/52–20/2/53.**G.**
Dar. 7/11–4/12/54.**G.**
Dar. 6/5–11/6/56.**G.**
Dar. 1–16/11/56.**C/L.**
Dar. 8/2–11/3/58.**G.**
Don. 3–24/12/59.**G.**
Don. 27/1–4/2/61.**N/C.**
Don. 5/7/62. *Not repaired.*

BOILERS:
9769.
9747 *(ex1161)* 4/3/49.
28318 *(ex3738)* 26/5/51.
28547 *(ex1192)* 20/2/53.
28117 *(ex1202)* 4/12/54.
28551 *(ex1053)* 11/6/56.
28304 *(ex61325)* 11/3/58.
28571 *(ex1631)* 24/12/59.

SHEDS:
Gorton.
Sheffield 10/8/47.

RENUMBERED:
61183 4/3/49.

CONDEMNED:
9/7/62.
Cut up at Doncaster.

1184

Vulcan 5542

To traffic 9/7/47.

REPAIRS:
Gor. 11–12/1/49.**C/L.**
Gor. 3/8–17/9/49.**G.**
Gor. 21-22/7/50.**C/L.**
Gor. 10/8–29/9/51.**G.**
Gor. 3–4/10/51.**N/C.**
Gor. 16–17/11/51.**N/C.**
Gor. 25/5–27/6/53.**G.**
Gor. 30/6–16/7/53.**C/L.**
Cow. 4/4–7/5/55.**L/I.**
Cow. 21/6–17/8/57.**G.**
Cow. 4–7/12/57.**N/C.**
Cow. 19–29/3/58.**N/C.**
Cow. 4–29/5/59.**L/I.**
*A.W.S.fitted. Mod.bogie
springs.*
Cow. 30/1–18/3/61.**L/I.**
Cow. 29/5–24/6/61.**C/L.**

BOILERS:
9770.
3706 *(ex1082)* 17/9/49.
28349 *(ex1209)* 29/9/51.
28130 *(ex1096)* 27/6/53.
28612 *(ex1197)* 17/8/57. 141
tubes

SHEDS:
Gorton.
St Margarets 13/9/53.

RENUMBERED:
61184 12/1/49.

CONDEMNED:
29/12/62.
*2/63 In for cut up at
Cowlairs.*

1185

Vulcan 5543

To traffic 9/7/47.

REPAIRS:
Dar. 15/1–4/3/49.**G.**
Gor. 20/9–8/11/50.**G.**
Gor. 9–13/11/50.**N/C.**
Dar. 18/6–10/7/52.**G.**
Gor. 31/10–21/11/53.**G.**
Dar. 26/5–2/7/55.**G.**
Dar. 19/3–12/4/57.**G.**
Don. 7/8–1/9/58.**C/H.**
Don. 22/7–21/8/59.**G.**
Don. 10/8–16/9/61.**G.**

BOILERS:
9771.
9748 *(ex1162)* 4/3/49.

28272 (ex1154) 8/11/50.
28251 (ex1157) 10/7/52.
28232 (ex1092) 21/11/53.
28206 (ex1176) 2/7/55.
28455 (ex1018) 12/4/57.
28954 (new) 1/9/58.
28981 (new) 21/8/59.
28450 (ex1272) 16/9/61.

SHEDS:
Gorton.
Leicester 2/11/47.
Colwick 11/11/56.
Immingham 6/12/59.

RENUMBERED:
61185 4/3/49.

CONDEMNED:
11/10/64.
Sold 12/64 for scrap to
W.F.Smith, Ecclesfield.

1186

Vulcan 5544

To traffic 16/7/47.

REPAIRS:
Dar. 5/1–24/2/49.**G.**
Gor. 29/8–1/10/49.**C/H.**
Cylinders ex1497.
Gor. 16/7–25/8/51.**G.**
Gor. 28–29/8/51.**N/C.**
Gor. 1/5–13/6/53.**G.**
Dar. 17/5–18/6/55.**G.**
Dar. 29/5–28/6/57.**G.**
Dar. 28/4–26/5/59.**G.**
Dar. 1–10/6/59.**N/C.**
Dar. 20/9–12/10/60.**C/L.**
Dar. 17/8–8/9/61.**G.**
Dar. 26/9–4/10/61.**N/C.**
Dar. 27/7–14/8/62.**C/L.**

BOILERS:
9772.
3869 (new) 24/2/49.
28337 (ex1188) 25/8/51.
28449 (ex61381) 13/6/53.
28457 (ex61309) 18/6/55.
28249 (ex1194) 28/6/57.
28348 (ex1028) 26/5/59.
28555 (ex1218) 8/9/61.

SHEDS:
Gorton.
Leicester 2/11/47.
Colwick 15/2/53.
Woodford 1/9/57.

RENUMBERED:
61186 24/2/49.

CONDEMNED:
5/11/62.
12/12/62 In for cut up at
Darlington.

1187

Vulcan 5545

To traffic 29/7/47.

REPAIRS:
Gor. 10/2–19/3/49.**G.**
Gor. 22/11/50–13/1/51.**G.**
Gor. 15–17/1/51.**N/C.**
Dar. 2/3–4/4/52.**G.**
Gor. 21/11–19/12/53.**G.**
Don. 27/6–22/7/55.**G.**
Don. 6/3–4/4/57.**G.**
Dar. 16/10–18/11/58.**G.**
Dar. 25/11–3/12/58.**N/C.**
Wfd. 4/11–20/12/59.**C/L.**
Dar. 29/7–2/9/60.**G.**

BOILERS:
9773.
9742 (ex1156) 19/3/49.
28280 (ex1145) 13/1/51.
28424 (ex1114) 4/4/52.
28334 (ex1209) 19/12/53.
28180 (ex1606) 22/7/55.
28177 (ex1645) 4/4/57.
28196 (ex1274) 18/11/58.
28226 (ex1295) 2/9/60.

SHEDS:
Gorton.
Leicester 2/11/47.
Neasden 26/12/54.
Woodford 3/10/59.
Neasden 9/1/60.
Leicester 13/11/61.
Woodford 17/3/62.

RENUMBERED:
61187 19/3/49.

CONDEMNED:
3/9/62.
19/9/62 In for cut up at
Darlington.

1188

Vulcan 5546

To traffic 29/7/47.

REPAIRS:
Gor. 27/1–19/3/49.**G.**
Gor. 10/5–23/6/51.**G.**
Gor. 21/3–25/4/53.**G.**
Gor. 4/12/54–15/1/55.**G.**
Dar. 11–20/1/56.**C/L.**
Dar. 19–26/4/56.**C/L.**
Dar. 18/4–17/5/57.**G.**
Don. 23/3–30/4/59.**G.**
Don. 1–8/3/60.**N/C.**
Don. 20/10–9/11/60.**N/C.**
Don. 8/5–3/6/61.**G.**

BOILERS:
9774.
9829 (ex1192) 19/3/49.
28810 (new) 23/6/51.

28841 (new) 25/4/53.
28279 (ex1194) 15/1/55.
28869 (ex1008) 17/5/57.
28807 (ex61406) 30/4/59.
28252 (ex1128) 3/6/61.

SHEDS:
Gorton.
Leicester 2/11/47.
Colwick 7/12/52.
Southern Region 19/5/53.
Colwick 27/5/53.
Leicester 1/6/58.
Colwick 7/9/58.

RENUMBERED:
61188 19/3/49.

CONDEMNED:
14/11/65.
Sold 12/65 for scrap to
Hughes, Bolckow, North
Blyth.

1189

Vulcan 5547

To traffic 8/8/47.

Named **SIR WILLIAM
GRAY** in 12/47.

REPAIRS:
Dar. 2/10/47.**N/C.** Stub axle
to weld.
Dar. 2–29/12/49.**G.**
Dar. 2–27/11/51.**G.**
Dar. 3–7/12/51.**N/C.**
Dar. 7/9–1/10/53.**H/I.**
Dar. 7–10/10/53.**N/C.**
Dar. 31/10–24/11/55.**G.**
Dar. 30/7–2/9/58.**G.**
A.T.C.Mech.fitted.
Dar. 9–30/9/58.**N/C.**
Dar. 3–16/2/59.**N/C.**
A.T.C.completed.
Dar. 12/11–12/12/62.**G.**

BOILERS:
9775.
9835 (ex1198) 29/12/49.
28820 (new) 27/11/51.
28398 (ex61315) 24/11/55.
28552 (ex1110) 2/9/58.
28419 (ex1271) 12/12/62.

SHEDS:
Stockton.
Ardsley 23/9/56.
Copley Hill 22/2/59.
Low Moor 20/8/61.
Mirfield 8/9/63.
Low Moor 12/4/64.
Wakefield 13/11/66.
York 15/1/67.

RENUMBERED:
61189 29/12/49.

CONDEMNED:
11/5/67.
Sold 7/67 for scrap to
A.Draper, Hull.

1190

North British Loco. 26091

To traffic 8/5/47.

REPAIRS:
Don. 22/2–25/3/49.**G.**
Gor. 16/3–28/4/51.**G.**
Gor. 11–14/5/51.**N/C.**
Don. 23/10–18/11/52.**G.**
Don. 15–22/4/53.**N/C.**
Gor. 26/6–10/7/54.**C/H.**
Dar. 15/2–18/3/55.**G.**
Don. 26/9–27/10/56.**G.**
Don. 1/4–1/5/59.**G.**
Don. 9/5–10/6/61.**G.**

BOILERS:
9827.
9752 (ex1166) 25/3/49.
28311 (ex1152) 28/4/51.
28116 (ex1194) 18/11/52.
28580 (ex1299) 10/7/54.
28114 (ex1015) 18/3/55.
28144 (ex1082) 27/10/56.
28512 (ex1622) 1/5/59.
28864 (ex1041) 10/6/61.

SHEDS:
Doncaster.
Immingham 18/6/50.
Canklow 10/1/65.
Colwick 13/6/65.

RENUMBERED:
61190 25/3/49.

CONDEMNED:
20/6/65.
Sold 8/65 for scrap to
T.W.Ward, Beighton.

1191

North British Loco. 26092

To traffic 13/5/47.

REPAIRS:
Don. 18/5–23/6/49.**G.**
Gor. 5/5–16/6/51.**G.**
Gor. 19/6/51.**N/C.**
Dar. 15/4–6/6/53.**G.**
StM. 16–30/11/54.**C/L.**
Cow. 1–26/3/55.**H/I.**
Cow. 31/3–1/4/55.**N/C.**
Cow. 30/9–26/10/57.**G.**
Mod.bogie springs.
Cow. 6–9/11/57.**N/C.**
Cow. 20–22/11/57.**N/C.**
Cow. 24/6–16/7/59.**H/I.**
A.T.C.fitted.
continued on page 56

WORKS CODES:– Cow – Cowlairs. Dar – Darlington. Dee – Dundee. Don – Doncaster. Ghd – Gateshead. Gor – Gorton. Inv – Inverurie. Str – Stratford. SRX – St Rollox.

REPAIR CODES:– **C/H** – Casual Heavy. **C/L** – Casual Light. **G** – General. **H** – Heavy. **H/I** – Heavy Intermediate. **L** – Light. **L/I** – Light Intermediate. **N/C** – Non–Classified.

The Norwich-London expresses were a regular duty for the first batch of the B1's built by N.B.Loco.Co and 61052 has one of them at Brentwood on 26th June 1948. Its clean condition is a tribute to Norwich shed as it was 3 months ex works.

After 61290 was transferred from Stockton in September 1953, all its further work was done from Carlisle Canal shed, much of it on the Waverley Route, to and from Edinburgh, and here it is passing through the station at Stobs. Although fitted with the correct 68E shed code plate, there was no excuse for those who would not make themselves familiar with codes, because CARLISLE (CANAL) was clearly shown on the buffer beam.

61197 was a regular performer on the West Highland line, and here is at Crianlarich with a Glasgow to Fort William train, in 1949. Note the duplicate water columns, enabling both engines of a double–headed train to be supplied simultaneously, so avoiding delay by having to draw up.

61289 on a Dairycoates goods working is approaching the end of its run to the marshalling yard at Healey Mills near Mirfield in West Yorkshire, in 1961. Its Automatic Warning System equipment can be seen, and although it was originally intended to have electric lighting, that was never fitted.

1191 continued
Cow. 20–26/4/61.**C/L.**
Cow. 27/6–25/8/61.**G.**
Cow. 29/9–25/10/62.**C/L.**
Cow. 30/12/63–8/2/64.**L/I.**

BOILERS:
 9828.
 9849 *(ex1212)* 23/6/49.
 28324 *(ex1110)* 16/6/51.
 28543 *(ex1044)* 6/6/53.
 28412 *(ex1246)* 26/10/57 141
 tubes.
 28462 *(ex61340)* 25/8/61.

SHEDS:
Doncaster.
Immingham 18/6/50.
Stratford 21/10/51.
St Margarets 13/9/53.

RENUMBERED:
61191 23/6/49.

CONDEMNED:
21/8/65.
*Sold 10/65 for scrap to
Motherwell Machinery &
Scrap Co., Wishaw.*

1192

North British Loco. 26093

To traffic 16/5/47.

REPAIRS:
Gor. 14/3–19/4/48.**L.** *After
collision.*
Gor. 27/11/48–15/1/49.**G.**
Gor. 1–2/7/49.**C/L.**
Str. 25/2–14/4/51.**G.**
Dar. 7–31/1/53.**G.**
Gor. 15–28/11/53.**C/L.**
Gor. 20/11/54–15/1/55.**G.**
Gor. 5–21/5/55.**C/L.**
Gor. 29/9–15/10/55.**C/L.**
Dar. 30/12/55–13/1/56.**C/L.**
Dar. 20/3–13/4/57.**G.**
Str. 4/11–29/12/58.**G.**
Dar. 26/7–8/9/60.**C/L.**
Dar. 30/8–23/9/61.**G.**
Dar. 10/10–16/11/61.**N/C.**
Dar. 17/4–2/5/62.**N/C.**

BOILERS:
 9829.
 9741 *(ex1155)* 15/1/49.
 28547 *(ex1286)* 14/4/51.
 28132 *(ex1018)* 31/1/53.
 28200 *(ex1156)* 15/1/55.
 28808 *(ex1177)* 13/4/57.
 28601 *(ex1182)* 29/12/58.
 28107 *(ex spare)* 23/9/61.

SHEDS:
Doncaster.
Leicester 6/6/47.
Gorton 6/2/49.
Stratford 21/8/49.
Parkeston 8/10/50.
Stratford 10/12/50.
Colwick 29/6/52.
Southern Region 19/5/53.

Colwick 27/5/53.
Woodford 27/6/54.
Leicester 24/9/60.
Woodford 12/3/62.

RENUMBERED:
61192 17/4/48.

CONDEMNED:
8/10/62.
*22/3/63 In for cut up at
Darlington.*

1193

North British Loco. 26094

To traffic 19/5/47.

REPAIRS:
Don. 15/12/48–27/1/49.**G.**
Don. 26/11–20/12/50.**G.**
Don. 4–11/1/51.**N/C.**
Don. 2/9–10/10/52.**G.**
Dar. 12/6–10/7/54.**G.**
Dar. 31/1–27/2/57.**G.**
Don. 7/7–7/8/59.**G.**

BOILERS:
 9830.
 9761 *(ex1175)* 27/1/49.
 28121 *(ex1124)* 20/12/50.
 28505 *(ex1043)* 10/10/52.
 28194 *(ex1087)* 10/7/54.
 28562 *(ex1220)* 27/2/57.
 28843 *(ex1284)* 7/8/59.

SHED:
Doncaster.

RENUMBERED:
61193 27/1/49.

CONDEMNED:
16/9/62.
*1/11/62 In for cut up at
Doncaster.*

1194

North British Loco. 26095

To traffic 21/5/47.

REPAIRS:
Don. 17/1–25/2/49.**G.**
Don. 6/11–6/12/50.**G.**
Don. 8/10–6/11/52.**G.**
Gor. 18/9–23/10/54.**G.**
Don. 16/1/56.*Weigh.*
Dar. 26/4–22/5/57.**G.**
Don. 8/12/59–8/1/60.**G.**
Don. 22/1–5/3/63.**G.**
Don. 15–26/3/63.**N/C.**
Don. 28/5–6/6/63.**C/L.**

BOILERS:
 9831.
 9730 *(ex1144)* 25/2/49.
 28116 *(ex1074)* 6/12/50.
 28279 *(ex1202)* 6/11/52.
 28249 *(ex1063)* 23/10/54.

28225 *(ex61327)* 22/5/57.
28954 *(ex1185)* 8/1/60.
28189 *(ex1105)* 5/3/63.

SHEDS:
Doncaster.
Mexborough 6/3/49.
Doncaster 11/9/49.
Mexborough 20/11/49.
Canklow 9/12/62.
New England 10/11/63.
Colwick 3/1/65.

RENUMBERED:
61194 25/2/49.

CONDEMNED:
29/8/65.
*Made S.B.Dept'l No.28.
Sold 8/66 for scrap to
R.A.King, Norwich.*

1195

North British Loco. 26096

To traffic 24/5/47.

REPAIRS:
Gor. 17/10–15/12/48.**G.**
Gor. 15/10–2/12/50.**G.**
Gor. 6/12/50–16/1/51.**N/C.**
Don. 22–29/5/51.**N/C.**
Dar. 11/7–23/8/52.**G.**
Str. 12/2–26/3/54.**G.**
Don. 13/4–14/5/55.**C/L.**
Don. 9/3–14/4/56.**G.**
Dar. 16/1–14/2/58.**G.**
Don. 20/8–23/9/59.**G.**
Don. 19/9–1/10/60.**N/C.**
Don. 1–29/7/61.**G.**

BOILERS:
 9832.
 9711 *(ex1123)* 15/12/48.
 28800 *(new)* 2/12/50.
 28261 *(ex1151)* 23/8/52.
 28597 *(ex61399)* 26/3/54.
 28204 *(ex61408)* 14/4/56.
 28146 *(ex1115)* 14/2/58.
 28438 *(ex1174)* 23/9/59.
 28575 *(ex1056)* 29/7/61.

SHEDS:
Immingham.
Frodingham 9/5/65.

RENUMBERED:
61195 15/12/48.

CONDEMNED:
14/11/65.
*Sold 12/65 for scrap to
A.Draper, Hull.*

1196

North British Loco. 26097

To traffic 27/5/47.

REPAIRS:
Don. 13/7–19/8/49.**G.**

Don. 21/5–13/6/51.**G.**
Don. 3–5/7/51.**N/C.**
Don. 16/2–13/3/53.**G.**
Don. 26/2–19/3/54.**C/L.**
Don. 27/1–25/2/55.**G.**
Dar. 23/1–22/2/57.**G.**
Don. 7/5–6/6/59.**G.**
Don. 18/8–30/9/61.**G.**

BOILERS:
 9833.
 9844 *(ex1207)* 19/8/49.
 28144 *(ex1027)* 13/6/51.
 28241 *(ex61328)* 13/3/53.
 28282 *(ex1112)* 25/2/55.
 28443 *(ex1237)* 22/2/57.
 28818 *(ex1600)* 6/6/59.
 28135 *(ex1127)* 30/9/61.

SHED:
Doncaster.

RENUMBERED:
61196 19/8/49.

CONDEMNED:
4/7/64 but returned to stock
21/7/64 until 26/9/65.
*Sold 11/65 for scrap to
T.W.Ward, Beighton.*

1197

North British Loco. 26098

To traffic 29/5/47.

REPAIRS:
Cow. 18/10–25/11/48.**G.**
Cow. 5–26/5/50.**L/I.**
Cow. 28/4–24/5/52.**G.**
Cow. 4–22/8/52.**C/L.**
Cow. 1–27/3/54.**H/I.**
Cow. 23–26/8/54.**N/C.**
Cow. 1–6/11/54.**C/L.**
Cow. 5–8/10/55.**N/C.**
Cow. 23/11–17/12/55.**L/I.**
Cow. 21–24/12/55.**N/C.**
Cow. 27/2–3/3/56.**N/C.**
Cow. 19–29/9/56.**N/C.**
Cow. 26/2–30/3/57.**G.**
Cow. 2/7/58.**N/C.**
Cow. 25/2–18/3/59.**L/I.**
Mod.bogie springs.
Cow. 19–20/5/59.**C/L.**
A.T.C. fitted.
Cow. 3–9/9/59.**C/L.**
Cow. 7–12/3/60.**N/C.**
Cow. 13/6–8/7/61.**G.**
Cow. 31/7–2/8/63.**C/L.**

BOILERS:
 9834.
 28612 *(ex1116)* 24/5/52.
 28631 *(ex1117)* 30/3/57.
 28703 *(ex61343)* 8/7/61.

SHEDS:
Eastfield.
Corkerhill 31/12/62.
Ayr 11/3/63.

RENUMBERED:
61197 25/11/48.

CONDEMNED:
8/6/64.
*Sold 8/64 for scrap to
Motherwell Machinery &
Scrap Co., Wishaw.*

1198

North British Loco. 26099

To traffic 2/6/47.

REPAIRS:
Ghd. 12–24/2/49.**L/I.**
Dar. 3/11–1/12/49.**G.**
Dar. 16/9–7/10/50.**C/L.**
Dar. 24/10–17/11/51.**G.**
Dar. 30/10–21/11/53.**G.**
Dar. 23–25/11/53.**N/C.**
Dar. 24/5–16/6/54.**C/H.**
Dar. 2–12/1/56.**C/L.**
Dar. 9/4–7/5/56.**G.**
Dar. 17/6–2/7/57.**C/L.**
Dar. 10/11–10/12/58.**G.**
A.T.C.Mech.fitted.
Dar. 10–22/6/59.**N/C.**
A.T.C.Elec.fitted.
Dar. 31/7–26/8/61.**G.**
Dar. 12/8–25/9/63.**C/L.**

BOILERS:
9835.
3702 *(ex1071)* 1/12/49.
Renumbered 28700 7/10/50.
28817 *(new)* 17/11/51.
28814 *(ex1111)* 21/11/53.
28537 *(ex1056)* 16/6/54.
28243 *(ex61368)* 7/5/56.
28535 *(ex1039)* 10/12/58.
28411 *(ex1206)* 26/8/61.

SHEDS:
Tweedmouth.
Borough Gardens 26/12/48.
Darlington 6/2/49.
Low Moor 14/6/59.
York 30/8/59.

RENUMBERED:
61198 6/10/48.

CONDEMNED:
5/4/65.
*Sold 5/65 for scrap to
A.Draper, Hull.*

1199

North British Loco. 26100

To traffic 4/6/47.

REPAIRS:
Ghd. 14/4–14/5/48.**L.**
Dar. 19/4–14/5/49.**G.**
Dar. 1–29/3/51.**G.**
Dar. 4–12/5/51.**N/C.**
Dar. 22–30/8/51.**C/L.**
Dar. 25–28/2/52.**C/L.**
Dar. 10–19/7/52.**C/L.**
Dar. 2–28/3/53.**G.**
Dar. 17–26/3/54.**C/L.**
Ghd. 2–14/9/54.**C/L.**

Dar. 31/1–26/2/55.**G.**
Dar. 4/12/56–1/1/57.**G.**
Dar. 14/5–17/6/59.**G.**
Complete A.T.C.fitted.
Dar. 9/4–11/5/62.**G.**
Dar. 22–25/5/62.**N/C.**
Dar. 15/11–5/12/62.**C/L.**
Dar. 20/3–21/4/64.**C/L.**

BOILERS:
9836.
9772 *(ex1186)* 14/5/49.
28603 *(ex1067)* 29/3/51.
28106 *(ex61309)* 28/3/53.
28229 *(ex1224)* 26/2/55.
28142 *(ex1182)* 1/1/57.
28228 *(ex1291)* 17/6/59.
28342 *(ex1039)* 11/5/62.

SHEDS:
Tweedmouth.
Gateshead 1/7/51.
Tweedmouth 25/9/55.
Blaydon 12/6/60.
Tyne Dock 16/6/63.
York 3/10/65.

RENUMBERED:
61199 11/5/48.

CONDEMNED:
5/1/67.
*Sold 3/67 for scrap to
A.Draper, Hull.*

1200

North British Loco. 26101

To traffic 6/6/47.

REPAIRS:
Don. 15/6–21/7/49.**G.**
Don. 21/3–18/4/51.**G.**
Don. 1/1–6/2/53.**G.**
Str. 5–15/4/54.**C/L.**
Don. 21/12/54–25/1/55.**G.**
Don. 2–12/5/55.**N/C.**
Don. 13/8–22/9/56.**G.**
Don. 9/6–19/7/58.**G.**
Don. 13/6–20/7/60.**G.**

BOILERS:
9837.
9828 *(ex1191)* 21/7/49.
28137 *(ex1167)* 18/4/51.
28124 *(ex1166)* 6/2/53.
28859 *(ex61325)* 25/1/55.
28109 *(ex1120)* 22/9/56.
28112 *(ex61366)* 19/7/58.
28100 *(ex1286)* 20/7/60.

SHEDS:
Kings Cross.
New England 19/4/59.
Kings Cross 27/3/60.

RENUMBERED:
61200 21/7/49.

CONDEMNED:
29/12/62.
*Sold 2/63 for scrap to
J.Cashmore, Great Bridge.*

1201

North British Loco. 26102

To traffic 10/6/47.

REPAIRS:
Don. 20/6–29/7/49.**G.**
Str. 17/1–3/3/51.**G.**
Str. 23/9–8/11/52.**G.**
Gor. 21/11/53.**C/L.**
Gor. 31/7–11/9/54.**G.**
Dar. 29/12/56–30/1/57.**G.**
Don. 2/6–3/7/58.**C/H.**
Dar. 2–26/2/59.**G.**
Dar. 18/11/59–26/1/60.**C/H.**

BOILERS:
9838.
9694 *(ex1105)* 29/7/49.
28534 *(ex1177)* 3/3/51.
28586 *(ex61336)* 8/11/52.
28585 *(ex1121)* 11/9/54.
28270 *(ex1078)* 30/1/57.
28576 *(ex1273)* 26/2/59.

SHEDS:
Doncaster.
Ipswich 30/4/50.
Colwick 20/9/53.
Leicester 19/12/54.
Colwick 20/2/56.·
Leicester 26/10/58.
Agecroft 29/8/59.

RENUMBERED:
61201 29/7/49.

CONDEMNED:
1/1/62.
*30/1/62 In for cut up at
Darlington.*

1202

North British Loco. 26103.

To traffic 12/6/47.

REPAIRS:
Gor. 6/2–12/3/49.**G.**
Gor. 7/10–23/12/50.**G.**
Gor. 28/12–4/1/51.**N/C.**
Gor. 13–29/9/51.**C/L.**
Gor. 2–6/10/51.**N/C.**
Don. 12/9–10/10/52.**G.**
Dar. 8/8–25/9/54.**G.**
Don. 26/10–30/11/56.**G.**
Don. 21–29/8/57.**N/C.**
Don. 22–30/4/58.**C/L.**
Str. 9/3–1/5/59.**G.**
Don. 6–16/10/59.**N/C.**
Don. 23/8–2/9/60.**N/C.**
Don. 25/3–12/4/61.**N/C.**

BOILERS:
9839.
3733 *(ex1018)* 12/3/49.
28279 *(ex1162)* 23/12/50.
28117 *(ex1091)* 10/10/52.
28450 *(ex1014)* 25/9/54.
28285 *(ex61405)* 30/11/56.
28101 *(ex61375)* 1/5/59.

SHEDS:
Immingham.
Lincoln 29/3/53.

RENUMBERED:
61202 12/3/49.

CONDEMNED:
16/9/62.
*Sold 1/63 for scrap to Cox
& Danks, Wadsley Bridge.*

1203

North British Loco. 26104.

To traffic 17/6/47.

REPAIRS:
Don. 1/5–3/6/49.**G.**
Don. 12/2–6/3/51.**G.**
Don. 19/11–12/12/52.**G.**
Don. 31/3–2/4/53.**N/C.**
Don. 24–27/8/53.**N/C.**
Don. 2–26/11/54.**G.**
Don. 24/4–25/5/56.**G.**
Str. 5/5–28/6/58.**G.**
Mod.bogie springs.
Don. 27/2–26/3/60.**G.**
Don. 18/7/62.*Not repaired.*

BOILERS:
9840.
9848 *(ex1211)* 3/6/49.
28131 *(ex1143)* 6/3/51.
28751 *(ex61371)* 12/12/52.
28327 *(ex1602)* 25/5/56.
28554 *(ex1006)* 28/6/58.
28320 *(ex1636)* 26/3/60.

SHEDS:
Kings Cross.
Cambridge 20/10/57.
March 11/9/60.

RENUMBERED:
61203 3/6/49.

CONDEMNED:
23/7/62.
Cut up Doncaster.

1204

North British Loco. 26105.

To traffic 19/6/47.

REPAIRS:
Gor. 10/7–28/8/48.**G.**
Gor. 17/9–29/10/49.**G.**
Gor. 12/8–13/10/51.**G.**
Gor. 16–23/10/51.**N/C.**
Don. 5/11–3/12/52.**G.**
Don. 23/2–23/3/54.**C/H.**
Don. 7/2–8/3/55.**G.**
Don. 19/8–24/9/57.**G.**
Str. 1/6–15/8/59.**G.**
Mod.bogie springs.
Complete A.T.C. fitted.
Don. 10/7–5/8/61.**G.**

BOILERS:
9841.
9699 (ex1111) 28/8/48.
9770 (ex1184) 29/10/49.
28352 (ex1111) 13/10/51.
28122 (ex1094) 3/12/52.
28758 (ex61393) 23/3/54.
28241 (ex1196) 8/3/55.
28178 (ex1159) 24/9/57.
28610 (ex61348) 15/8/59.
28438 (ex1195) 5/8/61.

SHEDS:
Immingham.
New England 20/9/53.
Peterborough 16/6/57.
March 31/1/60.

RENUMBERED:
61204 28/8/48.

CONDEMNED:
25/11/63.
Made S.B.Dept'l No.19.
Sold 3/66 for scrap to
R.A.King, Norwich.

1205

North British Loco. 26106.

To traffic 24/6/47.

REPAIRS:
Don. 28/3–28/4/49.G.
Str. 26/11/50–6/1/51.G.
Str. 24/6–16/8/52.G.
Don. 25/1–10/2/54.C/L.
Don. 12/10–12/11/54.G.
Don. 27/11/56–3/1/57.G.
Str. 9/2–20/3/59.G.
Mod.bogie springs.
Complete A.T.C.fitted.
Don. 5–10/8/60.N/C.
Don. 8/4–13/5/61.G.
Don. 18/7–3/8/61.C/L.

BOILERS:
9842.
3741 (ex1028) 28/4/49.
28520 (ex1603) 6/1/51.
28561 (ex1000) 16/8/52.
28156 (ex3924) 12/11/54.
28526 (ex61364) 3/1/57.
28292 (ex1058) 20/3/59.
28129 (ex3949) 13/5/61.

SHEDS:
Grantham.
Stratford 18/12/49.
New England 20/9/53.
Peterborough 16/6/57.
March 31/1/60.
Norwich 3/12/61.
March 4/2/62.

RENUMBERED:
61205 28/4/49.

CONDEMNED:
25/11/63.
Made S.B.Dept'l No.20.
Sold 2/65 for scrap to
R.A.King, Norwich.

1206

North British Loco. 26107.

To traffic 3/7/47.

REPAIRS:
Don. 8/10–10/11/49.G.
Don. 9/12/51–14/1/52.G.
Don. 18/8–2/9/52.N/C.
Str. 10/11–18/12/53.G.
Don. 23/11–22/12/55.G.
Dar. 16/8–12/9/57.G.
Dar. 13/4–8/5/59.G.
Dar. 15/5–13/6/61.G.
Dar. 14/8/62.Not repaired.

BOILERS:
9843.
9867 (ex1230) 10/11/49.
28166 (ex1073) 14/1/52.
28596 (ex3867) 18/12/53.
28294 (ex1608) 22/12/55.
28154 (ex1021) 12/9/57.
28411 (ex1214) 8/5/59.
28279 (ex1106) 13/6/61.

SHEDS:
New England.
Cambridge 5/2/50.
Ipswich 26/3/50.
New England 7/5/50.
Kings Cross 28/12/52.
Neasden 5/7/53.
Leicester 13/11/61.
Woodford 17/3/62.

RENUMBERED:
61206 10/11/49.

CONDEMNED:
3/9/62.
Cut up Darlington.

1207

North British Loco. 26108.

To traffic 27/6/47.

REPAIRS:
Don. 5/7–10/8/49.G.
Don. 9/5–7/6/51.G.
Don. 19/5–17/6/53.G.
Don. 23/2–18/3/55.G.
Don. 19/9–5/10/55.C/L.
Don. 2/5–6/6/57.G.
Don. 7–9/6/57.N/C.
Don. 11/6–17/7/59.G.
Don. 27/9–1/11/61.G.

BOILERS:
9844.
9837 (ex1200) 10/8/49.
28143 (ex1099) 7/6/51.
28532 (ex1177) 17/6/53.
28758 (ex1204) 18/3/55.
28507 (ex61378) 6/6/57.
28866 (ex1098) 17/7/59.
28138 (ex1299) 1/11/61.

SHED:
New England.

RENUMBERED:
61207 10/8/49.

CONDEMNED:
28/12/63.
28/2/64 In for cut up at
Doncaster.

1208

North British Loco. 26109.

To traffic 8/7/47.

REPAIRS:
Don. 2–31/10/49.G.
Don. 2–28/12/51.G.
Str. 2/3–10/4/54.G.
Don. 13/4–16/5/56.G.
Don. 29/8–10/10/58.G.
Don. 11–20/7/60.N/C.
Don. 6/7–2/8/61.G.

BOILERS:
9845.
9756 (ex1170) 31/10/49.
28164 (ex1213) 28/12/51.
28822 (ex1116) 10/4/54.
28370 (ex1666) 16/5/56.
28953 (new) 10/10/58.
28506 (ex1177) 2/8/61.

SHEDS:
Retford.
Doncaster 13/6/65.

RENUMBERED:
61208 31/10/49.

CONDEMNED:
26/9/65.
Sold 11/65 for scrap to
T.W.Ward, Beighton.

1209

North British Loco. 26110.

To traffic 1/7/47.

REPAIRS:
Gor. 18/7–27/8/49.G.
Gor. 12/6–4/8/51.G.
Gor. 9–11/8/51.N/C.
Dar. 24/8–19/9/52.C/L.
Gor. 9/9–22/10/53.G.
Gor. 27/10–26/11/53.N/C.
Gor. 27/10–4/12/54.C/L.
Gor. 7–11/12/54.N/C.
Dar. 7/7–13/8/55.G.
Dar. 7/11–5/12/57.G.
Don. 7–18/6/58.N/C.
Don. 10/10–14/11/59.G.
Don. 26/2–4/3/60.N/C.
Don. 22/10–12/11/60.N/C.

BOILERS:
9846.
9746 (ex1160) 27/8/49.
28334 (ex1183) 4/8/51.
28317 (ex3785) 22/10/53.
28232 (ex1185) 13/8/55.
28140 (ex1247) 5/12/57.

28291 (ex1281) 14/11/59.

SHEDS:
New England.
Colwick 12/2/48.
Annesley 21/3/48.
Colwick 14/10/56.

RENUMBERED:
61209 27/8/49.

CONDEMNED:
16/9/62.
Sold 2/63 for scrap to Albert
Looms, Spondon.

1210

North British Loco. 26111.

To traffic 3/7/47.

REPAIRS:
Don. 7/8–16/9/49.G.
Don. 12/8–6/9/51.G.
Don. 2–4/12/52.N/C.
Don. 26/10–20/11/53.G.
Don. 22/8–30/9/55.G.
Dar. 24/1–15/2/58.G.
Don. 5–19/8/59.N/C.
Don. 29/1–8/3/60.G.
Don. 17/10–23/11/62.G.

BOILERS:
9847.
9884 (ex1247) 16/9/49.
28148 (ex1247) 6/9/51.
28834 (ex1130) 20/11/53.
28221 (ex1251) 15/2/58.
28306 (ex1612) 8/3/60.
28532 (ex61392) 23/11/62.

SHEDS:
New England.
March 27/4/52.
New England 8/6/52.
Kings Cross 14/12/52.
New England 8/3/53.
Colwick 22/9/63.
Doncaster 28/11/65.

RENUMBERED:
61210 16/9/49.

CONDEMNED:
10/2/66.
Sold 3/66 for scrap to
A.Draper, Hull.

1211

North British Loco. 26112.

To traffic 14/7/47.

REPAIRS:
Don. 24/4–25/5/49.G.
Don. 24/9–18/10/51.G.
Don. 14/1–12/2/54.G.
Don. 19–28/4/55.N/C.
Don. 5/1–9/2/56.G.
Don. 23/4–28/5/58.G.
Don. 27/7–8/8/59.N/C.

Don. 4/4–10/5/61.**G.**
Don. 5/11/62.*Not repaired.*

BOILERS:
  9848.
  3747 *(ex1027)* 25/5/49.
28153 *(ex1210)* 18/10/51.
28821 *(ex1663)* 12/2/54.
28814 *(ex1079)* 9/2/56.
28347 *(ex1656)* 28/5/58.
28803 *(ex1073)* 10/5/61.

SHED:
Retford.

RENUMBERED:
61211 25/5/49.

CONDEMNED:
5/11/62.
Cut up Doncaster.

1212

North British Loco. 26113.

To traffic 8/7/47.

REPAIRS:
Don. 12/5–10/6/49.**G.**
Don. 7/6–10/7/50.**C/L.**
Don. 21/10–13/11/51.**G.**
Str. 24/3–14/5/54.**G.**
Don. 24/5–22/6/56.**G.**
Don. 26/11/58–3/1/59.**G.**
Don. 11–14/7/60.**N/C.**
Don. 21/9–21/10/61.**G.**

BOILERS:
  9849.
  9840 *(ex1203)* 10/6/49.
28157 *(ex1246)* 13/11/51.
28584 *(ex1089)* 14/5/54.
28817 *(ex1087)* 22/6/56.
28585 *(ex1177)* 3/1/59.
28539 *(ex1232)* 21/10/61.

SHED:
Retford.

RENUMBERED:
61212 10/6/49.

CONDEMNED:
1/11/64.
*Sold 1/65 for scrap to
A.Draper, Hull.*

1213

North British Loco. 26114.

To traffic 10/7/47.

REPAIRS:
Don. 15/8–21/9/49.**G.**
Don. 12/11–7/12/51.**G.**
Don. 15/12/53–6/1/54.**G.**
Don. 5/12/55–7/1/56.**G.**

Don. 19/2–21/3/58.**G.**
Don. 2–29/11/60.**G.**

BOILERS:
  9850.
  5124 *(ex1057)* 21/9/49.
28159 *(ex1212)* 7/12/51.
28221 *(ex1176)* 6/1/54.
28591 *(ex1044)* 7/1/56.
28755 *(ex1139)* 21/3/58.
28537 *(ex61371)* 29/11/60.

SHEDS:
Retford.
Doncaster 9/11/58.
Retford 22/11/59.

RENUMBERED:
61213 21/9/49.

CONDEMNED:
19/4/64.
*Sold 6/64 for scrap to
G.Haslewood, Attercliffe.*

1214

North British Loco. 26115.

To traffic 16/7/47.

REPAIRS:
Dar. 30/1–11/4/50.**G.**
Dar. 15/1–8/2/52.**G.**
Dar. 19/1–12/2/54.**G.**
Dar. 23–25/2/54.**N/C.**
Dar. 19/1–15/2/56.**G.**
Dar. 8/1–1/2/58.**G.**
Dar. 3–4/2/58.**N/C.**
Dar. 7–14/8/58.**C/L.**
Dar. 13/5–2/7/60.**G.**
A.T.C. elec.fitted.
Dar. 11/9–9/10/64.**C/L.**

BOILERS:
  9851.
  9975 *(ex61338)* 11/4/50.
28400 *(ex61367)* 8/2/52.
28244 *(ex1030)* 12/2/54.
28411 *(ex61316)* 15/2/56.
28211 *(ex1092)* 1/2/58.
28266 *(ex1229)* 2/7/60.

SHEDS:
Stockton.
Copley Hill 23/9/56.
Mirfield 8/9/63.
Low Moor 12/4/64.

RENUMBERED:
61214 11/4/50.

CONDEMNED:
3/5/65.
*Sold 6/65 for scrap to
Arnott Young, Dinsdale.*

1215

North British Loco. 26116.

To traffic 19/7/47.

Named **WILLIAM
HENTON CARVER** *in
12/47.*

REPAIRS:
Dar. 1–30/4/49.**G.**
Dar. 4–11/5/49.**N/C.**
Ghd. 28/3–25/4/50.**L/I.**
Ghd. 1–4/5/50.**N/C.**
Dar. 2/7–10/8/51.**G.**
Dar. 30/10–3/11/51.**C/L.**
Dar. 9/2–7/3/53.**G.**
Dar. 23/11–22/12/54.**G.**
Dar. 15/6–12/7/56.**G.**
Dar. 22–31/10/56.**N/C.**
Dar. 26/3–10/4/57.**C/L.**
Dar. 7–17/6/57.**C/L.**
Dar. 1/4–1/5/58.**G.**
Dar. 5–16/1/59.**C/L.**
Dar. 2–22/10/59.**C/L.**
Dar. 6/12/60–20/1/61.**G.**
A.W.S. fitted.

BOILERS:
  9852.
  3770 *(ex1023)* 30/4/49.
28223 *(ex61321)* 10/8/51.
28641 *(ex1035)* 7/3/53.
28453 *(ex1016)* 22/12/54.
28400 *(ex1037)* 12/7/56.
28318 *(ex61380)* 1/5/58.
28264 *(ex1030)* 20/1/61.

SHEDS:
Hull Botanic Gardens.
Hull Dairycoates 14/6/59.
Ardsley 25/11/62.

RENUMBERED:
61215 30/4/49.

CONDEMNED:
8/3/65.
*Sold 4/65 for scrap to
A.Draper, Hull.*

1216

North British Loco. 26117.

To traffic 15/7/47.

REPAIRS:
Dar. 18/2–19/3/49.**G.**
Dar. 11/7–19/8/50.**G.**
Dar. 21–22/8/50.**N/C.**
Dar. 28–31/8/50.**N/C.**
Dar. 7/4–3/5/52.**G.**
Dar. 3–26/9/53.**G.**
Dar. 8–14/10/53.**N/C.**
Dar. 27/3–3/4/54.**N/C.** *After
collision.*
Dar. 22/2–19/3/55.**G.**
Dar. 21–22/3/55.**N/C.**

Dar. 25/3–27/4/55.**N/C.**
Dar. 5/12/56–2/1/57.**H/I.**
Dar. 3–16/5/57.**C/L.**
Dar. 1/8–5/9/58.**G.** *A.T.C.
mech fitted.*
Dar. 10–16/9/58.**N/C.**
Dar. 3–14/10/58.**N/C.**
Dar. 9–19/6/59.**N/C.**
A.T.C. elec.fitted.
Dar. 24/11–8/12/59.**N/C.**
Dar. 18/10–15/12/61.**G.**

BOILERS:
  9853.
  9893 *(ex1256)* 19/3/49.
  9940 *(ex1303)* 19/8/50.
28418 *(ex1063)* 3/5/52.
28416 *(ex1237)* 26/9/53.
28293 *(ex1088)* 19/3/55.
28258 *(ex1044)* 5/9/58.
28545 *(ex1259)* 15/12/61.

SHEDS:
York.
Neville Hill 23/5/48.
Blaydon 15/1/61.
Heaton 9/9/62.
York 3/10/65.

RENUMBERED:
61216 19/3/49.

CONDEMNED:
23/1/67.
*Sold 3/67 for scrap to
T.W.Ward, Killamarsh.*

1217

North British Loco. 26118.

To traffic 11/8/47.

REPAIRS:
Cow. 29/9–28/10/48.**G.**
Cow. 3/11–1/12/50.**L/I.**
Cow. 30/11–25/12/51.**H/I.**
Cow. 1–26/11/53.**G.**
Cow. 11/4–5/5/55.**L/I.**
Cow. 8/11–14/12/56.**L/I.**
Cow. 1–31/12/58.**G.**

BOILERS:
  9854.
  3726 *(new)* 28/10/48.
  3726 renumbered 28640
25/12/51.
28650 *(ex61345)* 26/11/53.
28660 *(ex1178)* 31/12/58.

SHED:
Carlisle Canal.

RENUMBERED:
61217 19/9/48.

CONDEMNED:
21/3/62.
*5/62 In for cut up at
Cowlairs.*

WORKS CODES:- Cow – Cowlairs. Dar – Darlington. Dee – Dundee. Don – Doncaster. Ghd – Gateshead. Gor – Gorton. Inv – Inverurie. Str – Stratford. SRX – St Rollox.

REPAIR CODES:- **C/H** – Casual Heavy. **C/L** – Casual Light. **G** – General. **H** – Heavy. **H/I** – Heavy Intermediate. **L** – Light. **L/I** – Light Intermediate. **N/C** – Non–Classified.

1218

North British Loco. 26119.

To traffic 1/8/47.

REPAIRS:
Gor. 16/10–20/11/48.**G.**
Dar. 5/5–1/6/50.**G.**
Dar. 14/8–8/9/51.**G.**
Dar. 15/11–3/12/51.**C/L.**
Dar. 13/3–11/4/53.**G.**
Dar. 13–27/4/53.**N/C.**
Dar. 17–28/12/53.**N/C.**
Dar. 29/7–11/9/54.**G.**
Dar. 13–14/9/54.**N/C.**
Dar. 18/1–14/2/56.**G.**
Dar. 11/9–10/10/57.**G.**
Dar. 19/12/57–5/2/58.**N/C.**
Dar. 17/6–6/8/59.**G.**
Dar. 16/10–17/11/61.**H/I.**

BOILERS:
9855.
9913 *(ex1276)* 1/6/50.
28227 *(ex1215)* 8/9/51.
28224 *(ex61338)* 11/4/53.
28178 *(ex1267)* 11/9/54.
28259 *(ex1254)* 14/2/56.
28555 *(ex1050)* 10/10/57.
28209 *(ex61338)* 6/8/59.

SHEDS:
Neville Hill.
Thornaby 5/2/61.
Ardsley 25/11/62.

RENUMBERED:
61218 16/11/48.

CONDEMNED:
3/7/65.
Sold 8/65 for scrap to Ellis Metals, Swalwell.

1219

North British Loco. 26120.

To traffic 9/8/47.

REPAIRS:
Cow. 3/12/48–11/1/49.**G.**
Cow. 9/1–1/2/51.**H/I.**
Cow. 10/6–4/7/52.**G.**
Cow. 4/5–5/6/54.**H/I.**
Cow. 4/5–4/6/55.**H/I.**
W.P.U. gear removed.
Cow. 22–25/6/55.**N/C.**
Cow. 12/4–15/5/56.**N/C.**
Cow. 14/6–11/8/56.**G.**
Cow. 9/10–2/11/57.**J/I.**
Cow. 14/5–4/6/59.**N/C.**
Mod. bogie springs. A.W.S. fitted.
Cow. 8/8–12/9/59.**L/I.**
Cow. 2–6/10/59.**N/C.**
Cow. 23/3–23/4/60.**C/L.**
Cow. 4–18/5/61.**C/L.**
Cow. 8–27/1/62.**G.**

BOILERS:
9856.
9733 *(ex1147)* 11/1/49.

9733 renumbered 28618 1/2/51.
28610 *(ex1103)* 4/7/52.
28705 *(ex61397)* 11/8/56.
28823 *(ex61351)* 27/1/62.

SHEDS:
Carlisle Canal.
Southern Region 20/5/53.
Carlisle Canal 21/6/53.
Haymarket 9/12/57.
St Margarets 23/9/62.

RENUMBERED:
61219 19/9/48.

CONDEMNED:
8/6/64.
Sold 8/64 for scrap to P&W.McLellan, Langloan.

1220

North British Loco. 26121.

To traffic 6/8/47.

REPAIRS:
Dar. 8/6–1/7/50.**G.**
Dar. 1/5–1/6/51.**C/L.** *After collision.*
Dar. 3–21/6/52.**G.**
Dar. 5–31/12/52.**C/L.**
Dar. 3–27/11/54.**G.**
Dar. 29–30/11/54.**N/C.**
Dar. 18/3–15/4/55.**C/L.** *After collision.*
Dar. 21/12/56–18/1/57.**G.**
Dar. 31/10–2/12/58.**G.** *A.T.C. mech fitted.*
Dar. 22/6–2/7/59.**N/C.** *A.T.C. elec.fitted.*
Dar. 28/4–21/5/60.**C/L.**
Dar. 13/10–16/11/61.**H/I.**

BOILERS:
9857.
9875 *(ex1259)* 1/7/50.
28441 *(ex61364)* 21/6/52.
28562 *(ex1272)* 27/11/54.
28139 *(ex61305)* 18/1/57.
28208 *(ex1271)* 2/12/58.

SHEDS:
Stockton.
Thornaby 14/6/59.
West Hartlepool 24/3/63.

RENUMBERED:
61220 1/7/50.

CONDEMNED:
4/10/65.
Sold 11/65 for scrap to Hughes, Bolckow, North Blyth.

1221

North British Loco. 26122.

To traffic 16/8/47.

Named ***SIR ALEXANDER ERSKINE–HILL*** *in 12/47.*

REPAIRS:
Cow. 23/6–9/7/49.**L/I.**
Cow. 11/8–10/9/51.**G.**
Cow. 12/9–4/10/52.**L/I.**
Cow. 4–21/11/53.**C/L.**
Hay. 22–24/2/54.**C/L.**
Cow. 11–26/8/54.**N/C.**
Cow. 25/9–30/10/54.**H/I.**
Cow. 27/1–3/3/56.**G.**
Cow. 18/2–16/3/57.**H/I.**
Cow. 22–30/11/57.**C/L.**
Cow. 1–29/5/59.**G.** *Mod. bogie springs. A.W.S. fitted.*
Cow. 25/1–4/3/61.**H/I.**
Cow. 13–23/6/61.**N/C.**
Cow. 15/1–16/2/63.**H/I.**

BOILERS:
9858.
28628 *(ex1242)* 10/9/51.
28607 *(ex1076)* 3/3/56.
28653 *(ex61355)* 29/5/59.

SHEDS:
Carlisle Canal.
Haymarket 10/10/47.
Dalry Road 9/9/63.
St Margarets 18/11/63.
Thornton Junction 20/1/64.
Dundee 10/1/65.

RENUMBERED:
61221 9/7/49.

CONDEMNED:
27/3/65.
Sold 5/65 for scrap to Shipbreaking Industries, Faslane.

1222

North British Loco. 26123

To traffic 11/8/47.

REPAIRS:
Cow. 21/9–28/10/48.**G.**
Cow. 19/12/50–6/1/51.**L/I.**
Cow. 17/8–13/9/52.**G.**
Cow. 22/3–20/4/54.**H/I.**
Cow. 12/9–17/10/55.**L/I.**
Cow. 28/6–14/8/57.**G.**
Cow. 27/4–29/5/59.**L/I.**

BOILERS:
9859.
28618 *(ex1219)* 13/9/52.
28704 *(ex61396)* 14/8/57.

SHED:
Carlisle Canal.

RENUMBERED:
61222 19/9/48.

CONDEMNED:
18/1/62.
1/62 In for cut up at Cowlairs.

1223

North British Loco.26124.

To traffic 24/8/47.

REPAIRS:
Gor. 21/11–31/12/49.**G.**
Gor. 5–7/1/50.**N/C.**
Gor. 21–22/2/51.**N/C.**
Dar. 11/2–15/3/52.**G.**
Gor. 2–30/5/53.**G.**
Str. 24/1–18/3/55.**G.**
Str. 30/4–19/6/56.**C/L.**
Str. 18/3–17/4/57.**G.**
Str. 23/9–16/10/57.**N/C.**
Str. 2/2–20/3/59.**G.** *Mod. bogie springs. A.T.C. fitted.*
Str. 6–18/4/59.**N/C.**
Don. 3–5/8/60.**N/C.**
Don. 23/1–3/2/61.**N/C.**
Don. 3–27/1/62.**G.**

BOILERS:
9860.
9906 *(ex1269)* 31/12/49.
28410 *(ex61366)* 15/3/52.
28810 *(ex1188)* 30/5/53.
28527 *(ex1287)* 17/4/57.
28145 *(ex1233)* 20/3/59.
28312 *(ex61389)* 27/1/62.

SHEDS:
Leicester.
Gorton 2/11/47.
Newton Heath 2/7/50.
Gorton 11/8/50.
Cambridge 20/6/54.
Norwich 24/6/57.
Yarmouth 8/12/57.
Norwich 14/9/58.
Lowestoft 3/5/59.
Lincoln 28/2/60.
Immingham 20/3/60.
Lincoln 27/3/60.
Immingham 22/9/63.

RENUMBERED:
61223 31/12/49.

CONDEMNED:
2/1/66.
Sold 2/66 for scrap to Garnham,Harris & Elton, Chesterfield.

1224

North British Loco. 26125.

To traffic 15/8/47.

REPAIRS:
Dar. 26/4–20/5/49.**G.**
Dar. 17/5–9/6/51.**G.**
Dar. 11–12/6/51.**N/C.**
Don. 23–29/1/53.**N/C.**
Don. 29–31/1/53.**N/C.**
Dar. 26/5–20/6/53.**G.**
Dar. 22–23/6/53.**N/C.**
Dar. 29–30/6/53.**N/C.**
Dar. 31/12/54–29/1/55.**G.**
Dar. 19/11–12/12/56.**G.**

Dar. 16/4–30/5/58.**C/L.**
After collision.
Dar. 11/5–10/6/59.**G.**
Complete A.T.C. fitted.
Dar. 17–25/6/59.**N/C.**
Dar. 15/12/61–13/1/62.**G.**
Dar. 13/3–15/4/64.**C/L.**

BOILERS:
9861.
9894 *(ex1257)* 20/5/49.
28215 *(ex1035)* 9/6/51.
28229 *(ex1238)* 20/6/53.
28858 *(ex61328)* 29/1/55.
28456 *(ex1068)* 12/12/56.
28868 *(ex1167)* 10/6/59.
28453 *(ex61320)* 13/1/62.

SHEDS:
Heaton.
Darlington 7/11/48.
York 19/7/53.
Darlington 25/9/55.
Neville Hill 16/6/63.
Wakefield 7/6/64.

RENUMBERED:
61224 20/5/49.

CONDEMNED:
31/7/66.
*Sold 9/66 for scrap to
G.Hazlewood, Attercliffe.*

1225

North British Loco. 26126.

To traffic 28/8/47.

REPAIRS:
Gor. 5/9–1/10/49.**G.**
Gor. 14–15/2/51.**C/L.**
Gor. 16–19/4/51.**N/C.**
Gor. 7/8–29/9/51.**G.**
Gor. 2–6/10/51.**N/C.**
Dar. 1/4–2/5/53.**G.**
Dar. 4–7/5/53.**N/C.**
Dar. 5/2–2/3/55.**G.**
Dar. 20/2–20/3/57.**G.**
Don. 21/10–19/11/59.**G.**
Don. 21–22/11/60.**N/C.**
Don. 23/10–28/11/62.**G.**
Dar. 10–18/2/64.**N/C.**

BOILERS:
9862.
9920 *(ex1283)* 1/10/49.
28346 *(ex61406)* 29/9/51.
28308 *(ex1158)* 2/5/53.
28843 *(ex61381)* 2/3/55.
28176 *(ex61374)* 20/3/57.
28845 *(ex1661)* 19/11/59.
28410 *(ex1091)* 28/11/62.

SHEDS:
Leicester.
Gorton 2/11/47.
London Mid.Reg. 29/5/49.
Gorton 5/6/49.
Sheffield 29/6/52.
Doncaster 23/10/55.
Retford 17/1/60.
Doncaster 10/1/65.

RENUMBERED:
61225 1/10/49.

CONDEMNED:
20/6/65.
*Sold 8/65 for scrap to
T.W.Ward, Beighton.*

1226

North British Loco. 26127.

To traffic 21/8/47.

REPAIRS:
Str. 4/3–27/4/49.**G.**
Str. 16–26/11/49.**N/C.**
Str. 4/3–19/4/51.**G.**
Str. 3/6–25/7/53.**G.** *Mod.
bogie springs.*
Str. 14/9–1/10/55.**N/C.**
After collision.
Don. 12/1–17/2/56.**G.**
Str. 11–14/6/57.**N/C.**
Str. 31/3–30/5/58.**G.**
Str. 19–25/6/58.**N/C.**
Str. 3/3–6/5/60.**G.** *Part
A.T.C. fitted.*
Don. 21–23/9/60.**N/C.**

BOILERS:
9863.
9922 *(ex1285)* 27/4/49.
28545 *(ex1302)* 19/4/51.
28548 *(ex1047)* 25/7/53.
28821 *(ex1211)* 17/2/56.
28213 *(ex1111)* 30/5/58.
28269 *(ex1248)* 6/5/60.

SHEDS:
Stratford.
Parkeston 18/1/48.
March 8/10/50.
Parkeston 10/12/50.
Stratford 1/1/61.

RENUMBERED:
61226 27/4/49.

CONDEMNED:
16/9/62.
*22/11/62 In for cut up at
Doncaster.*

1227

North British Loco. 26128.

To traffic 21/8/47.

REPAIRS:
Gor. 9/1–18/2/50.**G.**
Gor. 23–24/2/50.**N/C.**
Gor. 14–15/3/50.**N/C.**
Str. 16/9–2/11/51.**G.**
Str. 14/8–19/9/53.**G.**
Str. 16/1–17/2/56.**G.**
Str. 3–4/10/57.**N/C.**
Str. 24/3–16/4/58.**C/L.**
Str. 25/9–7/11/58.**G.** *Mod.
bogie springs.*
Don. 15/3–20/4/61.**G.**
Don. 29/9–20/10/61.**C/L.**

Dar. 29/8–12/9/63.**C/L.**

BOILERS:
9864.
9917 *(ex1280)* 18/2/50.
28570 *(ex1232)* 2/11/51.
28567 *(ex1054)* 19/9/53.
28536 *(ex61360)* 17/2/56.
28533 *(ex1671)* 7/11/58.

SHEDS:
Leicester.
Gorton 2/11/47.
Stratford 30/4/50.
Cambridge 4/3/51.
Stratford 6/5/51.
Parkeston 28/10/56.
Colwick 27/11/60.

RENUMBERED:
61227 18/2/50.

CONDEMNED:
22/9/63.
*Sold 1/64 for scrap to
J.Cashmore, Great Bridge.*

1228

North British Loco. 26129.

To traffic 28/8/47.

REPAIRS:
Gor. 19/9–15/10/49.**G.**
Gor. 19–21/10/49.**N/C.**
Gor. 12/7–7/10/50.**C/H.**
Gor. 11–23/10/50.**N/C.**
Dar. 6–31/12/51.**G.**
Gor. 22/8–26/9/53.**G.**
Gor. 29/9–3/10/53.**N/C.**
Dar. 10/1–8/2/56.**G.**
Str. 30/4–9/11/57.**G.**
Str. 10/8–28/9/59.**G.** *Part
A.T.C. fitted.*
Don. 3–5/8/60.**N/C.**

BOILERS:
9865.
3744 *(ex1029)* 15/10/49.
3744 renumbered 28263
7/10/50.
28242 *(ex61328)* 31/12/51.
28253 *(ex3768)* 26/9/53.
28445 *(ex1288)* 8/2/56.
28592 *(ex1235)* 9/11/57.
28163 *(ex1109)* 28/9/59.

SHEDS:
Leicester.
Gorton 2/11/47.
March 17/6/48.
Gorton 31/10/48.
Ipswich 13/6/54.
Norwich 4/10/59.
Sheffield 17/1/60.

RENUMBERED:
61228 15/10/49.

CONDEMNED:
16/9/62.
*Sold 5/63 for scrap to Albert
Looms, Spondon.*

1229

North British Loco. 26130.

To traffic 2/9/47.

REPAIRS:
Don. 14/11–15/12/49.**G.**
Don. 20–23/12/49.**N/C.**
Don. 10/12/51–7/1/52.**G.**
Gor. 7–21/11/53.**C/L.**
Gor. 22/5–10/7/54.**G.**
Dar. 20/10–23/11/55.**C/H.**
Dar. 5/4–4/5/57.**G.**
Dar. 6–7/5/57.**N/C.**
Dar. 7–17/4/59.**N/C.**
A.T.C. mech fitted.
Dar. 23/3–30/4/60.**G.**
A.T.C. elec.fitted.
Dar. 22/11/60–1/2/61.**C/H.**
Dar. 6/9–23/10/62.**C/L.**

BOILERS:
9866.
9843 *(ex1206)* 15/12/49.
28165 *(ex1230)* 7/1/52.
28251 *(ex1185)* 10/7/54.
28266 *(ex1156)* 4/5/57.
28305 *(ex1077)* 30/4/60.

SHEDS:
Ardsley.
Bradford 21/9/47.

RENUMBERED:
61229 15/12/49.

CONDEMNED:
29/6/64.
*8/9/64 In for cut up at
Darlington.*

1230

North British Loco. 26131.

To traffic 4/9/47.

REPAIRS:
Don. 11/9–20/10/49.**G.**
Don. 20/11–14/12/51.**G.**
Gor. 13/2–20/3/54.**G.**
Dar. 8/11–22/12/55.**C/L.**
Dar. 22/10–16/11/56.**G.**
Dar. 26/6–11/7/58.**C/L.**
Dar. 10/3–10/4/59.**G.**
A.T.C. mech fitted.
Dar. 20–29/4/59.**N/C.**
Dar. 4–15/5/59.**N/C.**
Dar. 8–14/12/60.**N/C.**
A.W.S. elec.fitted.

BOILERS:
9867.
9850 *(ex1213)* 20/10/49.
28161 *(ex1251)* 14/12/51.
28420 *(ex61306)* 20/3/54.
28441 *(ex61381)* 16/11/56.
28105 *(ex61305)* 10/4/59.

SHEDS:
Ardsley.
Bradford 21/9/47.

RENUMBERED:
61230 20/10/49.

CONDEMNED:
19/11/62.
*9/1/63 In for cut up at
Darlington.*

1231

North British Loco. 26132.

To traffic 9/9/47.

REPAIRS:
Don. 4/12/49–6/1/50.**G.**
Don. 13/1–6/2/52.**G.**
Str. 7/4–21/5/54.**G.**
Str. 19/4–24/5/56.**G.**
Str. 31/10–19/12/58.**G.**
Don. 18–28/7/60.**N/C.**
Don. 6–28/1/61.**C/L.**
Don. 4–20/5/61.**C/L.**
Don. 12/6–4/7/61.**C/L.**
Don. 27/7/62.*Not repaired.*

BOILERS:
9868.
9438 *(ex3950)* 6/1/50.
28173 *(ex1265)* 6/2/52.
28112 *(ex1139)* 21/5/54.
28451 *(ex61326)* 24/5/56.
28584 *(ex1091)* 19/12/58.

SHEDS:
Doncaster.
Retford 2/11/47.

RENUMBERED:
61231 6/1/50.

CONDEMNED:
30/7/62.
Cut up at Doncaster.

1232

North British Loco. 26133.

To traffic 10/9/47.

REPAIRS:
Str. 15/6–20/8/49.**G.**
Str. 15–23/9/49.**N/C.**
Str. 7/8–29/9/51.**G.**
Str. 26/4–12/6/54.**G.**
Str. 8/1–15/2/57.**G.**
Str. 12/5–13/6/58.**C/L.**
Str. 23/3–8/5/59.**G.**
Complete A.T.C. fitted.
Don. 30/8–7/10/61.**G.**

BOILERS:
9869.
3841 *(ex1056)* 20/8/49.
28509 *(ex1046)* 29/9/51.
28262 *(ex1285)* 12/6/54.
28871 *(ex61375)* 15/2/57.
28539 *(ex1632)* 8/5/59.
28148 *(ex3938)* 7/10/61.

SHEDS:
Stratford.
Parkeston 8/2/48.

RENUMBERED:
61232 20/8/49.

CONDEMNED:
19/2/66.
*Sold 5/66 for scrap to Birds,
Long Marston.*

1233

North British Loco. 26134.

To traffic 10/9/47.

REPAIRS:
Str. 7/1–26/2/49.**G.**
Str. 17–24/6/49.**C/L.**
Str. 7/9–21/10/50.**G.**
Str. 24/3–25/4/52.**C/L.**
Str. 22/9–1/11/52.**G.**
Str. 1–4/12/52.**N/C.**
Str. 13/12/54–19/2/55.**G.**
Str. 8/4–31/5/57.**G.**
Str. 14/1–27/2/59.**G.** *Mod.
bogie springs. Part A.T.C.
fitted.*
Don. 25–30/8/60.**N/C.**
Don. 21/5–11/7/62.**G.**

BOILERS:
9870.
9873 *(ex1236)* 26/2/49.
28504 *(ex1049)* 21/10/50.
28524 *(ex61644)* 1/11/52.
28186 *(ex1070)* 19/2/55.
28145 *(ex1055)* 31/5/57.
28234 *(ex1279)* 27/2/59.
28180 *(ex1051)* 30/8/60.

SHEDS:
Stratford.
Parkeston 24/5/59.
Stratford 14/6/59.
March 24/9/61.

RENUMBERED:
61233 26/2/49.

CONDEMNED:
16/9/62 but put back in
stock 29/9/62. Finally
condemned 25/11/63.
*Made S.B.Dept'l No.21.
Sold 5/66 for scrap to Birds,
Long Marston.*

1234

North British Loco. 26135.

To traffic 16/9/47.

REPAIRS:
Str. 22/11–1/12/48.**L.**
Str. 18/2–15/4/49.**G.**
Str. 26/1–17/3/51.**G.**
Str. 7/5–19/6/53.**G.** *Mod.
bogie springs.*
Str. 13/6–5/8/55.**G.**

Str. 19/6–24/8/57.**G.**
Str. 24–28/2/58.**N/C.**
Don. 18/11–12/12/59.**G.**
Don. 9–24/2/61.**N/C.**
Don. 26/2–9/3/62.**C/L.**
Don. 7/8/62.*Not repaired.*

BOILERS:
9871.
9426 *(ex1001)* 15/4/49.
28535 *(ex1270)* 17/3/51.
28533 *(ex1301)* 19/6/53.
28553 *(ex1671)* 5/8/55.
28546 *(ex61336)* 24/8/57.
28158 *(ex1623)* 12/12/59.

SHEDS:
Stratford.
Sheffield 3/5/59.

RENUMBERED:
61234 14/4/49.

CONDEMNED:
13/8/62.
Cut up at Doncaster.

1235

North British Loco. 26136.

To traffic 18/9/47.

REPAIRS:
Str. 15/3–26/5/49.**G.**
Str. 20/3–13/4/50.**C/L.**
Str. 16/11/50–5/1/51.**G.**
Str. 1/4–23/5/53.**G.** *Mod.
bogie springs.*
Str. 18/4–4/6/55.**G.**
Str. 20/2–9/3/56.**C/L.**
Str. 15/2–2/3/57.**C/L.**
Str. 19/8–28/9/57.**G.**
Str. 24/3–21/5/58.**C/L.**
Don. 19/1–17/2/60.**G.**
Don. 9–17/3/60.**N/C.**

BOILERS:
9872.
9871 *(ex1234)* 26/5/49.
28519 *(ex1615)* 5/1/51.
28549 *(ex1282)* 23/5/53.
28592 *(ex1253)* 4/6/55.
28203 *(ex1254)* 28/9/57.
28151 *(ex1153)* 17/2/60.

SHEDS:
Stratford.
Norwich 12/10/58.
Immingham 3/1/60.

RENUMBERED:
61235 26/5/49.

CONDEMNED:
16/9/62.
*Sold 1/63 for scrap to Cox
& Danks, Wadsley Bridge.*

1236

North British Loco. 26137.

To traffic 26/9/47.

REPAIRS:
Str. 31/5–2/6/48.**L.**
Str. 19/12/48–12/2/49.**G.**
Str. 3–6/1/50.**N/C.**
Str. 5/10–11/11/50.**G.**
Str. 28/5–28/6/51.**C/L.**
Str. 5/11–20/12/52.**G.**
Str. 21–26/9/53.**N/C.**
Str. 19/10–20/11/54.**G.**
Str. 27/5–15/8/57.**G.**
Str. 21–23/8/57.**N/C.**
Str. 2/11/59–12/2/60.**G.**
A.T.C. fitted.

BOILERS:
9873.
9721 *(ex1135)* 12/2/49.
28510 *(ex1271)* 11/11/50.
28530 *(ex1253)* 20/12/52.
28521 *(ex1302)* 20/11/54.
28131 *(ex1059)* 15/8/57.
28810 *(ex61373)* 12/2/60.

SHEDS:
Stratford.
Cambridge 12/4/59.
March 20/11/60.

RENUMBERED:
61236 12/2/49.

CONDEMNED:
16/9/62.
*Sold 3/63 for scrap to
J.Cashmore, Great Bridge.*

1237

North British Loco. 26138.

To traffic 24/9/47.

*Named **GEOFFREY
H KITSON** in 12/47.*

REPAIRS:
Dar. 15/1–16/2/49.**G.**
Dar. 28/8–23/9/50.**G.**
Dar. 25–26/9/50.**N/C.**
Dar. 9/10/50.*Weigh.*
Dar. 3–25/3/52.**G.**
Dar. 24/6–16/7/53.**G.**
Dar. 12/6–22/7/54.**C/H.**
Dar. 3–26/3/55.**G.**
Dar. 28–31/3/55.**N/C.**
Dar. 26/4–31/5/55.**N/C.**
Dar. 16/7–9/8/55.**C/L.** *After
collision.*
Dar. 10–18/10/55.**N/C.**
Dar. 19/12/56–17/1/57.**G.**
Dar. 28/6–4/7/57.**C/L.**
Dar. 4–31/7/58.**C/L.**
Dar. 25/11–30/12/58.**G.**
A.T.C. mech.fitted.
Dar. 30/6–10/7/59.**N/C.**
A.T.C. elec.fitted.
Dar. 5/10/59.*Weigh.*
Dar. 26/3–27/4/62.**G.**

Dar. 25/11–21/12/63.**C/H.**
Derailment damage.
Dar. 23–27/12/63.**N/C.**

BOILERS:
9874.
   3866 *(new)* 16/2/49.
28104 *(ex1216)* 23/9/50.
28416 *(ex61305)* 25/3/52.
28461 *(ex61385)* 16/7/53.
28443 *(ex1038)* 26/3/55.
28858 *(ex1224)* 17/1/57.
28139 *(ex1220)* 30/12/58.
28113 *(ex1035)* 27/4/62.

SHEDS:
Neville Hill.
Gateshead 15/1/61.
Sunderland 30/4/61.
Blaydon 17/6/62.
Tyne Dock 16/6/63.
Wakefield 31/10/65.

RENUMBERED:
61237 16/2/49.

CONDEMNED:
6/12/66.
*Sold 16/2/67 for scrap to
Arnott Young, Parkgate.*

1238

North British Loco. 26139.

To traffic 26/9/47.

*Named LESLIE
RUNCIMAN in 12/47.*

REPAIRS:
Gor. 4/12/48–8/1/49.**G.**
Dar. 25/4–16/5/50.**G.**
Dar. 9/8–1/9/51.**H/I.**
Dar. 13/10–1/11/52.**G.**
Dar. 3–5/11/52.**N/C.**
Ghd. 2–9/12/53.**C/L.**
Dar. 25/5–19/6/54.**G.**
Ghd. 14/10–4/11/55.**C/L.**
Dar. 20/4–22/5/56.**G.**
Ghd. 21/9–9/10/56.**C/L.**
Dar. 4–28/3/58.**G.**
Dar. 20–29/4/59.**N/C.**
A.T.C.mech. fitted.
Dar. 9/1–18/2/61.**G.**
A.W.S. completed.
Dar. 25/3/61.**N/C.**
Dar. 19/5–4/7/61.**C/H.**
Dar. 29/9–26/11/64.**C/L.**

BOILERS:
9875.
9876 *(ex1239)* 8/1/49.
9943 *(ex61306)* 16/5/50.
*9943 renumbered 28229
1/9/51.*
28228 *(ex1259)* 1/11/52.
28406 *(ex1273)* 19/6/54.
28434 *(ex1154)* 22/5/56.
28424 *(ex1086)* 28/3/58.
28205 *(ex61387)* 18/2/61.

SHEDS:
Gateshead.

Blaydon 10/2/57.
Gateshead 14/6/59.
Tyne Dock 10/9/61.
Ardsley 7/6/64.
York 31/10/65.

RENUMBERED:
61238 11/7/48.

CONDEMNED:
17/2/67.
*Sold 24/4/67 for scrap to
Hughes, Bolckow, North
Blyth.*

1239

North British Loco. 26140.

To traffic 2/10/47.

REPAIRS:
Gor. 16/11–24/12/48.**G.**
Dar. 13/3–11/4/51.**G.**
Dar. 20/3–18/4/53.**G.**
Cow. 29/9–16/10/54.**H/I.**
Cow. 27/3–3/5/56.**H/I.**
Cow. 4/4–2/5/58.**G.**
Cow. 19/10–11/11/60.**H/I.**

BOILERS:
9876.
   5122 *(new)* 24/12/48.
28204 *(ex1013)* 11/4/51.
28223 *(ex1215)* 18/4/53.
28621 *(ex1277)* 2/5/58.

SHEDS:
York.
Neville Hill 16/5/48.
York 23/5/48.
Carlisle Canal 20/9/53.
Gorton 17/6/62.

RENUMBERED:
61239 24/12/48.

CONDEMNED:
27/8/62.
Gorton – Not repaired.

1240

North British Loco. 26141.

To traffic 6/10/47.

*Named HARRY
HINCHLIFFE in 12/47.*

REPAIRS:
Dar. 30/3–29/4/49.**G.**
Don. 13/11–12/12/50.**G.**
Dar. 9–31/5/52.**G.**
Dar. 19/11–12/12/53.**G.**
Dar. 9–17/12/54.**C/L.**
Dar. 19/5–18/6/55.**G.**
Dar. 12/12/55–18/1/56.**C/L.**
Dar. 31/7–30/8/56.**C/L.**
Dar. 27/8–20/9/57.**G.**
Dar. 30/9–3/10/57.**N/C.**
Dar. 8–21/10/57.**N/C.**
Dar. 31/3–30/4/59.**G.**

A.T.C. mech. fitted.
Dar. 6–26/5/59.**N/C.**
Dar. 8–18/6/59.**N/C.**
Dar. 25/6–2/7/59.**N/C.**
Dar. 19/2–28/3/62.**G.**
Dar. 28/5–5/6/62.**N/C.**

BOILERS:
9877.
   9853 *(ex1216)* 29/4/49.
28118 *(ex1060)* 12/12/50.
28430 *(ex61312)* 31/5/52.
28226 *(ex1241)* 12/12/53.
28308 *(ex1225)* 18/6/55.
28281 *(ex61306)* 20/9/57.
28222 *(ex1161)* 30/4/59.
28815 *(ex61353)* 28/3/62.

SHEDS:
York.
Neville Hill 16/5/48.
Thornaby 1/11/59.
York 11/9/60.
Ardsley 25/11/62.
Wakefield 31/10/65.

RENUMBERED:
61240 29/4/49.

CONDEMNED:
6/12/66.
*Sold 16/2/67 for scrap to
Arnott Young, Parkgate.*

1241

North British Loco. 26142.

To traffic 8/10/47.

*Named VISCOUNT
RIDLEY in 12/47.*

REPAIRS:
Dar. 19/5/49.*Weigh.*
Dar. 9/9–6/10/49.**G.**
Dar. 11–12/10/49.**N/C.**
Dar. 16/7–25/8/51.**G.**
Dar. 3–24/10/53.**G.**
Dar. 26–27/10/53.**N/C.**
Dar. 6–13/9/54.**N/C.**
Dar. 24/9–21/10/55.**G.**
Dar. 20/1–1/2/56.**N/C.**
Dar. 14/11–7/12/57.**G.**
Dar. 9–11/12/57.**N/C.**
Dar. 9/7–12/8/58.**N/C.**
Dar. 25/6–9/7/59.**N/C.**
Complete A.T.C. fitted.
Dar. 7/3–7/4/60.**G.**
Dar. 9–16/9/60.**N/C.**

BOILERS:
9878.
   9861 *(ex1224)* 6/10/49.
28226 *(ex1176)* 25/8/51.
28248 *(ex1298)* 24/10/53.
28559 *(ex61327)* 21/10/55.
28439 *(ex61385)* 7/12/57.
28456 *(ex1224)* 7/4/60.

SHEDS:
Heaton.
Darlington 7/11/48.
Tweedmouth 12/3/50.

Blaydon 12/6/60.
Heaton 9/9/62.

RENUMBERED:
61241 18/7/48.

CONDEMNED:
2/12/62.
*19/3/63 In for cut up at
Darlington.*

1242

North British Loco. 26143.

To traffic 10/10/47.

*Named ALEXANDER
REITH GRAY in 12/47.*

REPAIRS:
Inv. 9–12/11/47.**L.** *Tablet
catcher fitted.*
Cow. 25/2–9/4/49.**G.**
Cow. 8/6–2/7/51.**G.**
Cow. 5/4–5/5/54.**L/I.**
Cow. 9/11–11/12/54.**C/L.**
Inv. 24/2–11/3/55.**N/C.**
Inv. 29/3–15/4/55.**N/C.**
Inv. 25/7–3/8/55.**N/C.**
Cow. 6/12/55–14/1/56.**G.**
W.P.U. gear removed.
Kit. 28/5–10/6/57.**C/L.**
Abd. 17–21/6/57.**C/L.**
Cow. 25/11–21/12/57.**H/I.**
Cow. 4–17/4/58.**N/C.**
Cow. 14–30/1/59.**C/L.**
Inv. 28/4–7/5/59.**N/C.**
Cow. 13/8–19/9/59.**L/I.**
Cow. 29/12/59–5/2/60.**C/L.**
Inv. 5–6/12/60.**N/C.**
Cow.
27/12/60–21/1/61.**C/L.**
Cow. 22/11–23/12/61.**G.**
A.W.S. fitted.
Cow. 20/10–10/11/62.**N/C.**

BOILERS:
9879.
28633 *(ex1261)* 2/7/51.
28616 *(ex1081)* 14/1/56.
28611 *(ex61398)* 23/12/61.

SHEDS:
Kittybrewster.
St Margarets 16/11/49.
Dalry Road 15/4/51.
Keith 29/9/51.
Kittybrewster 28/1/57.
Carlisle Canal 17/6/61.
St Margarets 17/9/61.
Dalry Road 14/6/64.

RENUMBERED:
61242 9/4/49.

CONDEMNED:
23/7/64.
*11/64 In for cut up at
Darlington. Tender to
snowplough.*

61345 at Kittybrewster. It was a part of the order for ten built by Gorton from November 1948 to July 1949, numbered 61340 to 61349 and, apart from 61348, they did all their work in the Scottish Region. They had black paint, with red, cream and grey lining; letters and figures were both 10″, and correct Gill Sans 6 and 9 were used on cab side, but not on the cast plate on the smokebox door.

Darlington followed by building 61350 to 61359 from July to October 1949. All had standard black paint and lining, but only 61350 was lettered BRITISH RAILWAYS. 61351 to 61354 had no display on tender sides, but 61355 to 61359 acquired the lion and wheel emblem from new. That batch had the correct 6 and 9 on cab and plate. Apart from 61353 they too did all their work from Scottish Region sheds, and 61350 is again shown at Kittybrewster, its allocated shed for its first twelve years. Note the different smokebox door hinge strap spacing, and position for the number plate.

North British secured an order for a further forty, numbered 61360 to 61399. Shortage of materials caused delivery to stretch from May 1950 to April 1952, and whilst all carried the emblem and had the correct 6 and 9 on the smokebox plates, the cab side numbering incorporated the long out–dated LNER modification to correct Gill Sans, something which NBL continued with through to 61399 in 1952. This train, passing New Barnet South Box, was a combined one from King's Cross to Hitchin, where it split, New England 61392 taking on the Huntingdon portion, and 61121 the portion to Cambridge (where the loco was shedded).

This was a regular brake-fitted goods from Stockton to Hull which 61032 is taking through York station to Dringhouses yard from where it would return to its shed at Stockton to which it was allocated from new until that shed closed. A York engine and men then worked the goods to and from Hull.

1243

North British Loco. 26144.

To traffic 14/10/47.

*Named **SIR HAROLD MITCHELL** in 12/47.*

REPAIRS:
Cow. 22–23/12/47.**N/C.** *for naming only.*
Cow. 31/1–19/3/49.**G.**
Cow. 4–6/4/49.**N/C.**
Cow. 29/1–23/2/51.**L/I.**
Cow. 19/11–15/12/51.**C/L.**
Cow. 11–29/11/52.**G.**
Cow. 14/5/53.**N/C.**
Cow. 12/10/53.**N/C.**
Cow. 16/11/53.**N/C.**
Cow. 5/1/54.**N/C.**
Cow. 3–8/5/54.**N/C.**
Cow. 20/1–12/2/55.**H/I.**
W.P.U. gear removed.
Cow. 8/2–2/3/57.**G.**
Cow. 5–8/6/57.**N/C.**
Cow. 9–31/5/58.**L/I.**
Cow. 10–20/3/59.**N/C.**
A.T.C. fitted.
Cow. 31/3–6/5/61.**G.**

BOILERS:
9880.
9880 renumbered 28629 23/2/51.
28656 *(ex61351)* 29/11/52.
28668 *(ex61403)* 2/3/57.
28666 *(ex1103)* 6/5/61.

SHEDS:
Eastfield.
Corkerhill 31/12/62.
Ayr 11/3/63.

RENUMBERED:
61243 19/3/49.

CONDEMNED:
4/5/64.
Sold 7/64 for scrap to Arnott Young, West of Scotland Shipbreaking Co. Troon.

1244

North British Loco. 26145.

To traffic 20/10/47.

*Named **STRANG STEEL** in 12/47.*

REPAIRS:
Cow. 16/12/47.**N/C.** *for naming only.*
Cow. 10/3–30/4/49.**G.**
Cow. 31/3–27/4/51.**H/I.**
Cow. 12/11–14/12/51.**C/L.**
Cow. 22/5–6/6/52.**N/C.**
Cow. 2/2–28/3/53.**G.**
Cow. 8–23/1/54.**C/L.**
Hay. 28/9–6/11/54.**C/L.**
Cow. 24/10–19/11/55.**H/I.**

Cow. 1–2/2/57.**N/C.**
Hay. 15–25/3/57.**C/L.**
Cow. 1/7–23/8/57.**G.**
Cow. 23/4–9/5/59.**L/I.**
Cow. 26/7–5/8/60.**N/C.**
Cow. 3/4–12/5/62.**G.**
Cow. 30/5–1/6/62.**N/C.**
Cow. 3–11/7/62.**C/L.**
Cow. 17/2–4/4/64.**L/I.**

BOILERS:
9881.
9881 renumbered 28630 27/4/51.
28642 *(ex61308)* 28/3/53.
28623 *(ex61340)* 23/8/57.
28543 *(ex1007)* 12/5/62.

SHEDS:
Haymarket.
Dalry Road 30/6/60.
St Margarets 1/10/61.

RENUMBERED:
61244 30/4/49.

CONDEMNED:
29/10/65.
Sold 12/65 for scrap to Shipbreaking Industries, Faslane.

1245

North British Loco. 26146.

To traffic 20/10/47.

*Named **MURRAY OF ELIBANK** in 12/47.*

REPAIRS:
Cow. 7/7–19/8/49.**L/I.**
Cow. 6–31/12/51.**G.**
Cow. 7/7–12/8/53.**L/I.**
Cow. 14/5–3/6/54.**N/C.**
Cow. 5–13/7/54.**N/C.**
Cow. 4–14/5/55.**N/C.**
Cow. 3/2–10/3/56.**G.**
Hay. 28/4–9/5/57.**C/L.**
Cow. 4–27/6/58.**H/I.**
Cow. 19–26/3/59.**N/C.**
A.W.S. fitted.
Cow. 24/12/60–4/2/61.**G.**
Cow. 24/7–20/9/63.**L/I.**
Cow. 1–10/10/63.**N/C.**

BOILERS:
9882.
9882 renumbered 28631 1/51.
28608 *(ex1081)* 31/12/51.
28633 *(ex1242)* 10/3/56.
28706 *(ex1072)* 4/2/61.

SHEDS:
Haymarket.
Dalry Road 9/9/63.
St Margarets 2/12/63.
Dalry Road 12/10/64.

RENUMBERED:
61245 22/5/48.

CONDEMNED:
5/7/65.
Sold 8/65 for scrap to Motherwell Machinery & Scrap Co., Wishaw.

1246

North British Loco. 26147.

To traffic 22/10/47.

*Named **LORD BALFOUR OF BURLEIGH** in 12/47.*

REPAIRS:
Don. 18/10–17/11/49.**G.**
Don. 20/8–25/9/51.**G.**
Don. 8/6–14/7/53.**G.**
Cow. 20/9–29/11/55.**H/I.**
Cow. 12/11–17/12/55.**C/L.**
Cow. 7/8–17/9/57.**G.**
Cow. 24/3–2/4/59.**C/L.**
A.W.S. fitted.
Cow. 24/5–2/7/60.**L/I.**

BOILERS:
9883.
9845 *(ex1208)* 17/11/49.
28149 *(ex1294)* 25/9/51.
28412 *(ex61318)* 14/7/53.
28642 *(ex1244)* 17/9/57.

SHEDS:
Doncaster.
St Margarets 13/9/53.
Dalry Road 30/1/56.
St Margarets 17/2/58.

RENUMBERED:
61246 17/11/49.

CONDEMNED:
29/12/62.
2/63 In for cut up at Cowlairs.

1247

North British Loco. 26148.

To traffic 24/10/47.

*Named **LORD BURGHLEY** in 12/47.*

REPAIRS:
Don. 18/7–26/8/49.**G.**
Don. 28/5–21/6/51.**G.**
Don. 2–27/3/53.**G.**
Don. 23/2/54.*Weigh.*
Don. 1/9/54.*Weigh.*
Don. 15/2–15/3/55.**G.**
Don. 18/7/55.*Weigh.*
Don. 29/8/55.*Weigh.*
Don. 18/10/55.*Weigh.*
Dar. 18/9–12/10/57.**G.**
Dar. 17–18/10/57.**N/C.**
Don. 11/11–5/12/59.**G.**
Don. 16–27/1/60.**C/L.**
Don. 28/11–1/12/60.**N/C.**
Don. 1/6/62.*Not repaired.*

BOILERS:
9884.
9833 *(ex1196)* 26/8/49.
28145 *(ex1283)* 21/6/51.
28245 *(ex1269)* 27/3/53.
28140 *(ex1105)* 15/3/55.
28422 *(ex1296)* 12/10/57.
28188 *(ex1655)* 5/12/59.

SHEDS:
Doncaster.
Colwick 12/6/60.

RENUMBERED:
61247 26/8/49.

CONDEMNED:
12/6/62.
Cut up at Doncaster.

1248

North British Loco. 26149.

To traffic 27/10/47.

*Named **GEOFFREY GIBBS** in 12/47.*

REPAIRS:
Don. 8/5–2/6/50.**G.**
Don. 11–19/3/51.**C/L.**
Don. 13–22/8/51.**C/L.**
Don. 1–29/4/52.**G.**
Dar. 12/6–10/7/54.**G.**
Don. 15/8–21/9/55.**C/L.**
Don. 13/3–6/4/57.**G.**
Str. 6/5–19/6/59.**G.**
A.T.C. fitted.
Don. 14–28/10/59.**N/C.**
Don. 30/8–5/10/61.**G.**

BOILERS:
9885.
3755 *(ex1036)* 2/6/50.
28189 *(ex1297)* 29/4/52.
28433 *(ex1303)* 10/7/54.
28269 *(ex1144)* 6/4/57.
28152 *(ex61329)* 19/6/59.
28818 *(ex1196)* 5/10/61.

SHEDS:
Doncaster.
Lincoln 19/12/54.
Immingham 8/5/55.
Lincoln 19/2/56.
Immingham 22/11/59.
Colwick 10/1/65.

RENUMBERED:
61248 2/6/50.

CONDEMNED:
7/11/65.
Sold 12/65 for scrap to Hughes, Bolckow, North Blyth.

1249

North British Loco. 26150.

To traffic 31/10/47.

Named *FITZHERBERT WRIGHT* in 12/47.

REPAIRS:
Don. 1/5–1/6/50.**G.**
Don. 21/1–15/2/52.**G.**
Don. 13/1–3/2/53.**C/L.**
Don. 22/12/53–21/1/54.**G.**
Str. 31/8–8/10/55.**G.**
Str. 8–27/10/56.**C/L.**
Str. 6–16/2/57.**N/C.**
Str. 12/6–15/8/58.**G.** *Mod. bogie springs.*
Don. 10/5–16/6/61.**G.**
Don. 27–30/6/61.**N/C.**
Don. 23/8–5/9/62.**C/L.**

BOILERS:
9886.
9905 *(ex1268)* 1/6/50.
28175 *(ex1266)* 15/2/52.
28159 *(ex1213)* 21/1/54.
28349 *(ex1042)* 8/10/55.
28327 *(ex1203)* 15/8/58.
28292 *(ex1205)* 16/6/61.

SHEDS:
Doncaster.
Stratford 28/2/54.
Parkeston 8/2/59.
Sheffield 24/5/59.
Canklow 16/6/63.

RENUMBERED:
61249 1/6/50.

CONDEMNED:
4/6/64.
Sold 8/64 for scrap to Geo.Cohen, Ickles.

1250

North British Loco. 26151.

To traffic 31/10/47.

Named *A.HAROLD BIBBY* in 12/47.

REPAIRS:
Don. 16/5–14/6/50.**G.**
Don. 16/10/50.*Weigh.*
Don. 30/6–28/7/52.**G.**
Dar. 24/6–23/7/54.**G.**
Don. 29/8–13/10/56.**G.**
Don. 4/6–4/7/59.**G.**
Don. 6/12/61–10/1/62.**G.**

BOILERS:
9887.
9932 *(ex1295)* 14/6/50.
28197 *(ex61379)* 28/7/52.
28402 *(ex1039)* 23/7/54.
28859 *(ex1200)* 13/10/56.
28869 *(ex1188)* 4/7/59.
28861 *(ex1143)* 10/1/62.

SHEDS:
Doncaster.
New England 16/9/62.
Grantham 16/6/63.
Doncaster 8/9/63.
Immingham 22/9/65.

Doncaster 30/1/66.

RENUMBERED:
61250 14/6/50.

CONDEMNED:
17/4/66.
Sold 5/66 for scrap to Geo.Cohen, Kettering.

1251

North British Loco. 26152.

To traffic 4/11/47.

Named *OLIVER BURY* in 12/47.

REPAIRS:
Gor. 11–27/4/48.*Special.*
Don. 26/7–26/8/48.**L.**
Don. 9/11–9/12/49.**G.**
Don. 29/3–21/4/50.**C/L.**
Don. 30/10–22/11/51.**G.**
Don. 17/9–16/10/53.**G.**
Str. 20/7–8/9/54.**C/L.**
Don. 14/12/55–19/1/56.**G.**
Dar. 16/12/57–16/1/58.**G.**
Don. 19–31/10/59.**C/L.**
Don. 16/1–18/2/61.**G.**

BOILERS:
9888.
9883 *(ex1246)* 9/12/49.
28158 *(ex1211)* 22/11/51.
28162 *(ex1075)* 16/10/53.
28221 *(ex1213)* 19/1/56.
28153 *(ex1661)* 16/1/58.
28583 *(ex61408)* 18/2/61.

SHEDS:
Ipswich.
Kings Cross 20/11/47.
Hitchin 13/6/54.
Grantham 14/6/59.
Doncaster 8/9/63.
Immingham 22/9/63.

RENUMBERED:
61251 27/4/48.

CONDEMNED:
19/4/64.
Sold 6/64 for scrap to Central Wagon Co, Ince.

1252

North British Loco. 26153.

To traffic 6/11/47.

REPAIRS:
Str. 4/4–10/6/49.**G.**
Str. 10/12/50–3/2/51.**G.**
Str. 16/10–29/11/52.**G.**
Str. 14/6–30/7/54.**G.**
Str. 31/1–10/3/56.**G.**
Str. 11/10–15/11/57.**G.**
Mod. bogie springs.
Str. 20/4–5/6/59.**G.**
Complete A.T.C. fitted.

Don. 2/1–7/2/62.**G.**

BOILERS:
9889.
9891 *(ex1254)* 10/6/49.
28527 *(ex1235)* 3/2/51.
28581 *(ex1616)* 29/11/52.
28867 *(new)* 30/7/54.
28573 *(ex1302)* 10/3/56.
28593 *(ex61373)* 15/11/57.
28572 *(ex1089)* 5/6/59.

SHEDS:
Ipswich.
March 1/11/59.
Cambridge 10/1/60.
Norwich 20/11/60.
Stratford 10/9/61.
March 24/9/61.

RENUMBERED:
61252 10/6/49.

CONDEMNED:
25/11/63.
Made S.B.Dept'l No.22.
Sold 6/64 for scrap to R.A.King, Norwich.

1253

North British Loco. 26154.

To traffic 10/11/47.

REPAIRS:
Str. 24/4–16/6/49.**G.**
Str. 4/1–17/2/51.**G.**
Str. 8/9–18/10/52.**G.**
Str. 2–7/2/53.**N/C.**
Str. 30/3–8/4/53.**N/C.**
Str. 1/6–2/7/54.**G.**
Dar. 16/1–14/2/56.**G.**
Dar. 12/2–4/4/57.**C/L.**
Str. 11–28/6/57.**C/L.**
Str. 29/4–20/6/58.**G.** *Mod. bogie springs.*
Don. 11/3–16/4/60.**G.**

BOILERS:
9890.
9872 *(ex1235)* 16/6/49.
28530 *(ex1001)* 17/2/51.
28592 *(ex1639)* 18/10/52.
28102 *(ex1138)* 2/7/54.
28421 *(ex1013)* 14/2/56.
28397 *(ex1283)* 20/6/58.
28554 *(ex1203)* 16/4/60.

SHEDS:
Stratford.
Ipswich 16/11/47.
March 1/11/59.
Cambridge 10/1/60.
Norwich 20/11/60.
Stratford 10/9/61.

RENUMBERED:
61253 16/6/49.

CONDEMNED:
16/9/62.
19/11/62 In for cut up at Doncaster.

1254

North British Loco. 26155.

To traffic 12/11/47.

REPAIRS:
Str. 21/3–14/5/49.**G.**
Str. 2/11–16/12/50.**G.**
Str. 12/5–28/6/52.**G.**
Str. 15/12/53–23/1/54.**G.**
Dar. 7/12/55–11/1/56.**G.**
Str. 4/3–3/5/57.**G.**
Str. 23–25/6/58.**N/C.**
Str. 8/12/58–30/1/59.**G.**
Mod. bogie springs.
Don. 1/2–3/3/61.**G.**

BOILERS:
9891.
9908 *(ex1271)* 14/5/49.
28515 *(ex1236)* 16/12/50.
28587 *(ex1127)* 28/6/52.
28259 *(ex1608)* 23/1/54.
28203 *(ex61339)* 11/1/56.
28509 *(ex1617)* 3/5/57.
28867 *(ex1135)* 3/3/61.

SHEDS:
Stratford.
Norwich 10/12/47.
Ipswich 25/1/48.
March 1/11/59.
Cambridge 10/1/60.
Norwich 20/11/60.
March 4/2/62.

RENUMBERED:
61254 14/5/49.

CONDEMNED:
16/9/62.
Sold 6/63 for scrap to Central Wagon Co, Ince.

1255

North British Loco. 26156.

To traffic 14/11/47.

REPAIRS:
Ghd. 27/11/48.**L.**
Dar. 28/9–22/10/49.**G.**
Dar. 25–27/10/49.**N/C.**
Dar. 15/10–9/11/51.**G.**
Dar. 8–30/1/54.**G.**
Dar. 1–2/2/54.**N/C.**
Dar. 7–13/9/55.**N/C.**
Dar. 6/3–4/4/56.**G.**
Dar. 2/5–5/6/58.**G.**
Dar. 10–18/6/58.**N/C.**
Dar. 24–27/6/58.**N/C.**
Dar. 23/12/58.*Weigh.*
Dar. 13–22/4/59.**N/C.**
A.T.C. mech. fitted.
Dar. 20–23/12/60.**N/C.**
A.W.S. elec. fitted.
Dar. 14/4–10/5/61.**G.**
Dar. 20/1–6/3/64.**G.**

BOILERS:
9892.
9878 *(ex1241)* 22/10/49.

28233 *(ex61339)* 9/11/51.
28403 *(ex61305)* 30/1/54.
28440 *(ex1153)* 4/4/56.
28513 *(ex1037)* 5/6/58.
28142 *(ex1199)* 10/5/61.
28576 *(ex spare 2 years)*
6/3/64.

SHEDS:
Heaton.
Darlington 7/11/48.
Haverton Hill 15/2/59.
Thornaby 14/6/59.
Hull Dairycoates 4/3/62.

RENUMBERED:
61255 27/11/48.

CONDEMNED:
24/6/67.
*Sold 8/67 for scrap to
Garnham, Harris & Elton,
Chesterfield.*

1256

North British Loco. 26157.

To traffic 17/11/47.

REPAIRS:
Dar. 3/2–14/3/49.**G.**
Dar. 23/8–16/9/50.**G.**
Dar. 14/2–8/3/52.**G.**
Dar. 9/7–23/8/52.**C/H.**
Dar. 10–31/10/53.**G.**
Dar. 2–7/11/53.**N/C.**
Dar. 14–19/11/53.**N/C.**
Dar. 9/11–11/12/54.**C/H.**
Dar. 5–29/9/55.**G.**
Dar. 29/3–26/4/57.**G.**
Dar. 7/7–22/8/58.**C/H.**
Dar. 25/8–25/9/59.**G.**
Complete A.T.C. fitted.
Dar. 19/3–17/4/62.**G.**
Dar. 16/3–21/5/64.**C/H.**

BOILERS:
9893.
9874 *(ex1237)* 14/3/49.
28103 *(ex61337)* 16/9/50.
28408 *(ex1214)* 8/3/52.
28418 *(ex1216)* 31/10/53.
28900 *(ex61376)* 29/9/55.
28280 *(ex1026)* 26/4/57.
28137 *(ex1015)* 25/9/59.
28868 *(ex1224)* 17/4/62.
28187 *(ex1032)* 21/5/64.

SHEDS:
Neville Hill.
Gateshead 15/9/57.
Hull Dairycoates 14/9/58.
York 6/9/64.

RENUMBERED:
61256 14/3/49.

CONDEMNED:
7/11/65.
*Sold 12/65 for scrap to
A.Draper, Hull.*

1257

North British Loco. 26158.

To traffic 19/11/47.

REPAIRS:
Dar. 29/3–28/4/49.**G.**
Dar. 4–30/9/50.**G.**
Dar. 1–25/4/52.**G.**
Dar. 27/8–19/9/53.**G.**
Dar. 29/9–1/10/53.**N/C.**
Dar. 5–8/10/53.**N/C.**
Dar. 5/5–2/6/54.**C/L.**
Dar. 15–22/6/54.**C/L.**
Dar. 14/4–12/5/55.**G.**
Dar. 7–30/11/56.**H/I.**
Dar. 4–5/12/56.**N/C.**
Dar. 13–18/12/56.**N/C.**
Dar. 29/1–22/2/57.**C/L.**
Dar. 9/12/58–13/1/59.**G.**
A.T.C.Mech. fitted.
Dar. 28/1–2/2/59.**N/C.**
Dar. 6–18/8/59.**N/C.**
A.T.C.Elec. fitted.
Dar. 12/2–3/3/60.**C/L.**
Dar. 4/9–5/10/61.**H/I.**
Dar. 16–27/10/61.**N/C.**
Dar. 2–24/11/61.**N/C.**

BOILERS:
9894.
9896 *(ex1259)* 28/4/49.
9895 *(ex1258)* 30/9/50.
28203 *(ex1274)* 25/4/52.
28219 *(ex61321)* 19/9/53.
28547 *(ex1183)* 12/5/55.
28407 *(ex1275)* 13/1/59.

SHEDS:
Neville Hill.
Thornaby 1/11/59.
West Hartlepool 9/12/62.

RENUMBERED:
61257 28/4/49.

CONDEMNED:
4/10/65.
*Sold 11/65 for scrap to
Hughes,Bolckow, North
Blyth.*

1258

North British Loco. 26159.

To traffic 21/11/47.

REPAIRS:
Dar. 3/1–11/2/49.**G.**
Dar. 27/6–5/8/50.**G.**
Dar. 2/10–8/11/51.**G.**
Don. 12/10–6/11/53.**G.**
Don. 3–4/11/54.**N/C.**
Don. 26/9–27/10/55.**G.**
Dar. 6–31/1/58.**G.**
Don. 2–7/2/58.**N/C.**
Don. 24/8–3/9/59.**C/L.**
Don. 10/3–9/4/60.**G.**
Don. 13–23/9/60.**N/C.**

BOILERS:
9895.

9941 *(ex61304)* 5/8/50.
28231 *(ex1259)* 8/11/51.
28753 *(ex61391)* 6/11/53.
28302 *(ex1145)* 27/10/55.
28248 *(ex61339)* 31/1/58.
28549 *(ex1283)* 9/4/60.

SHEDS:
Neville Hill.
Doncaster 27/1/52.
Lincoln 29/6/52.

RENUMBERED:
61258 11/2/49.

CONDEMNED:
5/1/64.
*18/3/64 In for cut up at
Doncaster. The last B1 sent
to Doncaster to be scrapped
by that works.*

1259

North British Loco. 26160.

To traffic 24/11/47.

REPAIRS:
Gor. 31/12/48–29/1/49.**G.**
Dar. 10/5–6/6/50.**G.**
Dar. 13–16/6/50.**N/C.**
Dar. 22/8–14/9/51.**G.**
Dar. 12/6–3/7/52.**C/L.**
Dar. 16/7–23/8/52.**G.**
Dar. 25–27/8/52.**N/C.**
Dar. 10–28/11/53.**G.**
Dar. 30/11–4/12/53.**N/C.**
Dar. 9–15/12/53.**N/C.**
Dar. 29/4–1/6/55.**G.**
Dar. 17/1–9/2/57.**G.**
Dar. 11–12/2/57.**N/C.**
Dar. 12/11–16/12/58.**G.**
A.T.C. Mech. fitted.
Dar. 18–22/12/58.**N/C.**
Dar. 13–26/8/59.**N/C.**
A.T.C. Elec. fitted.
Dar. 25/9–19/10/61.**G.**

BOILERS:
9896.
9875 *(ex1238)* 29/1/49.
9912 *(ex1275)* 6/6/50.
28228 *(ex1241)* 14/9/51.
28445 *(ex1268)* 23/8/52.
28230 *(ex61339)* 28/11/53.
28113 *(ex1152)* 1/6/55.
28641 *(ex1141)* 9/2/57.
28545 *(ex1014)* 16/12/58.
28245 *(ex61644)* 19/10/61.

SHEDS:
Neville Hill.
Thornaby 5/2/61.
Ardsley 25/11/62.

RENUMBERED:
61259 29/1/49.

CONDEMNED:
26/8/65.
*Sold 10/65 for scrap to
Hughes,Bolckow, North
Blyth.*

1260

North British Loco. 26161.

To traffic 26/11/47.

REPAIRS:
Cow. 29–30/11/48.**L.**
Cow. 24/5–11/6/49.**L/I.**
Cow. 24/8–13/9/50.**C/L.**
Cow. 29/12/50–20/1/51.**H/I.**
Cow. 31/10–15/11/52.**G.**
Cow. 27/3/53.**N/C.**
Cow. 19/5/53.**N/C.**
Cow. 14/1–12/2/54.**H/I.**
Efd. 2–25/11/54.**C/L.**
Cow. 29/11–1/12/54.**N/C.**
Cow. 11–18/3/55.**N/C.**
Cow. 5–24/9/55.**L/I.**
W.P.U. gear removed.
Cow. 14–25/8/56.**C/L.**
Cow. 20–21/9/56.**N/C.**
Hay. 1–10/7/57.**C/L.**
Cow. 6/11–7/12/57.**G.**
Cow. 26/3–8/4/59.**C/L.**
A.W.S. fitted.
Cow. 23/12/59–16/1/60.**H/I.**
Cow. 14/6–1/7/61.**C/L.**

BOILERS:
9897.
*9897 renumbered 28632
20/1/51.*
28627 *(ex1222)* 15/11/52.
28212 *(ex1029)* 7/12/57.

SHEDS:
Eastfield.
Haymarket 21/3/57.
Dalry Road 18/4/60.
St Margarets 1/10/61.

RENUMBERED:
61260 11/6/49.

CONDEMNED:
29/12/62.
*7/63 In for cut up at
Inverurie.*

1261

North British Loco. 26162.

To traffic 28/11/47.

REPAIRS:
Cow. 17/5–4/6/49.**L/I.**
Cow. 23/5–19/6/51.**G.**
Cow. 11/7/51.**N/C.**
Cow. 16/1–19/2/53.**L/I.**
Cow.
31/12/53–16/1/54.**C/L.**
Cow. 29/3–17/4/54.**C/L.**
Cow. 6/8–11/9/54.**G.**
Cow. 17/5–16/6/56.**L/I.**
Hay. 26/10–8/11/57.**C/L.**
Cow. 1/7–15/8/58.**G.**
Cow. 20–30/10/58.**C/L.**
Cow. 9–20/3/59.**N/C.**
Cow. 27/5–5/6/59.**C/L.**
Cow. 19/9–29/10/60.**L/I.**
Cow. 10/1–2/3/63.**G.**
Cow. 4–17/10/63.**N/C.**
Cow. 9/5–3/6/66.**C/L.**

BOILERS:
 9898.
28635 (ex1263) 19/6/51.
28652 (ex61347) 11/9/54.
28625 (ex61344) 15/8/58.
28619 (ex1102) 2/3/63.

SHEDS:
Eastfield.
Haymarket 21/3/57.
Eastfield 26/1/59.
Corkerhill 31/12/62.
Ayr 11/3/63.
Thornton Junction 31/7/64.

RENUMBERED:
61261 4/6/49.

CONDEMNED:
23/9/66.
Sold 11/66 for scrap to
Motherwell Machinery &
Scrap Co, Wishaw.

1262

North British Loco. 26163.

To traffic 1/12/47.

REPAIRS:
Cow. 2–18/6/49.**L/I.**
Cow. 7/3–3/4/51.**G.**
Cow. 15/12/52–7/2/53.**G.**
Cow. 12/1–12/2/55.**H/I.**
Cow. 31/10–12/11/55.**N/C.**
Cow. 10/11–8/12/56.**G.**
Cow. 23/5–14/6/58.**H/I.**
Cow. 26/1–3/2/59.**C/L.**
Cow. 8/7–15/8/59.**H/I.**
Cow. 17/1–10/2/62.**G.**
Inv. 23/4–5/6/65.**L/I.**

BOILERS:
 9899.
28702 (ex1290) 3/4/51.
28629 (ex1243) 7/2/53.
28644 (ex61343) 8/12/56.
28631 (ex1197) 10/2/62.

SHEDS:
Thornton Junction.
Dundee 18/4/60.
Dunfermline 28/8/66.

RENUMBERED:
61262 18/6/49.

CONDEMNED:
22/4/67.
Sold 1/68 for scrap to
Arnott Young, Parkgate.

1263

North British Loco. 26164.

To traffic 3/12/47.

REPAIRS:
Cow. 23/4–21/5/49.**L/I.**
Cow. 1–28/5/51.**G.**
Cow. 17/9–31/10/53.**G.**
Cow. 21/6–16/8/56.**H/I.**
Cow. 20–29/11/57.**N/C.**
Cow. 7/4–3/5/58.**G.**
Cow. 1–9/12/58.**N/C.**
Cow. 16–23/12/58.**N/C.**
Inv. 29/5–24/6/59.**N/C.**
Inv. 10–22/10/59.**N/C.**
Cow. 18/1–18/2/61.**L/I.**
Cow. 25/1–10/2/62.**N/C.**
Cow. 25/5–7/6/62.**C/L.**
Inv. 17–18/7/62.**N/C.**
Cow. 10/1–7/2/63.**C/L.**
Cow. 10/7–6/9/63.**G.**
Inv. 9–13/3/65.**C/L.**
Inv. 24/5–1/6/65.**N/C.**

BOILERS:
 9900.
28619 (ex1148) 28/5/51.
28643 (ex1180) 3/5/58.
28207 (ex61344) 6/9/63.

SHEDS:
Dundee.
Perth 19/2/50.
Dundee 13/3/50.

RENUMBERED:
61263 21/5/49.

CONDEMNED:
31/12/66.
Sold 27/2/67 for scrap to
G.McWilliam, Shettleston.

1264

North British Loco. 26165.

To traffic 5/12/47.

REPAIRS:
Str. 17–28/6/49.**C/L.**
Str. 5/9–22/10/49.**G.**
Str. 28/9–17/11/51.**G.**
Str. 23/12/53–30/1/54.**C/L.**
Don. 1/3–1/4/55.**G.**
Str. 19/3–24/5/57.**G.**
Str. 3/2–8/4/58.**C/L.**
Str. 15/6–20/8/59.**G.** Mod.
bogie springs. Complete
A.T.C. fitted.
Don. 9/7–7/9/62.**G.**

BOILERS:
 9901.
 9745 (ex1159) 22/10/49.
28571 (ex1227) 17/11/51.
28245 (ex1247) 1/4/55.
28520 (ex1109) 24/5/57.
28278 (ex1156) 20/8/59.
28592 (ex1000) 7/9/62.
SHEDS:
Stratford.
Parkeston 18/12/47.
Colwick 27/11/60.

RENUMBERED:
61264 22/10/49.

CONDEMNED:
21/11/65.
Made S.B.Dept'l No.29 to
7/67. Sold for scrap 3/68 to
Woodham Bros., Barry.
But re-sold for preservation
& left Barry 7/76 for Main
Line Steam Trust at
Loughborough.

1265

North British Loco. 26166.

To traffic 8/12/47.

REPAIRS:
Gor. 25/5–5/6/48.Spec.
Don. 30/1–21/3/50.**G.**
Don. 10–17/4/51.**N/C.**
Don. 28/12/51–21/1/52.**G.**
Gor. 10/4–22/5/54.**G.**
Gor. 19/4–7/6/58.**C/L.**
Dar. 20/8–17/9/58.**G.**
Dar. 23/9–22/11/60.**C/L.**

BOILERS:
 9902.
 3695 (ex1073) 21/3/50.
28170 (ex1229) 21/1/52.
28565 (ex61317) 22/5/54.
28103 (ex1152) 17/9/58.

SHEDS:
Doncaster.
Gorton 27/6/54.
Leicester 30/5/59.
Gorton 20/7/59.
Leicester 31/7/61.

RENUMBERED:
61265 5/6/48.

CONDEMNED:
19/2/62.
10/4/62 In for cut up at
Darlington.

1266

North British Loco. 26167.

To traffic 10/12/47.

REPAIRS:
Gor. 11–31/5/48.Spec.
Don. 14–29/9/48.**L.**
Don. 29/1–31/3/50.**G.**
Don. 4–25/1/52.**G.**
Don. 24/9–23/10/53.**G.**
Dar. 27/5–1/7/55.**G.**
Don. 24/9–22/10/57.**G.**
Don. 12/12/59–15/1/60.**G.**
Don. 15–17/12/60.**N/C.**

RENUMBERED:
61264 22/10/49.

BOILERS:
 9903.
 9934 (ex1297) 31/3/50.
28172 (ex1665) 25/1/52.
28281 (ex1665) 23/10/53.
28219 (ex1257) 1/7/55.
28550 (ex1100) 22/10/57.
28546 (ex1234) 15/1/60.

SHEDS:
Kings Cross.
Doncaster 21/12/52.
Sheffield 12/6/60.

RENUMBERED:
61266 29/5/48.

CONDEMNED:
16/9/62.
Sold 1/63 for scrap to Albert
Looms, Spondon.

1267

North British Loco. 26168.

To traffic 12/12/47.

REPAIRS:
Don. 10/12/48–28/1/49.**G.**
Don. 22–28/2/49.**N/C.**
Don. 15/3–28/4/50.**G.**
Don. 31/1–5/3/52.**G.**
Don. 7–15/5/52.**N/C.**
Don. 19/6–17/7/54.**G.**
Dar. 7–31/1/57.**G.**
Dar. 2/4–7/5/60.**G.** A.W.S.
fitted.
Dar. 17/6–2/7/60.**N/C.**
Dar. 1/8/61.Weigh.

BOILERS:
 9904.
 9902 (ex1265) 28/4/50.
28178 (ex1231) 5/3/52.
28240 (ex1040) 17/7/54.
28850 (ex1056) 31/1/57.
28179 (ex1166) 7/5/60.

SHEDS:
Ardsley.
Bradford 10/4/49.
Wakefield 16/6/57.
Copley Hill 15/9/57.
West Hartlepool 14/9/58.

RENUMBERED:
61267 28/1/49.

CONDEMNED:
10/12/62.
13/2/63 In for cut up at
Darlington.

1268

North British Loco. 26169.

To traffic 16/12/47.

WORKS CODES:– Cow – Cowlairs. Dar – Darlington. Dee – Dundee. Don – Doncaster. Ghd – Gateshead. Gor – Gorton. Inv – Inverurie. Str – Stratford. SRX – St Rollox.

REPAIR CODES:– **C/H** – Casual Heavy. **C/L** – Casual Light. **G** – General. **H** – Heavy. **H/I** – Heavy Intermediate. **L** – Light. **L/I** – Light Intermediate. **N/C** – Non–Classified.

REPAIRS:
Don. 14/4–12/5/50.**G.**
Don. 19/5–7/6/52.**G.**
Don. 6/8–17/9/54.**G.**
Dar. 15–25/8/56.**C/L.**
Dar. 9/7–22/8/57.**G.**
Dar. 5/4–4/5/61.**G.**
Complete A.W.S. fitted.

BOILERS:
9905.
9904 *(ex1267)* 12/5/50.
28105 *(ex1257)* 7/6/52.
28444 *(ex61322)* 17/9/54.
28409 *(ex1298)* 22/8/57.
28863 *(ex1023)* 4/5/61.

SHEDS:
Ardsley.
Bradford 10/4/49.
Wakefield 16/6/57.
Ardsley 25/11/62.

RENUMBERED:
61268 12/5/50.

CONDEMNED:
28/12/64.
Sold 3/65 for scrap to
A.Draper, Hull.

1269

North British Loco. 26170.

To traffic 24/12/47.

REPAIRS:
Gor. 27/10–9/12/49.**G.**
Gor. 13–15/12/49.**N/C.**
Gor. 19–23/12/49.**N/C.**
Dar. 5/12/51–22/1/52.**G.**
Don. 19/11–12/12/52.**C/H.**
Gor. 20/2–27/3/54.**G.**
Dar. 17/5–19/6/56.**G.**
Dar. 4–19/3/57.**C/L.**
Dar. 8/8–5/9/58.**G.**
Dar. 12/5–9/6/61.**G.**

BOILERS:
9906.
9949 *(ex61312)* 9/12/49.
28245 *(ex61304)* 22/1/52.
28342 *(ex61406)* 12/12/52.
28854 *(new)* 27/3/54.
28800 *(ex1169)* 19/6/56.
28155 *(ex1053)* 5/9/58.
28270 *(ex1106)* 9/6/61.

SHEDS:
Lincoln.
Colwick 6/4/52.
Lincoln 20/4/52.
Colwick 27/9/53.
Leicester 11/11/56.
Agecroft 3/10/59.
Woodford 21/7/62.
Gorton 19/11/62.

RENUMBERED:
61269 9/12/49.

CONDEMNED:
21/12/63.
Sold 12/64 for scrap to
T.W.Ward, Killamarsh.

1270

North British Loco. 26171.

To traffic 25/12/47.

REPAIRS:
Str. 24/6–2/9/49.**G.**
Str. 31/12/50–17/2/51.**G.**
Str. 28/5–7/6/51.**N/C.**
Str. 11/8–27/9/52.**G.**
Str. 10/11/53–9/1/54.**H/I.**
Collision at Goodmayes.
Str. 14/4–11/6/55.**C/L.**
Str. 13/5–29/6/56.**G.**
Str. 7/11–13/12/57.**C/L.**
Str. 29/4–30/5/58.**N/C.**
Str. 30/9–14/11/58.**G.** *Mod.*
bogie springs.
Don. 4–24/3/60.**C/L.**
Don. 2/1–1/2/61.**G.**

BOILERS:
9907.
9939 *(ex1302)* 2/9/49.
28531 *(ex1252)* 17/2/51.
28835 *(new)* 27/9/52.
28542 *(ex1287)* 29/6/56.
28276 *(ex1001)* 14/11/58.
28753 *(ex1141)* 1/2/61.

SHEDS:
Norwich.
Ipswich 7/8/55.
Norwich 23/10/55.
Doncaster 18/10/59.

RENUMBERED:
61270 2/9/49.

CONDEMNED:
22/9/63.
31/10/63 In for cut up at
Doncaster.

1271

North British Loco. 26172.

To traffic 26/12/47.

REPAIRS:
Str. 7/3–7/5/49.**G.**
Str. 20/8–29/9/50.**G.**
Str. 21/2–10/3/51.**C/L.**
Str. 2/2–5/4/52.**G.**
Str. 21/10–20/11/52.**C/L.**
Gor. 15/5–26/6/54.**G.**
Dar. 22/8–22/9/56.**G.**
Dar. 18/8–23/9/58.**G.**
Dar. 26/2–31/3/60.**G.**

BOILERS:
9908.
9870 *(ex1233)* 7/5/49.
28503 *(ex1285)* 29/9/50.
28583 *(ex1042)* 5/4/52.
28864 *(ex61366)* 26/6/54.

28208 *(ex1181)* 22/9/56.
28398 *(ex1189)* 23/9/58.
28419 *(ex61380)* 31/3/60.

SHEDS:
Norwich.
Colwick 20/9/53.
Woodford 16/6/57.

RENUMBERED:
61271 7/5/49.

CONDEMNED:
30/7/62.
20/8/62 In for cut up at
Darlington.

1272

North British Loco. 26173.

To traffic 29/12/47.

REPAIRS:
Str. 6–19/3/49.**C/L.**
Str. 27/5–28/7/49.**G.**
Str. 31/8–2/9/49.**N/C.**
Str. 26/2–17/3/50.**C/L.**
Str. 5/11–16/12/50.**G.**
Str. 19/5–4/7/52.**G.**
Dar. 14/7–11/8/54.**G.**
Dar. 9/7–21/8/56.**G.**
Don. 31/1–7/3/59.**G.**
Don. 9/8–16/9/61.**G.**

BOILERS:
9909.
9924 *(ex1287)* 28/7/49.
28518 *(ex1144)* 16/12/50.
28562 *(ex1089)* 4/7/52.
28189 *(ex1248)* 11/8/54.
28415 *(ex1274)* 21/8/56.
28450 *(ex61364)* 7/3/59.
28854 *(ex61348)* 16/9/61.

SHEDS:
Norwich.
Colwick 20/9/53.
Leicester 19/12/54.
Colwick 20/2/55.
Annesley 17/2/57.
Sheffield 26/1/58.
Kings Cross 19/10/58.
New England 19/4/59.

RENUMBERED:
61272 19/3/49.

CONDEMNED:
3/1/65.
Made S.B.Dept'l No.25.
Sold 1/66 for scrap to
Garnham,Harris & Elton,
Chesterfield.

1273

North British Loco. 26174.

To traffic 30/12/47.

REPAIRS:
Dar. 25/1–21/3/50.**G.**
Dar. 6/2–6/3/52.**G.**
Dar. 12/2–6/3/54.**G.**
Dar. 12–25/5/54.**C/L.**
Dar. 14–27/7/55.**C/L.**
Dar. 19/4–14/5/56.**G.**
Dar. 30/5–8/6/56.**N/C.**
Dar. 23/6–7/8/58.**G.**
Dar. 13–19/8/58.**N/C.**
Dar. 12–25/2/59.**N/C.**
A.T.C.Mech. fitted.
Dar. 12/6–8/7/61.**G.**

BOILERS:
9910.
9976 *(ex61339)* 21/3/50.
28406 *(ex1298)* 6/3/52.
28214 *(ex61320)* 6/3/54.
28576 *(ex1289)* 14/5/56.
28181 *(ex1130)* 7/8/58.
28409 *(ex1268)* 8/7/61.

SHEDS:
Darlington.
Southern Region 17/5/53.
Darlington 21/6/53.
York 14/6/59.

RENUMBERED:
61273 21/3/50.

CONDEMNED:
7/5/63.
16/5/63 In for cut up at
Darlington.

1274

North British Loco. 26175.

To traffic 2/1/48.

REPAIRS:
Dar. 17/1–2/3/50.**G.**
Ghd. 6–10/3/50.**N/C.**
Dar. 22–23/3/50.*Weigh.*
Dar. 19/2–14/3/51.**C/L.**
Dar. 23/2–21/3/52.**G.**
Dar. 15/3–10/4/54.**G.**
Dar. 26/5–24/6/54.**C/L.**
Dar. 15–27/3/56.**C/L.**
Dar. 5/6–2/7/56.**G.**
Dar. 9–11/7/56.**N/C.**
Dar. 19/9–21/10/58.**G.**
A.T.C.mech. fitted.
Dar. 7–15/10/59.**N/C.**
A.T.C.elec. fitted.
Dar. 4/1–17/2/62.**H/I.**

BOILERS:
9911.
3739 *(ex1032)* 2/3/50.
3739 renumbered 28203
14/3/51.
28417 *(ex1280)* 21/3/52.
28415 *(ex1276)* 10/4/54.
28196 *(ex61325)* 2/7/56.
28417 *(ex1068)* 21/10/58.

SHEDS:
Darlington.
Southern Region 17/5/53.
Darlington 21/6/53.

York 26/6/55.
Darlington 25/9/55.
Low Moor 14/6/59.
Wakefield 23/12/62.

RENUMBERED:
61274 2/3/50.

CONDEMNED:
23/11/64.
Sold 1/65 for scrap to Cox
& Danks, Wadsley Bridge.

1275

North British Loco. 26176.

To traffic 12/1/48.

REPAIRS:
Dar. 13/4–6/5/50.**G.**
Dar. 1/8/50.Weigh.
Dar. 30/4–24/5/52.**G.**
Dar. 26–27/5/52.**N/C.**
Dar. 26/4–15/5/54.**G.**
Dar. 17–20/5/54.**N/C.**
Dar. 9–17/1/56.**C/L.**
Dar. 26/4–23/5/56.**G.**
Dar. 9/12/57–15/1/58.**C/H.**
Dar. 1/10–6/11/58.**G.**
A.T.C.mech. fitted.
Dar. 10–14/11/58.**N/C.**
Dar. 11–12/8/59.Not
repaired.
Dar. 21/12/60–7/1/61.**N/C.**
A.W.S. elec. fitted.
Dar. 27/12/61–27/1/62.**G.**

BOILERS:
9912.
9851 (ex1214) 6/5/50.
28428 (ex1071) 24/5/52.
28407 (ex1037) 15/5/54.
28403 (ex1255) 23/5/56.
28233 (ex61381) 6/11/58.
28258 (ex)1216 27/1/62.

SHEDS:
Darlington.
Stockton 4/11/51.
West Hartlepool 7/11/54.
York 12/5/63.

RENUMBERED:
61275 6/5/50.

CONDEMNED:
28/10/65.
Sold 12/65 for scrap to
Hughes,Bolckow, North
Blyth.

1276

North British Loco. 26177.

To traffic 14/1/48.

REPAIRS:
Dar. 28/2–7/3/49.**C/L.**
Dar. 3/4–3/5/50.**G.**
Dar. 10/3–2/4/52.**G.**
Dar. 8/2–4/3/54.**G.**

Dar. 15–23/3/54.**N/C.**
Dar. 3–16/8/55.**C/L.**
Dar. 14/8–10/9/56.**G.**
Dar. 24/10–21/11/58.**G.**
A.T.C. mech. fitted.
Dar. 18/4–18/5/61.**G.**
A.W.S. completed.
Dar. 9/9–19/10/63.**G.**

BOILERS:
9913.
9911 (ex1274) 3/5/50.
28415 (ex1273) 2/4/52.
28103 (ex1288) 4/3/54.
28837 (ex61314) 10/9/56.
28102 (ex1011) 21/11/58.
28232 (ex1037) 18/5/61.
28222 (ex1240) 19/10/63.

SHEDS:
Darlington.
York 14/6/59.

RENUMBERED:
61276 3/5/50.

CONDEMNED:
28/6/65.
Sold 8/65 for scrap to Ellis
Metals, Swalwell.

1277

North British Loco. 26178.

To traffic 16/1/48.

REPAIRS:
Inv. 3–5/2/48.**L.** Tab.
catcher fitted.
Inv. 14–15/12/48.**L.**
Cow. 10/3–6/5/49.**G.**
Cow. 12/9–6/10/51.**L/I.**
Cow. 21/9–22/10/53.**G.**
Cow. 11/11–10/12/55.**H/I.**
W.P.U. gear removed.
Cow. 10–13/4/57.**N/C.**
Cow. 24/12/57–25/1/58.**G.**
Cow. 16/7–15/8/59.**H/I.**
A.W.S. fitted.
Cow. 26–27/8/59.**N/C.**
Mod. bogie springs.
Cow. 25/4–19/5/62.**G.**

BOILERS:
9914.
9914 renumbered 28636
6/10/51.
28621 (ex1178) 22/10/53.
28143 (ex61407) 25/1/58.
28628 (ex1148) 19/5/62.

SHEDS:
Kittybrewster.
Keith 11/9/49.
St Margarets 1/12/49.
Parkhead 4/3/51.
Eastfield 18/3/51.
Thornton Junction 4/5/57.
Dundee 18/4/60.

RENUMBERED:
61277 6/5/49.

CONDEMNED:
2/6/64.
Sold 8/64 for scrap to
P&W.McLellan,
Langloan.

1278

North British Loco. 26179.

To traffic 19/1/48.

REPAIRS:
Cow. 5/9–1/10/49.**L/I.**
Cow. 31/5–23/6/51.**L/I.**
Cow. 26/6–11/7/53.**G.**
Cow. 7/7–20/8/55.**H/I.**
Cow. 16/10–16/11/57.**L/I.**
Cow. 2–27/3/59.**G.**
Cow. 2–13/10/59.**N/C.**
Cow. 23/10–12/11/59.**L/C.**
Cow. 25/10–1/12/61.**H/I.**
Cow. 21/11–8/12/62.**C/L.**
Inv. 31/10–21/11/63.**N/C.**
Inv. 5–10/12/63.**N/C.**
Cow. 24/9–31/10/64.**H/I.**
Cow. 23/6–13/8/66.**C/L.**

BOILERS:
9915.
9915 renumbered 28637
23/6/51.
28664 (ex1359) 11/7/53.
28655 (ex61307) 27/3/59.

SHED:
Dundee.

RENUMBERED:
61278 1/10/49.

CONDEMNED:
22/4/67.
Sold 1/68 for scrap to
Arnott Young, Carmyle.

1279

North British Loco. 26180.

To traffic 21/1/48.

REPAIRS:
Gor. 22/9–29/10/49.**G.**
Gor. 3–5/11/49.**N/C.**
Dar. 16/2–15/3/52.**G.**
Gor. 28/3–22/5/54.**G.**
Gor. 25–31/5/54.**N/C.**
Dar. 3/6–7/7/56.**G.**
Str. 8–21/10/58.**G.** Mod.
bogie springs.
Don. 17/11–22/12/60.**G.**

BOILERS:
9916.
9862 (ex1225) 29/10/49.
28413 (ex61318) 15/3/52.
28342 (ex1269) 22/5/54.
28234 (ex61383) 7/7/56.
28857 (ex61363) 21/10/58.
28597 (ex61334) 22/12/60.

SHEDS:
Lincoln.
Norwich 12/9/54.
Lincoln 21/11/54.
Stratford 17/2/57.
Norwich 10/8/58.
Doncaster 4/10/59.

RENUMBERED:
61279 29/10/49.

CONDEMNED:
22/9/63.
30/10/63 In for cut up at
Doncaster.

1280

North British Loco. 26181.

To traffic 23/1/48.

REPAIRS:
Gor. 27/11/49–28/1/50.**G.**
Gor. 1–2/2/50.**N/C.**
Dar. 30/1–7/3/52.**G.**
Str. 10/12/52–24/1/53.**C/H.**
Str. 16/2–2/4/54.**G.**
Str. 5/3–21/4/56.**G.**
Str. 21/4–1/6/58.**G.** Mod.
bogie springs.
Str. 13/4–27/5/60.**G.**
A.T.C. fitted.
Don. 20–23/7/60.**N/C.**

BOILERS:
9917.
9918 (ex1281) 28/1/50.
28243 (ex1284) 7/3/52.
28587 (ex1254) 2/4/54.
28867 (ex1252) 21/4/56.
28581 (ex1301) 1/6/58.
28432 (ex spare & 3897)
27/5/60.

SHEDS:
Lincoln.
Colwick 6/4/52.
Lincoln 20/4/52.
Stratford 14/9/52.
Parkeston 8/2/59.
Cambridge 12/4/59.
Norwich 20/11/60.
March 4/2/62.

RENUMBERED:
61280 28/1/50.

CONDEMNED:
16/9/62.
Sold 11/63 for scrap to
Central Wagon Co., Ince.

1281

North British Loco. 26182.

To traffic 27/1/48.

REPAIRS:
Gor. 12/11–22/12/49.**G.**
Gor. 23–29/12/49.**N/C.**
continued on page 76

This double-heading, seen at New Southgate on 13th June 1957 was deliberate, and regular. The train is the 4.12 p.m. from King's Cross to Peterborough and Cambridge, which split at Hitchin, B1 class 61139 going forward with the Peterborough portion and L1 class 67749 taking the other to Cambridge.

61015 was one of those loaned to Southern Region in May/June 1953 to work between London Victoria and Dover or Ramsgate in place of Bullied Pacifics withdrawn for their axles to be checked.

During March and April 1951, 61370 and 61373 worked a series of dynamometer car tests on the mainly level line between Peterborough and Grimsby, the London Midland Region braking units being included in the train. To measure wind velocity and direction, an anemometer and indicator were mounted in front of the leading engine. Due to the gear being so close to the front of the engine, it proved difficult to get accurate readings.

Another example of 'mixed traffic' working is seen leaving Bulwell Common station working the railway employees special known as the Annesley 'Dido'. 61063 shedded at Annesley was no doubt filling in between more important (certainly heavier) jobs when seen here on 22nd March 1952.

This B1 was allocated to Wakefield shed in 1960 when it was working this special excursion, and is included for the excellent portrayal of the front end. Note the 61131 plate on the door − which was fitted by Gorton in September 1948 has the 6 with the curled tail − and is likely then to have been kept to withdrawal. Wakefield's first shed code was 25A, but changed to 56A when it was taken over by North Eastern Region, and the plate has been duly kept in line.

The B1 selected for the B.R. Interchange Trials was given a special repair at Gorton in April 1948 when its number had the modified 6 added to it, and on the tender BRITISH RAILWAYS naturally replaced LNER. Here on 18th June 1948 it is leaving St Pancras, and the leading coach is the LMS dynamometer car.

When they were new, 1018 – 1034 and 1140 – 1089 were fitted with an axle mounted electric generator on the near side rear bogie wheel. They came adrift easily and many were soon discarded, in 61024's case before December 1948 – that is, with less than twenty months use. Although the lamps and conduit remained in place, 61024 never had any alternative generator fitted. Note change from LNER to BR numbering by patching, and addition of plate on smokebox door.

Electric equipment was never really accepted by those who had to work the engines. Its maintenance was frequently neglected, and here is a by no means unusual example, 61237 (a Director named engine!) in August 1963 with one lamp fitting gone completely and another with the glass missing. Note absence of allocation plate, due to a recent transfer from Blaydon to Tyne Dock shed.

1281 continued
Gor. 29/8–3/11/51.**G.**
Gor. 6–10/11/51.**N/C.**
Don. 29/9–28/10/53.**G.**
Dar. 20/7–2/9/55.**G.**
Dar. 17/5–14/6/57.**G.**
Don. 12/5–10/6/59.**G.**
Don. 2–14/3/60.**N/C.**
Don. 10/10–1/11/60.**N/C.**
Don. 14/2–9/3/62.**G.**
Dar. 29/8–11/9/63.**N/C.**

BOILERS:
9918.
  3699 *(ex1111)* 22/12/49.
28356 *(ex61408)* 3/11/51.
28409 *(ex61366)* 28/10/53.
28449 *(ex1186)* 2/9/55.
28291 *(ex61369)* 14/6/57.
28404 *(ex1179)* 10/6/59.
28859 *(ex1168)* 9/3/62.

SHEDS:
Lincoln.
Immingham 19/2/56.
Colwick 1/6/58.
To LMR Stock 1/2/66.

RENUMBERED:
61281 22/12/49.

CONDEMNED:
19/2/66.
*Sold 5/66 for scrap to Birds,
Long Marston.*

1282

North British Loco. 26183.

To traffic 28/1/48.

REPAIRS:
Gor. 8/3–23/4/49.**G.**
Str. 23–30/1/50.**N/C.**
Str. 30/3–5/5/51.**G.**
Str. 9/2–10/4/53.**G.** *Mod.
bogie springs.*
Don. 11/1–10/2/55.**G.**
Don. 15/4–4/5/55.**C/L.**
Dar. 19/10–13/11/57.**G.**
Dar. 17–20/11/57.**N/C.**
Don. 23/9–23/10/59.**G.**

BOILERS:
9919.
  9773 *(ex1187)* 23/4/49.
28549 *(ex1192)* 5/5/51.
28508 *(ex1615)* 10/4/53.
28124 *(ex1200)* 10/2/55.
28418 *(ex61316)* 13/11/57.
28443 *(ex1196)* 23/10/59.

SHEDS:
Colwick.
Leicester 21/11/48.
Gorton 15/5/49.
Stratford 21/8/49.
New England 27/9/53.

RENUMBERED:
61282 23/4/49.

CONDEMNED:
16/9/62.
*Sold 1/63 for scrap to
R.A.King, Norwich.*

1283

North British Loco. 26184.

To traffic 2/2/48.

REPAIRS:
Gor. 15–27/11/48.**L.**
Gor. 24/5–1/7/49.**G.**
Gor. 19–20/7/49.**N/C.**
Don. 29/3–3/5/51.**G.**
Don. 27/2–18/4/52.**H/I.**
Gor. 22/8–19/9/53.**G.**
Gor. 22/9–22/11/53.**N/C.**
Dar. 1–26/10/55.**G.**
Dar. 17–24/10/56.**N/C.**
Ghd. 19/2–15/3/57.**C/L.**
Str. 17/2–25/4/58.**G.**
Don. 22/2–19/3/60.**G.**

BOILERS:
9920.
  9919 *(ex1282)* 1/7/49.
28138 *(ex1240)* 3/5/51.
28237 *(ex61304)* 19/9/53.
28397 *(ex61313)* 26/10/55.
28549 *(ex1615)* 25/4/58.
28750 *(ex1652)* 19/3/60.

SHEDS:
Colwick.
Leicester 6/11/49.
Colwick 18/12/49.
Leicester 5/2/50.
Colwick 12/3/50.
Woodford 7/11/54.
Colwick 20/2/55.
Leicester 15/11/56.
Colwick 9/12/56.
Kings Cross 5/5/57.
Cambridge 20/10/57.
Norwich 20/11/60.
Stratford 10/9/61.

RENUMBERED:
61283 27/11/48.

CONDEMNED:
16/9/62.
*26/11/62 In for cut up at
Doncaster.*

1284

North British Loco. 26185.

To traffic 6/2/48.

REPAIRS:
Gor. 19/1–25/2/50.**G.**
Gor. 3–4/3/50.**N/C.**
Dar. 18/11–20/12/51.**G.**
Don. 30/10–2/12/52.**C/H.**
Don. 27/11–29/12/53.**G.**
Don. 14/4–6/5/55.**C/L.**
Dar. 9/7–11/8/55.**G.**
Dar. 13–24/9/55.**N/C.**
Dar. 31/3–4/5/57.**G.**

Dar. 8–15/5/57.**N/C.**
Don. 5/5–6/6/59.**G.**
Don. 5–24/10/60.**N/C.**

BOILERS:
9921.
  9700 *(ex1092)* 25/2/50.
28239 *(ex61369)* 20/12/51.
28135 *(ex1170)* 2/12/52.
28151 *(ex1165)* 29/12/53.
28226 *(ex1240)* 11/8/55.
28843 *(ex1225)* 4/5/57.
28344 *(ex1093)* 6/6/59.

SHEDS:
Immingham.
Lincoln 22/11/59.

RENUMBERED:
61284 25/2/50.

CONDEMNED:
16/9/62.
*Sold 1/63 for scrap to Albert
Looms, Spondon.*

1285

North British Loco. 26186.

To traffic 9/2/48.

REPAIRS:
Str. 7/2–26/3/49.**G.**
Str. 7/6–29/7/50.**G.** *Speed
indic. gear fitted.*
Str. 21/8–14/9/51.**C/L.**
Str. 2/3–10/4/52.**G.**
Str. 30/7–24/9/52.**C/H.**
Str. 15/12/52–17/1/53.**C/H.**
Str. 11/12/53–23/1/54.**G.**
Str. 2/8–16/9/55.**G.**
Dar. 14/6–12/7/57.**G.**
Don. 22–28/4/59.**N/C.**
Don. 29/10–25/11/59.**G.**
Don. 15–17/12/60.**N/C.**
Don. 22/1–24/2/62.**G.**

BOILERS:
9922.
  3464 *(ex8309)* 26/3/49.
  9434 *(ex1616)* 29/7/50.
  9434 renumbered 28566
14/9/51.
28262 *(ex1299)* 10/4/52.
28577 *(ex1043)* 23/1/54.
28582 *(ex1615)* 16/9/55.
28200 *(ex1192)* 12/7/57.
28751 *(ex1158)* 25/11/59.

SHEDS:
Cambridge.
Doncaster 28/10/56.
Colwick 12/6/60.

RENUMBERED:
61285 26/3/49.

CONDEMNED:
19/12/65.
*Sold 2/66 for scrap to
Steelbreaking &
Dismantling Co,
Chesterfield.*

1286

North British Loco. 26187.

To traffic 11/2/48.

REPAIRS:
Str. 11/1–9/2/49.**L.**
Str. 1/7–10/9/49.**G.**
Str. 11/2–7/4/51.**G.**
Str. 20–22/5/52.**N/C.**
Str. 23/10–13/12/52.**G.**
Str. 17–20/11/53.**N/C.**
Str. 12/5–25/6/54.**G.**
Str. 30/8–10/9/54.**N/C.**
Str. 5/10–6/1/55.**C/L.**
Str. 18/9–26/10/56.**G.**
Str. 1/7–4/9/58.**G.** *Mod.
bogie springs.*
Str. 19/5–5/6/59.**C/L.**
Complete A.T.C. fitted.
Don. 11/5–10/6/60.**G.**
Don. 21/11–16/12/61.**C/L.**

BOILERS:
9923.
  5110 *(new)* 10/9/49.
28542 *(ex1300)* 7/4/51.
28534 *(ex1201)* 13/12/52.
28560 *(ex1003)* 25/6/54.
28544 *(ex1603)* 26/10/56.
28100 *(ex1083)* 4/9/58.
28980 *(new)* 10/6/60. *This
boiler only worked 2 years
& 3 months.*

SHEDS:
Cambridge.
Stratford 16/9/56.
March 17/6/62.

RENUMBERED:
61286 10/9/49.

CONDEMNED:
16/9/62.
*Sold 6/63 for scrap to
Central Wagon Co., Ince.*

1287

North British Loco. 26188.

To traffic 13/2/48.

REPAIRS:
Str. 19/5–1/7/49.**G**
Str. 13/3–21/4/51.**G.**
Str. 22–29/6/51.**N/C.**
Str. 4/2–4/4/52.**C/H.**
Str. 15/12/52–31/1/53.**G.**
Str. 29/6–23/7/53.**N/C.**
Str. 5/8–10/9/53.**N/C.**
Str. 24–25/3/54.*Weigh.*
Str. 11/10–20/11/54.**G.**
Str. 7/8–8/9/56.**G.**
Str. 15/5–25/7/58.**G.** *Mod.
bogie springs.*
Don. 28/1–3/3/60.**G.**

BOILERS:
9924.
  9890 *(ex1253)* 1/7/49.

28546 *(ex spare & 1059)*
21/4/51.
28542 *(ex1286)* 31/1/53.
28527 *(ex1052)* 20/11/54.
28835 *(ex1270)* 8/9/56.
28821 *(ex1226)* 25/7/58.
28203 *(ex1235)* 3/3/60.

SHEDS:
Cambridge.
March 17/6/62.

RENUMBERED:
61287 1/7/49.

CONDEMNED:
16/9/62.
*Sold 3/63 for scrap to
J.Cashmore, Great Bridge.*

E1288

North British Loco. 26189.

To traffic 16/2/48.

REPAIRS:
Dar. 31/5–24/6/50.**G.**
Dar. 26–27/6/50.**N/C.**
Dar. 11/3–3/4/52.**G.**
Ghd. 7–10/4/52.**N/C.**
Dar. 30/12/53–23/1/54.**G.**
Dar. 14/11–10/12/55.**G.**
Dar. 12–14/12/55.**N/C.**
Dar. 31/1–1/3/58.**G.**
Dar. 2/8–7/9/60.**G.**
Complete A.W.S. fitted.
Dar. 14/3–10/4/62.**C/H.**
Dar. 5–29/11/62.**C/L.**

BOILERS:
9925.
9855 *(ex1218)* 24/6/50.
28103 *(ex1256)* 3/4/52.
28445 *(ex1259)* 23/1/54.
28430 *(ex61306)* 10/12/55.
28210 *(ex61376)* 1/3/58.
28588 *(spare 1 year ex 1616)*
7/9/60.

SHEDS:
Darlington.
York 26/9/48.

RENUMBERED:
61288 24/6/50.

CONDEMNED:
6/1/64.
*27/1/64 In for cut up at
Darlington.*

E1289

North British Loco. 26190.

To traffic 18/2/48.

REPAIRS:
Dar. 1–24/11/49.**G.**
Dar. 28–30/11/49.**N/C.**
Dar. 30/11–28/12/51.**G.**
Dar. 14/5/53.*Weigh.*

Dar. 16/12/53–8/1/54.**G.**
Dar. 13/2–8/3/56.**G.**
Dar. 7–14/6/57.**C/L.**
Dar. 21/5–25/6/58.**G.**
Dar. 14/11–13/12/60.**G.**
Complete A.W.S. fitted.
Dar. 23/10–14/11/61.**C/L.**
Dar. 7/4–28/5/64.**G.**

BOILERS:
9926.
9892 *(ex1255)* 24/11/49.
28238 *(ex61368)* 28/12/51.
28576 *(ex61311)* 8/1/54.
28364 *(ex1061)* 8/3/56.
28187 *(ex1169)* 25/6/58.
28309 *(ex1115)* 13/12/60.
28177 *(ex spare for 2 years)*
28/5/64.

SHEDS:
Darlington.
Hull Botanic Gardens
13/1/57.
Hull Dairycoates 14/6/59.

RENUMBERED:
61289 24/11/49.

CONDEMNED:
24/6/67.
*Sold 8/67 for scrap to
Garnham, Harris & Elton,
Chesterfield.*

E1290

North British Loco. 26191.

To traffic 20/2/48.

REPAIRS:
Dar. 25/7–18/8/49.**C/L.**
After collision.
Cow. 21/8–2/10/50.**G.**
Dar. 26/8–13/9/52.**G.**
Cow. 1–30/8/54.**L/I.**
Cow. 2/11–7/12/55.**G.**
Cow. 1/11–10/12/57.**L/I.**
Cow. 3/8–8/9/59.**G.**

BOILERS:
9927.
9925 *(ex1288)* 2/10/50.
28437 *(ex1227)* 13/9/52.
28669 *(ex61404)* 7/12/55.
28640 *(ex61358)* 8/9/59.

SHEDS:
Darlington.
Stockton 14/11/48.
Carlisle Canal 20/9/53.

RENUMBERED:
61290 18/8/49.

CONDEMNED:
21/3/62.
*7/62 In for cut up at
Cowlairs.*

E1291

North British Loco. 26192.

To traffic 24/2/48.
REPAIRS:
Dar. 15/5–8/6/50.**G.**
Dar. 12–15/6/50.**N/C.**
Dar. 13/5–6/6/52.**G.**
Dar. 26/3–3/4/54.**C/L.**
Dar. 2–26/6/54.**G.**
Dar. 28–29/6/54.**N/C.**
Dar. 6–9/7/54.**N/C.**
Dar. 22/7–11/8/54.**N/C.**
Dar. 20/8–17/9/56.**G.**
Dar. 5/12/58–9/1/59.**G.**
Dar. 8/9–6/10/61.**G.**
Complete A.W.S. fitted.
Dar. 19/10–10/11/61.**N/C.**

BOILERS:
9928.
9942 *(ex61305)* 8/6/50.
28435 *(ex1216)* 6/6/52.
28417 *(ex1274)* 26/6/54.
28228 *(ex61322)* 17/9/56.
28243 *(ex1198)* 9/1/59.
28224 *(ex1062)* 6/10/61.

SHEDS:
Darlington.
Borough Gardens 25/7/48.
Darlington 6/2/49.
York 26/6/55.
Darlington 25/9/55.
York 14/6/59.
Ardsley 25/11/62.

RENUMBERED:
61291 8/6/50.

CONDEMNED:
20/5/65.
*Sold 6/65 for scrap to Ellis
Metals, Swalwell.*

E1292

North British Loco. 26193.

To traffic 25/2/48.

REPAIRS:
Cow. 26/5–25/6/48.**L.** *LMS
tab. catcher fitted.*
Cow. 8–25/3/50.**L/I.**
Cow. 20/11–8/12/51.**H/I.**
Cow. 17/12/51–5/1/52.**C/L.**
Cow. 12–17/1/52.**N/C.**
Cow. 29/4–26/5/53.**G.**
Cow. 21/10–6/11/54.**N/C.**
Dee. 8–30/4/55.**C/L.**
Cow. 24/8–24/9/55.**H/I.**
Cow. 17–22/10/55.**N/C.**
Cow. 27/12/56–30/1/57.**L/I.**
Cow. 16–26/4/57.**N/C.**
Cow. 20/11–6/12/58.**G.**
Mod. bogie springs.
Cow. 8–21/5/59.**C/L.**
A.W.S. fitted.
Cow. 2/5–10/6/61.**L/I.**
Cow. 30/3–6/4/62.**N/C.**
Cow. 24/4–25/5/63.**C/L.**
Cow. 24/9–30/11/63.**G.**

BOILERS:
9929.
9929 renumbered 28638
8/12/51.
28630 *(ex1244)* 26/5/53.
28167 *(ex1108)* 6/12/58. *141
tubes.*
28233 *(ex Dar & spare)*
30/11/63.

SHEDS:
Thornton Junction.
Haymarket 28/3/48.
Dundee 25/7/48.

RENUMBERED:
61292 25/6/48.

CONDEMNED:
10/9/65.
*Sold 10/65 for scrap to
Shipbreaking Industries,
Faslane.*

E1293

North British Loco. 26194.

To traffic 27/2/48.

REPAIRS:
Cow. 28/11–17/12/49.**L/I.**
Cow. 4–23/2/52.**L/I.**
Dee. 30/10–30/11/53.**C/L.**
Cow. 22/3–1/5/54.**G.**
Cow. 5/9–13/10/56.**H/I.**
Cow. 17–19/10/56.**N/C.**
Cow. 31/10–1/11/56.**C/L.**
Cow. 18/10–2/11/57.**N/C.**
Cow. 20–25/1/58.**N/C.**
Cow. 9/7–16/8/58.**G.**
Cow. 1–11/7/59.**N/C.**
Cow. 17/5–24/6/61.**L/I.**
Cow. 30/9–30/11/63.**G.**
Cow. 23/2–12/3/66.**N/C.**

BOILERS:
9930.
9930 renumbered 28639
23/2/52.
28600 *(ex1067)* 1/5/54.
28223 *(ex1239)* 16/8/58.
28280 *(from spare 2 years)*
30/11/63.

SHED:
Dundee.

RENUMBERED:
61293 17/12/49.

CONDEMNED:
17/8/66.
*Sold 10/66 for scrap to
Motherwell Machinery &
Scrap Co, Wishaw.*

E1294

North British Loco. 26195.

To traffic 1/3/48.

REPAIRS:
Don. 23/10–25/11/49.**G.**
Don. 1–11/1/50.**N/C.**
Don. 28/5–22/6/51.**G.**
Dar. 4/7–14/8/53.**G.**
Cow. 15/6–9/7/55.**H/I.**
Cow. 8/2–16/3/57.**G.**
Cow. 6/9–4/10/58.**L/I.**
Mod. bogie springs.
Cow. 11/11–12/12/59.**C/L.**
Cow. 10/2–31/3/61.**G.**
Complete A.W.S. fitted.
Cow. 19/6–10/8/63.**L/I.**

BOILERS:
9931.
9444 *(ex3932)* 25/11/49.
28146 *(ex1105)* 22/6/51.
28462 *(ex61386)* 14/8/53.
28632 *(ex61348)* 16/3/57.
141 tubes.
28437 *(ex61397)* 31/3/61.

SHEDS:
Bradford.
Eastfield 13/9/53.
Kittybrewster 9/6/54.
St Margarets 30/5/60.

RENUMBERED:
61294 25/11/49.

CONDEMNED:
13/11/64.
*Sold 1/65 for scrap to
Shipbreaking Industries,
Faslane.*

E1295

North British Loco. 26196.

To traffic 3/3/48.

REPAIRS:
Don. 31/12/48–10/1/49.**C/L.**
Tender Damaged.
Don. 3/5–13/6/50.**G.**
Don. 10/2–6/3/52.**G.**
Gor. 8/5–19/6/54.**G.**
Dar. 20/5–15/6/57.**G.**
Dar. 17–27/6/57.**N/C.**
Dar. 25/9–2/10/58.**N/C.**
Dar. 12/2–24/3/60.**G.**
Complete A.W.S. fitted.
Dar. 7–13/4/60.**N/C.**
Dar. 6–10/11/61.**C/L.**
Dar. 15–30/1/62.**C/L.**

BOILERS:
9932.
9701 *(ex1113)* 13/6/50.
28179 *(ex1249)* 6/3/52.
28369 *(ex3869)* 19/6/54.
28226 *(ex1284)* 15/6/57.
28528 *(ex1031)* 24/3/60.

SHEDS:
Ardsley.
Copley Hill 26/9/48.
Ardsley 11/10/53.

RENUMBERED:
61295 13/6/50.

CONDEMNED:
25/11/62.
*7/2/63 In for cut up at
Darlington.*

E1296

North British Loco. 26197.

To traffic 6/3/48.

REPAIRS:
Don. 23/5–3/7/50.**G.**
Dar. 12/6–6/7/52.**G.**
Gor. 21/8–9/10/54.**G.**
Dar. 12/8–7/9/57.**G.**
Dar. 3/7–14/9/59.**C/H.**

BOILERS:
9933.
9968 *(ex61331)* 3/7/50.
28118 *(ex1240)* 6/7/52.
28422 *(ex61312)* 9/10/54.
28582 *(ex1285)* 7/9/57.
28194 *(ex61369)* 14/9/59.

SHEDS:
Ardsley.
Bradford 4/6/50.
Wakefield 16/6/57.

RENUMBERED:
61296 3/7/50.

CONDEMNED:
19/11/62.
*1/2/63 In for cut up at
Darlington.*

E1297

North British Loco. 26198.

To traffic 10/3/48.

REPAIRS:
Don. 23/1–10/3/50.**G.**
Don. 24/2–20/3/52.**G.**
Dar. 20/7–2/9/54.**G.**
Dar. 5/6–4/7/57.**G.**
Dar. 14/10–20/11/57.**C/H.**
Dar. 31/12/59–3/2/60.**G.**
A.W.S. mech. fitted.
Dar. 17–18/10/60.**N/C.**
A.W.S. elec. fitted.

BOILERS:
9934.
9868 *(ex1231)* 10/3/50.
28182 *(ex1267)* 20/3/52.
28197 *(ex1250)* 2/9/54.
28230 *(ex61386)* 4/7/57.
28582 *(ex1296)* 3/2/60.

SHEDS:
Ardsley.
Copley Hill 10/4/49.
Ardsley 2/10/49.

RENUMBERED:
61297 10/3/50.

CONDEMNED:
25/11/62.
*8/2/63 In for cut up at
Darlington.*

E1298

North British Loco. 26199.

To traffic 11/3/48.

REPAIRS:
Gor. 4–20/10/48.**L.**
Gor. 13/11/49–7/1/50.**G.**
Gor. 12–13/1/50.**N/C.**
Dar. 10/1–6/2/52.**G.**
Dar. 11–17/9/52.**N/C.** *Elec.
equipment to fit.*
Dar. 1–25/9/53.**G.**
Dar. 6/9–5/10/55.**G.**
Dar. 4–5/12/56.**N/C.**
Dar. 20/6–9/8/57.**G.**
Dar. 29/7–19/8/58.**C/L.**
Dar. 16/3–17/4/59.**G.**

BOILERS:
9935.
9936 *(ex1299)* 7/1/50.
28248 *(ex1030)* 6/2/52.
28146 *(ex1194)* 25/9/53.
28409 *(ex1281)* 5/10/55.
28449 *(ex1281)* 9/8/57.
28177 *(ex1187)* 17/4/59.

SHEDS:
Leicester.
Agecroft 3/10/59.
Gorton 5/5/62.

RENUMBERED:
61298 20/10/48.

CONDEMNED:
14/6/62.
*2/7/62 In for cut up at
Darlington.*

E1299

North British Loco. 26200.

To traffic 12/3/48.

REPAIRS:
Gor. 6/11–17/12/49.**G.**
Gor. 22–23/12/49.**N/C.**
Gor. 10/7–30/10/50.**C/H.**
After collision.
Str. 28/1–8/3/52.**G.**
Gor. 1–29/5/54.**G.**
Dar. 26/6–9/8/56.**G.**
Str. 10/11/58–2/1/59.**G.**
Don. 10–19/3/60.**N/C.**
Don. 29/9/60.*Weigh.*

Don. 1–15/11/60.**N/C.**
Don. 19/9–14/10/61.**G.**

BOILERS:
9936.
5059 *(ex1079)* 17/12/49.
5059 renumbered 28262
30/10/50.
28580 *(ex61363)* 8/3/52.
28535 *(ex1270)* 29/5/54.
28854 *(ex1269)* 9/8/56.
28138 *(ex61317)* 2/1/59.
28955 *(ex1098)* 14/10/61.

SHEDS:
Leicester.
Colwick 17/11/57.

RENUMBERED:
61299 17/12/49.

CONDEMNED:
25/7/65.
*Sold 9/65 for scrap to
Geo.Cohen, Ickles,
Rotherham.*

E1300

North British Loco. 26201.

To traffic 15/3/48.

REPAIRS:
Str. 3–23/12/48.**L.**
Str. 16/5–25/6/49.**G.**
Str. 4/2–22/3/51.**G.**
Str. 17–21/6/52.**N/C.**
Str. 17/11/52–10/1/53.**G.**
Mod. bogie springs.
Str. 9/11–2/12/53.**N/C.**
Str. 13/9–16/10/54.**G.**
Str. 19–23/3/56.**N/C.**
Str. 10/9–19/10/56.**G.**
Str. 3/10–28/11/58.**G.**
Str. 10–26/6/59.**N/C.**
B.T.H. speed indic. fitted.
Complete A.T.C. fitted.
Str. 19–22/6/60.**C/L.**
Don. 4/5–3/6/61.**G.**
Don. 13/8–1/9/62.**C/L.**

BOILERS:
9937.
9889 *(ex1252)* 25/6/49.
28539 *(ex1135)* 22/3/51.
28504 *(ex1233)* 10/1/53.
28557 *(ex61335)* 16/10/54.
28452 *(ex1052)* 19/10/56.
28349 *(ex1249)* 28/11/58.
28542 *(ex61384)* 3/6/61.

SHEDS:
March.
Cambridge 21/3/49.
Colchester 14/12/58.
Stratford 6/12/59.
March 13/12/59.
Cambridge 10/1/60.
March 17/6/62.

RENUMBERED:
61300 25/6/49.

CONDEMNED:
25/11/63.
Made S.B.Dept'l No23.
Sold 1/66 for scrap to
Garnham,Harris & Elton,
Chesterfield.

E1301

North British Loco. 26202.

To traffic 17/3/48.

REPAIRS:
Str. 17/10–10/12/49.**G.**
Str. 27/11–9/12/50.**C/L.**
Str. 22/3–7/4/51.**C/L.**
Str. 22/7–1/9/51.**G.**
Str. 24/2–24/4/53.**G.**
Str. 11/5–19/6/53.**N/C.**
Str. 5/1–25/2/55.**G.**
Str. 24/8–5/10/56.**G.**
Str. 10/4–13/6/58.**G.**
Don. 3/5–3/6/60.**G.**

BOILERS:
9938.
 9938 renumbered 28523
9/12/50.
28533 (ex1617) 1/9/51.
28147 (ex1048) 24/4/53.
28152 (ex1054) 25/2/55.
28581 (ex spare 2 years)
5/10/56.
28147 (ex1054) 13/6/58.
28979 (new) 3/6/60.

SHEDS:
Cambridge.
Stratford 17/6/62.

RENUMBERED:
61301 10/12/49.

CONDEMNED:
16/9/62.
3/12/62 In for cut up at
Doncaster.

E1302

North British Loco. 26203.

To traffic 22/3/48.

REPAIRS:
Str. 16/6–20/8/49.**G.**
Str. 12/2–31/3/51.**G.**
Str. 16/9–1/11/52.**G.**
Str. 8–10/2/54.**N/C.**
Str. 2/3–23/4/54.**G.** Mod.
bogie springs.
Str. 24/10/55–28/1/56.**G.**
Don. 7–30/11/57.**G.**
Don. 6/7–4/8/60.**G.**
Don. 19/11/62–1/1/63.**G.**

BOILERS:
9939.
 9909 (ex1272) 20/8/49.
28541 (ex1056) 31/3/51.
28521 (ex1045) 1/11/52.
28573 (ex61363) 23/4/54.

28504 (ex1300) 28/1/56.
28120 (ex1620) 30/11/57.
28195 (ex61393) 4/8/60.
28963 (ex3965) 1/1/63.

SHEDS:
Cambridge.
New England 7/10/56.
Colwick 3/1/65.
To LMR Stock 2/1/66.

RENUMBERED:
61302 20/8/49.

CONDEMNED:
2/4/66.
Sold 5/66 for scrap to
J.Cashmore, Great Bridge.

E1303

North British Loco. 26204.

To traffic 26/3/48.

REPAIRS:
Dar. 19/6–1/8/50.**G.**
Dar. 21/5–12/6/52.**G.**
Dar. 6–29/5/54.**G.**
Dar. 29/8–3/9/55.**C/L.**
Dar. 4–24/10/55.**C/L.** After
collision.
Dar. 28/8–24/9/56.**G.**
Dar. 10/9–10/10/58.**G.**
A.T.C. Mech. fitted.
Dar. 23/10–3/11/58.**N/C.**
Dar. 10–12/8/59.Not
repaired.
Dar. 21/9–2/10/59.**N/C.**
A.T.C. Elec. fitted.
Dar. 25/5–21/6/61.**G.**
Dar. 3–6/7/61.**N/C.**
Dar. 28/9–28/11/64.**H/I.**
Dar. 30/11–4/12/64.**N/C.**

BOILERS:
9940.
 5138 (new) 1/8/50.
28433 (ex61316) 12/6/52.
28658 (ex1013) 29/5/54.
28353 (ex1049) 24/9/56.
28346 (ex61388) 10/10/58.
28102 (ex1276) 21/6/61.

SHEDS:
Darlington.
Stockton 14/11/48.
Thornaby 14/6/59.
Hull Dairycoates 4/3/62.
York 6/9/64.

RENUMBERED:
61303 1/8/50.

CONDEMNED:
21/11/66.
Sold 2/67 for scrap to
Arnott Young, Parkgate.

61304

North British Loco. 26205.

To traffic 31/3/48.

REPAIRS:
Dar. 24/5–17/6/50.**G.**
Dar. 28/11–21/12/51.**G.**
Gor. 3/6–4/7/53.**G.**
Dar. 15/12/54–14/1/55.**G.**
Dar. 16/8–12/9/56.**G.**
Dar. 14–29/4/58.**N/C.**
Dar. 28/7–26/8/58.**G.**
Dar. 29/11/60–7/1/61.**G.**

BOILERS:
9941.
 9876 (ex1238) 17/6/50.
28237 (ex1255) 21/12/51.
28590 (ex61370) 4/7/53.
28458 (ex61338) 14/1/55.
28342 (ex1279) 12/9/56.
28428 (ex61320) 26/8/58.
28244 (ex1016) 7/1/61.

SHEDS:
Hull Dairycoates.
Hull Botanic Gardens
16/5/48.
Scarborough 14/6/59.
Darlington 27/3/60.
Ardsley 7/6/64.

CONDEMNED:
31/10/65.
Sold 12/65 for scrap to
Hughes,Bolckow, North
Blyth.

61305

North British Loco. 26206.

To traffic 1/4/48.

REPAIRS:
Dar. 17/4–12/5/50.**G.**
Dar. 24/1–16/2/52.**G.**
Dar. 23/11–19/12/53.**G.**
Dar. 21–23/12/53.**N/C.**
Dar. 26/4–27/5/55.**G.**
Dar. 27/11–28/12/56.**G.**
Dar. 28/10–4/12/58.**G.**
A.T.C. Mech. fitted.
Dar. 21/9–8/10/59.**N/C.**
A.T.C. completed.
Dar. 5/12/61–6/1/62.**G.**
Dar. 2/10/63.Not repaired.

BOILERS:
9942.
 9910 (ex1273) 12/5/50.
28403 (ex61365) 16/2/52.
28408 (ex1256) 19/12/53.
28139 (ex61318) 27/5/55.
28105 (ex1062) 28/12/56.
28431 (ex1008) 4/12/58.
28117 (ex61306) 6/1/62.

SHEDS:
Hull Dairycoates.
Hull Botanic Gardens
16/5/48.

Scarborough 14/6/59.
Hull Dairycoates 20/3/60.

CONDEMNED:
21/10/63.
Cut up at Darlington.

61306

North British Loco. 26207.

To traffic 5/4/48.

REPAIRS:
Dar. 7/2–18/4/50.**G.**
Dar. 24–28/4/50.**N/C.**
Don. 24/10–15/11/50.**C/L.**
Dar. 17/3–9/4/52.**G.**
Dar. 12–21/3/53.**N/C.**
Dar. 20/4–2/5/53.**C/L.**
Dar. 9/12/53–5/1/54.**G.**
Dar. 9/8–17/9/55.**G.**
Dar. 20/3–9/4/56.**C/L.**
Dar. 30/1–8/2/57.**N/C.**
Dar. 1–29/5/57.**G.**
Dar. 11–15/8/58.**N/C.** New
Smokebox door.
Dar. 1–31/12/58.**G.** A.T.C.
Mech. fitted.
Dar. 26/7–5/10/60.**C/L.**
A.W.S. Elec. fitted.
Dar. 5–28/10/61.**G.**
Dar. 16/4–28/5/64.**G.**

BOILERS:
9943.
 3604 (ex1037) 18/4/50.
28420 (ex1037) 9/4/52.
28430 (ex1240) 5/1/54.
28281 (ex1266) 17/9/55.
28752 (ex1107) 29/5/57.
28117 (ex1078) 31/12/58.
28547 (ex61338) 28/10/61.
28285 (ex61319) 28/5/64.

SHEDS:
Hull Dairycoates.
Hull Botanic Gardens
16/5/48.
Hull Dairycoates 14/6/59.
Low Moor 25/6/67.

CONDEMNED:
30/9/67.
Sold 1/2/68 for preservation
in working condition.

61307

North British Loco. 26208.

To traffic 7/4/48.

REPAIRS:
Inv. 22–26/4/48.**N/C.** Tab.
catcher fitted.
Cow. 12/1–17/2/50.**L/I.**
Cow. 25/1–24/2/51.**G.**
Cow. 14/8–6/9/52.**L/I.**
Cow. 18/6–17/7/54.**H/I.**
Cow. 15/9–26/10/56.**L/I.**
Cow. 27/9–27/10/58.**G.**
Cow. 28/8–6/10/61.**H/I.**

Cow. 6/63.**G.**
Cow. 10/64.**C/L.**
Cow. 3/65.**C/L.**

BOILERS:
9944.
28701 *(ex1038)* 24/2/51.
28655 *(ex61350)* 17/7/54.
28652 *(ex1261)* 27/10/58.
28519 *(ex61180)* 6/63.

SHEDS:
Kittybrewster.
Keith 7/7/54.
Kittybrewster 18/2/57.
St Margarets 31/7/57.
Dalry Road 14/6/64.
St Margarets 4/10/65.
Bathgate 9/1/66.
Thornton Junction 24/4/66.
St Margarets 28/8/66.

CONDEMNED:
19/11/66.
Sold 12/66 for scrap to
Motherwell Machinery &
Scrap, Wishaw.

61308

North British Loco. 26209.

To traffic 9/4/48.

REPAIRS:
Inv. 27–29/4/48.**N/C.** *Tab.*
catcher fitted.
Cow. 4/7–13/8/49.**L/I.**
Cow. 11/10–2/11/51.**H/I.**
Cow. 2–22/2/53.**G.**
Cow. 10/2–8/3/55.**L/I.**
Cow. 5/1–7/2/57.**L/I.**
Cow. 26/1–3/3/58.**G.**
Cow. 17/8–30/9/60.**L/I.**
Cow. 20/11–21/12/62.**G.**

BOILERS:
9945.
9945 renumbered 28642
2/11/51.
28615 *(ex1132)* 22/2/53.
28844 *(ex61332)* 3/3/58.
28640 *(ex1290)* 21/12/62.

SHEDS:
Kittybrewster.
Keith 8/1/50.
Kittybrewster 18/2/57.
St Margarets 19/8/57.
Kittybrewster 21/5/60.
St Margarets 19/6/61.
Dalry Road 12/10/64.
St Margarets 4/10/65.
Thornton Junction 3/4/66.

CONDEMNED:
19/11/66.
Sold 12/66 for scrap to
Motherwell Machinery &
Scrap Co, Wishaw.

61309

North British Loco. 26210.

To traffic 15/4/48.

REPAIRS:
Don. 29/8–4/10/50.**G.**
Don. 16/1–12/2/53.**G.**
Dar. 10/3–5/4/55.**G.**
Dar. 29/4–6/5/57.**C/L.**
Dar. 2–10/7/57.**N/C.**
Dar. 26/3–25/4/58.**G.**
Dar. 29/7–5/8/58.**C/L.**
Dar. 14–25/9/59.**C/L.**
Dar. 8/3–15/4/61.**G.**
A.W.S. fitted.
Dar. 19/6–3/9/64.**C/L.**

BOILERS:
9946.
28106 *(ex1028)* 4/10/50.
28457 *(ex61378)* 12/2/53.
28106 *(ex1199)* 5/4/55.
28134 *(ex1123)* 25/4/58.
28123 *(ex61319)* 15/4/61.

SHEDS:
Ardsley.
Copley Hill 29/7/51.
Low Moor 8/9/63.
Mirfield 5/1/64.
Low Moor 12/4/64.
Wakefield 13/11/66.

CONDEMNED:
23/1/67.
Sold 3/67 for scrap to
T.W.Ward, Killamarsh.

61310

North British Loco. 26211.

To traffic 19/4/48.

REPAIRS:
Don. 11/7–3/8/50.**G.**
Don. 14/5–7/6/52.**G.**
Don. 11/12/54–22/1/55.**G.**
Dar. 2–26/10/57.**G.**
Dar. 28–29/10/57.**N/C.**
Dar. 11/3–8/4/59.**C/L.**
Dar. 29/3–9/5/60.**G.**
A.W.S. fitted.
Dar. 18–28/5/60.**N/C.**

BOILERS:
9947.
9443 *(ex1085)* 3/8/50.
28432 *(ex61326)* 7/6/52.
28116 *(ex1190)* 22/1/55.
28260 *(ex1010)* 26/10/57.
28242 *(ex61315)* 9/5/60.

SHEDS:
Ardsley.
Copley Hill 18/2/51.
Ardsley 6/1/52.

CONDEMNED:
5/1/65.
Sold 5/65 for scrap to
A.Draper, Hull.

61311

North British Loco. 26212.

To traffic 21/4/48.

REPAIRS:
Gor. 1–8/9/48.**L.**
Gor. 25–30/10/48.**L.**
Gor. 24/11/48–22/1/49.**C/L.**
Gor. 3/3–1/4/50.**G.**
Gor. 6–22/4/50.**N/C.**
Str. 13/2–22/3/52.**G.**
Gor. 3–31/10/53.**G.**
Don. 19/7–18/8/55.**G.**
Don. 25–31/8/55.**N/C,**
Str. 9/9–19/10/57.**G.**
Str. 23/9–20/11/59.**G.**

BOILERS:
9948.
9955 *(ex61318)* 1/4/50.
28576 *(ex1058)* 22/3/52.
28845 *(new)* 31/10/53.
28218 *(ex1100)* 18/8/55.
28553 *(ex1234)* 19/10/57.
28658 *(ex1060)* 20/11/59.

SHEDS:
Sheffield.
Lincoln 26/9/54.
Kings Cross 7/10/56.
Stratford 10/2/57.
Parkeston 10/8/58.
Colchester 14/12/58.
Parkeston 1/11/59.
Stratford 1/1/61.

CONDEMNED:
16/9/62.
14/11/62 In for cut up at
Doncaster.

61312

North British Loco. 26213.

To traffic 23/4/48.

REPAIRS:
Gor. 17/10–19/11/49.**G.**
Gor. 25–28/11/49.**N/C.**
Dar. 26/3–19/4/52.**G.**
Gor. 5/12/53–30/1/54.**G.**
Gor. 2–8/2/54.**N/C.**
Str. 27/5–3/8/56.**G.**
Str. 30/9–14/11/58.**G.**
Don. 29/6–1/8/61.**G.**

BOILERS:
9949.
9916 *(ex1279)* 19/11/49.
28422 *(ex61313)* 19/4/52.
28848 *(new)* 30/1/54.
28201 *(ex1363)* 3/8/56.
28579 *(ex61371)* 14/11/58.
28108 *(ex1157)* 1/8/61.

SHEDS:
Sheffield.
Norwich 3/10/54.
Yarmouth 29/1/56.
Norwich 1/4/56.
Sheffield 3/5/59.

Staveley 20/9/59.
Canklow 3/1/60.
Sheffield 10/9/61.
Staveley 23/9/62.
Kings Cross 10/3/63.
Mexborough 16/6/63.

CONDEMNED:
1/3/64.
Sold 5/64 for scrap to
Geo.Cohen, Ickles,
Rotherham.

61313

North British Loco. 26214.

To traffic 27/4/48.

REPAIRS:
Gor. 21/2–25/3/50.**G.**
Gor. 28–29/3/50.**N/C.**
Dar. 18/2–22/3/52.**G.**
Gor. 19/12/53–23/1/54.**G.**
Dar. 5–30/9/55.**G.**
Dar. 17/5–13/6/57.**G.**
Dar. 18–24/6/57.**N/C.**
Dar. 25/6–11/7/58.**C/L.**
Dar. 29/9–7/10/58.**C/L.**
Don. 21/8–1/10/59.**G.**
Don. 14/2–1/3/61.**C/L.**
Don. 12/7–7/9/62.**G.**

BOILERS:
9950.
9921 *(ex1284)* 25/3/50.
28411 *(ex1039)* 22/3/52.
28397 *(ex61383)* 23/1/54.
28242 *(ex61369)* 30/9/55.
28251 *(ex1229)* 13/6/57.
28507 *(ex1207)* 1/10/59.
28851 *(ex3646)* 7/9/62.

SHEDS:
Gorton.
Sheffield 3/10/48.
Canklow 16/6/63.
Langwith 13/6/65.

CONDEMNED:
14/11/65.
Sold 12/65 for scrap to
Hughes,Bolckow, North
Blyth.

61314

North British Loco. 26215.

To traffic 29/4/48.

REPAIRS:
Gor. 25–30/10/48.**L.**
Gor. 2/1–11/2/50.**G.**
Gor. 17–20/2/50.**N/C.**
Str. 3/2–8/3/52.**G.**
Dar. 6/10–3/11/54.**G.**
Dar. 25/6–8/8/56.**G.**
Str. 11/8–25/9/58.**G.** *Mod.*
bogie springs.
Don. 1/12/60–5/1/61.**G.**

BOILERS:
9951.
9935 (ex1298) 11/2/50.
28568 (ex1009) 8/3/52.
28837 (ex3807) 3/11/54.
28537 (ex1198) 8/8/56.
28595 (ex1052) 25/9/58.
28522 (ex1142) 5/1/61.

SHEDS:
Gorton.
Sheffield 3/10/48.
Cambridge 29/9/57.
Doncaster 11/10/59.
New England 16/9/62.

CONDEMNED:
28/12/63.
4/3/64 In for cut up at
Doncaster.

61315

North British Loco. 26216.

To traffic 30/4/48.

REPAIRS:
Gor. 25/3–6/5/50.**G.**
Gor. 22–25/5/50.**N/C.**
Dar. 16/4–9/5/52.**G.**
Gor. 9/1–13/2/54.**G.**
Dar. 6/10–5/11/55.**G.**
Dar. 30/8–21/9/57.**G.**
Dar. 29/9–6/11/59.**G.**
Don. 31/1–17/2/61.**N/C.**
Don. 22/1–3/3/62.**G.**

BOILERS:
9952.
9964 (ex61327) 6/5/50.
28425 (ex1276) 9/5/52.
28398 (ex61387) 13/2/54.
28217 (ex61386) 5/11/55.
28242 (ex61313) 21/9/57.
28186 (ex1048) 6/11/59.

SHEDS:
Gorton.
Sheffield 3/10/48.
Canklow 16/6/63.
Langwith 13/6/65.

CONDEMNED:
10/2/66.
Made S.B.Dept'l No.32.
Sold 2/10/68 for cut up
eng.only. Tender to snow
plough. Engine scrap to
G.Haselwood, Attercliffe.

61316

North British Loco. 26217.

To traffic 4/5/48.

REPAIRS:
Gor. 9–13/6/48.**L.**
Gor. 11/4–13/5/50.**G.**
Gor. 17–19/5/50.**N/C.**
Gor. 22–26/5/50.**N/C.**
Dar. 4/4–3/5/52.**G.**

Dar. 5–6/5/52.**N/C.**
Gor. 27/12/53–13/2/54.**G.**
Gor. 17/2–10/3/54.**N/C.**
Gor. 23/5–5/6/54.**N/C.**
Dar. 21/11–20/12/55.**G.**
Dar. 9/9–9/10/57.**G.**
Don. 4/2–11/3/60.**G.**
Don. 14–24/5/62.**C/L.**

BOILERS:
9953.
9952 (ex61315) 13/5/50.
28426 (ex1288) 3/5/52.
28411 (ex61313) 13/2/54.
28418 (ex1256) 20/12/55.
28401 (ex1025) 9/10/57.
28559 (ex1151) 11/3/60.

SHEDS:
Gorton.
Sheffield 13/10/48.
Mexborough 15/5/60.
Canklow 11/3/62.

CONDEMNED:
29/12/62.
Sold 6/63 for scrap to
J.Cashmore, Great Bridge.

61317

North British Loco. 26218.

To traffic 6/5/48.

REPAIRS:
Gor. 2–3/11/49.**N/C.**
Gor. 6/6–27/7/50.**G.**
Gor. 29/7–2/8/50.**N/C.**
Dar. 17/3–15/4/52.**G.**
Gor. 6/3–10/4/54.**G.**
Gor. 13–23/4/54.**N/C.**
Str. 6–15/4/55.**N/C.**
Str. 21/1–25/2/56.**G.**
Str. 29/10–7/12/57.**G. Mod.
bogie springs.**
Str. 19/8–2/10/59.**G. Part
A.T.C. fitted.**
Don. 18/7–12/8/60.**C/L.**
Don. 10/11–8/12/61.**C/L.**

BOILERS:
9954.
9963 (ex61326) 27/7/50.
28565 (ex1040) 15/4/52.
28138 (ex1283) 10/4/54.
28374 (ex1033) 25/2/56.
28836 (ex61644) 7/12/57.
28262 (ex1046) 2/10/59.

SHEDS:
Gorton.
Sheffield 19/6/49.
Norwich 12/9/54.
Lincoln 14/2/60.
Immingham 20/3/60.

CONDEMNED:
16/9/62.
Sold 1/63 for scrap to
Geo.Cohen, Ickles,
Rotherham.

61318

North British Loco. 26219.

To traffic 11/5/48.

REPAIRS:
Gor. 26/1–4/3/50.**G.**
Gor. 9–12/3/50.**N/C.**
Dar. 20/1–27/2/52.**G.**
Don. 2/5–10/6/53.**G.**
Gor. 25/3–13/5/54.**C/L.**
Dar. 17/1–16/2/55.**G.**
Don. 19/9/55.**Weigh.**
Don. 7–24/5/56.**C/L.**
Don. 14/11–13/12/56.**G.**
Don. 18–26/2/58.**N/C.**
Don. 24/4–23/5/59.**G.**
Don. 27/9–8/10/60.**N/C.**
Don. 7/2–10/3/61.**G.**

BOILERS:
9955.
9951 (ex61314) 4/3/50.
28412 (ex1281) 27/2/52.
28139 (ex1105) 10/6/53.
28590 (ex61304) 16/2/55.
28523 (ex1094) 13/12/56.
28229 (ex61374) 23/5/59.

SHED:
Immingham.

CONDEMNED:
22/9/63.
Sold 2/64 for scrap to
R.A.King, Norwich.

61319

North British Loco. 26220.

To traffic 14/5/48.

REPAIRS:
Ghd. 11–19/5/49.**C/L.**
Ghd. 16/6–7/7/49.**C/L.
After collision.**
Dar. 24/4–19/5/51.**G.**
Dar. 27/1–18/2/54.**G.**
Ghd.
15/12/54–21/1/55.**C/H.
After collision.**
Ghd. 21–24/3/55.**C/L.**
Dar. 30/5–28/6/56.**G.**
Ghd. 27/12/56–1/1/57.**N/C.**
Ghd. 31/1–1/2/57.**N/C.**
Dar. 30/12/57–18/3/58.**C/H.**
Dar. 12/12/60–27/1/61.**G.**
Dar. 25/2–11/4/64.**G.**

BOILERS:
9956.
28209 (ex1239) 19/5/51.
28238 (ex1289) 18/2/54.
28123 (ex1168) 28/6/56.
28285 (ex1202) 27/1/61.
28170 (ex spare 2 years)
11/4/64.

SHEDS:
Borough Gardens.
Wakefield 8/6/58.
Darlington 14/9/58.

York 14/6/59.

CONDEMNED:
16/12/66.
Sold 16/2/67 for scrap to
A.Draper, Hull.

61320

North British Loco. 26221.

To traffic 18/5/48.

REPAIRS:
Dar. 9/5–7/6/51.**G.**
Dar. 21/9–15/10/53.**G.**
Ghd. 10–24/5/54.**C/L. After
collision.**
Dar. 28/12/55–23/1/56.**G.**
Dar. 13/5–11/6/58.**G.**
Dar. 19–27/6/58.**N/C.**
Dar. 31/7–26/8/61.**G.**
Complete A.W.S. fitted.
Dar. 12–23/9/61.**N/C.**

BOILERS:
9957.
28214 (ex61319) 7/6/51.
28463 (ex61390) 15/10/53.
28428 (ex1035) 23/1/56.
28453 (ex1069) 11/6/58.
28951 (ex1672) 26/8/61.

SHEDS:
Borough Gardens.
Bradford 23/9/56.
Wakefield 16/6/56.
Copley Hill 15/9/57.
Wakefield 5/1/64.

CONDEMNED:
19/8/65.
Sold 10/65 for scrap to
Hughes, Bolckow, North
Blyth.

61321

North British Loco. 26222.

To traffic 20/5/48.

REPAIRS:
Dar. 3–15/11/49.**C/L.**
Dar. 11/6–5/7/51.**G.**
Ghd. 13–27/3/52.**Not
repaired.**
Dar. 27/3–17/4/52.**N/C.**
Dar. 15/6–9/7/53.**G.**
Dar. 7/11–3/12/55.**G.**
Dar. 5–7/12/55.**N/C.**
Dar. 3–29/1/58.**G.**
Dar. 5–12/2/58.**N/C.**
Dar. 17/6–1/7/59.**N/C.**
Complete A.T.C. fitted.
Dar. 23/9–3/11/60.**G.**

BOILERS:
9958.
28219 (ex1224) 5/7/51.
28346 (ex1225) 9/7/53.
28419 (ex1115) 3/12/55.

continued on page 84

The fifty engines numbered 1140 to 1189 were built by Vulcan Foundry and delivered from April to August 1947. None were named when they first went into traffic, but 1189 was named later. All had the current standard green passenger livery. Note axle–mounted generator on the rear bogie wheel for electric lighting equipment. No.1164 is outside Neasden shed, where it was then allocated.

From July 1949 until April 1951 the electric lighting on 61174 came from a Metropolitan Vickers compressed air turbine driven generator. That must have been fitted on the right hand side, as this photo shows no evidence of it, and was taken during that period – confirmed by the plain sides of the tender. The axle mounted generator has been removed, but the stub on which it was fitted can be seen.

61310 at Ardsley shed. It was one of the order for 150 which North British Loco. Co. built from May 1947 to September 1948, numbered 1190 to 1287, E1288 to E1303, and 61304 to 61339. None of them were named when new. The electric lighting was provided by a Stone's steam turbine driven generator.

The fifty built by Vulcan, 1140 to 1189, had the bracket by the rear coupled wheel fitted to carry a speedometer but neither the instrument nor the drive to it were available when the engines were delivered. The equipment only came from B.T.H. in May 1950 for that fitting to be completed.

61321 continued

28308 *(ex1240)* 29/1/58.
28578 *(ex61339)* 3/11/60.

SHEDS:
Borough Gardens.
Wakefield 8/6/58.
Darlington 14/9/58.
Ardsley 7/6/64.

CONDEMNED:
10/8/64.
*7/9/64 In for cut up at
Darlington.*

61322

North British Loco. 26223.

To traffic 25/5/48.

REPAIRS:
Cow. 8/9–12/10/50.**H/I.**
Dar. 30/6–18/7/52.**G.**
Dar. 5–31/7/54.**G.**
Dar. 3/7–17/8/56.**G.**
Dar. 24/1–20/2/59.**G.**
A.T.C. Mech. fitted.
Dar. 4–7/8/59.**N/C.**
A.T.C. Elec. fitted.
Dar. 6/6–29/7/61.**H/I.**

BOILERS:
 9959.
28444 *(ex61310)* 18/7/52.
28228 *(ex1238)* 31/7/54.
28214 *(ex1273)* 17/8/56.
28837 *(ex1276)* 20/2/59.

SHEDS:
Borough Gardens.
St Margarets 29/8/48.
Darlington 31/10/48.
Tweedmouth 12/3/50.
Blaydon 12/6/60.
Heaton 9/9/62.
Gateshead 16/6/63.
Hull Dairycoates 31/10/65.

CONDEMNED:
20/2/66.
*Sold 4/66 for scrap to
A.Draper, Hull.*

61323

North British Loco. 26224.

To traffic 27/5/48.

REPAIRS:
Inv. 13–15/7/48.**N/C.** *Tab.
catcher fitted.*
Cow. 16/3–14/4/50.**L/I.**
Cow. 10/5–14/6/52.**G.**
Cow. 28/4–22/5/54.**H/I.**
Cow. 7–9/6/54.**N/C.**
Cow. 1–25/12/54.**N/C.**
Cow. 19/4–13/5/55.**C/L.**
Cow. 27/6–18/8/56.**G.**
Don. 24/1–4/2/58.**C/L.**
Str. 1–25/7/58.**C/L.**

Str. 27/10–12/12/58.**G.**
Mod. bogie springs.
Don. 19/7–19/8/61.**G.**

BOILERS:
 9960.
28605 *(ex1101)* 14/6/52.
28634 *(ex1148)* 18/8/56.
28569 *(ex1055)* 12/12/58.
28953 *(ex1208)* 19/8/61.

SHEDS:
Kittybrewster.
Peterborough 25/2/57.
March 31/1/60.

CONDEMNED:
25/11/63.
*Allocated S.B.Dep't'l No 24
but into Doncaster 17/2/64
for cut up instead.*

61324

North British Loco. 26225.

To traffic 1/6/48.

REPAIRS:
Inv. 8/7/48.**N/C.** *Tab.
catcher fitted.*
Cow. 15–26/11/48.**L.**
Cow. 29/3–21/4/50.**L/I.**
Inv. 9/4/51.**N/C.**
Cow. 25/6–13/7/51.**H/I.**
Inv. 8/1/52.**N/C.**
Cow. 3/9–3/10/53.**G.**
Inv. 17/2/54.**N/C.**
Cow. 10/9–22/10/55.**H/I.**
Cow. 31/12/56–26/1/57.**L/I.**
Cow. 4/4–17/5/58.**G.**
Inv. 11–21/5/59.**N/C.**
Inv. 18–25/8/59.**N/C.**
Inv. 22/9–14/10/59.**C/L.**
Cow. 4/12/59–29/1/60.**H/I.**
Cow. 15/4–7/5/60.**N/C.**
Inv. 13–14/3/61.**N/C.**
Cow. 28/7–2/9/61.**C/L.**
Cow. 9/10–9/11/62.**G.**
Cow. 7/1–23/2/63.**C/L.**

BOILERS:
 9961.
 *9961 renumbered 28644
13/7/51.*
28649 *(ex61344)* 3/10/53.
28638 *(ex61357)* 17/5/58.
28704 *(ex1222)* 9/11/62.

SHEDS:
Kittybrewster.
Carlisle Canal 17/6/61.
Dalry Road 23/8/61.
St Margarets 5/11/62.

CONDEMNED:
12/10/65.
*Sold 12/65 for scrap to
Geo.H.Campbell, Airdrie.*

61325

North British Loco. 26226.

To traffic 3/6/48.

REPAIRS:
Gor. 15/5–29/6/50.**G.**
Gor. 1–5/7/50.**N/C.**
Dar. 6/1–2/2/52.**G.**
Dar. 5–8/2/52.**N/C.**
Don. 5/3–13/4/53.**G.**
Don. 29/5–3/7/53.**N/C.**
Gor. 10/4–8/5/54.**C/L.**
Gor. 5/7–7/8/54.**C/L.**
Don. 23/11–30/12/54.**G.**
Dar. 14/5–12/6/56.**G.**
Dar. 16–25/6/56.**N/C.**
Dar. 14/1–15/2/58.**G.**
Don. 18–27/9/58.**C/L.**
Don. 29/6–9/7/59.**N/C.**
Don. 10/8–16/9/60.**G.**
Don. 23/11–5/12/60.**N/C.**

BOILERS:
 9962.
 9953 *(ex61316)* 29/6/50.
28263 *(ex1228)* 2/2/52.
28859 *(new)* 13/4/53.
28196 *(ex1658)* 30/12/54.
28304 *(ex1159)* 12/6/56.
28253 *(ex1151)* 15/2/58.
28239 *(ex1113)* 16/9/60.

SHED:
Immingham.

CONDEMNED:
22/9/63.
*Sold 11/63 for scrap to
J.Cashmore, Great Bridge.*

61326

North British Loco. 26227.

To traffic 8/6/48.

REPAIRS:
Gor. 6–27/5/50.**G.**
Dar. 31/3–26/4/52.**G.**
Gor. 27/2–27/3/54.**G.**
Don. 23/3–28/4/56.**G.**
Don. 18/8–4/9/56.**N/C.**
Don. 5/6–18/7/58.**G.**
Don. 20–29/7/59.**N/C.**
Don. 8/7–10/8/60.**G.**
Don. 6–27/7/61.**C/L.**
Don. 6/3–18/4/63.**G.**
Don. 14/6–22/7/63.**C/L.**

BOILERS:
 9963.
 9948 *(ex61311)* 27/5/50.
28104 *(ex1237)* 26/4/52.
28451 *(ex61380)* 27/3/54.
28136 *(ex1130 & spare)*
28/4/56.
28757 *(ex1036)* 18/7/58.
28119 *(ex1112)* 10/8/60.
28402 *(ex1097)* 18/4/63.

SHEDS:
Gorton.
Newton Heath 11/8/50.
Gorton 24/9/50.
Doncaster 27/6/54.

CONDEMNED:
20/3/66.
*Sold 5/66 for scrap to
Station Steel, Wath.*

61327

North British Loco. 26228.

To traffic 11/6/48.

REPAIRS:
Gor. 5/9–23/10/48.**H.**
Gor. 12/2–11/3/50.**G.**
Gor. 16/3–20/4/50.**N/C.**
Don. 28/3–17/4/51.**C/L.**
Dar. 20/4–17/5/52.**G.**
Dar. 2–23/3/53.**N/C.**
Gor. 15/8–3/10/53.**G.**
Gor. 18–25/12/54.**C/L.**
Dar. 17/6–13/7/55.**G.**
Dar. 6/10–1/11/55.**C/L.**
Dar. 13/2–15/3/57.**G.**
Dar. 10–21/10/58.**C/L.**
Dar. 19/12/58–23/1/59.**G.**
Don. 26/5–29/6/61.**G.**

BOILERS:
 9964.
 9864 *(ex1227)* 11/3/50.
28429 *(ex61317)* 17/5/52.
28559 *(ex61332)* 3/10/53.
28225 *(ex61377)* 13/7/55.
28240 *(ex1267)* 15/3/57.
28403 *(ex1275)* 23/1/59.
28544 *(ex61370)* 29/6/61.

SHEDS:
Gorton.
Sheffield 19/6/49.
Canklow 2/12/62.

CONDEMNED:
14/2/65.
*Sold 4/65 for scrap to
Marples & Gillott,
Sheffield.*

61328

North British Loco. 26229.

To traffic 16/6/48.

REPAIRS:
Gor. 12/2–11/3/50.**G.**
Gor. 15–23/3/50.**N/C.**
Dar. 30/10–5/12/51.**G.**
Don. 9/2–6/3/53.**G.**
Don. 26/1–19/2/54.**C/H.**
Dar. 5/12/54–8/1/55.**G.**
Dar. 11–17/1/55.**N/C.**
Don. 29/3/55.*Weigh.*
Don. 11/10/56–15/1/57.**G.**
Don. 11/8–20/9/58.**G.**
Don. 1–10/11/58.**C/L.**

Don. 11–30/12/58.**C/L.**
Don. 16–21/7/59.**N/C.**
Don. 26/10–24/11/60.**H/I.**

BOILERS:
 9965.
 5140 (*ex61407*) 11/3/50.
28241 (*ex61407*) 5/12/51.
28858 (*new*) 6/3/53.
28583 (*ex1271*) 8/1/55.
28423 (*ex1125*) 15/1/57.
28136 (*ex61326*) 20/9/58.

SHED:
Immingham.

CONDEMNED:
22/9/63.
*Sold 1/64 for scrap to
J.Cashmore, Great Bridge.*

61329

North British Loco. 26230.

To traffic 18/6/48.

REPAIRS:
Gor. 13/8–7/10/50.**G.**
Gor. 14–25/10/50.**N/C.**
Str. 22/12/52–21/2/53.**G.**
Str. 18/1–12/3/55.**G.**
Str. 11/2–28/3/57.**G.**
Str. 21/2–9/5/58.**C/L.**
Str. 17/3–7/5/59.**G.**
Complete A.T.C. fitted.
Str. 12–21/5/59.**N/C.**
Str. 21/12/59–8/1/60.**N/C.**
Don. 6/9–26/10/62.**G.**

BOILERS:
 9966.
28264 (*ex61325*) 7/10/50.
28539 (*ex1300*) 21/2/53.
28841 (*ex1188*) 12/3/55.
28152 (*ex1301*) 28/3/57.
28527 (*ex1223*) 7/5/59.
28304 (*ex1079*) 26/10/62.

SHEDS:
New England.
March 12/6/49.
Lincoln 20/10/49.
Stratford 21/10/51.
Southern Region 19/5/53.
Stratford 23/5/53.
March 16/9/62.
Doncaster 28/10/62.

CONDEMNED:
17/4/66.
*Sold 5/66 for scrap to
Geo.Cohen, Kettering.*

61330

North British Loco. 26231.

To traffic 23/6/48.

REPAIRS:
Don. 20/6–26/7/50.**G.**

Don. 26/9–5/10/51.**C/L.**
Don. 14/7–15/8/52.**G.**
Cow. 1–26/2/55.**H/I.**
Cow. 15/7–13/8/55.**N/C.**
Cow. 10/8–15/9/56.**L/I.**
Cow. 25/11–28/12/57.**G.**
Cow. 12–20/3/58.**N/C.**
Cow. 4–11/6/58.**C/L.**
Cow. 5–22/1/59.**N/C.**
Cow. 26/1–27/2/59.**C/H.**
Cow. 2/7–8/8/59.**L/I.**
Cow. 25–26/8/59.**N/C.**
Cow. 16/3–26/4/62.**G.**
Dar. 7/9–17/10/64.**L/I.**
Dar. 19–20/10/64.**N/C.**
Inv. 25/1–5/2/65.**C/L.**

BOILERS:
 9967.
 9887 (*ex1250*) 26/7/50.
28198 (*ex1250*) 15/8/52.
28702 (*ex1007*) 28/12/57.
28644 (*ex1262*) 26/4/62.

SHEDS:
New England.
St Margarets 13/9/53.
Carstairs 6/12/54.
St Margarets 27/2/56.
Thornton Junction 2/5/57.

CONDEMNED:
19/11/66.
*Sold 12/66 for scrap to
Motherwell Mcy & Scrap
Co., Wishaw.*

61331

North British Loco. 26232.

To traffic 25/6/48.

REPAIRS:
Don. 1/4–10/5/50.**G.**
Don. 3–26/3/52.**G.**
Str. 6/4–3/6/54.**G.**
Don. 26/3–1/5/56.**G.**
Don. 9–12/5/56.**N/C.**
Don. 19–23/5/56.**N/C.**
Don. 1–11/1/57.**C/L.**
Don. 18/4–14/5/58.**G.**
Don. 21/9–15/10/60.**G.**

BOILERS:
 9968.
 9903 (*ex1266*) 10/5/50.
28184 (*ex1295*) 26/3/52.
28556 (*ex1104*) 3/6/54.
28271 (*ex1623*) 1/5/56.
28950 (*new*) 14/5/58.
28213 (*ex1226*) 15/10/60.

SHEDS:
New England.
Kings Cross 28/12/52.
New England 27/3/60.

CONDEMNED:
22/9/63.
*Sold 22/1/64 for scrap to
R.A.King & Sons,
Norwich.*

61332

North British Loco. 26233.

To traffic 30/6/48.

REPAIRS:
Str. 4/9–22/10/49.**G.**
Str. 25/2–30/3/50.**C/L.**
Str. 5/5–21/7/51.**G.**
Gor. 18/3–9/5/53.**G.**
Gor. 12–14/5/53.**N/C.**
Cow. 26/5–25/6/55.**H/I.**
Cow. 29/11/57–3/1/58.**G.**
Cow. 4–18/5/59.**N/C.** *Mod.
bogie springs. A.W.S.
fitted.*
Cow. 23/6–13/8/60.**L/I.**

BOILERS:
 9969.
 9907 (*ex1270*) 22/10/49.
28559 (*ex1041*) 21/7/51.
28844 (*new*) 9/5/53.
28618 (*ex1222*) 3/1/58. *141
tubes.*

SHEDS:
Cambridge.
Norwich 11/7/48.
St Margarets 13/9/53.
Thornton Junction
12/11/62.

CONDEMNED:
29/12/62.
*4/63 In for cut up at
Cowlairs.*

61333

North British Loco. 26234.

To traffic 2/7/48.

REPAIRS:
Str. 14/11/49–14/1/50.**G.**
Str. 30/7–15/9/51.**G.**
Str. 2/2–27/3/53.**G.**
Str. 28/4–24/8/53.**C/H.**
Cow. 1/9–15/10/55.**H/I.**
Cow. 27/2–17/3/56.**N/C.**
Cow. 12–25/1/57.**C/L.**
Cow. 27/5–29/6/57.**G.**
Cow. 30–31/12/57.**N/C.**
Cow. 4–25/4/59.**L/I.** *Mod.
bogie springs. A.W.S.
fitted.*

BOILERS:
 9970.
28544 (*ex1003*) 15/9/51.
28538 (*ex1055*) 27/3/53.
28519 (*ex1235*) 24/8/53.
28645 (*ex61351*) 29/6/57.
141 tubes.

SHEDS:
Cambridge.
Norwich 11/7/48.
Cambridge 15/8/48.
Haymarket 29/8/48.
Cambridge 15/11/48.

St Margarets 13/9/53.
Bathgate 31/1/54.
Eastfield 19/4/54.
Kittybrewster 9/6/54.
St Margarets 17/7/57.
Haymarket 21/10/57.
Eastfield 26/1/59.
Parkhead 12/3/59.

CONDEMNED:
29/12/62.
*7/63 In for cut up at
Cowlairs.*

61334

North British Loco. 26235.

To traffic 7/7/48.

REPAIRS:
Str. 13–27/10/48.**L.**
Str. 18/10–31/12/49.**G.**
Str. 30/4–22/6/51.**G.**
Str. 10/12/52–31/1/53.**G.**
Str. 9/8–25/9/54.**G.**
Dar. 25/3–30/4/56.**G.**
Dar. 1–15/12/56.**C/L.**
Dar. 15/1–8/2/57.**C/L.**
Dar. 21/1–22/2/58.**G.**
Dar. 6–13/3/58.**N/C.**
Don. 14/10–5/11/60.**G.**

BOILERS:
 9971.
28555 (*ex1282*) 22/6/51.
28513 (*ex1175*) 31/1/53.
28244 (*ex1214*) 30/4/56.
28597 (*ex61408*) 22/2/58.
28581 (*ex1280*) 5/11/60.

SHEDS:
Norwich.
Cambridge 15/8/48.
Sheffield 28/10/56.
Millhouses 8/11/59.
Canklow 3/1/60.
Sheffield 29/4/61.
Canklow 2/12/62.
Gorton 1/12/63.

CONDEMNED:
1/12/63.
*Sold 10/64 for scrap to
W.Rigley, Bulwell Forest.*

61335

North British Loco. 26236.

To traffic 15/7/48.

REPAIRS:
Str. 12/3–20/5/50.**G.**
Str. 27/4–15/5/51.**C/L.**
Str. 13/4–7/6/52.**G.**
Str. 23/2–17/3/54.**N/C.**
Str. 19/7–3/9/54.**G.**
Str. 14/2–8/3/57.**G.**
Str. 23/11/59–4/3/60.**G.**

BOILERS:
9972.
 9972 renumbered 28556
15/5/51.
28557 *(ex1607)* 7/6/52.
28173 *(ex1231)* 3/9/54.
28560 *(ex1286)* 8/3/57.
28836 *(ex61317)* 4/3/60.

SHEDS:
Stratford.
Haymarket 29/8/48.
Stratford 8/11/48.
Norwich 18/6/61.
Stratford 10/9/61.

CONDEMNED:
16/9/62.
14/11/62 In for cut up at
Doncaster.

61336

North British Loco. 26237.

To traffic 5/8/48.

REPAIRS:
Str. 27/3–2/4/49.**C/L.**
Str. 3/2–20/4/50.**G.**
Str. 28/1–9/2/51.**C/L.**
Str. 11–28/3/52.**C/L.**
Str. 1/9–11/10/52.**G.**
Str. 8/11–24/12/54.**G.**
Str. 23/5–22/7/55.**C/L.**
Str. 13/11/56–15/1/57.**G.**
Str. 14/3–5/4/57.**C/L.**
Str. 31/12/58–6/2/59.**G.**
Mod. bogie springs.
Str. 14/4–8/5/59.**N/C.**
Complete A.T.C. fitted.
Str. 29/7–24/8/59.**C/L.**
Don. 18/1–27/2/60.**C/H.**
Don. 25/4–19/5/61.**C/L.**

BOILERS:
9973.
 9973 renumbered 28586
28/3/52.
28520 *(ex1205)* 11/10/52.
28546 *(ex61373)* 24/12/54.
28538 *(ex1121)* 15/1/57.
28451 *(ex1231)* 6/2/59.
28317 *(ex1079)* 27/2/60.

SHEDS:
Stratford.
St Margarets 29/8/48.
Stratford 7/11/48.
Colchester 30/10/56.
Stratford 6/12/59.
Parkeston 13/12/59.
Colwick 27/11/60.

CONDEMNED:
22/9/63.
Sold 12/63 for scrap to
J.Cashmore, Great Bridge.

61337

North British Loco. 26238.

To traffic 12/8/48.

REPAIRS:
Dar. 5/7–12/8/50.**G.**
Dar. 11/6–4/7/52.**G.**
Dar. 9–10/7/52.**N/C.**
Dar. 6–19/12/53.**C/L.**
Dar. 20/5–18/6/54.**G.**
Dar. 27/9–16/10/54.**C/L.**
Dar. 21–30/4/55.**C/L.**
Dar. 5–15/3/56.**C/L.**
Dar. 5/7–20/8/56.**G.**
Dar. 29/12/58–27/1/59.**G.**
A.T.C. Mech. fitted.
Dar. 5–19/8/59.**N/C.**
A.T.C. Elec. fitted.
Dar. 18/8–15/9/61.**G.**
Dar. 27/9–16/10/61.**N/C.**
Dar. 23/9–6/11/64.**G.**

BOILERS:
9974.
 9857 *(ex1220)* 12/8/50.
28442 *(ex1275)* 4/7/52.
28438 *(ex61353)* 18/6/54.
28238 *(ex61319)* 20/8/56.
28454 *(ex1022)* 27/1/59.
28206 *(ex1041)* 15/9/61.
28449 *(ex1030)* 6/11/64.

SHEDS:
Neville Hill.
St Margarets 29/8/48.
York 31/10/48.
Low Moor 25/6/67.

CONDEMNED:
30/9/67.
Sold 11/67 for scrap to
T.W.Ward, Killamarsh.

61338

North British Loco. 26239.

To traffic 20/8/48.

REPAIRS:
Dar. 6/1–2/2/50.**G.**
Dar. 9–15/2/50.**N/C.**
Dar. 27/6–20/7/51.**G.**
Dar. 23/2–21/3/53.**G.**
Dar. 25–28/3/53.**N/C.**
Dar. 11–24/3/54.**N/C.**
Dar. 18/10–13/11/54.**G.**
Dar. 5/9–3/10/56.**G.**
Dar. 14–19/3/57.**G.**
Dar. 9–24/9/58.**N/C.**
Dar. 16/2–13/3/59.**G.**
A.T.C. Mech. fitted.
Dar. 28–29/7/59.**N/C.**
A.T.C. Elec. fitted.
Dar. 14/8–8/9/61.**G.**
Dar. 14/10–21/12/62.**C/L.**

BOILERS:
9975.
 4045 *(new)* 2/2/50.
 4045 renumbered 28224
20/7/51.
28458 *(ex61377)* 21/3/53.
28224 *(ex1218)* 13/11/54.
28209 *(ex1039)* 3/10/56.
28547 *(ex1257)* 13/3/59.
28318 *(ex1215)* 8/9/61.

SHEDS:
Neville Hill.
Heaton 19/11/50.
Neville Hill 1/1/51.
York 2/9/51.
Southern Region 19/5/53.
York 21/6/53.
Darlington 25/9/55.
Neville Hill 16/6/63.
Wakefield 7/6/64.

CONDEMNED:
11/1/65.
Sold 3/65 for scrap to
A.Draper, Hull.

61339

North British Loco. 26240.

To traffic 8/9/48.

REPAIRS:
Dar. 30/12/49–26/1/50.**G.**
Dar. 24/9–16/10/51.**G.**
Dar. 5–30/10/53.**G.**
Dar. 26/10–24/11/55.**G.**
Dar. 5–29/11/57.**G.**
Dar. 22/4–3/6/60.**G.**
A.W.S. fitted.
Dar. 13–22/6/60.**N/C.**

BOILERS:
9976.
 3600 *(ex1039)* 26/1/50.
28230 *(ex1218)* 16/10/51.
28203 *(ex1257)* 30/10/53.
28248 *(ex1241)* 24/11/55.
28578 *(ex spare 2 years)*
29/11/57.
28447 *(ex1049)* 3/6/60.

SHEDS:
Neville Hill.
York 2/9/51.
Copley Hill 8/6/58.

CONDEMNED:
25/11/62.
31/1/63 in for cut up at
Darlington.

61340

Gorton.

To traffic 27/11/48.

REPAIRS:
Cow. 15/8–1/9/50.**L/I.**
Cow. 6/6–7/7/52.**G.**
Cow. 13/4–15/5/54.**L/I.**
Cow. 11/2/55.**N/C.**
Cow. 27/1–10/3/56.**H/I.**
Cow. 24/5–29/6/57.**G.**
SRX. 25/3–11/4/59.**N/C.**
Cow. 20/5–6/6/59.**H/I.**
Cow. 6–18/3/61.**N/C.**
Cow. 17/5–24/6/61.**G.**
Cow. 27/3–12/4/62.**C/L.**
Cow. 28/3–16/5/64.**L/I.**
Inv. 29–30/10/64.**C/L.**

BOILERS:
5121.
28623 *(ex1197)* 7/7/52.
28462 *(ex1294)* 29/6/57.
28637 *(ex1147)* 24/6/61.

SHEDS:
Eastfield.
Grangemouth 30/1/61.
Thornton Junction
16/10/61.
Dundee 12/11/61.
Dunfermline 28/8/66.
Dundee 13/11/66.

CONDEMNED:
22/4/67.
Sold 7/7/67 for scrap to P &
W McLellan, Langloan.

61341

Gorton.

To traffic 18/12/48.

REPAIRS:
Cow. 7/3–7/4/51.**H/I.**
Cow. 16/12/52–7/1/53.**L/I.**
Cow. 30/4–12/6/54.**G.**
Cow. 6/6–7/7/56.**H/I.**
Cow. 24/4–24/5/57.**C/L.**
Cow. 10/12/58–10/1/59.**G.**
Cow. 16–24/2/59.**N/C.**
Cow. 16/6–12/8/61.**L/I.**
A.W.S. fitted 28/12/59.

BOILERS:
5107.
 5107 renumbered 28646
7/4/51.
28657 *(ex61352)* 12/6/54.
28627 *(ex1260)* 10/1/59. *141*
tubes.

SHEDS:
Eastfield.
Parkhead 16/1/49.
St Margarets 20/11/49.

CONDEMNED:
28/12/63.
2/64 In for cut up at
Cowlairs.

WORKS CODES:– Cow – Cowlairs. Dar – Darlington. Dee – Dundee. Don – Doncaster. Ghd – Gateshead. Gor – Gorton. Inv – Inverurie. Str – Stratford. SRX – St Rollox.
REPAIR CODES:– **C/H** – Casual Heavy. **C/L** – Casual Light. **G** – General. **H** – Heavy. **H/I** – Heavy Intermediate. **L** – Light. **L/I** – Light Intermediate. **N/C** – Non–Classified.

61342

Gorton.

To traffic 3/1/49.

REPAIRS:
Cow. 23/8–16/9/50.**L/I.**
Cow. 25/12/50–5/1/51.**N/C.**
Cow. 10–22/5/51.**N/C.**
SRX. 13–16/8/51.**N/C.**
SRX. 7–14/11/51.**N/C.**
Cow. 14/1–2/2/52.**L/I.**
Cow. 1–15/5/52.**N/C.**
Cow. 2–12/9/52.**N/C.**
Cow. 18/11–6/12/52.**C/L.**
Cow. 15–31/10/53.**C/L.**
Cow. 23/2–27/3/54.**G.**
Cow. 23/4/54.**N/C.**
Cow. 18–19/11/54.**N/C.**
Efd. 1–16/11/54.**C/L.**
Cow. 28/11–24/12/55.**H/I.**
Cow. 24/2–10/3/56.**C/L.**
Cow. 15–24/5/57.**C/L.**
Cow. 24/12/57–29/1/58.**H/I.**
Cow. 26/2–6/3/59.**N/C.**
Cow. 23/3–23/4/59.**C/L.**
Cow. 13/2–2/4/60.**G.**
Cow. 30/6–13/7/61.**C/L.**
Cow. 6–10/8/62.**N/C.**
Cow. 10/12/62–5/1/63.**L/I.**
Cow. 6/10–7/11/64.**C/L.**

BOILERS:
5108.
5108 renumbered 28647
5/1/51.
28663 (ex61358) 27/3/54.
28669 (ex1290) 2/4/60.

SHEDS:
Eastfield.
Motherwell 10/11/66.

CONDEMNED:
31/12/66.
Sold 27/2/67 for scrap to
G.McWilliam, Shettleston.

61343

Gorton.

To traffic 4/2/49.

REPAIRS:
Cow. 26/10–23/11/50.**L/I.**
Cow.
18/12/50–13/1/51.**C/L.**
Kit. 14/8–13/9/52.**L/I.**
Cow. 5/10–14/11/53.**G.**
Inv. 14/1/54.**N/C.**
Cow. 10/8–3/9/55.**L/I.**
Cow. 14/1–4/2/56.**C/L.**
Cow. 19/3–21/4/56.**C/H.**
Cow. 24/8–20/9/57.**H/I.**
Cow. 21/11–13/12/58.**C/L.**
Cow. 23/4–16/5/59.**H/I.**
Cow. 23/2–22/4/61.**G.**
Cow. 5/12/63–18/1/64.**L/I.**

BOILERS:
5127.
5127 renumbered 28648

13/9/52.
28644 (ex61324) 14/11/53.
28703 (ex61395) 21/4/56.
28613 (ex61350) 22/4/61.

SHEDS:
Aberdeen.
Kittybrewster 16/5/49.
Thornton Junction 24/3/59.

CONDEMNED:
3/3/66.
Sold 4/66 for scrap to
Motherwell Mcy & Scrap
Co., Wishaw.

61344

Gorton.

To traffic 5/3/49.

REPAIRS:
Cow. 23/3–13/4/51.**H/I.**
Cow. 21/1–16/2/52.**C/L.**
Cow. 21–28/2/52.**N/C.**
Cow. 23/3–25/4/53.**G.**
Cow. 29/4–17/6/54.**L/I.**
Cow. 20–29/1/55.**N/C.**
Cow. 30/11–24/12/55.**C/L.**
Cow. 20/3–28/4/56.**L/I.**
Cow. 30/5–22/6/57.**C/L.**
Cow. 6/3–5/4/58.**G.**
Cow. 20–27/4/59.**N/C.**
Cow. 7/7–20/8/60.**H/I.**
Cow. 20–24/12/60.**N/C.**
Cow. 13–16/3/61.**N/C.**
Cow. 10–21/9/62.**C/L.**
Cow. 29/6–17/8/63.**G.**

BOILERS:
5128.
5128 renumbered 28649
13/4/51.
28625 (ex61007) 25/4/53.
28207 (ex1099) 5/4/58.
28431 (ex spare) 17/8/63.

SHEDS:
Eastfield.
Parkhead 28/10/57.
St Margarets 13/8/62.
Thornton Junction 24/4/66.

CONDEMNED:
23/9/66.
Sold 11/66 for scrap to
Motherwell Mcy & Scrap
Co., Wishaw.

61345

Gorton.

To traffic 8/4/49.

REPAIRS:
Inv. 12–13/7/49.**N/C.** Tab.
catcher fitted.
Cow. 5–30/10/51.**H/I.**
Cow. 30/11–28/12/51.**H/I.**
Cow. 14/9–12/10/53.**G.**
Inv. 11/3/54.**N/C.**

Cow. 22/9–29/10/55.**H/I.**
Cow. 19–29/3/56.**N/C.**
Cow. 30/5–6/7/57.**G.**
Cow. 12/9–23/10/58.**H/I.**
Cow. 24/9–7/10/59.**N/C.**
Cow. 26/4–18/6/60.**L/I.**
Cow. 30/8–12/10/60.**C/L.**
Cow. 29/5–30/6/62.**G.**
Cow. 3–15/7/64.**N/C.**
Cow. 26/2–20/3/65.**N/C.**

BOILERS:
5129.
5129 renumbered 28650
30/10/51.
28637 (ex1278) 12/10/53.
28636 (ex61356) 6/7/57.
28702 (ex61330) 30/6/62.

SHEDS:
Aberdeen.
Kittybrewster 16/5/49.
St Margarets 19/6/61.

CONDEMNED:
14/7/66.
Sold 9/66 for scrap to
G.H.Campbell, Airdrie.

61346

Gorton.

To traffic 30/4/49.

REPAIRS:
Inv. 2–3/8/49.**N/C.** Tab.
catcher fitted.
Cow. 27/9–18/10/51.**H/I.**
Cow. 11/2–1/4/52.**C/H.**
Cow. 26/10–12/12/53.**G.**
Inv. 20/4/54.**N/C.**
Cow. 18/4–14/5/55.**L/I.**
W.P.U. gear removed.
Cow. 24/4–30/5/57.**H/I.**
Cow. 1–23/11/57.**C/L.**
Cow. 13/3–18/4/59.**G.**
Inv. 12/12/60–13/1/61.**L/I.**
Cow. 14/7–2/9/61.**C/L.**
Cow. 11–19/4/63.**N/C.**
Inv. 17–18/7/63.**N/C.**

BOILERS:
5130.
5130 renumbered 28651
18/10/51.
28648 (ex61343) 12/12/53.
28650 (ex1217) 18/4/59. 141
tubes.

SHEDS:
Kittybrewster.
Keith 9/1/50.
Kittybrewster 21/12/50.
Aberdeen 19/6/61.
Thornton Junction
26/12/62.

CONDEMNED:
8/6/64.
Sold 8/64 for scrap to P &
W McLellan, Langloan.

61347

Gorton.

To traffic 21/5/49.

REPAIRS:
Inv. 12–14/12/49.**N/C.** Tab.
catcher fitted.
Cow. 6/11–1/12/51.**H/I.**
Cow. 26/4–29/5/54.**G.**
Cow. 7–10/6/54.**N/C.**
Inv. 15–18/3/55.**N/C.**
Cow. 7/6–2/7/55.**N/C.**
Cow. 28/1–10/3/56.**H/I.**
Cow. 10/5–15/6/57.**G.**
Cow. 2–27/12/58.**H/I.**
Cow. 8/10–19/11/60.**L/I.**
Cow. 23/11–21/12/62.**C/H.**
Cow. 25/1–13/3/65.**L/I.**
Cow. 16/6–3/7/65.**C/L.**
Cow. 4–7/8/65.**N/C.**
Cow. 29/10–20/11/65.**C/L.**

BOILERS:
5131.
5131 renumbered 28652
1/12/51.
28639 (ex1293) 29/5/54.
28185 (ex1140) 15/6/57.
28648 (ex61395) 21/12/62.

SHEDS:
Kittybrewster.
Keith 9/1/50.
Kittybrewster 21/12/50.
Aberdeen 19/6/61.
Dalry Road 9/8/64.
St Margarets 4/10/65.
Thornton Junction 24/4/66.

CONDEMNED:
4/4/67.
Sold 7/7/67 for scrap to P &
W McLellan, Langloan.

61348

Gorton.

To traffic 9/6/49.

REPAIRS:
Cow. 27/2–19/3/51.**H/I.**
Cow. 26/11–23/12/52.**G.**
Cow. 17/9–23/10/54.**L/I.**
Cow. 1–6/11/54.**N/C.**
Cow. 11–13/7/55.**N/C.**
Cow. 2/8–10/9/55.**C/L.**
Cow. 24/11–17/12/55.**C/L.**
Cow. 13/10–10/11/56.**G.**
Don. 4–14/5/57.**C/L.**
Don. 23–28/9/57.**C/L.**
Str. 17/2–8/4/59.**G.** A.T.C.
fitted.
Don. 6–9/12/60.**N/C.**
Don. 26/7–25/8/61.**G.**
Don. 9/4–9/5/63.**C/L.**
Dar. 13–28/9/63.**C/L.**

BOILERS:
5132.
5132 renumbered 28653
19/3/51.

28632 *(ex1260)* 23/12/52.
28610 *(ex1219)* 10/11/56.
28854 *(ex1299)* 8/4/59.
28183 *(ex1088)* 25/8/61.

SHEDS:
Kittybrewster.
Peterborough 25/2/57.
March 31/1/60.
Lincoln 3/4/60.
Retford 5/1/64.
Doncaster 13/6/65.
Frodingham 11/7/65.
Colwick 14/11/65.

CONDEMNED:
26/12/65.
*Sold 2/66 for scrap to
Garnham, Harris & Elton,
Chesterfield.*

61349

Gorton.

To traffic 2/7/49.

REPAIRS:
Inv. 21–23/11/49.**N/C.**
Cow. 13/3–3/4/51.**H/I.**
Cow. 22/9–11/10/52.**H/I.**
Cow. 13/5–13/6/53.**C/L.**
Inv. 7/6–10/7/53.**N/C.**
Inv. 23–25/9/53.**N/C.**
Cow. 15/4–29/5/54.**G.**
Cow. 28/5–2/7/55.**L/I.**
Cow. 9/2–10/3/56.**N/C.**
Cow. 9/2–9/3/57.**L/I.**
Cow. 18–20/3/57.**N/C.**
Cow. 1–31/10/58.**G.**
Cow. 7–11/11/58.**N/C.**
Cow. 13–24/3/59.**N/C.**
Inv. 13/3–28/4/61.**H/I.**
Cow. 26/10–15/11/61.**C/L.**
Cow. 14–26/5/62.**C/L.**
Cow.
17/12/62–12/1/63.**C/L.**
Cow. 25/5–29/6/63.**G.**
Cow. 1/7–21/8/65.**L/I.**

BOILERS:
5133.
*5133 renumbered 28654
3/4/51.*
28647 *(ex61342)* 29/5/54.
28600 *(ex1293)* 31/10/58.
28618 *(ex61332)* 29/6/63.

SHEDS:
Kittybrewster.
St Margarets 22/8/57.
Thornton Junction 24/4/66.

CONDEMNED:
17/8/66.
*Sold 10/66 for scrap to
Motherwell Machinery &
Scrap Co., Wishaw.*

61350

Darlington 2072.

To traffic 28/7/49.

REPAIRS:
Inv. 8–10/11/49.**N/C.**
Cow. 1–18/9/51.**H/I.**
Inv. 17–19/6/52.**N/C.**
Inv. 5–10/7/52.**N/C.**
Cow. 6–7/11/52.**C/L.**
Cow. 26/5–3/7/54.**G.**
Cow. 8/10–12/11/55.**C/L.**
Cow. 19/6–4/8/56.**G.**
Cow. 21–23/8/56.**N/C.**
Cow. 22/11–21/12/57.**H/I.**
Cow. 20/3–5/4/58.**C/L.**
Cow. 18/4–1/5/58.**N/C.**
Cow. 7–29/11/58.**L/I.**
Cow. 9/5–25/6/60.**G.**
Cow. 20/5–22/6/63.**L/I.**
Cow. 30/10–7/12/63.**C/L.**
Cow.
13/12/63–25/1/64.**C/H.**

BOILERS:
3874.
*3874 renumbered 28655
18/9/51.*
28654 *(ex61349)* 3/7/54.
28613 *(ex1133)* 4/8/56.
28607 *(ex1221)* 25/6/60.
28518 *(ex61383)* 25/1/64.

SHEDS:
Kittybrewster.
Aberdeen 19/6/61.
St Margarets 16/5/62.
Dunfermline 24/4/66.

CONDEMNED:
19/11/66.
*Sold 12/66 for scrap to
Motherwell Machinery &
Scrap Co., Wishaw.*

61351

Darlington 2073.

To traffic 16/8/49.

REPAIRS:
Dar. 7–11/2/50.**N/C.**
*Special exam of copper
firebox liner.*
Cow. 9–28/4/51.**L/I.**
Cow. 20/8–19/9/52.**G.**
Inv. 4/2/54.**N/C.**
Inv. 2/6/54.**N/C.**
Cow. 14/4–14/5/55.**H/I.**
W.P.U. gear removed.
Cow. 2/4–11/5/57.**G.**
Cow. 17–18/9/58.**N/C.**
Cow. 23/1–20/2/59.**L/I.**
A.T.C. fitted.
Cow. 24/11–20/12/60.**N/C.**
Cow. 23/8–14/10/61.**G.**

BOILERS:
3878.
28645 *(ex61340)* 19/9/52.
28823 *(ex1118)* 11/5/57.

28632 *(ex1294)* 14/10/61.

SHEDS:
Kittybrewster.
St Margarets 19/8/57.
Dalry Road 14/6/64.

CONDEMNED:
13/7/64.
*9/64 In for cut up at
Darlington. Tender to
snowplough.*

61352

Darlington 2074.

To traffic 25/8/49.

REPAIRS:
Dar. 31/8–5/9/49.**N/C.**
Adjust.
Dar. 14/9/49.**N/C.** *Tender
to lower.*
Dar. 7–12/11/49.**N/C.**
Pistons.
Inv. 15–16/12/49.**N/C.** *Tab.
catcher fitted.*
Cow. 4–22/12/51.**H/I.**
Cow. 31/3–1/5/54.**G.**
Cow. 16/11–17/12/55.**L/I.**
W.P.U. gear removed.
Cow. 18/10–3/11/56.**N/C.**
Cow. 18–20/6/57.**H/I.**
Cow. 5–22/5/58.**C/L.**
Cow. 9–31/1/59.**G.**
Cow. 22/9–7/10/59.**N/C.**
Cow. 9/4–28/5/60.**L/I.**
A.T.C. fitted.
Cow. 27/6–5/7/62.**C/L.**

BOILERS:
3880.
*3880 renumbered 28657
22/12/51.*
28624 *(ex1146)* 1/5/54.
28662 *(ex61401)* 31/1/59.

SHEDS:
Kittybrewster.
Mallaig 19/6/61.
Gorton 12/8/62.

CONDEMNED:
22/10/62.
*1/63 In for cut up at
Cowlairs.*

61353

Darlington 2075.

To traffic 6/9/49.

REPAIRS:
Inv. 5–6/12/49.**N/C.** *Tab.
catcher fitted.*
Dar. 18–25/10/49.**N/C.**
Dar. 15–19/11/49.**N/C.**
Dar. 15/8–21/9/50.**C/L.**
Mod. for Rugby test plant.
Dar. 12–28/12/50.**N/C.**
Dar. 28/8–10/9/51.**C/L.**

Blast pipe modification.
Dar. 27/5–18/6/52.**G.**
Dar. 4–15/11/52.**C/L.**
Dar. 6–7/1/53.**N/C.**
Dar. 31/8/53.*Weigh.*
Dar. 23/3–22/4/54.**G.**
Dar. 20/6–1/8/56.**G.**
Dar. 23–27/5/57.**N/C.**
Dar. 15–21/11/57.**N/C.**
Dar. 12–22/5/58.**N/C.**
Dar. 15–21/8/58.**N/C.**
Dar. 31/12/58–30/1/59.**G.**
A.T.C. Mech. fitted.
Dar. 6–18/9/59.**N/C.**
A.T.C. Elec. fitted.
Dar. 8/3–13/4/60.**C/H.**
Dar. 3/8–2/9/61.**G.**
Dar. 17/8–12/9/62.**C/L.**

BOILERS:
3881.
*3881 renumbered 28658
21/9/50.*
28438 *(ex61315)* 18/6/52.
28426 *(ex61316)* 22/4/54.
28128 *(ex1086)* 1/8/56.
28815 *(ex61368)* 30/1/59.
28293 *(ex1002)* 2/9/61.

SHEDS:
Kittybrewster.
Keith 12/12/49.
Rugby Test Station 4/10/50.
Keith 28/8/51.
Darlington 2/9/51.
Neville Hill 16/6/63.
Wakefield 7/6/64.

CONDEMNED:
16/8/65.
*Sold 10/65 for scrap to
Hughes, Bolckow, North
Blyth.*

61354

Darlington 2076.

To traffic 14/9/49.

REPAIRS:
Dar. 25/10–1/11/49.**N/C.**
Cow. 14/8–6/9/51.**L/I.**
Cow. 17–19/9/51.**N/C.**
Cow. 13/1–6/2/53.**L/I.**
Cow. 25/8–9/10/54.**G.**
Cow. 24/12/54–8/1/55.**C/L.**
Cow. 13/12/56–19/1/57.**H/I.**
Cow. 27/3–25/4/59.**G.**
Cow. 20/10–9/12/61.**L/I.**
Cow. 6/6–3/8/63.**G.**
Cow. 18/1–6/2/64.**C/L.**
Cow. 5/3–26/4/65.**N/C.**

BOILERS:
3883.
*3883 renumbered 28659
6/9/51.*
28635 *(ex1261)* 9/10/54.
28664 *(ex1278)* 25/4/59.
28400 *(ex spare & 1068)*
3/8/63.

SHEDS:
St Margarets.
Dalry Road 11/3/51.
St Margarets 29/9/51.
Southern Region 20/5/53.
St Margarets 25/6/53.
Thornton Junction 24/4/66.
Dundee 13/11/66.

CONDEMNED:
22/4/67.
*Sold 7/7/67 for scrap to P &
W. McLellan, Langloan.*

61355

Darlington 2077.

To traffic 21/9/49.

REPAIRS:
Dar. 1–4/11/49.**N/C.**
Cow. 4/6–12/7/51.**H/I.**
Cow. 18/5–27/6/53.**G.**
Cow. 31/10–26/11/55.**H/I.**
Cow. 9/1–8/2/57.**H/I.**
Cow. 30/4–11/5/57.**C/L.**
Cow. 4–14/3/58.**N/C.**
Cow. 16/12/58–16/1/59.**G.**
Cow. 23–26/2/59.**N/C.**
Cow. 18–21/5/59.**N/C.**
A.W.S. fitted.
Cow. 11–25/12/59.**C/L.**
Cow. 6–8/7/60.**N/C.**
Cow. 7/10–12/11/60.**L/I.**
Cow. 18–26/4/61.**N/C.**
Cow. 19–27/1/62.**N/C.**
Cow. 7–15/5/62.**C/L.**
Cow. 17–21/9/62.**N/C.**

BOILERS:
3886.
3886 renumbered 28660
12/7/51.
28653 *(ex61348)* 27/6/53.
28630 *(ex1292)* 16/1/59. *141
tubes.*

SHEDS:
St Margarets.
Haymarket 27/9/54.
Eastfield 24/1/59.
Corkerhill 31/12/62.
Ayr 11/3/63.

CONDEMNED:
8/6/64.
*Sold 8/64 for scrap to
Motherwell Machinery &
Scrap Co., Wishaw.*

61356

Darlington 2078.

To traffic 28/9/49.

REPAIRS:
Dar. 14–19/11/49.**N/C.**
Cow. 1–23/10/51.**H/I.**
Cow. 30/10–5/12/53.**G.**
Cow. 31/10–26/11/55.**H/I.**
Cow. 7–17/12/55.**N/C.**

Cow. 7/3–13/4/57.**G.**
Cow. 19/7–3/8/57.**N/C.**
Cow. 22/5–21/6/58.**L/I.**
Cow. 7–21/4/59.**N/C.**
A.W.S. fitted.
Cow. 12/10–3/11/59.**N/C.**
Cow. 9/9–15/10/60.**L/I.**
Cow. 25–27/10/60.**N/C.**
Cow. 2/3–7/4/62.**G.**

BOILERS:
3996.
3996 renumbered 28661
23/10/51.
28636 *(ex1277)* 5/12/53.
28654 *(ex61350)* 13/4/57.
28705 *(ex1219)* 7/4/62.

SHEDS:
St Margarets.
Dalry Road 15/4/51.
St Margarets 29/9/51.

CONDEMNED:
23/7/64.
*11/64 In for cut up at
Darlington. Tender to
Snowplough.*

61357

Darlington 2079.

To traffic 10/10/49.

REPAIRS:
Dar. 21–25/11/49.**N/C.**
Cow. 29/5–18/6/51.**H/I.**
Cow. 12/6–4/7/53.**L/I.**
Cow. 25/8–25/9/54.**G.**
Cow. 21/6–14/7/56.**H/I.**
Cow. 3/2–8/3/58.**G.**
Cow. 11/4–9/5/59.**H/I.**
A.W.S. fitted.
Cow. 7–20/10/60.**N/C.**
Cow. 21/9–4/11/61.**H/I.**
Cow. 26/3–27/4/63.**C/H.**

BOILERS:
5134.
5134 renumbered 28662
18/6/51.
28638 *(ex61359)* 25/9/54.
28198 *(ex61330)* 8/3/58. *141
tubes.*
28625 *(ex1261)* 27/4/63.

SHEDS:
St Margarets.
Carstairs 3/2/55.
St Margarets 28/3/55.

CONDEMNED:
8/6/65.
*Sold 11/65 for scrap to
Motherwell Machinery &
Scrap Co., Wishaw.*

61358

Darlington 2080.

To traffic 18/10/49.

REPAIRS:
Dar. 30/11–2/12/49.**N/C.**
Cow. 3/8–7/9/51.**L/I.**
Cow. 20/11–19/12/53.**G.**
Cow. 17/1–18/2/56.**H/I.**
Cow. 14/3–14/4/56.**C/L.**
Cow. 19/9–3/10/56.**N/C.**
Cow. 29/11/57–7/1/58.**H/I.**
Cow. 13–20/9/58.**N/C.**
Cow. 7/2–5/3/59.**G.** *Mod.
bogie springs.*
Cow. 2–18/6/59.**C/L.**
Cow. 18/8–10/9/59.**C/L.**
A.W.S. fitted.
Cow. 21/10–17/11/61.**L/I.**
Thj. 14/2–1/3/63.**C/L.**

BOILERS:
3999.
3999 renumbered 28663
7/9/51.
28640 *(ex1217)* 19/12/53.
28647 *(ex61349)* 5/3/59. *141
tubes.*

SHEDS:
St Margarets.
Thornton Junction 2/5/57.

CONDEMNED:
25/12/63.
*1/64 In for cut up at
Cowlairs.*

61359

Darlington 2081.

To traffic 26/10/49.

REPAIRS:
Cow. 15/6–10/7/51.**H/I.**
Cow. 1–20/6/53.**G.**
Inv. 29/12/53–5/2/54.**N/C.**
Cow. 21/5–10/6/54.**N/C.**
Cow. 7/7–7/8/54.**N/C.**
Cow. 17/8–4/9/54.**C/H.**
Cow. 10–17/9/54.**N/C.**
Cow. 3–28/5/55.**H/I.**
Cow. 23/1–18/2/56.**N/C.**
Cow. 6/1–15/2/58.**H/I.**
Cow. 3–25/12/58.**C/L.**
Cow. 6–18/4/59.**N/C.**
A.W.S. fitted.
Cow. 7–11/7/59.**N/C.**
Cow. 18/9–24/10/59.**G.**
Cow. 5/9–21/10/61.**H/I.**

BOILERS:
5135.
5135 renumbered 28664
10/7/51.
28638 *(ex1292)* 20/6/53.
28646 *(ex61341)* 4/9/54.
28659 *(ex1081)* 24/10/59.
141 tubes.

SHED:
St Margarets.

CONDEMNED:
28/12/63.
*1/64 In for cut up at
Cowlairs.*

61360

North British Loco. 26819.

To traffic 22/3/50.

REPAIRS:
Str. 5/12/51–12/1/52.**G.**
Str. 8/10–14/11/53.**G.**
Str. 7/11/55–4/2/56.**G.**
Str. 8–17/4/57.**N/C.**
Str. 14/5–4/7/58.**G.** *Mod.
bogie springs.*
Don. 17/10–12/11/60.**G.**
Dar. 29/7–12/9/63.**G.**

BOILERS:
10810.
28572 *(ex61361)* 12/1/52.
28536 *(ex1135)* 14/11/53.
28515 *(ex61372)* 4/2/56.
28577 *(ex61362)* 4/7/58.
28184 *(ex1149)* 12/11/60.
28858 *(ex1065)* 12/9/63.

SHEDS:
Stratford.
Colchester 6/1/57.
Cambridge 12/4/59.
Doncaster 1/11/59.

CONDEMNED:
17/4/66.
*Sold 5/66 for scrap to
Geo.Cohen, Kettering.*

61361

North British Loco. 26820.

To traffic 24/3/50.

REPAIRS:
Str. 5/11–15/12/51.**G.**
Str. 7/12/53–16/1/54.**G.**
Str. 13/2–24/3/56.**G.**
Str. 25/3–2/4/57.**N/C.**
Str. 20/11/58–16/1/59.**G.**
Mod. bogie springs.
Str. 18–29/9/59.**N/C.** *New
smokebox front & door.*
Don. 26/9–27/10/61.**G.**

BOILERS:
10811.
28540 *(ex spare)* 15/12/51.
28572 *(ex61360)* 16/1/54.
28295 *(ex61370)* 24/3/56.
28201 *(ex61312)* 16/1/59.
28152 *(ex1248)* 27/10/61.

SHEDS:
Stratford.
Colchester 6/1/57.
Parkeston 6/12/59.
Colwick 27/11/60.

CONDEMNED:
26/12/65.
*Sold 2/66 for scrap to
Garnham, Harris & Elton,
Chesterfield.*

The Vulcan batch started without speed indicators, and in their later years had it discarded. 61165, at Sheffield (Midland) on 4th May 1963, shows that both bracket and connection to the rear coupled wheel had been removed.

For working on the former LMS line between Inverness and Perth in the 1948 locomotive exchanges, 61292 had its cab side fitted with tablet exchanging apparatus of ex–Highland Railway type, but that was removed at the end of the trials. Its use of discs instead of lamps for express train indication was rare.

One must give credit to the Great Western for knowing how to fill a sandwich. 61369 of Leicester shed shows up well at Swindon on 22nd January 1956 between the two nondescript items flanking it.

Definitely a "one-off"; a B1 heading an LM Region 'Duchess'. 61353 piloting 46236 CITY OF BRADFORD at Nuneaton on 9th August 1951 was being returned from its trials at the Rugby Testing Station, and is surely letting the Pacific do all the work. It is a perfect example of an old saying by my mother–in–law "that idleness was nowt unless properly carried out".

61077 did all its sixteen years work on the former Great Central main line, almost all of it from Neasden and Leicester sheds. Here passing the milk depot outside Marylebone station it has an outer suburban stopping train for Rickmansworth.

61362

North British Loco. 26821.

To traffic 31/3/50.

REPAIRS:
Str. 10/9–20/10/51.**G.**
Str. 31/8–26/9/53.**G.**
Str. 29/12/54–21/5/55.**C/L.**
Str. 26/9/55–13/1/56.**G.**
Str. 27/1–22/3/58.**G.** *Mod. bogie springs.*
Don. 20/7–25/8/60.**G.**

BOILERS:
10812.
10812 renumbered 28569 20/10/51.
28564 *(ex1046)* 26/9/53.
28577 *(ex1285)* 13/1/56.
28503 *(ex61399)* 22/3/58.
28147 *(ex1301)* 25/8/60.

SHEDS:
Stratford.
Parkeston 8/2/59.
Stratford 1/1/61.

CONDEMNED:
16/9/62.
4/12/62 In for cut up at Doncaster.

61363

North British Loco. 26822.

To traffic 5/4/50.

REPAIRS:
Str. 17/12/51–19/1/52.**G.**
Str. 5–29/8/52.**C/H.**
Str. 23/2–2/4/54.**G.**
Str. 30/4–16/6/56.**G.**
Str. 26/8–3/10/58.**G.** *Mod. bogie springs.*
Str. 6–17/4/59.**N/C.**
Complete A.T.C. fitted.
Don. 28/3–6/5/61.**G.**

BOILERS:
10813.
28573 *(ex1059)* 19/1/52.
28201 *(ex61378)* 2/4/54.
28857 *(ex1160)* 16/6/56.
28421 *(ex1253)* 3/10/58.
28755 *(ex1213)* 6/5/61.

SHEDS:
Stratford.
Colchester 6/1/57.
Stratford 6/12/59.
March 13/12/59.
Cambridge 10/1/60.
Stratford 17/6/62.
March 16/9/62.

CONDEMNED:
23/9/62.
Sold 6/63 for scrap to Central Wagon Co., Ince.

61364

North British Loco. 26823.

To traffic 19/4/50.

REPAIRS:
Dar. 18/4–16/5/52.**G.**
Don. 16/11–11/12/53.**C/L.**
Str. 15/6–13/8/54.**G.**
Don. 14/9–28/10/55.**C/H.**
Don. 15/11–19/12/56.**G.**
Don. 6/10–6/11/58.**G.**
Str. 16/2–13/3/59.**C/L.**
Don. 25/7–3/8/60.**N/C.**

BOILERS:
10814.
28427 *(ex61306)* 16/5/52.
28526 *(ex1614)* 13/8/54.
28450 *(ex1202)* 19/12/56.
28423 *(ex61328)* 6/11/58.

SHEDS:
Lincoln.
New England 20/9/53.
Kings Cross 13/2/55.
New England 3/6/62.

CONDEMNED:
16/9/62.
Sold 1/63 for scrap to R.A.King, Norwich.

61365

North British Loco. 26824.

To traffic 21/4/50.

REPAIRS:
Dar. 9/12/51–24/1/52.**G.**
Don. 1/6–6/7/53.**G.**
Don. 15/9/53.*Weigh.*
Don. 15/3–7/4/55.**G.**
Don. 14/2–5/3/57.**C/L.**
Don. 3/9–9/10/57.**G.**
Don. 30/9–24/10/59.**G.**
Don. 19/3–19/4/62.**G.**
Don. 3–15/1/63.**N/C.**

BOILERS:
10815.
28246 *(ex1289)* 24/1/52.
28866 *(new)* 6/7/53.
28532 *(ex1207)* 7/4/55.
28521 *(ex1236)* 9/10/57.
28251 *(ex61313)* 24/10/59.
28958 *(ex1092)* 19/4/62.

SHEDS:
Immingham.
Doncaster 1/11/53.
Immingham 30/12/62.

CONDEMNED:
11/7/65.
Sold 8/65 for scrap to A.Draper, Hull.

61366

North British Loco. 26825.

To traffic 24/4/50.

REPAIRS:
Dar. 27/1–23/2/52.**G.**
Don. 9/4–18/5/53.**G.**
Gor. 16/3–1/5/54.**C/H.**
Gor. 4–7/5/54.**N/C.**
Don. 28/10–8/12/54.**G.**
Don. 8/7–11/8/56.**G.**
Don. 11–19/1/57.**C/L.**
Don. 5/5–9/6/58.**G.**
Don. 11–20/11/58.**C/L.**
Don. 20–28/5/59.**N/C.**
Don. 24/11–30/12/60.**G.**
Don. 30/11/62.*Not repaired.*

BOILERS:
10816.
28409 *(ex1225)* 23/2/52.
28864 *(new)* 18/5/53.
28104 *(ex61326)* 1/5/54.
28112 *(ex1231)* 11/8/56.
28952 *(new)* 9/6/58.
28166 *(ex1104)* 30/12/60.

SHED:
Immingham.

CONDEMNED:
17/12/62.
Cut up at Doncaster.

61367

North British Loco. 26826.

To traffic 28/4/50.

REPAIRS:
Dar. 11/12/51–12/1/52.**G.**
Gor. 12/9–17/10/53.**G.**
Dar. 12/4–5/5/55.**C/H.**
Dar. 29/12/55–24/1/56.**H/I.**
Dar. 30–31/1/56.**N/C.**
Dar. 7/8–4/9/58.**G.**
Dar. 4/10–1/11/61.**G.**

BOILERS:
10817.
28700 *(ex1198)* 12/1/52.
28429 *(ex61327)* 17/10/53.
28461 *(ex1237)* 5/5/55.
28463 *(ex1024)* 4/9/58.
28585 *(ex1212)* 1/11/61.

SHEDS:
Colwick.
Woodford 27/5/51.
Colwick 30/12/51.
Leicester 27/1/52.
Colwick 27/4/52.
Kings Cross 5/5/57.
New England 20/10/57.
Hitchin 23/2/58.
Grantham 14/6/59.
Doncaster 8/9/63.

CONDEMNED:
22/8/65.
Sold 9/65 for scrap to Hughes, Bolckow, N.Blyth.

61368

North British Loco. 26827.

To traffic 30/4/50.

REPAIRS:
Dar. 17/10–22/11/51.**G.**
Dar. 4–28/2/53.**G.**
Dar. 2–3/3/53.**N/C.**
Gor. 13/11/54–8/1/55.**G.**
Dar. 27/2–28/3/56.**C/H.**
Dar. 15/11–13/12/56.**H/I.**
Dar. 18–20/12/56.**N/C.**
Dar. 17/10–19/11/58.**G.**
Dar. 3–9/12/58.**N/C.**
Str. 20–29/7/59.**N/C.**
Dar. 20/7–18/10/60.**C/H.**
Dar. 27/10–10/11/60.**N/C.**

BOILERS:
10818.
28236 *(ex1258)* 22/11/51.
28459 *(ex61376)* 28/2/53.
28243 *(ex1280)* 8/1/55.
28815 *(ex1024)* 28/3/56.
28800 *(ex1269)* 19/11/58.

SHEDS:
Colwick 5/5/50.
Woodford 20/5/51.

CONDEMNED:
29/1/62.
31/1/62 In for cut up at Darlington.

61369

North British Loco. 26828.

To traffic 16/5/50.

REPAIRS:
Dar. 18/10–10/11/51.**G.**
Dar. 10–11/7/52.**N/C.**
Gor. 26/9–31/10/53.**G.**
Dar. 25/6–22/7/55.**G.**
Dar. 1/4–1/5/57.**G.**
Dar. 28/11/58–5/1/59.**C/L.**
Dar. 27/2–31/3/59.**G.**
Dar. 23/11–4/12/59.**N/C.**
Dar. 1/2–1/3/61.**G.**

BOILERS:
10819.
28234 *(ex1291)* 10/11/51.
28242 *(ex61328)* 31/10/53.
28291 *(ex1106)* 22/7/55.
28194 *(ex1193)* 1/5/57.
28240 *(ex61327)* 31/3/59.
28596 *(ex61382)* 1/3/61.

SHEDS:
Colwick.
Leicester 12/10/52.
Agecroft 3/10/59.
Woodford 21/7/62.

Gorton 17/11/62.

CONDEMNED:
21/12/63.
*Sold 12/64 for scrap to
T.W.Ward, Killamarsh.*

61370

North British Loco. 26829.

To traffic 10/10/50.

REPAIRS:
Str. 23/6–22/8/52.**C/H.**
Gor. 27/3–16/5/53.**G.**
Str. 14/9–3/10/53.**N/C.**
Str. 31/10/55–2/2/56.**G.**
Str. 6/8–19/9/58.**G.** *Mod.
bogie springs.*
Don. 18/5–17/6/61.**G.**

BOILERS:
10820.
10820 renumbered 28590
22/8/52.
28295 *(ex3740)* 16/5/53.
28159 *(ex1249)* 2/2/56.
28544 *(ex1286)* 19/9/58.
28512 *(ex1190)* 17/6/61.

SHEDS:
Lincoln.
New England 4/3/51.
March 8/4/51.
Lincoln 17/6/51.
Stratford 21/10/51.
Colchester 6/1/57.
Sheffield 14/6/59.
Canklow 3/4/60.
Immingham 28/3/65.
Frodingham 9/5/65.

CONDEMNED:
4/7/65.
*Sold 8/65 for scrap to
A.Draper, Hull.*

61371

North British Loco. 26830.

To traffic 24/10/50.

REPAIRS:
Don. 30/10–27/11/52.**G.**
Don. 15/11–10/12/54.**G.**
Str. 22/10–8/12/56.**G.**
Str. 1/9–10/10/58.**G.** *Mod.
bogie springs.*
Str. 5–20/1/59.**C/L.**
Str. 3–17/4/59.**N/C.** *B.T.H.
speed recorder. Complete
A.T.C. fitted.*
Don. 19/8–30/9/60.**G.**

BOILERS:
10821.
28818 *(ex61407)* 27/11/52.
28163 *(ex1666)* 10/12/54.
28579 *(ex61399)* 8/12/56.
28537 *(ex1314)* 10/10/58.
28110 *(ex1126)* 30/9/60.

SHEDS:
Lincoln.
Cambridge 23/10/55.
March 17/6/62.

CONDEMNED:
16/9/62.
*Sold 3/63 for scrap to
J.Cashmore, Great Bridge.*

61372

North British Loco. 26841.

To traffic 8/12/50.

REPAIRS:
Str. 9/6–2/8/52.**G.**
Str. 4–15/8/53.**C/L.**
Str. 30/8–9/10/54.**G.**
Str. 29/10–22/12/56.**G.**
Str. 11/11/58–9/1/59.**G.**
Mod. bogie springs.
Don. 28/7–31/8/61.**G.**

BOILERS:
10822.
28515 *(ex1254)* 2/8/52.
28164 *(ex1208)* 9/10/54.
28536 *(ex1227)* 9/1/59.
28426 *(ex1138)* 31/8/61.

SHEDS:
Immingham.
Stratford 21/10/51.
Parkeston 8/2/59.
Sheffield 27/11/60.
Canklow 16/6/63.
Langwith 13/6/65.

CONDEMNED:
20/6/65.
*Sold 8/65 for scrap to
T.W.Ward, Beighton.*

61373

North British Loco. 26842.

To traffic 26/12/50.

REPAIRS:
Str. 6/2–29/3/52.**C/H.**
Str. 30/12/52–7/2/53.**G.**
Str. 2/11–4/12/54.**G.**
Str. 20/5–27/7/57.**G.**
Str. 23/9–13/11/59.**G.**
A.T.C. fitted.

BOILERS:
10823.
10823 renumbered 28582
29/3/52.
28546 *(ex1287)* 7/2/53.
28593 *(ex61375)* 4/12/54.
28810 *(ex1223)* 27/7/57.
28520 *(ex1264)* 13/11/59.

SHEDS:
Immingham.
New England 4/3/51.
March 8/4/51.
Immingham 17/6/51.

Stratford 21/10/51.
Colchester 6/1/57.
Parkeston 25/10/59.
Sheffield 27/11/60.

CONDEMNED:
16/9/62.
*Sold 11/63 for scrap to
Albert Looms, Spondon.*

61374

North British Loco. 26833.

To traffic 12/2/51.

REPAIRS:
Don. 12/9–15/10/52.**G.**
Don. 26/1/53.*Weigh.*
Don. 2–25/3/53.**N/C.**
Don. 12–13/5/53.**N/C.**
Don. 24/1–11/2/54.**C/H.**
Dar. 11/10–6/11/54.**G.**
Dar. 7–10/11/54.**N/C.**
Don. 13/2–16/3/56.**C/H.**
Dar. 18/1–15/2/57.**G.**
Don. 30/10–6/12/58.**G.**
Don. 24–28/7/59.**N/C.**
Don. 11/11–14/12/60.**G.**
Don. 2/1–2/2/62.**C/L.**

BOILERS:
10824.
28511 *(ex1130)* 15/10/52.
28175 *(ex1249)* 11/2/54.
28413 *(ex1279)* 6/11/54.
28176 *(ex1165)* 16/3/56.
28229 *(ex1199)* 15/2/57.
28370 *(ex1208)* 6/12/58.
28345 *(ex spare 2 years)*
14/12/60.

SHED:
Immingham.

CONDEMNED:
22/9/63.
*Sold 1/64 for scrap to
J.Cashmore, Great Bridge.*

61375

North British Loco. 26834.

To traffic 23/2/51.

REPAIRS:
Str. 10/11–24/12/52.**G.**
Str. 11/10–13/11/54.**G.**
Str. 17/12/56–8/2/57.**G.**
Str. 10/2–3/4/59.**G.** *Mod.
bogie springs. Complete
A.T.C. fitted.*
Str. 18–23/3/60.**N/C.**
Str. 8–12/8/60.**N/C.**
Don. 22–25/8/60.**N/C.**
Don. 11/1–10/2/62.**G.**

BOILERS:
10825.
10825 renumbered 28593
24/12/52.
28871 *(new)* 13/11/54.

28101 *(ex1119)* 8/2/57.
28114 *(ex1171)* 3/4/59.
28145 *(ex1223)* 10/2/62.

SHEDS:
Immingham.
Stratford 21/10/51.
March 16/9/62.

CONDEMNED:
25/11/63.
*Made S.B.Dept'l 24. Sold
5/66 for scrap to Birds,
Long Marston.*

61376

North British Loco. 26835.

To traffic 12/4/51.

REPAIRS:
Dar. 19/12/52–21/1/53.**G.**
Gor. 29/5–19/6/54.**C/H.**
Dar. 9–31/5/55.**G.**
Dar. 26/11–21/12/57.**G.**
Dar. 15/9–10/10/58.**C/H.**
Don. 12/8–18/9/59.**G.**

BOILERS:
10826.
28452 *(ex61322)* 21/1/53.
28900 *(new)* 19/6/54.
28210 *(ex1068)* 31/5/55.
28124 *(ex1282)* 21/12/57.
28427 *(ex1162)* 18/9/59.

SHEDS:
Colwick.
Woodford 30/9/51.
Colwick 30/12/51.
Leicester 10/12/56.

CONDEMNED:
5/2/62.
*1/3/62 In for cut up at
Darlington.*

61377

North British Loco. 26836.

To traffic 1/5/51.

REPAIRS:
Dar. 23/1–21/2/53.**G.**
Dar. 23–26/2/53.**N/C.**
Gor. 16/9–10/10/53.**C/L.**
Dar. 22/4–13/5/55.**G.**
Dar. 15–18/5/55.**N/C.**
Dar. 24/11–27/12/57.**G.**
Dar. 31/12/57–5/1/58.**N/C.**
Don. 2–3/12/59.**N/C.**
Don. 30/12/59–30/1/60.**G.**
Don. 4–6/1/61.**N/C.**

BOILERS:
10827.
28225 *(ex1062)* 21/2/53.
28416 *(ex1216)* 13/5/55.
28442 *(ex61377)* 27/12/57.
28534 *(ex1635)* 30/1/60.

SHEDS:
Colwick.
Norwich 9/12/51.
Ardsley 27/1/52.
Copley Hill 29/6/52.
Ardsley 7/3/54.
Doncaster 18/12/55.
Sheffield 12/6/60.
Langwith 24/9/61.

CONDEMNED:
16/9/62.
Sold 1/63 for scrap to
T.W.Ward, Broughton
Lane, Sheffield.

61378

North British Loco. 26837.

To traffic 25/5/51.

REPAIRS:
Dar. 20/2–12/3/52.**C/L.**
After collision.
Dar. 30/9–11/10/52.**C/H.**
Str. 14/9–24/10/53.**G.**
Str. 17/2–7/4/56.**G.**
Str. 21/10–12/12/58.**G.**
Mod. bogie springs.
Don. 14/6–22/7/61.**G.**

BOILERS:
10828.
28201 *(ex1013)* 11/10/52.
28507 *(ex1058)* 24/10/53.
28138 *(ex61317)* 7/4/56.
28159 *(ex61370)* 12/12/58.
28109 *(ex1074)* 22/7/61.

SHEDS:
Colwick.
Stratford 19/10/52.
Parkeston 8/2/59.
Stratford 1/1/61.
March 16/9/62.

CONDEMNED:
25/11/63.
14/1/64 In for cut up at
Doncaster.

61379

North British Loco. 26838.

To traffic 14/6/51.

Named MAYFLOWER
13/7/51.

REPAIRS:
Don. 1–5/7/51.**N/C.**
Don. 9/6–15/7/52.**G.**
Don. 14/11–3/12/52.**N/C.**
Don. 21–23/12/52.*Exam.*
Don. 30/3–16/4/53.**C/L.**
Don. 8/10–6/11/53.**C/H.**
Dar. 8/7–7/8/54.**G.**

Dar. 30/8–11/9/54.**N/C.**
Don. 25/2–5/4/56.**G.**
Don. 27/10–23/11/57.**G.**
Don. 5–18/3/59.**N/C.**
Don. 10/9–1/10/59.**C/L.**
Don. 10/5–10/6/60.**G.**
Don. 6–17/3/61.**C/L.**
Don. 31/7/62.*Not repaired.*

BOILERS:
10829.
28111 *(ex1143)* 15/7/52.
28181 *(ex1077)* 6/11/53.
28442 *(ex61337)* 7/8/54.
28217 *(ex61315)* 23/11/57.
28202 *(ex1111)* 10/6/60.

SHEDS:
Colwick.
Immingham 8/7/51.

CONDEMNED:
6/8/62.
Cut up at Doncaster.

61380

North British Loco. 26839.

To traffic 22/8/51.

REPAIRS:
Dar. 8/7–28/8/52.**C/H.**
Gor. 23/1–27/2/54.**G.**
Dar. 15/2–12/3/56.**G.**
Dar. 23/4–1/5/57.**C/L.**
Dar. 2–5/9/57.**C/L.**
Dar. 5/2–5/3/58.**G.**
Dar. 18/8–14/9/59.**G.**
Dar. 15–24/3/60.**N/C.**

BOILERS:
10830.
10830 renumbered 28451
28/8/52.
28545 *(ex1226)* 27/2/54.
28318 *(ex1129)* 12/3/56.
28419 *(ex61321)* 5/3/58.
28441 *(ex1230)* 14/9/59.

SHEDS:
Colwick.
Leicester 25/1/53.
Woodford 17/3/62.

CONDEMNED:
26/3/62.
13/4/62 In for cut up at
Darlington.

61381

North British Loco. 26840.

To traffic 7/9/51.

REPAIRS:
Dar. 11–22/9/52.**C/H.**
Gor. 28/3–25/4/53.**G.**

Dar. 14/1–12/2/55.**G.**
Dar. 14/9–15/10/56.**G.**
Dar. 22–24/10/56.**N/C.**
Dar. 26/10–1/11/56.**N/C.**
Dar. 10/7–6/9/57.**C/L.**
Dar. 17/9–20/10/58.**G.**
Dar. 30/10–7/11/58.**N/C.**
Dar. 2/5–2/6/60.**G.**

BOILERS:
10831.
28449 *(ex1296)* 22/9/52.
28843 *(new)* 25/4/53.
28441 *(ex1220)* 12/2/55.
28233 *(ex1069)* 15/10/56.
28565 *(ex1265)* 20/10/58.
28230 *(ex1297)* 2/6/60.

SHEDS:
Colwick.
Woodford 25/11/51.
Leicester 28/2/54.
Woodford 7/11/54.
Leicester 20/2/55.
Gorton 11/5/62.
Leicester 17/5/62.
Gorton 19/7/62.

CONDEMNED:
1/11/62.
2/11/62 In for cut up at
Darlington.

61382

North British Loco.26831.

To traffic 18/9/51.

REPAIRS:
Gor. 27/3–8/5/54.**G.**
Dar. 12/11–6/12/56.**G.**
Dar. 22/5–23/6/59.**G.**
Complete A.T.C. fitted.
Dar. 2–6/7/59.**N/C.**
Dar. 13/10–25/11/61.**G.**
Dar. 4–9/12/61.**N/C.**

BOILERS:
10832.
28425 *(ex61315)* 8/5/54.
28596 *(ex1206)* 6/12/56.
28172 *(ex1018)* 23/6/59.
28237 *(ex1110)* 25/11/61.

SHEDS:
Ardsley.
Bradford 15/9/57.
Low Moor 12/1/58.
Darlington 14/9/58.
Copley Hill 16/6/63.
Ardsley 6/9/64.

CONDEMNED:
7/12/64.
Sold 2/65 for scrap to Slag
Reduction Co., Ickles.

61383

North British Loco. 26832.

To traffic 3/10/51.

REPAIRS:
Don. 7–30/4/52.**C/L.**
Gor. 14/11–12/12/53.**G.**
Dar. 23/4–23/5/56.**G.**
Dar. 18/11–18/12/58.**G.**
A.T.C. mech. fitted.
Dar. 3–29/6/60.**C/L.**
Dar. 19/1–3/3/61.**C/L.**
Dar. 7/2–10/3/62.**G.**

BOILERS:
10833.
28234 *(ex61369)* 12/12/53.
28602 *(ex1011)* 23/5/56.
28353 *(ex1303)* 18/12/58.
28518 *(ex1017)* 10/3/62.

SHEDS:
Ardsley.
Bradford 15/9/57.
Low Moor 12/1/58.

CONDEMNED:
21/1/63.
14/3/63 In for cut up at
Darlington.

61384

North British Loco. 26843.

To traffic 17/10/51./
REPAIRS:
Str. 19/1–21/2/53.**C/H.**
Str. 22/3–30/4/54.**G.**
Str. 19/5/54.**N/C.**
Str. 11–22/10/54.**C/L.**
Don. 25/1–29/2/56.**G.**
Str. 30/5–8/6/56.**C/L.**
Str. 3–15/2/58.**C/L.**
Str. 10–15/4/58.**N/C.**
Str. 12–24/6/58.**C/L.**
Str. 13/10–28/11/58.**G.**
Mod. bogie springs.
Str. 22–29/1/60.**N/C.**
Don. 12/4–17/5/61.**G.**

BOILERS:
10834.
10834 renumbered 28595
21/2/53.
28161 *(ex1230)* 30/4/54.
28542 *(ex1270)* 28/11/58.
28529 *(ex1073)* 17/5/61.

SHEDS:
Ardsley.
Bradford 20/7/52.
Stratford 19/10/52.
Parkeston 16/9/56.
Lincoln 10/4/60.
Immingham 22/9/63.
Retford 7/3/65.
Doncaster 13/6/65.
Immingham 3/10/65.

WORKS CODES:– Cow – Cowlairs. Dar – Darlington. Dee – Dundee. Don – Doncaster. Ghd – Gateshead. Gor – Gorton. Inv – Inverurie. Str – Stratford. SRX – St Rollox.

REPAIR CODES:– **C/H** – Casual Heavy. **C/L** – Casual Light. **G** – General. **H** – Heavy. **H/I** – Heavy Intermediate. **L** – Light. **L/I** – Light Intermediate. **N/C** – Non–Classified.

CONDEMNED:
9/1/66.
*Sold 2/66 for scrap to
Garnham, Harris & Elton,
Chesterfield.*

61385

North British Loco. 26844.

To traffic 25/10/51.

REPAIRS:
Dar. 3–19/6/53.**C/H.**
Gor. 22/5–3/7/54.**G.**
Dar. 12–25/3/55.**C/L.**
Dar. 24/9–8/10/56.**C/L.**
Dar. 11–19/10/56.**N/C.**
Dar. 6–31/8/57.**G.**
Dar. 13–18/2/58.**N/C.**
Dar. 13–18/3/58.**N/C.**
Dar. 25/8–4/10/60.**G.**
Complete A.W.S. fitted.
Dar. 13–27/10/60.**N/C.**

BOILERS:
10835.
28204 *(ex1239)* 19/6/53.
28439 *(ex1161)* 3/7/54.
28197 *(ex1297)* 31/8/57.
28586 *(ex1080)* 4/10/60.

SHEDS:
Ardsley.
Leicester 27/7/52.
Ardsley 10/8/52.
Wakefield 22/2/59.
Copley Hill 25/11/62.
Ardsley 6/9/64.

CONDEMNED:
31/10/65.
*Sold 12/65 for scrap to
Hughes, Bolckow, North
Blyth.*

61386

North British Loco. 26845.

To traffic 30/10/51.

REPAIRS:
Dar. 19/6–11/7/53.**G.**
Gor. 21–28/8/54.**C/L.**
Dar. 24–29/1/55.**C/L.**
Dar. 12/6–15/7/55.**G.**
Dar. 3–30/5/57.**G.**
Dar. 26/10–21/11/59.**G.**
Complete A.T.C. fitted.
Dar. 17/9–19/10/62.**G.**
Dar. 10/6–30/7/64.**C/H.**

BOILERS:
10836.
28217 *(ex1068)* 11/7/53.
28230 *(ex1259)* 15/7/55.
28433 *(ex1248)* 30/5/57.
28516 *(ex1021)* 21/11/59.
28137 *(ex1256)* 19/10/62.

SHEDS:
Ardsley.

Copley Hill 6/1/52.
Low Moor 20/8/61.
Mirfield 8/9/63.
Low Moor 12/4/64.
North Blyth 21/8/66.

CONDEMNED:
31/12/66.
*Sold 1/3/67 for scrap to
Willoughby's,
Choppington.*

61387

North British Loco. 26846.

To traffic 2/11/51.

REPAIRS:
Gor. 28/11–26/12/53.**G.**
Dar. 29/9–22/10/55.**G.**
Dar. 16/9–11/10/57.**G.**
Dar. 24–30/10/57.**N/C.**
Dar. 7/10/58.*Weigh.*
Dar. 18/2–2/3/59.**C/L.**
Dar. 2/11–24/12/60.**G.**
Complete A.W.S. fitted.

BOILERS:
10837.
28700 *(ex61367)* 26/12/53.
28317 *(ex1209)* 22/10/55.
28205 *(ex1106)* 11/10/57.
28260 *(ex61310)* 24/12/60.

SHEDS:
Ardsley.
Copley Hill 6/1/52.
Darlington 14/9/58.
Low Moor 14/6/59.
Wakefield 23/12/62.

CONDEMNED:
31/10/65.
*Sold 12/65 for scrap to
Hughes, Bolckow, North
Blyth.*

61388

North British Loco. 26847.

To traffic 9/11/51.

REPAIRS:
Gor. 1/5–5/6/54.**G.**
Dar. 19/12/55–16/1/56.**G.**
Dar. 17–25/10/57.**N/C.**
Dar. 13/8–11/9/58.**G.**
A.T.C. mech. fitted.
Dar. 3–14/10/58.**N/C.**
Dar. 2–16/2/59.**N/C.**
A.T.C. completed.
Dar. 18/12/61–18/1/62.**G.**
Dar. 6–22/3/62.**N/C.**
Dar. 7/4–25/5/64.**C/H.**

BOILERS:
10838.
28399 *(ex61382)* 5/6/54.
28346 *(ex61321)* 16/1/56.
28801 *(ex1181)* 11/9/58.
28454 *(ex61337)* 18/1/62.

28142 *(ex1255)* 25/5/64.

SHEDS:
Ardsley.
Copley Hill 2/11/52.
York 30/8/59.
Ardsley 25/11/62.
Low Moor 31/10/65.
Wakefield 13/11/66.

CONDEMNED:
24/6/67.
*Sold 8/67 for scrap to
Hughes, Bolckow, North
Blyth.*

61389

North British Loco. 26848.

To traffic 30/11/51.

REPAIRS:
Don. 13–18/1/52.**N/C.**
Don. 24/11–23/12/53.**G.**
Don. 31/10–26/11/55.**G.**
Don. 25/3–25/4/58.**G.**
Don. 18–28/8/59.**N/C.**
Don. 12/10–11/11/61.**G.**

BOILERS:
10839.
28754 *(ex3882)* 23/12/53.
28231 *(ex1127)* 26/11/55.
28312 *(ex1668)* 25/4/58.
28150 *(ex1145)* 11/11/61.

SHEDS:
New England.
Grantham 6/10/57.
Doncaster 8/9/63.
Immingham 14/6/64.
Frodingham 9/5/65.

CONDEMNED:
14/11/65.
*Sold 12/65 for scrap to
A. Draper, Hull.*

61390

North British Loco. 26849.

To traffic 12/12/51.

REPAIRS:
Don. 21/8–14/9/53.**G.**
Gor. 27/3/54.**C/L.**
Don. 2–14/2/55.**C/L.**
Don. 23/5–30/6/55.**G.**
Don. 20/9–4/10/55.**C/L.**
Don. 24/11–8/12/55.**C/L.**
Dar. 2–27/9/57.**G.**
Don. 23/10–20/11/59.**G.**
Don. 7–19/11/60.**N/C.**
Don. 6/7–28/8/62.**G.**
Don. 17–19/9/62.**N/C.**

BOILERS:
10840.
28215 *(ex1224)* 14/9/53.
28309 *(ex1646)* 30/6/55.
28580 *(ex1179)* 27/9/57.

28418 *(ex1282)* 20/11/59.
28978 *(ex1050)* 28/8/62.

SHEDS:
New England.
Colwick 29/6/52.
Immingham 24/10/54.
Doncaster 13/12/59.
Colwick 12/6/60.
To LMR Stock 2/1/66.

CONDEMNED:
19/2/66.
*Sold 5/66 for scrap to Birds,
Long Marston.*

61391

North British Loco. 26850.

To traffic 18/12/51.

REPAIRS:
Don. 27/9–30/10/53.**G.**
Don. 25/4–18/5/55.**C/L.**
Don. 25/7–29/8/55.**G.**
Don. 30/4–7/6/57.**G.**
Don. 11–17/6/57.**N/C.**
Str. 20/7–28/8/59.**G.**
A.T.C. fitted.
Don. 5/9/62. *not repaired.*

BOILERS:
10841.
28158 *(ex1251)* 30/10/53.
28845 *(ex61311)* 29/8/55.
28180 *(ex1187)* 7/6/57.
28236 *(ex1095)* 28/8/59.

SHED:
New England.

CONDEMNED:
10/9/62.
Cut up at Doncaster.

61392

North British Loco. 26851.

To traffic 27/12/51.

REPAIRS:
Don. 9/12/53–19/1/54.**G.**
Don. 9/11–3/12/55.**G.**
Don. 15–28/2/56.**C/L.**
Don. 3/1–1/2/58.**G.**
Don. 25/7–6/8/60.**N/C.**
Don. 23/8–6/10/62.**G.**

BOILERS:
10842.
28755 *(ex61389)* 19/1/54.
28754 *(ex61389)* 3/12/55.
28532 *(ex61365)* 1/2/58.
28278 *(ex1264)* 6/10/62.

SHEDS:
New England.
Stratford 25/3/56.
Cambridge 25/3/56.
New England 7/10/56.
Grantham 6/10/57.

Doncaster 8/9/63.
Immingham 14/6/64.
Canklow 10/1/65.
Colwick 13/6/65.

CONDEMNED:
20/6/65.
*Sold 8/65 for scrap to
T.W.Ward, Killamarsh.*

61393

North British Loco. 26852.

To traffic 11/1/52.

REPAIRS:
Don. 14/1–19/2/54.**G.**
Don. 31/8–6/10/55.**G.**
Don. 28/2–3/3/56.**N/C.**
Don. 30/4–4/5/57.**N/C.**
Don. 14/1–13/2/58.**G.**
Don. 24/5–1/7/60.**G.**

BOILERS:
10843.
28160 (ex1073) 19/2/54.
28540 (ex1116) 6/10/55.
28195 (ex1663) 13/2/58.
28822 (ex1606) 1/7/60.

SHEDS:
Doncaster.
Kings Cross 21/12/52.
Hitchin 11/1/53.
Kings Cross 13/6/54.
New England 8/11/59.
Kings Cross 24/1/60.
Mexborough 16/6/63.

CONDEMNED:
22/9/63.
*Sold 12/63 for scrap to
J.Cashmore, Great Bridge.*

61394

North British Loco. 26853.

To traffic 23/1/52.

REPAIRS:
Don. 16/2–11/3/54.**G.**
Don. 10/8–17/9/55.**G.**
Don. 16/12/57–18/1/58.**G.**
Don. 15/10–13/11/59.**G.**
Don. 28/8–23/10/62.**G.**
Don. 19–21/11/62.**N/C.**
BOILERS:
10844.
28522 (ex1171) 11/3/54.
28169 (ex1627) 17/9/55.
28241 (ex1204) 18/1/58.
28121 (ex1175) 13/11/59.
28507 (ex61313) 23/10/62.

SHEDS:
Doncaster.
Kings Cross 21/12/52.

Hitchin 11/1/53.
Kings Cross 13/6/54.
Neasden 17/3/57.
Kings Cross 19/5/57.
Mexborough 16/6/63.
Canklow 1/3/64.
Langwith 13/6/65.

CONDEMNED:
14/11/65.
*Sold 12/65 for scrap to
Hughes,Bolckow, North
Blyth.*

61395

North British Loco. 26854.

To traffic 1/2/52.

REPAIRS:
Cow. 24–29/11/52.**C/L.**
Cow. 1–27/2/54.**L/I.**
Cow. 7/12/55–7/1/56.**G.**
W.P.U. gear removed.
Cow. 14/11–19/12/56.**C/L.**
Cow. 27/1–1/3/58.**H/I.**
Cow. 5–8/8/58.**C/L.**
Cow. 9–13/9/58.**N/C.**
Cow. 5–31/12/59.**G.**

BOILERS:
10845.
10845 renumbered 28703
27/2/54.
28606 (ex1064) 7/1/56.
28648 (ex61346) 31/12/59.

SHEDS:
Carlisle.
Gorton 17/6/62.

CONDEMNED:
1/10/62.
*10/62 In for cut up at
Cowlairs.*

61396

North British Loco. 26855.

To traffic 20/2/52.

REPAIRS:
Cow. 2–26/12/53.**L/I.**
Efd. 4–9/2/54.**C/L.**
Cow. 24/5–25/6/55.**L/I.**
W.P.U. gear removed.
Cow. 20/10–5/11/55.**C/L.**
Cow.
16/12/55–18/1/56.**C/L.**
Cow. 27/5–22/6/57.**G.**
Cow. 17/3–10/4/59.**H/I.**
*Mod. bogie springs.
A.W.S. fitted.*
Cow. 7/8–16/9/61.**G.**
Cow. 20/5–6/7/63.**C/L.**
Cow. 10/64.**C/L.**

BOILERS:
10846.
10846 renumbered 28704
20/2/52.
28656 (ex1243) 22/6/57.
28605 (ex61403) 16/9/61.

SHEDS:
Eastfield.
Corkerhill 31/12/62.
Ayr 11/3/63.
St Margarets 31/7/64.

CONDEMNED:
10/9/65.
*Sold 4/12/65for scrap to
Shipbreaking Industries,
Faslane.*

61397

North British Loco. 26856.

To traffic 13/3/52.

REPAIRS:
Cow. 7/6–3/7/54.**L/I.**
Cow. 23/4–9/6/56.**G.**
Cow. 21–23/6/56.**N/C.**
Cow. 14/4–17/5/58.**H/I.**
Cow. 10–31/12/58.**C/L.**
Cow. 21/4–6/5/59.**N/C.**
*Mod. bogie springs.
A.W.S. fitted.*
Cow. 11/11–17/12/60.**G.**
Cow. 3–16/2/62.**N/C.**
Inv. 19/10–14/12/62.**L/I.**

BOILERS:
10847.
10847 renumbered 28705
3/7/54.
28437 (ex1290) 9/6/56.
28701 (ex61404) 17/12/60.

SHED:
St Margarets.

CONDEMNED:
26/6/65.
*Sold 6/8/65 for scrap to
Shipbreaking Industries,
Faslane.*

61398

North British Loco. 26857.

To traffic 28/3/52.

REPAIRS:
Cow. 3–27/3/54.**L/I.**
Cow. 24/5–23/6/56.**G.**
Cow. 30/10–22/11/58.**L/I.**
Mod. bogie springs.
Cow. 12–26/5/59.**N/C.**
A.W.S. fitted.
Cow. 28/1–2/3/60.**C/L.**
Cow. 27/5–10/6/60.**C/L.**

Cow. 24/8–21/10/61.**G.**
Cow. 21–30/6/62.**N/C.**
Cow. 25/9–4/10/62.**N/C.**
Cow. 8–15/5/63.**N/C.**
Cow.
19/12/63–10/1/64.**N/C.**

BOILERS:
10848.
10848 renumbered 28706
27/3/54.
28611 (ex1101) 23/6/56.
28626 (ex1101) 21/10/61.

SHEDS:
St Margarets.
Carstairs 11/11/54.
St Margarets 17/2/56.
Thornton Junction 15/6/64.
Dundee 20/7/64.

CONDEMNED:
5/11/64.
*Sold 1/65 for scrap to
Shipbreaking Industries,
Faslane.*

61399

North British Loco. 26858.

To traffic 22/4/52.

REPAIRS:
Str. 21/12/53–30/1/54.**G.**
Str. 2/2–17/3/56.**G.**
Str. 15/10–9/11/56.**C/L.**
Str. 8/1–1/3/58.**G.** *Mod.
bogie springs.*
Don. 31/3–30/4/60.**G.**

BOILERS:
10849.
28579 (ex1671) 30/1/54.
28503 (ex1000) 17/3/56.
28218 (ex61311) 1/3/58.
28334 (ex1663) 30/4/60.

SHEDS:
Doncaster.
Stratford 19/10/52.
Norwich 8/2/59.
Sheffield 31/1/60.
Canklow 2/12/62.

CONDEMNED:
22/9/63.
*Sold 12/63 for scrap to
Marples & Gillott,
Sheffield.*

61400

Darlington 2102.

To traffic 30/3/50.

REPAIRS:
Cow. 4–28/2/52.**L/I.**

WORKS CODES:– Cow – Cowlairs. Dar – Darlington. Dee – Dundee. Don – Doncaster. Ghd – Gateshead. Gor – Gorton. Inv – Inverurie. Str – Stratford. SRX – St Rollox.
REPAIR CODES:– C/H – Casual Heavy. C/L – Casual Light. G – General. H – Heavy. H/I – Heavy Intermediate. L – Light. L/I – Light Intermediate. N/C – Non–Classified.

97

Inv. 23/2/54.**N/C.**
Cow. 18/8–25/9/54.**G.**
Cow. 20/2–24/3/56.**H/I.**
Cow. 13–14/4/56.**N/C.**
Cow. 7–23/3/57.**N/C.**
Cow. 19/2–22/3/58.**L/I.**
Cow. 4/7–15/8/59.**G.**
Inv. 20/5–1/6/60.**N/C.**
Inv. 10–27/1/61.**L/I.**
Cow. 3/8–28/9/61.**C/L.**
Inv. 27/11/63–10/1/64.**C/L.**

BOILERS:
 4047.
 4047 renumbered 28665
28/2/52.
28877 *(new)* 25/9/54.
28651 *(ex1146)* 15/8/59. *141
tubes.*

SHEDS:
Kittybrewster.
Aberdeen 19/6/61.
Dalry Road 9/8/64.
Thornton Junction 5/10/64.

CONDEMNED:
17/12/64.
*Sold 2/65 for scrap to
Motherwell Machinery &
Scrap Co., Wishaw.*

61401

Darlington 2103.

To traffic 12/4/50.

REPAIRS:
Cow. 11/1–2/2/52.**H/I.**
Inv. 25–26/6/52.**N/C.**
Cow. 16–21/2/53.**N/C.**
Cow. 8–31/10/53.**H/I.**
Inv. 12/4/54.**N/C.**
Cow. 4/10–13/11/54.**G.**
W.P.U. gear removed.
Cow. 17/12/55–7/1/56.**L/I.**
Cow. 8/1–2/2/57.**H/I.**
Cow. 25/11–13/12/58.**G.**
Cow. 20–27/5/59.**N/C.**
A.T.C. fitted.
Cow. 27–28/5/60.**N/C.**
Cow. 22/11–16/12/61.**L/I.**

BOILERS:
 5136.
 5136 renumbered 28666
2/2/52.
28662 *(ex61357)* 13/11/54.
28617 *(ex1102)* 13/12/58.
141 tubes.

SHEDS:
Kittybrewster.
Thornton Junction
15/10/56.
Eastfield 13/4/60.
Grangemouth 3/1/61.
Thornton Junction
16/10/61.

CONDEMNED:
17/4/64.
*Sold 6/64 for scrap to
Shipbreaking Industries,
Faslane.*

61402

Darlington 2104.

To traffic 27/4/50.

REPAIRS:
Cow. 7–31/5/52.**L/I.**
Cow. 20/10–13/11/54.**G.**
Cow. 22/3–20/4/57.**H/I.**
Cow. 10–28/3/59.**G.**
Cow. 17/4–24/6/59.**N/C.**
A.W.S. fitted.
Cow. 22–24/10/59.**N/C.**
Mod. bogie springs.
Cow. 18–20/7/60.**N/C.**
Cow. 23/11–22/12/61.**L/I.**
Cow. 12/6/62.**C/L.**
Cow. 26–28/11/62.**N/C.**
Cow. 14–19/12/62.**N/C.**
Cow. 12–16/2/63.**C/L.**
Inv. 27–29/5/63.**N/C.**
Inv. 11–16/7/63.**C/L.**
Cow. 15–16/8/63.**N/C.**

BOILERS:
 4051.
 4051 renumbered 28667
31/5/52.
28665 *(ex61400)* 13/11/54.
28624 *(ex61352)* 28/3/59.
141 tubes.

SHEDS:
Kittybrewster.
Dundee 2/7/50.

CONDEMNED:
8/6/64.
*Sold 8/64 for scrap to P&W
McLellan, Langloan.*

61403

Darlington 2105.

To traffic 27/4/50.

REPAIRS:
Cow. 11–26/4/52.**L/I.**
Dee. 27/4–18/5/53.**C/L.**
Cow. 14/4–15/5/54.**L/I.**
Cow. 20/5/54.**N/C.**
Dee. 6–14/6/55.**C/L.**
Cow. 7/8–6/10/56.**G.**
Cow. 20/2–22/3/58.**H/I.**
Cow. 19–29/10/59.**N/C.**
Cow. 24/5–1/7/61.**G.**
Cow. 10/5–7/9/63.**L/I.**
Inv. 16–26/3/65.**C/L.**
Inv. 26–30/7/65.**C/L.**

BOILERS:
 4025.
 4025 renumbered 28668
26/4/52.
28605 *(ex61323)* 6/10/56.

28639 *(ex1099)* 1/7/61.

SHEDS:
Kittybrewster.
Dundee 2/7/50.
Thornton Junction 7/3/55.
Eastfield 9/4/60.
Grangemouth 3/1/61.
Dunfermline 16/10/61.
Dundee 11/11/63.

CONDEMNED:
14/7/66.
*Sold 9/66 for scrap to
Geo.H.Campbell, Airdrie.*

61404

Darlington 2106.

To traffic 4/5/50.

REPAIRS:
Hay. 24–31/8/51.**C/L.**
Hay. 1–6/12/51.**C/L.**
Cow. 14/2–7/3/53.**L/I.**
Hay. 10/12/53–9/1/54.**C/L.**
Cow. 11–30/1/54.**C/L.**
Cow. 26/5–19/6/54.**C/L.**
Cow. 11/3–16/4/55.**G.**
Cow. 24/10–26/11/55.**C/L.**
Cow. 10/2–15/3/58.**H/I.**
Cow. 10–24/6/59.**N/C.**
Cow. 29/8–15/9/59.**N/C.**
Cow. 11/4–4/6/60.**G.**
Inv. 19/4–7/6/63.**L/I.**

BOILERS:
 4033.
 4033 renumbered 28669
7/3/53.
28701 *(ex61307)* 16/4/55.
28877 *(ex61400)* 4/6/60.

SHEDS:
Kittybrewster.
Haymarket 12/11/50.
St Rollox 19/1/59.
Parkhead 24/3/59.
St Margarets 13/8/62.

CONDEMNED:
9/11/65.
*Sold 12/65 for scrap to
Motherwell Machinery &
Scrap Co., Wishaw.*

61405

Darlington 2107.

To traffic 10/5/50.

REPAIRS:
Gor. 7–23/6/51.**C/L.**
Gor. 26/6–4/7/51.**N/C.**
Don. 10/8–5/9/52.**G.**
Don. 21/8–27/9/54.**G.**
Don. 23/9–20/10/56.**G.**
Don. 7–25/1/58.**C/L.**
Str. 24/2–10/4/59.**G.**
Don. 26/5–3/6/59.**N/C.**
Don. 27/9–13/10/60.**N/C.**

BOILERS:
 4042.
 4042 renumbered 28330
23/6/51.
28833 *(new)* 5/9/52.
28285 *(ex1623)* 27/9/54.
28402 *(ex1250)* 20/10/56.
28804 *(ex1136)* 10/4/59.

SHED:
Lincoln.

CONDEMNED:
16/9/62.
*Sold 1/63 for scrap to Cox
& Danks, Wadsley Bridge.*

61406

Darlington 2108.

To traffic 20/5/50.

REPAIRS:
Dar. 23–27/5/50.**N/C.**
Dar. 15–16/6/50.**N/C.**
Gor. 8/7–15/9/51.**G.**
Don. 18/6/52.*Weigh.*
Don. 11/11–5/12/52.**G.**
Don. 1–8/7/53.**N/C.**
Gor. 28/8–4/9/54.**C/H.**
Dar. 14/3–7/4/55.**H/I.**
Don. 29/12/56–26/1/57.**G.**
Don. 30/12/58–31/1/59.**G.**
Don. 3–29/10/60.**G.**
Don. 23/10/61.*Weigh.*
Don. 30/5–9/8/63.**G.**

BOILERS:
 5139.
28342 *(ex61409)* 15/9/51.
28311 *(ex1190)* 5/12/52.
28179 *(ex1295)* 4/9/54.
28807 *(ex1651)* 26/1/57.
28563 *(ex1642)* 31/1/59.
28356 *(ex3966)* 29/10/60.
28269 *(ex1226)* 9/8/63.

SHEDS:
Lincoln.
Immingham 21/5/50.
Doncaster 6/2/66.

CONDEMNED:
17/4/66.
*Sold 5/66 for scrap to
Geo.Cohen, Kettering.*

61407

Darlington 2109.

To traffic 10/6/50.

REPAIRS:
Don. 6–7/3/51.**N/C.**
Gor. 13/8–17/10/51.**G.**
Gor. 21–27/10/51.**N/C.**
Don. 5–16/5/52.**C/L.**
Don. 6–20/10/52.**C/H.**
Don. 14/7–11/8/53.**G.**
Cow. 11/10–5/11/55.**H/I.**
Cow. 15/11–1/12/56.**N/C.**

Cow. 12/10–16/11/57.**G.**
Cow. 13–25/1/58.**C/L.**
Cow. 4–16/4/59.**C/L.**
Cow. 16–25/5/59.**C/L.**
Cow. 22/9–21/10/59.**C/L.**
Cow. 20/2–15/4/61.**L/I.**
Cow. 8–13/9/62.**N/C.**
Cow. 4–15/2/63.**N/C.**
Cow. 18/6–6/7/63.**N/C.**
Cow. 25/11/63–4/1/64.**G.**

BOILERS:
 5141.
28818 *(new)* 17/10/51.
28750 *(ex61374)* 20/10/52.
28143 *(ex1207)* 11/8/53.
28130 *(ex1184)* 16/11/57.
28232 *(ex1276)* 4/1/64.

SHEDS:
Immingham.
St Margarets 13/9/53.
Dalry Road 30/1/56.
Dunfermline 12/4/57.
Thornton Junction 14/8/66.

CONDEMNED:
22/4/67.
*Sold 7/7/67 for scrap to
P&W McLellan, Langloan.*

61408

Darlington 2110.

To traffic 13/6/50.

REPAIRS:
Gor. 29/7–22/9/51.**G.**
Gor. 26–27/9/51.**N/C.**
Gor. 8/11–6/12/51.**C/L.**
Don. 15/5–16/6/52.**C/L.**
Don. 1/5–11/6/53.**G.**
Gor. 19/8–16/10/54.**G.**
Don. 8/3–14/4/56.**G.**
Dar. 2/12/57–11/1/58.**G.**
Dar. 24/4–27/5/58.**C/L.**
Don. 8–15/4/59.**N/C.**
Don. 20/5–17/6/60.**G.**
Don. 28/11–8/12/60.**N/C.**

BOILERS:
 5137.
28344 *(ex1186)* 22/9/51.
28288 *(ex1605)* 11/6/53.
28204 *(ex61385)* 16/10/54.
28597 *(ex1195)* 14/4/56.
28583 *(ex61328)* 11/1/58.
28169 *(ex1036)* 17/6/60.

SHED:
Immingham.

CONDEMNED:
29/12/62.
*Sold 2/63 for scrap to
J. Cashmore, Great Bridge.*

61409

Darlington 2111.

To traffic 15/6/50.

REPAIRS:
Gor. 5/6–28/7/51.**G.**
Don. 25/7–27/8/52.**G.**
Don. 13/8–24/9/53.**G.**
Don. 28/11–29/12/54.**G.**
Don. 1/3/55.*Weigh.*
Don. 9–20/4/55.**C/L.**
Don. 1–22/3/56.**C/H.**
Don. 11/1–9/2/57.**G.**
Don. 13–15/2/57.**N/C.**
Don. 4/12/58–10/1/59.**G.**
Don. 19/12/60–18/1/61.**G.**

BOILERS:
 5142.

28331 *(ex1158)* 28/7/51.
28750 *(ex61407)* 24/9/53.
28861 *(ex1171)* 29/12/54.
28141 *(ex1646)* 9/2/57.
28413 *(ex1650)* 10/1/59.
28515 *(ex1083)* 18/1/61.

SHEDS:
Immingham.
Lincoln 29/11/59.

CONDEMNED:
22/9/63.
*Sold 1/64 for scrap to
R. A. King, Norwich.*

The first – and fortunately sole – casualty and early withdrawal was 61057, seen here at Stratford works on 18th March 1950 awaiting a decision about which there could be little doubt; indeed it was withdrawn from stock on 17th April 1950. It had been attached at Ipswich in the early hours of 7th March to work the mail train from Peterborough East to Liverpool Street and in dense fog near Witham, had crashed into a goods train.

To be able to see both sides of the same train simultaneously is rather unusual, but is achieved on this Dundee to Edinburgh and Glasgow train calling at Perth, and which would be split for the two destinations when it reached Stirling. 61102 had Dundee as its only shed and carries that name on its buffer beam in addition to having the usual shed code on its smokebox door.

Cowlairs bank posed no difficulty for 1118 to surmount on only six coaches and a bogie parcels van which it was working from Glasgow Queen Street to the Fife coast. That engine did all its work allocated to Thornton Junction shed.

Doncaster shedded 61329 on 21st October 1964 has paused on the former Midland main line at Apperley Bridge & Rawdon station for examination of the two preserved locos 4771 and 1217E which it was taking from Doncaster works for temporary storage in Hellifield shed. By sheer coincidence, in which I played no part whatever, this view shows the wall (to the left of the B1's top lamp) over which I did my first spotting in the school holidays of 1919–22 after a 2½ mile walk there – and back – from my home in Yeadon, where my forbears can be traced back to the year 1379.

Of the ten which Gorton built and numbered 61340 to 61349, only 61348 did not spend its whole life working from Scottish sheds. For some reason in February 1957 it was transferred from as far north as Kittybrewster to Peterborough (Midland) and here on 31st July 1959 is about to go under the East Coast Main Line on the link between Peterborough North and East stations.

When steam was withdrawn from East Anglia in September 1962, the replacement diesels found difficulty not only in carriage warming but also preventing their engines from freezing. In the severe conditions of January 1963, on one morning at March shed, there was a row of 18 frozen–up diesel engines. For the following winter withdrawn B1 class engines were used to thaw out diesels and pre-heat carriages. As they were only insured for stationary work, their front and rear couplings were removed. Whilst cab numbers were changed into the Departmental List, many of the sixteen so used retained their smokebox number plate. 61181 withdrawn at March on 25th November 1963 became Departmental No.18 and remained at that shed for heating purposes until sold for cutting up in December 1965.

The application of the Departmental numbers took many and varied forms, even when done by the same shed. No.20 at Norwich got the full treatment, in contrast to 22, which simply had those two digits and no wording whatever.